Engaging with Historical Traumas

This book provides case-studies of how teachers and practitioners have attempted to develop more effective "experiential learning" strategies in order to better equip students for their voluntary engagements in communities, working for sustainable peace and a tolerant society free of discrimination.

All chapters revolve around this central theme, testing and trying various paradigms and experimenting with different practices, in a wide range of geographical and historical arenas. They demonstrate the innovative potentials of connecting know-how from different disciplines and combining experiences from various practitioners in this field of shaping historical memory, including non-formal and formal sectors of education, non-governmental workers, professionals from memorial sites and museums, local and global activists, artists, and engaged individuals. In so doing, they address the topic of collective historical traumas in ways that go beyond conventional classroom methods.

Interdisciplinary in approach, the book provides a combination of theoretical reflections and concrete pedagogical suggestions that will appeal to educators working across history, sociology, political science, peace education and civil awareness education, as well as memory activists and remembrance practitioners.

Nena Močnik is a researcher at CY Cergy Paris Université, France. She is the author of *Sexuality after War Rape: From Embodied to Narrative Research* and *Trauma Transmission and Sexual Violence: Peacebuilding and Reconciliation in Post-Conflict Societies*.

Ger Duijzings is Professor of Social Anthropology (with focus on Southeastern and Eastern Europe) at Universität Regensburg, Germany. He has published extensively on the conflicts in the former Yugoslavia, and was a researcher and expert witness at the International Criminal Tribunal for the former Yugoslavia (ICTY).

Hanna Meretoja is Professor of Comparative Literature and Director of SELMA: Centre for the Study of Storytelling, Experientiality and Memory at the University of Turku, Finland. She has authored *The Ethics of Storytelling* (2018) and co-edited (with Colin Davis) *The Routledge Companion to Literature and Trauma* (2020).

Bonface Njeresa Beti is an African multidisciplinary practitioner. He has co-published book chapters and journal articles. He is a committee member of NADTA and board member of Pedagogy and Theatre of the Oppressed. He has an MA degree in Peace and Conflict Studies from the University of Manitoba in Canada and has been admitted to the European Graduate School to pursue his PhD.

Routledge Studies in Modern History

Food History
A Feast of the Senses in Europe, 1750 to the Present
Edited by Sylvie Vabre, Martin Bruegel and Peter J. Atkins

Labour and Economic Change in Southern Africa c.1900–2000
Zimbabwe, Zambia and Malawi
Rory Pilossof and Andrew Cohen

Engaging with Historical Traumas
Experiential Learning and Pedagogies of Resilience
Edited by Nena Močnik, Ger Duijzings, Hanna Meretoja, and Bonface Njeresa Beti

Sun Yatsen, Robert Wilcox and Their Failed Revolutions, Honolulu and Canton 1895
Dynamite on the Tropic of Cancer
Patrick Anderson

Histories of Surveillance from Antiquity to the Digital Era
The Eyes and Ears of Power
Edited by Andreas Marklund and Laura Skouvig

Children Born of War
Past, Present and Future
Edited by Barbara Stelzl-Marx, Sabine Lee and Heide Glaesmer

The Cold War, the Space Race, and the Law of Outer Space
Space for Peace
Albert K. Lai

Experiences of War in Europe and the Americas, 1792–1815
Soldiers, Slaves, and Civilians
Mark Lawrence

For more information about this series, please visit: https://www.routledge.com/history/series/MODHIST

Engaging with Historical Traumas
Experiential Learning and
Pedagogies of Resilience

Edited by
Nena Močnik, Ger Duijzings, Hanna
Meretoja, and Bonface Njeresa Beti

LONDON AND NEW YORK

First published 2021
by Routledge
2 Park Square, Milton Park, Abingdon, Oxon OX14 4RN

and by Routledge
605 Third Avenue, New York, NY 10158

Routledge is an imprint of the Taylor & Francis Group, an informa business

© 2021 selection and editorial matter, Nena Močnik, Ger Duijzings, Hanna Meretoja, and Bonface Njeresa Beti; individual chapters, the contributors

The right of Nena Močnik, Ger Duijzings, Hanna Meretoja, and Bonface Njeresa Beti to be identified as the authors of the editorial material, and of the authors for their individual chapters, has been asserted in accordance with sections 77 and 78 of the Copyright, Designs and Patents Act 1988.

All rights reserved. No part of this book may be reprinted or reproduced or utilised in any form or by any electronic, mechanical, or other means, now known or hereafter invented, including photocopying and recording, or in any information storage or retrieval system, without permission in writing from the publishers.

Trademark notice: Product or corporate names may be trademarks or registered trademarks, and are used only for identification and explanation without intent to infringe.

British Library Cataloguing-in-Publication Data
A catalogue record for this book is available from the British Library

Library of Congress Cataloging-in-Publication Data
A catalog record has been requested for this book

ISBN: 978-0-367-49615-9 (hbk)
ISBN: 978-1-032-01329-9 (pbk)
ISBN: 978-1-003-04687-5 (ebk)

Typeset in Times New Roman
by MPS Limited, Dehradun

Contents

List of figures viii
Editors ix
List of contributors xi

Introduction 1
NENA MOČNIK, HANNA MERETOJA, GER DUIJZINGS, AND
BONFACE NJERESA BETI

PART I
Creative engagements with "ghosts from the past" in traditional classroom contexts 15

1 Why would you use a Fascist greeting to celebrate a football victory? Discussing historical revisionism and genocide memory with Danish high school teenagers 17
  TEA SINDBÆK ANDERSEN AND TIPPE EISNER

2 Breaking the nationalistic master-narrative: the case of teaching history in contemporary Croatia 32
  STEVO ĐURAŠKOVIĆ

3 Fictional family tree: storytelling and short film project 45
  TAINA KILPELÄ AND ELINA MÄKILÄ

4 From traditional to the moving classroom: empathy as a key component of the classroom teaching 59
  ALMA JEFTIĆ

PART II
Places of pain as sites of critical knowledge production   69

5 The last ones: Serbian and Russian prisoners on the Alpine front   71
NICCOLÒ CARANTI, LUISA CHIODI, AND MARCO ABRAM

6 #Never Forget: teaching trauma experience at historical places   86
NERINGA LATVYTĖ

7 Exploring the 1991 Battle of Vukovar through experiential learning   103
SANDRA CVIKIĆ

8 Speak Your Mind but Mind Your Speech   115
BENEDIKT HIELSCHER

PART III
Using artistic strategies to respond, reflect, and overcome   135

9 Atomic poetry and active learning: from Japan to Newfoundland   137
SHOSHANNAH GANZ

10 "Through the Refugee's Eyes": experiences with the experiential and interactive theatre show   147
MANCA ŠETINC VERNIK

11 The gestalt of historical research, art, and education: the circus theme and performing arts in remembering the tyranny of the Nazi Regime   160
MALTE GASCHE

PART IV
Healing and embodied strategies of learning   171

12 Utilising the breath as an experiential tool to teach, learn and manage trauma   173
ANNA WALKER

13 Art therapy and integral education with traumatised youths in Bosnia-Herzegovina 193
ANNA DRUKA AND HANNAH SCARAMELLA

14 Poetry against Trump: shared experience and creative resistance 202
ADAM BEARDSWORTH

PART V
Playing (with) the past, rehearsing (for) the future **215**

15 Performative experiential learning strategies: reenacting the historical, enacting the everyday 217
GER DUIJZINGS, FREDERIK LANGE, AND EVA-MARIA WALTHER

16 Escaping the Thucydides Trap in IR class 233
MIKAEL MATTLIN

17 Designing videogames for teaching about transmission of historical traumas: a case study of *Memory Gliders* 244
NENA MOČNIK

18 In memory of *Memory Gliders*: preservation of EU-funded serious games as digital heritage 257
MARIA B. GARDA AND JAAKKO SUOMINEN

Index 271

List of Figures

2.1	Blackboard notes, example 1: New Absolutism	35
2.2	Blackboard notes, example 2: Austro-Hungarian Empire	37
2.3	Blackboard notes, example 3: Representation of Croatian Serbs in Socialist Croatia	39
2.4	Blackboard notes, example 4: Socialist history and Croatian and Serbian nationalism	41
3.1	Family tree made with collage technique	49
3.2	Students grouping themes that came up from the family trees	51
3.3	Students filming scenes outside University of Applied Science of Metropolia	53
4.1	Moving classroom	61
5.1	The church on Carè Alto build by Russian prisoners in 1917	75
5.2	Participants at the Castle of Castellano	76
5.3	The Wikipedia workshop	78
5.4	Memorial of the victims of the Venzan landslide	81
10.1	Image from one of the performances – the boat landing scene, in Ljubljana underground shelter, 2016	152
10.2	Author with actors Hasan and Payman after the performance in Vienna, September 11th 2018	156
12.1	Interior of Fabrica Art Gallery	174
12.2	Interior of Fabrica Art Gallery	175
12.3	Stills from *Breath Wind into Me, Chapter 1* (Walker, 2019)	177
12.4	Stills from *Breath Wind into Me, Chapter 1* (Walker, 2019)	177
15.1	Participants in Regensburg in conversation with viewers in Cluj-Napoca	220
15.2	Image from the public intervention in Regensburg on 31 January 2019	223
15.3	Example of a textile patch quoting from a conversation	225
15.4	The accompanying poster and flyer	226

Editors

Nena Močnik is a researcher at CY Cergy-Paris Université, France. She is the author of S*exuality after War Rape: From Narrative to Embodied Research* (2017) and *Trauma Transmission and Sexual Violence: Reconciliation and Peacebuilding in Post Conflict Settings* (2020). In 2018, she was invited as the external expert at EUROCLIO – European Association of History Educators, developing experiential and embodied pedagogical practices in history teaching and she was the initiator and co-leader of the European Commission funded project *#Never Again: Teaching Transmission of Trauma and Remembrance through Experiential Learning*.

Hanna Meretoja is a professor of Comparative Literature and Director of *SELMA: Centre for the Study of Storytelling, Experientiality and Memory* at the University of Turku (Finland) and in 2019–2021 a visiting fellow at the University of Oxford. Her research is mainly in the fields of narrative theory, narrative ethics, trauma studies, and cultural memory studies. Her monographs include *The Ethics of Storytelling: Narrative Hermeneutics, History, and the Possible* (2018, Oxford University Press) and *The Narrative Turn in Fiction and Theory: The Crisis and Return of Storytelling from Robbe-Grillet to Tournier* (2014) and she has co-edited, with Colin Davis, *The Routledge Companion to Literature and Trauma* (2020) and *Storytelling and Ethics: Literature, Visual Arts and the Power of Narrative* (2018).

Ger Duijzings is a professor of Social Anthropology at Universität Regensburg. He published extensively on the conflicts in the former Yugoslavia, and was a researcher and expert witness at the International Criminal Tribunal for the former Yugoslavia (ICTY).

Bonface Njeresa Beti is a Kenyan multidisciplinary practitioner working at the intersection between the arts, trauma-healing, and peacebuilding. He is working with the Green String Network (GSN) as a senior program manager. GSN's work is currently being implemented in Kenya and South Sudan.

Bonface Njeresa Beti holds, BA in communication from Daystar University in Kenya, an MA degree in Peace and Conflict Studies from University of Manitoba in Canada and is currently admitted at the European Graduate School in Saas Fee, Switzerland to pursue his PhD in Expressive Arts for Conflict Transformation. He is the co-author of *Forum Theatre for Conflict Transformation in East Africa: The Domain of the Possible* (2015).

Contributors

Marco Abram holds PhD in History at the University of Udine, Master in History of Europe at the University of Bologna. He spent research periods in different countries and worked for the Center for Advanced Studies – South-Eastern Europe, the Department of History of the University of Rijeka and the University of British Columbia, where he was a lecturer of history of South-East Europe. His research has been devoted to Yugoslav and post-Yugoslav history, and his articles have been published in several Italian and international academic journals. He was involved in many dissemination projects promoted by different organizations and has been collaborating with OBCT since 2009, mainly on projects focused on history, memory, and the dealing with the past.

Tea Sindbæk Andersen teaches East European Studies at the University of Copenhagen. Tea's research focuses on the contemporary history of Southeastern Europe, especially on issues related to cultural memory, uses of history, identity politics, and popular culture in the Yugoslav area. Tea is a member of the executive board of the Memory Studies Association. She is the author of *Usable History? Representations of Yugoslavia's difficult past from 1945 to 2002* (2012) and, with Barbara Törnquist-Plewa, editor of *Disputed Memory* (2016) and *The Twentieth Century in European Memory: Transcultural Mediation and Reception* (2018).

Adam Beardsworth is an associate professor of English at Grenfell Campus, Memorial University of Newfoundland. He has published many articles on American and Canadian poetry, and his research interests include Cold War poetry and environmental poetics. He is currently the president of the Canadian Association for American Studies.

Niccolò Caranti has a Master's degree in law, expert Wikipedian, in addition to volunteer work he has collaborated with Wikimedia Italy and Wikimedia Foundation. He has collaborated as an editor with Sanbaradio, the student radio of Trento, and as a photojournalist with Corriere del Trentino, the local edition of Corriere della Sera. After the first collaboration with OBCT in 2017, since 2018 he has been an editor and researcher.

xii *Contributors*

Luisa Chiodi obtained her PhD at the European University Institute of Fiesole (Florence), a degree in Political Science at the University of Milan, director of Osservatorio Balcani e Caucaso since 2006. From 2003 to 2008 she taught Eastern European studies at the Faculty of Political Science of the University of Bologna and lectured in other university courses in Italy and abroad. She has edited several academic publications and coordinated many research projects. Her research interests focus on civil society and the transnational social dynamics of post-communism.

Sandra Cvikić is employed by the Institute of Social Sciences Ivo Pilar, Regional Center Vukovar. She studied at the University of Western Ontario, has an MA Degree from the University of Sussex, and a PhD from the University of Zagreb.

Anna Druka, artist, entrepreneur, and consultant graduated from the University of Dundee, holds BA degree in Time Based Art. Anna works as an artist and runs her private art studio in Latvia where she teaches children and adults in group and private settings. Her work experience comes from a diverse background in various creative fields in the UK including Fine Art (Glasgow Center for Contemporary Art, Dundee Contemporary Arts), Commercial Art (The Film Museum), Film, Television and video (Domino Records, The Aged Care Channel), Photography (Lambeth County Council) and even modelling (The Model Team). She also helped launch Reel Angels, one of the first all female film companies. Anna is currently doing research on design thinking and the prospects of interdisciplinary design and group processes as part of her MA.

Stevo Đurašković, PhD, assistant professor at the Faculty of Political Sciences, University of Zagreb, where he teaches the courses in Politics of history and in Modern and Contemporary Croatian history. He received his PhD in Political Science from the Faculty of Social Sciences at the University of Ljubljana and his MA in Central European History from the History Department at the Central European University, Budapest. His research interests include the politics of history, intellectual history and national identity-building processes in East Central and Southeastern Europe. He published the book *The Politics of History in Croatia and Slovakia in the 1990s* (2016).

Tippe Eisner has a background in cross-cultural studies with a focus on Indonesia. She works at the University of Copenhagen, Department of Cross-Cultural and Regional Studies as a research outreach consultant and project coordinator. Tippe is co-organiser of the project events in Copenhagen and co-author of the project report.

Shoshannah Ganz is an associate professor of Canadian literature at Grenfell Campus, Memorial University, in Newfoundland, Canada. In 2008 she co-edited a collection of essays with University of Ottawa Press on the poet Al

Purdy. In 2017 she published *Eastern Encounters: Canadian Women's Writing about the East, 1867–1929* with National Taiwan University Press. Shoshannah just completed a manuscript entitled *Now I Am Become Death: Industry and Disease in Canadian and Japanese Literature*. This book is currently being revised for McGill-Queen's University Press.

Maria B. Garda, PhD, is an expert in media history, and her current work focuses on comparative history of digital game cultures. Maria's recent publications have dealt with indie games and early computer art, and she was previously involved with several research projects, including: "Alternative Usage of New Media Technology During The Decline of People's Republic of Poland" (University of Lodz, 2013–2017) and "Creative Micro-computing in Australia, 1976-1992" (Flinders University, 2017–2018).

Malte Gasche received his PhD in Scandinavian Studies from the Humboldt University of Berlin (Germany). He is a researcher at the Centre for Nordic Societies at the University of Helsinki (Finland). Gasche is Finland's representative in the committee "Genocides on the Roma" within the International Holocaust Remembrance Alliance (IHRA).

Benedikt Hielscher is a trainer, mediator, and co-founder of the Berlin-based social enterprise Conflict Consultancy. He holds a master's degree in Political Psychology and combines academic insights with practical experience to develop evidence-based interventions to social and political conflicts.

Alma Jeftić is a research fellow at the Peace Research Institute, International Christian University and a co-chair of the Research Network on Transnational Memory and Identity in Europe (Council for European Studies at Columbia University).

Taina Kilpelä is a drama teacher and has her master's in cultural anthropology. She has been working widely in the field of drama and global education connecting people through storytelling. Her passion is community art. In her latest project *Muistomuokkaamo*, participants explored memories, time, and remembering through storytelling and photomanipulation.

Frederik Lange, MA, studied history, art history, and Southeast European Studies in Göttingen and Jena. Since 2017 he is a doctoral student at the Graduate School for East and Southeast European Studies in Regensburg, doing research on the Drina river.

Neringa Latvytė is a historian and a PhD candidate at the Faculty of Communication, Vilnius University. Her dissertation project concentrates on Holocaust sites in Lithuania, with special focus on diverse practices of institutionalization of traumatic heritage in different political regimes. She worked at the Vilna Gaon Jewish History Museum for two decades, led the history research department, and was a curator of the Holocaust

Exhibition. She is currently a lecturer of communication of traumatic memory at the Faculty of Communication, Vilnius University.

Elina Mäkilä has MA in social and cultural anthropology and studies in documentary film directing in Aalto University. She has years of experience in a field of communications, media and participatory community-based filmmaking as well as artistic and documentary short films. She has worked as a project coordinator, producer as well as educator in multicultural projects and workshops. She is interested in exploring intergenerational relations, transmission, and communication through filmmaking and storytelling.

Mikael Mattlin is Professor of Political Science (act.) in the University of Turku, and Principal Investigator of the Academy of Finland-funded ForAc-research project (funding nr 338145). He was recently also Professor of Chinese Studies in the University of Helsinki, and Collegium Researcher in the Turku Institute for Advanced Studies (TIAS), during which time this paper was written. Professor Mattlin's most recent book *Politicized Society: Taiwan's Struggle with its One-Party Past* was published in 2018 by NIAS Press (Copenhagen University). The book is a revised and expanded second edition of his acclaimed 2011 book. His peer-reviewed journal articles have appeared e.g. in The China Quarterly, Information, Communication & Society, Cooperation and Conflict, Journal of Contemporary China, Simulation & Gaming, Journal of Political Science Education, Asia-Europe Journal, European Political Science, Issues & Studies, Internasjonal Politikk, China Perspectives and East Asia.

Hannah Scaramella, artist, art therapist graduated from at Art Therapy Italiana, member of APIART, holds BA – Degree in Art Psychotherapy from – Goldsmiths University of London. Hannah works as an art therapist individually and/or with groups of men, women, teenagers and, children within the public and private institutions in Europe and Middle East. Hannah has been teaching in Academies of Art, Universities and Social Areas. She frequently collaborates with social workers and psychologists in Russia and Israel, in particular with Art and History Museum in St Petersburg. Her work in Bosnia-Herzegovina has been performed in collaboration with the ArtReach Foundation Tuzlanska Amica (Tuzla), Accademia Psicologia Applicata (Palermo) psychological support services of Tuzla municipality, the orphanage and refugee camps. The project of psychological support to the kids of Srebrenica was carried out in collaboration with Associazione Alexander Langer (Bolzano).

Jaakko Suominen, PhD, is professor of Digital Culture (UTU), with a focus on cultural history of media and information technologies; he has studied computers and popular media, Internet, social media, digital games, and theoretical and methodological aspects of the study of digital culture.

Jaakko has (co-)authored over 100 scholarly publications (e.g. Media History, Technology & Culture, New Media & Society, Routledge). He has led several multi-disciplinary research projects, funded by AKA, Tekes, private companies and municipal bodies.

Manca Šetinc Vernik is a Communication Science Graduate with years of experience in the field of human rights, in particular the field of protection against discrimination. Her professional career path led her from the research work at the Institute for Ethnic Studies to the Human Rights Ombudsman of the Republic of Slovenia, where she had worked in the department of prevention of discrimination as a promotion and education officer. She is a qualified antidiscrimination trainer since 2006 (Ludwig Boltzmann Institute and European Peer Training Organization). She is currently working as a project coordinator at the NGO Humanitas – Centre for global learning and cooperation, leading various domestic and international projects and conducting numerous workshops on human rights, migration and global education in Slovenia and abroad, also as an independent expert advisor in the field of non-discrimination for organization like COE, the EU Commission, and the OSCE.

Anna Walker, PhD, is an artist, writer, and researcher working in mixed media, specifically moving image and sound. She has been exploring trauma in her arts practice research for many years, how the body responds to overwhelming traumatic and stressful situations and how it reorganises itself to cope with or manage the trauma. She was awarded an MA in Fine Art from Southampton University in 1998, and a certificate in Psychotherapy from CBPC, Cambridge, in 2010. An interest in the effects of trauma on the body led her to a PhD in Arts and Media at Plymouth University, which she completed in May 2017. Her arts-practice balances the auto-ethnographic with the critical, utilising personal experiences to facilitate a greater understanding of memory, trauma and its wider cultural implications. Most recently, Anna is researching storytelling as performance, bridging technology with traditional storytelling.

Eva-Maria Walther, MSc, studied Social Anthropology and Slavic Studies in Tübingen, Pécs, and Stockholm. Since 2016 she is a doctoral student at the Graduate School for East and Southeast European studies in Regensburg, doing research on refugee care services in Slovakia.

Introduction

Nena Močnik, Hanna Meretoja, Ger Duijzings, and Bonface Njeresa Beti

The growing interest in the exploration of trauma and its short- and longterm effects by scholars outside of the clinical domain has shed new light on the links between violent, contested pasts and current threats to peace and security. These entanglements are most visible in divided societies with rich multicultural histories and persistent structures of social injustice. The rise of such historical divisions has been exacerbated by the current COVID-19 pandemic, plaguing the world at a pivotal historic epoch when this edited volume is being put together. While collective historical resentments can be mobilised to spur radical political movements or fuel authoritarian (neo-) nationalist, populist governments, the pain of historic injustice and the silence surrounding it can escalate into vicious cycles of violence, causing further marginalisation, social and political division and, eventually, political unrest. The traditional historical narratives used in educational institutions regarding the recurrence of violence too often allow the learners to isolate themselves as members of a particular community rather than seeing themselves as members of humanity as a whole. Especially for those individuals or generations that are lucky enough not to have first-hand experience of war and mass political crimes, such distancing can further cause "Othering", both in the sense of temporality and identity, whereby the cruelties, beheadings, mass rape, torture, detentions, and other outrageous acts do not belong to *us*: they do not belong to *our times* or *our cultures*. Because this is not *our* war, we can judge, and we can be horrified, disgusted, enraged, and frightened. We remain spectators only, witnesses of *their* war, *their* barbarism, and *their* primitivism. But what, in the end, is the learning outcome of such a lesson? How can it be used for the betterment of society and justice, and how can it be directly used in our everyday lives to promote coexistence and resist the historically established unequal power structures? How can we think of specific historical atrocities as one human race, globally? And, last but not least, how is such knowledge and global perspective useful for us as individuals and as a collective?

History as a school subject contains unimaginable amounts of traumatic content, which has, for decades, been dealt with in classrooms through emotionally detached and temporally decontextualised pedagogical practices.

Only when we come to consciously address the past and its violence and injustice, we – educators and learners – might start to recognise ourselves as active and/or passive agents in shaping contemporary sociopolitical dynamics. However, history scholars and, above all, history educators are yet to find a common ground on how to meaningfully integrate these personalised and contextualised questions of traumatic experience into history education. When we say *personalised* and *contextualised*, we refer to educators and learners being engaged in a process whereby everyone becomes responsible for the past, the present, and the future. Such a method means approaching collective historical traumas through the Freirean lens of the *pedagogy of hope* – that is, by using different pedagogies as a collective road to liberation from oppressive systems, which were commonly established using brutal colonial and imperial force and various forms of collective/political violence. It also means acknowledging the collective responsibility that emerges from us, and our societies, being implicated in past injustices, even when we are not directly responsible for them (Rothberg 2019; Meretoja 2018) – it is to acknowledge, as Judith Butler puts it, that "our lives are profoundly implicated in the lives of others" (2004, 7).

Clinical educators in the field of trauma studies (see, for instance, Mattar 2011; Newman 2011; Zurbriggen 2011) provide several recommendations on how to integrate historical trauma, understood very broadly, with the demands and needs of contemporary learners. Accommodating trauma-informed pedagogical approaches in teaching mostly means adopting the principles of empathic witnessing, an alert and active response to triggers, and the dialogical approach that does not ignore or deny the risks of traumatisation but embraces them in a transformative process of constructive, critical learning. The scholars who advocate for incorporating an active approach to trauma in history education (Felman 1995; Berman 2001) often assume that exposure to traumatic pasts can be "used to shock students into feeling 'appropriate' responses to atrocity" (Rak 2003, 64). There is, however, little to no evidence that learning through shock results in a transformational, ethical, and empowering understanding of the past. Such learning allegedly happens through the practice of "witnessing" and "active listening" to past atrocities that helps the learners to experience the "bewilderment, injury, confusion, dread and conflicts that the victim feels" (Laub 1992, 58).

Teachers who are proactive and responsive to the potential triggers and/or unhealed (intergenerational) traumas of the students might aim to foster a safe and supportive atmosphere in the classroom, but some students may not respond with empathy and critical understanding. The trauma-informed classroom does not guarantee that students will feel safe and willing to take risks; they might not learn with curiosity or even "heal." Students may not aim to bring decades of trauma to a close in order to start reconciliation and collective healing but can, instead, potentially perpetuate further violence related to these same traumas (Zembylas 2008). Students might react with pity, guilt, vengeance, or disinterest: the legacies of traumatic histories are often so embedded in our present political, social, and private worlds that they constitute an essential, "naturalized" part of our behaviours, values, and moral guidelines. These traumas are also often hard to access, explore, and deal with using the critical and (self-)reflective pedagogical principles.

Keeping in mind that there are risks when engaging with trauma as well as the evidence that most (history) teachers are ill-prepared in this regard (Taylor & Guyver 2012; Bentrovato et al. 2016; Psaltis et al. 2017), we believe that engaging with historical traumas, in fact, can offer opportunities to counteract the perpetuation of shame, stigma, and different aspects of violence rooted in historical injustices. With the collection of different pedagogical approaches in this edited volume, we aim to respond to the needs of history teachers when discussing traumatic events and trauma-triggering narratives in the history classroom. The challenges in teaching the darker aspects of our pasts have been discussed by several scholars (see, for instance, Bekerman & Zembylas 2011; Ahonen 2012), yet we believe there is still plenty of room for improvement when it comes to understanding teaching and learning beyond cognitive recognition and conventional classroom explanations. We have tried to explore pedagogical practices that can help to minimise the re-traumatisation or/and vicarious trauma when exposing students to distressing material. Therefore, the focus of this book is on the diverse interactive pedagogical practices that can support constructive and transformative learning. While history educators are the main target group, we hope to reach out beyond history education to all the educators whose practice is informed or inspired by or based on traumatic historical events and who are committed to addressing traumatic pasts using critical and justice-oriented pedagogies.

We particularly focus on exploring the potential of "experiential learning" strategies in secondary and higher education, aiming at innovative, creative, and inter- and cross-disciplinary ways of teaching young people about collective historical traumas at the local, national, and international levels. Consequently, the contributors not only offer helpful theoretical and practical insights but specific advice on how concrete historical cases can be addressed. They look at how to counter, through new experiential learning formats, the potentially toxic consequences of transmitting such traumas from one generation to another and how to imbue young people with a clear sense of how the unaddressed traumatic past can affect the future of peaceful coexistence in Europe and beyond. Therefore, the collected practices centre on the different innovative modes of experiential learning whereby the active participation of learners helps to stimulate sociopolitical engagement.

While in this book we refer to the terminology and the circular model of *experiential learning* (including active experimentation, concrete experience, abstract conceptualisation and reflective observation) developed by David Kolb (1984), the presented practices advance and intersect with rich and diverse traditions of *engaged pedagogy* as understood by bell hooks (1994), *the pedagogy of the oppressed* and *the pedagogy of hope* by Paolo Freire (1994), and *critical pedagogy* by Henry Giroux (2011). The commonality of all these traditions and practices collected in this book lies in the power of "first-hand experience" through cognitive understanding as well as emotional and embodied (physical) re-enactment in the process of generating knowledge and transformation. While integrating trauma in the class curricula always adds a certain level of emotional and psychological burden, we aim to explore what hooks calls "the pleasure" and the "erotic" in the process of learning. Using these concepts, she emphasises the importance of the sensual, physical, and emotional "energy" (1994, 195) that can charge a learning process and "excite the critical imagination" (1994, 195). She calls for the creation of an "open learning community" (1994, 8), which brings us back to recognising learners not only as individuals with their own (family) pasts but also as constitutive parts of the (traumatic) historical continuum that continues to "manifest" itself in the present. Once we open the floor and engage in dialogue with the students, we allow everyone to equally draw from their own experiences, beliefs, values, and relationships outside of the classroom; but in this way we also "invite" everyone's past or current trauma(s) to enter the classroom and to become part of the pedagogical situation.

Using the teaching practices presented in this edited volume, educators try to move away from the instructor-focused approaches by taking the subjects and the learners outside of the traditional classroom, either physically (in-situ learning) or emotionally (for instance, via simulations and re-enactments). Despite the diversity in their approaches and perspectives, in general the contributors agree that non-traditional approaches to learning offer many advantages and benefits. First and foremost, experiential learning acknowledges the idea that individuals and groups learn in different ways that extend way beyond cognitive comprehension, categorisation of data, and/or memorisation, just to give some examples. By including learning through visuals, visits, mutual exchanges, listening, feelings, and so on, teachers encourage learners to fully explore and use individually specific potentials, talents, skills, knowledges, (family) backgrounds, and experiences in an active exchange with others. Many people learn better when they are engaged in the process of exploration and creation of knowledge rather than simply consuming facts and theories.

Because experiential learning extends beyond "cognitive" (conventionally one-directional) learning, it includes immersive emotional and embodied ways of gaining knowledge and understanding, which might trigger very subjective and also painful responses. Central to this process is active engagement, exchanging of roles (educator-learner) and de-hierarchisation of knowledge through forms of hands-on learning and problem-solving, addressing concrete and real-world problems, encouraging genuine student interaction around "uncomfortable" content, and providing students with direct "field" experiences outside of schools and campuses at the intersection of past traumas and current socio-political dynamics and developments. Above all, by bridging the split between the mind and the body, experiential learning "humanizes" education (Freire 1994, 36).

All these aspects are covered in the 18 chapters of this book, which is a follow-up to the project *#Never Again: Teaching Transmission of Trauma and Remembrance through Experiential Learning*, coordinated by the University of Turku, Finland, and funded by the European Commission's Europe for Citizens Programme in 2018.[1] The book is divided into four sections, each revolving around a central theme that connects the know-how from different disciplines and professionals, including the non-formal and formal sectors of education, non-governmental workers, professionals from memorial sites and museums, local and global activists, artists, and engaged individuals from a wide range of geographical and historical arenas. The authors demonstrate the innovative potential of connecting, intersecting, and readjusting various global traditions while dealing with very specific local cases.

In *Creative engagements with 'ghosts from the past' in traditional classroom contexts*, the first section of the book, the contributors focus on the teacher's role and the requirement of establishing a creative classroom context which would help addressing the general ignorance and widespread indifference amongst students in respect of Europe's dark history including mass atrocities inspired by radical ideologies. Contributors explore how in a context of rather fixed and prescribed institutional curricula teachers can nevertheless open new spaces for thinking about collective traumas and trigger contemporary reflections. These chapters try to reflect on how teaching in traditional classroom contexts may still contribute to the prospective breaking of future cycles of violence.

In the first chapter, Tea Sindbæk Andersen and Tippe Eisner reflect on the increasing far-right tendencies and a general rise in xenophobic nationalism in Europe, seemingly accompanied by a general ignorance or even indifference towards Europe's dark history. They explore the level and nature of indifference among Danish teenagers through three qualitative case studies of how Danish high school youth react to examples of right-wing and fascist revisionism. Drawing on experiential learning methods, the case studies confront the teenagers with examples of blatant representations of fascist and extreme nationalist ideology and symbolism within the emotionally and aesthetically appealing world of top football.

Historical memory in Croatia is also approached with a range of different didactic methods in the second chapter by Stevo Djurašković. In his teaching of the course in Modern Croatian Political History, he focuses on the comprehension of complexity and contingency of history, and for this he introduces the students into the skill of a cause–effect thinking thus making students eventually grasp comprehensively a specific historical event. He observes that gradually students get skilled in understanding the complexity of historical events and embrace multiple perspectives towards the national history. On the basis of his insights through the course, the author argues that these classes contribute to prospective break of a future cycle of violence, especially in respect to the legacy of the war for independence that Croatia relatively recently went through.

A very different approach, but in a format that can easily be applied in the classroom, is described by Elina Mäkilä and Taina Kilpelä. The premise of their project "Fictional Family Tree" is in the invisible stories and intergenerational knowledge that people carry and transfer to future generations. The idea combines together a concept of "transmission of the burden", explored with creation of family trees and ethnofiction, a blend of documentary and fictional film that has been used in the field of visual anthropology. The project was organised as experimental storytelling and participatory filmmaking workshop that combined reality and fiction in exploring the past and the future. The project was carried out for students of social services at University of Applied Science of Metropolia and Diak in spring 2019 and resulted in a short movie.

In the last chapter in this section, Alma Jeftić demonstrates the importance of empathy in promoting dialogue between teachers and students while discussing sensitive topics related to history and in-group wrongdoings. While practicing active listening and perspective-taking, teachers gathered in two workshops were exposed to different narratives related to the same events from 1992–1995 war in Bosnia-Herzegovina. She observed their behavioural and verbal responses for the purpose of developing a new concept of moving classroom. In this chapter, further implications for a moving classroom development are discussed in line with the proposed theoretical framework.

The four chapters in the second section *Places of pain as sites of critical knowledge production* explore the experiential learning potentials of site visits, that is, of organised visits or "excursions" to historically charged places and spaces that carry a strong significance in the collective memory of the community or for others affected by or interested in the history of these places. This phenomenon, which has been on the rise in recent decades, has been labelled "dark tourism" in the literature: as a rule, traumatic sites or destinations of this form of "dark tourism" are located outside conventional educational settings, such as schools, campuses, and other didactic environments including museums, even though some selected sites may indeed be transformed into museums or "regimented" places for commemoration, as one of the chapters illustrates. All the authors in this section emphasise the nature of immersive learning, which encourages learners to understand the role of traumatic events in the context of their concrete social and spatial environments and landscapes. They ask how these forms of in situ learning can be integrated into formal and institutional curricula and what kind of preparatory steps educators can and should undertake to offer thought-provoking and reflective "field" experiences.

In the first chapter, Niccolò Carranti, Luisa Chiodi, and Marco Abram discuss two site trainings carried out in the region of Trentino-Alto Adige. The local interventions drew attention to an aspect of the First World War which is virtually ignored in the master narratives of the war: the experiences of prisoners of war from the "enemy" side. Apart from site visits, the project included a Wikipedia workshop teaching students how to write online articles related to the topic. Both projects represent attempts at retrieving silenced experiences and creating new *lieux de mémoires*, either in situ or online.

To follow up, Neringa Latvytė similarly starts from the notion that traumatic places are often forgotten or silenced in local memory narratives. It describes a specific in situ learning project with site visits related to the Holocaust in Lithuania. Involving teachers, educators, librarians, and memory institution specialists, the memorial site of Paneriai, a site of mass extermination, was visited with a view of replicating such site visits with Lithuanian youth. The chapter explores the theme of the "genius loci" of such killing sites.

Sandra Cvikić discusses an experiential learning project in Vukovar, sponsored by the government of Croatia. Since the 2016/2017 school year a field trip to the Memorial Centre of the Homeland War is mandatory for all Croatian 8th Graders, to commemorate the victims of the Battle of Vukovar, and moderate the transgenerational transmission of trauma and remembering of the war in post-war Croatia. This is an example of an "official" experiential learning practice, organised, designed, and regimented on the national level and implemented in the local contexts in which historical traumatic events occurred.

In the last chapter of this section, Benedikt Hielscher describes a training course carried out in Cluj-Napoca (Romania) where participants learned to navigate and negotiate diverging individual experiences and opposing perspectives and antagonisms, in order to prevent political polarisation. One of the root causes is the lack of real communication and empathy for the plight of others, which poisons the political climate. Although this chapter does not deal with in situ learning in traumatic places of the past, new contemporary situations and "sites of pain" were created: through enacted "provocations" and deliberate "exposure", participants were trapped into painful situations bringing about changes in their attitude and behaviour.

Section three, *Using artistic strategies to respond, reflect, and overcome*, explores the ways in which different artistic media address historical trauma and can be mobilised to support experiential learning. The emphasis is particularly on the use of literature, creative writing, and experiential theatre. The chapters discuss the affordances of artistic exercises and workshops in reflecting on cultural trauma in ways that foreground links to students' own experiences of hurt, vulnerability, anxiety, and suffering. This section also brings forth the ability of artistic engagement to foster awareness of the connections between the global and local, past and present, distant suffering and mechanisms of the everyday that perpetuate such suffering.

Shoshannah Ganz's chapter focuses on the creation of global awareness of the connected impacts of nuclear energy and arms. Although Canada has never had a nuclear weapons programme and the impacts of atomic warfare and accidents can seem historically distant and geographically remote, the uranium mined and used in the bombs detonated over Hiroshima and Nagasaki was taken from Canadian ground, it decimated a generation of Dene (Indigenous) people in Canada's north, and Canada has been a storage place for nuclear weapons. Ganz's chapter discusses three English literature courses in which she took her students for a tour of the former air force base where these weapons were stored. This allowed the students to see that the distant events of Hiroshima and Fukushima have a real-life corollary in their own landscape. There was measurable success in the areas of historical awareness, student motivation, scholastic achievement, and ethical accountability.

Manca Šetinc Vernik describes the process of co-creation that took place within the interactive experiential theatre play *Through the Refugee's Eyes*, which emerged in response to the inhumane asylum policy of "fortress Europe" and the problematic treatment of people fleeing war, persecution, or poverty. As a tool for confronting prejudices and intolerance, the play was co-created with people with real-life experience of being refugees, who at the same time processed their own traumas, built personal social networks, and promoted intercultural dialogue. In this experiential play, the participants step into the refugee shoes on their way to the "promised" Europe and in the end they meet the true persons behind the performed life stories.

Malte Gasche brings forward the case of European circuses that have for centuries been run by "marginalized groups" (i.e. Sinti and Roma, Jewish, immigrants, people with physical disabilities) and therefore the "Other." However, the evidence on their life and survival during the Nazi regime is rather poorly evidenced. The author explores the prospects of using research-based performances and artistic elements in educational work and remembrance activities.

Section Four focuses on *Healing and embodied strategies of learning*. Contributors in this section deeply reflect on ways in which embodied, creative artistic, and experiential learning spaces are critical in transforming intergenerational trauma and historical memories. Drawing upon their lessons from practical use and application of a creative artistic workshop and a short video showcase shown at various exhibition spaces, the authors of this section demonstrate what kind of challenges trauma and memory poses for individuals and collective societies coming from divided pasts. Through their use of artistic experiential learning processes, the authors strongly showcase how imaginative artistic approaches can provide psychological support for processing historical memories, heal trauma, and create new connections.

This section highlights how embodied, artistic, and experiential approaches play a critical role in learning and imagining new ways of relating.

In her chapter, Anna Walker, showcases ways of managing trauma and transforming historical memories through an exploration of her 23-minute video on the importance of use of breath as an experiential method. The author explores the relationship of the breath to communicable states of affect and shared spaces. She approaches this theoretical premise through several propositions including the spectral breath, breathing with the other, the haptic breath creating a new narrative through sense, and the mimetic breath. In the end, she concludes that breath as an experiential tool can be used to transform memories, heal trauma, and support our own self-connection as well as community wellbeing.

Anna Druka and Hannah Scaramella describe their methodological findings from a creative trauma recovery project for teens and preteens who participated in an experiential learning workshop after the war in Bosnia-Herzegovina during 2007–2009. The project registered positive outcomes witnessed through youth attitude change at the very end. The reflections of these two authors showcase how use of creative arts provided psychological support to build connections among these young generations after the war. In the end, both authors argue that use of creative artistic therapies offered experiential opportunities for young people's healing of historical traumatic memories and afforded new ways of connecting after a divisive war.

Through an analysis of contemporary affective politics, Adam Beardsworth examines how Donald Trump's presidency has perpetuated cycles of violence. He focuses on a case study that aimed to teach university students how creative activities engaging with cultural traumas can function as testimonials that promote both healing and dissent in uncertain times. By challenging students to share the various ways in which the politics of the Trump era made them feel vulnerable, threatened, and anxious, this activity sought to help them find ways in which aesthetic activities could provide solidarity and mitigate the experience of trauma on both individual and collective levels.

The last section of the book, *Playing (with) the past, rehearsing (for) the future*, explores the potential of reenactment in online and physical spaces by introducing imaginary contexts that go beyond the factual and well-recorded historical events. In the first chapter of this section, the authors Ger Duijzings, Frederik Lange, and Eva-Maria Walther introduce two different types of performance they engaged with and evaluated their respective pedagogical potential. One was a reenactment of a concrete historical event, the 1941 massacre of the Jewish population of Odessa, as depicted and reenacted in a film screened and discussed in a transnational exchange, Radu Jude's film *"I don't care if we go down in history as barbarians."* The second was a public art intervention staged in the Old Town of Regensburg, in which they used metal bunk beds from a nuclear bunker, a historically contingent but evocative symbol, to get into conversation with passers-by. Both performances exemplify the potential of historical reenactments and mundane enactments to forge a new perspective on the past and present in dialogue with others.

In the second chapter, Mikael Mattlin describes a course concept that he has developed and taught for years, using a board game and negotiation simulation that, in its original form, is steeped in Structural Realism. Adjusting the board game for the needs of teaching war within International Relations, from an exercise in seeking dominance and sowing distrust, the negotiations turn into an exercise in building peaceful, negotiated solutions and enhancing communal aspects in the classroom.

Nena Močnik remains in the domain of using games and gaming as pedagogical tools and focuses particularly in applying videogames for opening up new possibilities for disseminating knowledge about the dynamics of structural violence and its connection to historical traumas. She presents the evidence that shows how the dynamic interplay between designers (teachers) and players (learners) might lead to the development of empathy and understanding and contribute in the end to forms of moral behaviour. Building on the example of *Memory Gliders* videogame, she reflects on challenges in providing content materials while aiming to address global, culturally diverse and complex audiences.

The last chapter in this section and in the book is sort of an echo to the previous examples, as it describes possible preservation strategies of videogame-based experiential learning tools in order to reflect on the lifespan, sustainability, and long-term accessibility of these digital artefacts. Maria B. Garda and Jaakko Suominen focus on the case study of the videogame *Memory Gliders*, but their main paradigm could easily be expanded in broader consideration of how to develop preservation strategies of the experiential learning methods that demand a lot of different types of explorations and investments. *Memory Gliders*, and other educational games, cannot rely on fan engagement in the preservation work like in the case of entertainment games and retrogaming communities. Specifically for the videogames, the authors ask should the weight of the efforts rest on the shoulders of project coordinators (i.e. scientific network members), game developers (as a part of company's portfolio and legacy), funding bodies (e.g. EU centralised solutions), research centres (e.g. on history of education), or memory institutions (e.g. local libraries). All these questions are strikingly relevant when it comes to the broader call for didactic reforms and investments.

While one of the most important elements of experiential learning is the idea that the knowledge learnt can be immediately applied in the learner's everyday life and real situation, this aspect becomes harder to grasp (or to "measure" and "monitor" in the traditional ways) when engaging with questions related to intergenerational traumas and the transmission and historical recurrence of collective violence. From a practical perspective, these questions are more often addressed in other domains, like peace education, social work, or even civic education. Nonetheless, history education remains in a powerful position within the institutional educational settings because it participates in national culture and memory which explains why most of the learning that enhances critical thinking and holistic engagement for individuals and communities must come from the enthusiastic and critically reflective individuals first before we can hope for serious systematic changes.

Teaching about traumatic historic events as presented through the different teaching practices in this book enables not only transmitting the historical evidence and archival data but also teaching these events in such a manner that they would not be repeated ever again. However, history education is not (yet) a practical domain and an applied science that would allow learners to become professionals in dealing with the violence or trauma transmission in the field. Experiential learning, therefore, intervenes in the established institutional agendas to overcome the temporal, spatial, and political/ideological distances between the past and the present by awakening in the learners their critical consciousness – that is, the core of any critical pedagogical practice. Namely, experiential learning encourages learners to think about education as a tool for emancipation not only from the taken-for-granted concepts, evidence, and data but also from the real-life dynamics, systems, and power structures that very often reinforce and further existing inequalities and structural violence. We believe that such education about past mass atrocities sparks the desire for change among the learners not only by encouraging critical thinking but also political and/or social action. The outcome of such education should be understanding rather than knowing in terms of self-engagement, self-reflection, re-self-positioning of our own roles, social dynamics, and power structures. But the processes that lead to the transition from knowledge to understanding can occur only if the learner is engaged at least on some level. Active engagement connects the intrinsic inner world of the learner with the regulated outer environment that dictates our lifestyle choices through assigned and expected social roles and relations. Such learning is essentially very intimate, personal and, for some individuals, also very transformative as it can provoke the deconstruction of our own (or our community's) morals, values, and self as such. Therefore, not only the poor training of history educators in experiential learning methods but also more systematic resistance prevents the experiential history education from being more widespread and applied, particularly in (public) schools.

We hope that this edited volume that offers perspectives and practical guidelines from a diverse range of experts who have piloted, tested, and/or exercised a variety of pedagogical approaches over the course of several years will be a source of inspiration for new generations of educators who are willing to engage (with) learners. While the cases provided in this edited volume serve as illustrations and the methods presented should be carefully adjusted according to the specific needs of the context, the underlying idea – to imbue the learners with the sense that the violence which leaves communities with lasting traumas should "never happen again" – remains the most important argument for further exploration of experiential learning principles.

Note

1 Over the 18-month long project, run by Nena Mocnik and Hanna Meretoja, we organised a kick-off meeting, 12 local events, one university short course, and an international symposium. The project involved 461 citizens; the symposium attracted 85 professionals from 20 countries. We launched a 45-minute long videogame that has been so far downloaded 1431 times (by February 2021) and published the pilot version of two sets of online tools.

References

Ahonen, S. (2012) *Coming To Terms with A Dark Past. How Post-conflict Societies Deal with History*. Frankfurt: Peter Lang.

Bekerman, Z. & Zembylas, M. (2011) *Teaching Contested Narratives: Identity, Memory and Reconciliation in Peace Education and Beyond*. New York, NY: Cambridge University Press.

Bentrovato, D., Korostelina V. K., & Schulze, M. (2016) *History Can Bite. History Education in Divided and Postwar Societies*. Göttingen: V&R Unipress.

Berman, J. (2001) *Risky writing: Self-disclosure and Self-transformation in the Classroom*. Amherst, MA: University of Massachusetts Press.

Butler, J. (2004) *Precarious Life: The Powers of Mourning and Violence*. New York: Verso.

Felman, S. (1995) Education and Crisis, or the Vicissitudes of Teaching. In C. Caruth, ed. *Trauma: Explorations in Memory*. Baltimore, MD: The Johns Hopkins University Press: 13–60.

Freire, P. (1994) *Pedagogy of Hope: Reliving Pedagogy of the Oppressed*. New York: Continuum.

Giroux, Henry (2011) *On Critical Pedagogy*. London: Continuum.

Hooks, B. (1994) *Teaching to Transgress Education as the Practice of Freedom*. New York: Routledge.

Kolb, D. A. (1984) *Experiential Learning: Experience as the Source of Learning and Development*. Englewood Cliffs, N.J: Prentice-Hall.

Laub, D. (1992) Bearing Witness in the Viccisitudes of Listenint. In S. Felman & D. Laub, eds. *Testimony: Crises of Witnessing in Literature, Psychoanalysis, and History*. New York: Routledge.

Mattar, S. (2011) Educating and Training The Next Generations of Traumatologists: Development of Cultural Competencies, *Psychological Trauma: Theory, Research, Practice, and Policy*, 3 (3): 258–265.

Meretoja, H. (2018) *The Ethics of Storytelling: Narrative Hermeneutics, History, and the Possible*. Oxford & New York: Oxford University Press.

Newman, E. (2011) Teaching Clinical Psychology Graduate Students about Traumatic Stress Studies, *Psychological Trauma: Theory, Research, Practice, and Policy*, 3 (3): 235–242.

Psaltis, C., Carretero, M., & Čehajić-Clancy, S. (2017) Conflict Transformation and History Teaching: Social Psychological Theory and Its Contributions. In C. Psaltis, M. Carretero, & S. Čehajić-Clancy, eds. *History Education and Conflict Transformation: Social Psychological Theories, History Teaching and Reconciliation*. London: Palgrave Macmillan: 1–34.

Rak, J. (2003) Do Witness: Don't: A Woman's Word and Trauma as Pedagogy, *Topia*, 10: 53–71.

Rothberg, M. (2019) *The Implicated Subject. Beyond Victims and Perpetrators*. Stanford: Stanford University Press.

Taylor, T. & Guyver, R. (2012) *History Wars and The Classroom: Global Perspectives*. Charlotte: Information Age Publishing.

Zembylas, M. (2008) *The Politics of Trauma in Education*. New York: Palgrave Macmillan.

Zurbriggen, E. L. (2011) Preventing Secondary Traumatization in The Undergraduate Classroom: Lessons from Theory and Clinical Practice, *Psychological Trauma: Theory, Research, Practice, and Policy*, 3 (3): 223–228.

Part I
Creative engagements with "ghosts from the past" in traditional classroom contexts

1 Why would you use a Fascist greeting to celebrate a football victory? Discussing historical revisionism and genocide memory with Danish high school teenagers

Tea Sindbæk Andersen and Tippe Eisner

Introduction

European societies of the 21st century seem to cherish history and curate the sense of a shared past as much as human collectives have ever done. If we recognise that ideas of shared memories are a crucial element of establishing states, societies, and other social groups (Connerton 1989; Gillis 1994; Assmann 2010; Smith 1991, 11–15) this is perhaps not so surprising. Yet, given the resources and energy invested in creating and sustaining historical memories, it is worth questioning what it is such memories teach us as members of 21st-century societies. Does historical memory primarily give us a much-needed sense of collectivity and social belonging? Does it help us find anchor and orientate ourselves as humans in time and space? Does it perhaps allow us to reflect on the past as an archive of human experience, constituting in a way a catalogue of successes and mistakes to learn from and try to improve? Can we use historical memory to learn to be careful empathic creatures, or at least to be wary of repeating crimes and human-made catastrophes of the past?

In Denmark of the 2010s, history as a school topic has rather high priority. It is taught continuously from the early primary school to the end of high school. Moreover, history remains among the biggest study programmes within the Arts and Humanities faculties of Danish universities. History teaching is politically administered with the Ministry of Education supplying directives in the form of so-called "teaching plans" pointing out which issues and topics are to be taught, including national history, the establishment of democracy in Denmark and the welfare state. As a new addition within the last decades, pupils are introduced to the idea of "uses of history", that is, ways in which history and memory are being appropriated for various purposes (Ministry's webpage, Børne- og Undervisningsministeriet 2017).

Yet, which lessons the Danish public are able to draw from history and memory are uncertain. It is clear from the public debates of the last decades that direct historical parallels may serve to mobilise attention and affective reactions, but they do not seem to foster much empathy or reflection. The political rise of right-wing Danish nationalism with its outspoken anti-immigrant and anti-refugee rhetoric has been accompanied by frequent comparisons to the memory of Nazism made by the right wing itself and by its opponents as well as by mainstream media. Yet, these discussions are usually packed in confusing meta-discussions about the validity of making such historical parallels, often referred to as "playing the Nazi-card" (e.g. Vistisen 2016; Hedegaard 2011; Center for Vild Analyse 2014; Engelbreth 2009). Thus, when a new extreme right-wing party, *Stram Kurs* (roughly translatable as "Hard Line") ran in the Parliamentary elections in May 2019 with an explicit agenda to deport all Muslims from Denmark, an argument unfolded in Danish media about whether the party and its front figure, Rasmus Paludan, were Nazi or not (Krasnik 2019; Larsen 2019; Boffey 2019). A group of university historians discussed the question and concluded that the party's views were certainly worrisome, but it was not a Nazi party as such (Ringgaard 2019). Here, history was involved more as a source of exact comparison and definition, and less a source of general knowledge of the risks of far-right thinking, stigmatisation, and potential ostracism of particular population groups.

Created initially as an internet and social media phenomenon, Stram Kurs became famous by visiting predominantly Muslim neighbourhoods and filming themselves loudly insulting Islam and Muslim populations. The party became an internet sensation especially among the young, and by May 2019 the party's around 400 videos had been watched more than 20 million times on Youtube (Ringberg & Kristiansen 2019). Stram Kurs' wide Youtube audience may be watching the videos with deep disapproval or ironic distance. Nevertheless, the party's powerful presence on the internet and the fact that its videos were being quoted in Danish schoolyards are certainly disturbing factors in a democratic state. Equally troubling is the knowledge that the party managed to gather the 20,000 signatures that allowed it to run for elections and though it did not make it into Parliament, it still gathered 1.8% of all ballots (Hvilsom 2019). Even though the party may not adhere to National socialism as such, its party programme called for the general deportation of several hundred thousand Danish Muslim citizens (Stram Kurs undated). Such rhetoric should remind most people with some knowledge of Europe's 20th-century history of other cases where discourses of extreme othering, segregation, and dehumanisation have existed, and also of cases where such discourses have been acted out in practice, resulting in mass violence, deportation, or even genocide.

It was against this context that we set out in the spring of 2019 to explore if we could find a way of drawing on history and historical memory to make Danish teenagers reflect about histories of mass murder and genocide in relation to processes of othering and dehumanisation of today. We were hoping to find a way of battling the playful indifference that seemed to be behind some of the reactions from teenagers following the party Stram

Kurs' videos; indeed, this attitude seemed to us a widespread reaction to the rise of the right wing. Thus, our ambition was to somehow make youngsters really think about and relate to genocide history and its presence and role in contemporary societies.

Within the framework of the *#Never Again: Teaching Transmission of Trauma and Remembrance through Experiential Learning*, we created a one-day teaching pack aimed for high-school pupils. The teaching pack was based on our own research into memory, history, and popular culture in contemporary Croatia and Serbia, and it was built around the project's idea of using experiential learning as a tool to engage and include participants and audiences in teaching and learning experiences. As a pilot project, we tried out the teaching pack on two groups of high school pupils in the Copenhagen area. The results were interesting, though rather mixed, we think. Some feedback was thoughtful and rather encouraging, whereas other reactions were quite puzzling and not along the lines of our aims. The following pages will present the ideas and theories behind our teaching pack and the results of our pilot project. Before that, however, we would like to express our warm gratitude to our great collaborative partners and high school teachers at Hvidovre Gymnasium and Niels Brock innovation high school, to their kind and funny pupils and not least to our wonderful students who helped us prepare the course pack and realise our teaching events.[1]

Memory and historical empathy

Following the thinking of Astrid Erll, we propose to understand history as a specific "mode" of cultural memory (Erll 2010, 7), one of the organised and institutionalised ways in which "societies remember" (Connerton 1989). Cultural memory, of which history and history teaching constitutes important parts, serves to orientate people in time and space and to establish individual and collective identities (Karlsson 2003, 33, 43–44). Thus, school teaching in history contributes both to consolidating a consensual public memory in future citizens and, more fundamentally, to help students understand their time and place in the world. This is done through historical narratives. Historical narratives, as presented in history books, school textbooks and historical teaching, connect past, present, and future into concepts of continuity. They mobilise experiences of the past, engraved into archives of memory, to make the present understandable and to make expectations of future time possible (Rüsen 2008, 11). Thus, historical narratives create a certain logic of the connection between past, present, and future. They suggest what is to be learned from the past and what should be expected of the future. We learn from history by reflecting on experiences from the shared past of human beings, and we use these reflections to imagine future scenarios and conditions for actions. Hence, ideally, history should make us wiser and better prepared for our future.

The capacity to understand and learn from history may be thought of as "historical empathy." Recent scholarship on history didactics views historical empathy as comprised of several aspects, the first of which is a primarily intellectual endeavour to understand and explain historical events and developments based on a "distinctly cognitive act of reconstructing past perspectives from available historical evidence" (Brooks 2011, 166–167). This act of trying to understand the acts of historical figures based on their worldview and conditions is also referred to as "perspective recognition" (Endacott 2014, 5–6; Barton & Levstik 2004, 206–227).

Yet, whereas perspective recognition is a useful tool to explain actions in the past, it does not help us to evaluate these actions. According to Barton and Levstik, to be able to do so, students of history need to be emotionally engaged; to actually *care*. The absence of emotional commitment, they argue, leave historical enquiry "vulnerable to indifference" (2004, 241). For Barton and Levstik, emotional commitment and feelings of personal relevance are necessary to make students of history engage in understanding, to consider the issues at stake and to be willing to react and behave according to what they have learnt. As such, history teaching and the formation of historical empathy become means to develop democratic participation. "The ultimate purpose of history education", they argue, "is to enable students to take action in the present, and if they are going to take action, they must care to do so – that is, they must be willing, based on what they have learned, to make changes in their own values, attitudes, beliefs, or behavior" (Barton & Levstik 2004, 237).

Thus, if we hope to make Danish teenagers reflect about the threats of right-wing nationalism, the dangers of dehumanisation of minority groups, and the risks of repeating politics that lead to mass violence, one way to do that could be by trying to foster historical empathy. Yet, in order to do that, we needed to develop teaching tools aimed particularly for this by drawing on the idea of experiential learning.

Experiential learning

We work with a simple understanding of experiential learning as "the process whereby knowledge is created through the transformation of experience" (Kolb 1984, 41). This understanding combines experience, perception, cognition and behaviour (Kolb 1984, 21). Kolb presents a model, experiential learning cycle, in which he describes four elementary forms of knowledge: two different ways of grasping experience, either by concrete experience or by abstract conceptualisation, and two types of transforming experience, either via reflective observation or via active experimentation. Critics called this model too simplistic as it did not consider factors such as emotion and individual differences, which may play a role in the ability to learn (Beard & Wilson 2018, 42–43). Consequently, Kolb's experiential learning cycle was altered into a *spiral of learning* (Kolb & Kolb 2009, 309;

Beard & Wilson 2018, 43), which allows for the notion of continuity of experience to be included (Kolb & Kolb 2009, 309–310).

The thoughts behind the spiral of learning are useful for our purpose: Examining if the high school students (can) reflect upon the experiences gained during the event(s) and, upon that, whether they (can), simultaneously or afterwards, conceptualise and eventually apply what they have learned, or even take it further. Nonetheless, we acknowledge, along with the model's critics (Beard & Wilson 2018, 43), that experiential learning does not happen in a closed space, neither spatially nor timewise. Various contexts may influence the individual's possibilities to learn, and we acknowledge these contexts as relevant and omnipresent.

For the learning to actually take place, some significant conditions have to be present. These involve motivation, engagement, and immersion, what can help in creating emotional investment (Beard & Wilson 2018, 52; Schwartz 2012, 2), which was also pointed out as crucial to historical empathy. We as facilitators can take part in creating motivation and engagement, making sure that there is a certain quality to the experience to make it memorable (Beard & Wilson 2018: 52). The following section describes how we attempted to implement experiential learning as a tool in the development of our teaching pack in order to engage and motivate the high school students.

The teaching pack

We prepared the teaching sessions in collaboration with two teachers from each high school. Through explorative and creative group work, we were hoping to make the students engage themselves, investigate, reflect, and make a stand. Thus, we were trying to encourage enough emotional investment to make these students care enough to move beyond indifference and, if we were truly successful, to perhaps also draw that reflection back to wondering about the dangers of indifference in contemporary Danish society.

In order to do this, we needed to create a teaching material that initially gave enough knowledge to try to grasp the historical cases, but also allowed the students to engage themselves in investigating the cases and somehow encouraged them to reflect and consider what they learned. We decided to use cases from Yugoslavia's recent history, both because this is where we ourselves have some expertise, and because we were hoping that by drawing on a non-Danish material we could create the experience of learning something completely new. At the same time, we were hoping to benefit from the students having a more open approach to examples from Yugoslav history, since they would know relatively little about this in advance. We prepared a very brief written introduction to Yugoslav history with a focus on political changes and on moments of mass violence and genocide in connection to the Second World War and the Yugoslav wars of the early 1990s. The text was also prepared as an audio file by one of the teachers at

Hvidovre Gymnasium. By giving them a certain factual knowledge on the topic of the historical cases chosen for the group work, we wanted to enable the students to work in an experiential way with expanding this knowledge.

For the group work, we prepared three different cases that the students were to investigate further. We had selected three examples of Yugoslav histories of genocide or mass violence that were appropriated for various purposes in Serbian or Croatian football culture. Examples from the world of international professional football seemed particularly appealing to us, both because of the fame and glamour that surrounds football culture and because of the strange paradox inherent in the meeting between the sports entertainment industry and the references to historical memories of mass violence and genocide.

The first of our examples was that of Croatian national football team captain Josip Šimunić celebrating a victory in 2013 by chanting a salute associated with the Fascist Ustasha regime that ruled Croatia and Bosnia during the Second World War. The Ustasha are infamous for committing genocide against Serbs, Jews, and Roma and for having contributed to the Holocaust (Sindbæk Andersen 2016; Brentin 2016). The second example was the fans of Red Star Belgrade parading banners with the city name Vukovar in Cyrillic, thus reminding of war crimes committed by Serbian paramilitary units during the war in Croatia in the early 1990s (Mills 2009; Anon 2018; MČ 2017). And the final example was that of Serbian national coach Mladen Krstajić' reference to the international war crimes tribunal for the former Yugoslavia, ICTY, where, among others, the perpetrators of the massacre at Srebrenica were trialled and convicted. Krstajić referred to the ICTY as an example of selective justice, in his eyes apparently comparable to the use of video referencing (VAR) at the 2018 World Championship in football. Krstajić' even suggested sending one of the referees to the tribunal in the Hague (Danas online 2018; Iljukić 2018; Bates 2018).

For each of these examples, we had outlined a brief introduction as well as a collection of easily accessible online sources, where the students could investigate further into the cases. The purpose of this was to foster students' personal engagement by enabling them to make their own investigations, hopefully based on their ideas of relevance. To support their investigations and enrich their discussions, our group included four university students of Balkan studies at the University of Copenhagen, who made themselves available as another source of information about Yugoslav history and the football examples. The university students were all women, which we thought of as a strength, since women are often underrepresented in football culture and rarely figure as football experts. Most of our students were in their early twenties, while one was slightly older, and about half of them had a family background in Bosnia or Montenegro. The aim was to give the high school students an experience of working through the sources themselves, with informed and interesting guidance, and thus make them truly engage with and think about the cases.

As the final element of our teaching pack, we asked the student groups to create a product as a comment, a reflection or a statement in reaction to the cases they had investigated. This was intended to create some sort of impetus and obligation to make up their minds and somehow take a stance in relation to this kind of history and the problems involved in letting it be appropriated or forgotten. We were hoping that this process of deciding their own stance would make them reflect more carefully on their own position. So how did that work out?

Experiential learning event 1: Hvidovre Gymnasium

In early April 2019, we visited the Danish high school, Hvidovre Gymnasium, to conduct our first experiential learning event. The event was prepared in collaboration with two high school teachers in history, and it was their groups of students (40 students in total) we were to work with on this day. The teachers had prepared groups of 4–5 high school students, mixing them across classes and personalities. Moreover, the high school students had read or listened to the audio version of our brief introduction to Yugoslav history, and the teachers had informed them in advance about us and our research project.

The first element of our event was a brief lecture that repeated and elaborated on their concise reading of Yugoslav history with the aim to remind them of the background for some of the historical metaphors and associations that are being used in contemporary football culture in Serbia and Croatia. This was followed by an introduction to the three cases of appropriation of genocide history in football culture. We then asked the student groups to discuss what these uses of genocide and war crimes history were about and why anyone might want to draw on such historical references to celebrate or make particular statements in football culture.

The idea with the group work was to make the high school students spend some time reflecting on these questions. We gave them access to the prepared selection of accessible online sources, and the students could consult these in order to explore certain aspects of the three cases further. By doing this, we were hoping to make the students immerse themselves in the questions and somehow take ownership of their own investigation as a basis of reflecting over the questions. During the group work, many of the high school students seemed both interested and engaged in the cases we presented and the wider meaning of them. The main aspect of this reflection was the presence of our university students, who walked among the groups, made their knowledge and insights available and helped facilitate the discussions. This created thoughtful talks, allowing the high school students to explore issues and pose more fundamental questions. After the event, our university students described these chats as surprisingly open and engaged, as the high school students had been truly curious both about the football cases and the Balkan contexts of these cases. Indeed, this dialogue between the teenagers and the university students may have been the most fruitful experiential element of the event.

After the group work, we had a plenum feedback discussion that concentrated on the role of nationalist ideology and the ways in which it may dominate the perspective on history, to the extent that any sensitivity to historical experience and genocide history may be excluded. The high school students also pointed to the ambiguity of football culture, the highly affective character of international sports, and the possible inability of sporting personalities to actually know what they are saying. It seemed to us that a significant number of the high school students actually *cared* enough about our cases to both learn and really think about them. Thus, the first element of our experiential learning spiral appeared at least partly successful.

The groups were then asked to create a "product" in whichever form they would prefer – a poster, a meme, a written statement, an audio file – as their reaction to this type of use of war crimes and genocide history in football culture. We were hoping to make them position themselves as persons and subjects, and as members of a small teenage collective, in relation to these questions.

Did we succeed? The "products" were truly interesting. Some of them testified to thoughtful discussions among the high school students. Several groups pointed out how they thought these actualisations of genocide history by football heroes could create anger and hate, resulting in deep divisions among groups in society and potential ostracism of groups and individuals. Also, some students pointed out the negative effects such uses of genocide history could have upon the relationships between different states and nations. Many groups produced "memes" often based on widely recycled and remediated images from the internet and edited these images to express sophisticated and humorous condemnations of the football heroes and their uses of history. One group produced a meme that neatly emphasised the use and manipulation of affect; it showed the hand of "soccer" speeding towards a blue button with the caption "bring up the past to support your national feeling", thus suggesting a somehow automatic and unreflective actualisation of the use of history to stir national passions from the side of football heroes.

The same group quite thoughtfully pointed out what is somehow a dilemma in relation to nationalist discourse between ensuring freedom of speech and keeping emotional expressions within the acceptable. They chose a well-known image of a male person holding hands with one woman, presumably his girlfriend, while obviously enjoying the look of another woman passing by. Adding in captions, the group made the guy in this meme represent "nations", while his disregarded girlfriend represented "political correctness" whereas the attractive flirting object represented "freedom of speech."

Interestingly, a different group used the same image to illustrate how they understood the case of Croatian football captain Šimunić celebrating a victory with an Ustasha greeting. They made the male person represent Šimunić, whereas the attractive other woman represented Fascism and Fifa was the girlfriend looking hurt and appalled. Thus, they apparently suggested that the football captain was flirting irresponsibly and disrespectfully with Fascism in a way that was unacceptable to the international footballing world.

Other groups made presentations and statements condemning abuse of history in general, and specifically Serbian football manager Mladen Krstajić's disrespectful references to the Hague tribunal. Others created posters calling for mutual respect and understanding and more "LOVE" within the world of football or emphasising that we should use sports to create communities across borders. One group composed a letter to the world of football requesting collaboration and forgiveness. And one group simply argued, a bit naïvely perhaps, that "the past should be shelved!"

The experiences of researching and discussing these issues and actually *producing* a lasting statement about them seem to have pushed some thinking among our high school students. There was certainly awareness of the problems, and also some quite sensitive reflections about the risks connected to irresponsible and disrespectful uses of genocide history. Did we manage to return the reflections to consider the problem of indifference in Denmark? Probably not. Indeed, one high school student asked as a concluding remark if anything like the wars of the 1990s, the campaigns of ethnic cleansing and genocide could ever happen again in Yugoslavia. He and his fellow students looked highly sceptical at the suggestion that this could happen anywhere – even in Denmark. Yet, a few actually looked a bit frightened at the thought of this possibility.

Afterwards, we received feedback from the two high school teachers, who had participated in the event. They informed us that their students had been satisfied and enthusiastic about the event, in particular working with the subject in a different style than usual classroom teaching, and they felt that they had learned a lot. So perhaps in the longer term, more reflections will pop up.

Experiential learning event 2: Niels Brock business and innovation high school

For our second event, at the end of May 2019 we visited a Copenhagen high school, with a business and innovation profile. Though we intended to follow exactly the same programme, our interaction with these high school students developed quite differently. The introductory lecture was similar to the one given at Hvidovre, and our group of university students was almost identical (one student was replaced by another). Following the lecture, the high school students were supposed to start the group work on investigating the cases of use of genocide history in post-Yugoslav football. Yet, the group work somehow collapsed, and the high school students dispersed across the school buildings, in part because the event took place around their lunchtime break. Moreover, unlike the pupils at Hvidovre, they seemed quite unenthusiastic about the topic under discussion, and they were rather hesitant to enter into discussions or even informal chats with our university students. In hindsight, we obviously did not succeed in making the issues relevant to the pupils, nor to engage them emotionally and make them care about the cases.

The Niels Brock groups' reporting on the cases they had looked into was less informed and not very well researched, and the groups often seemed to have misunderstood the cases and sources. In general, they seemed quite indifferent to the uses of genocide history that we introduced. Indeed, a couple of students suggested that this way of using history was not very surprising, given "the emotions at play in football" and "the strong nationalism of the Balkans." It seems to us that the high school students' lack of emotional engagement made it hard for them to grasp what we were talking about. Few of them seemed to gain any particular experience of new knowledge or learning.

In the next group work, like at Hvidovre, we asked the groups to deliver a "product" in the form of a meme or something similar, reflecting and commenting on the uses of genocide history. The students at Niels Brock seemed very apt at the technical side of producing memes; using memes as a product in school projects and teaching was clearly something they were quite familiar with. Yet, they seemed much more challenged when asked to reflect upon the meaning and potential implications of the uses of genocide history that their memes were supposed to comment on. A number of the products did not relate to the questions of using genocide history at all. One group broke down completely due to internal disagreements and therefore had to refrain from presenting a product. Instead, they played out a debate where they presented different views on their case. Another group produced several memes, some that seemed rather confused or even somehow indifferent to the use of genocide history, and some that seemed to condemn it. Among the first was a meme showing the actor Chris Pratt with the caption "I don't know why everyone is hating on Simunic and at this point I'm too afraid to ask." According to Imgflip, one of the internet's many meme generator sites, the image of Pratt is supposed to suggest that the author has no idea what is happening (Imgflip undated). We understood this as a statement that the group could not quite see the problem with Šimunić's use of the Fascist greeting, which they vaguely confirmed during the following discussion. Other memes from the same group showed a worried-looking sea parrot saying "I don't think Simunic did anything wrong. He just loves his country and was happy they won" and an image of SpongeBob SquarePants holding a rainbow while exclaiming "genocide wonderful." This last rather grotesque meme was never really explained.

One group reacted specifically to the question of whether the use of history and radical nationalistic mobilisation could happen in Denmark by suggesting that this would demand a complete change of attitude within Danish football culture. They illustrated this by replacing all the faces of the Danish men's national football team with that of the radical nationalist and islamophobe party leader of Stram Kurs, Rasmus Paludan, who was then running for parliament. When we asked about this, they explained that they were quite confident this was not a likely development in contemporary Danish society in spite of the presence of discourses like those promoted by Paludan. Whether this makes them less careful and less aware of such risks is a different question.

One important aspect of working with products such as memes is the complexity and vagueness of meaning that characterise them. They are often massively recycled and remediated images with an original meaning that tends to drift and change through repeated reinterpretations in new contexts. Moreover, memes usually convey their messages in a supposedly humoristic or ironic way, which further complicates the reading of their actual meaning. They are inherently ambiguous, which may cause both thoughtful reflection and utter confusion.

Luckily, we had time to discuss the products from the group works, and thus we were allowed to question, challenge, and explore the views presented by the students. Indeed, the students seemed quite confused and uncertain about the whole topic of using history of genocide and mass violence, as well as their own position towards it. Often they had difficulties in explaining what kind of messages their memes were actually intended to convey. When directly questioned, one student agreed that use of genocide history was perhaps "a bit worse" than other types of national mobilisation within football culture. Another student suggested that it is "completely up to individual opinion" whether the use of genocide history within football culture is problematic. However, when asked if he thought it was ok, he strongly argued that he thought it "completely unacceptable." From here, the discussion developed quite widely into a more general consideration of the meanings of national identity, and whether it is possible to combine more than one such identity – a question that seemed quite pregnant, since several of the high school students had parts of their personal backgrounds in the Balkans or the Middle East. Nevertheless, they seemed to have rather little reflections about the implications of this.

We left this event in a rather puzzled mood, wondering if we had in any way succeeded in challenging the widespread indifference about traumatic pasts and future threats. Yet, as one of our university students pointed out: perhaps this group needed this discussion much more than the bright and well-informed students at Hvidovre Gymnasium. At least, as she said, we had tried to pose the questions. Nevertheless, we still left the Niels Brock high school students with a sense that what we had tried to communicate to them was basically not understood as relevant or meaningful.

Comparing the events

At a meeting with our group of university students and some of the high school teachers we pondered the reasons for the very different experiences of the two events: why had they seemingly grasped the problem so much easier and with much more interest in Hvidovre than at Niels Brock?

There may be several factors contributing to these two very different experiences of our event. First of all, it is worth mentioning that the two groups of high school students were quite dissimilar. The first event took place in a high school with a standard or classic profile including a stronger focus on history as a subject of study. At the business and innovation high school, the students seemed less knowledgeable about and less interested in history. The profiles of the high schools also influence the way that history is taught; in a classic high school, history is taught during all three years, while a high school with a business profile teaches history for two years only. Also, they may have a slight difference in age and maturity. At Hvidovre, it was a mixture of both second and third-year students, while at Niels Brock they were all second-year students. Finally, the two groups of high school teachers seemed to have different teaching styles, and the teachers at Hvidovre seemed more closely engaged in managing the event and keeping the students involved.

Secondly, the timing may have played a role. Our first event was in April, still in the active part of the school year. The second event was late May, when Danish high school students prepare for exams. In this period, students only need to be present at school if they have been illegally absent too often during the school year. Some of those present in the Niels Brock classroom may have been less dedicated students, and their motivation may not have been as focused as that of the first group of students. Another timing-related aspect may be that the second event had to include a lunch break, which led the groups to break up in the middle of the programme and some never returning.

Thirdly, as mentioned briefly above, at the second event the pupils were not eager to enter into discussions or even informal chats with the university students during group work. At Hvidovre Gymnasium this interaction had seemed crucial as a way of opening perspectives on the examined cases and gaining a sense of accessibility and familiarity with the topics.

In conclusion: what did we learn from our events?

In our efforts to make two groups of Danish high school teenagers actually think about and react to examples of appropriation of histories of mass violence and genocide, we created a teaching day and a teaching pack that were meant to reflect Kolb's learning spiral (Kolb 1984, 2009), which argues that knowledge is created through transformation of experience. Asking the question "why would you use a Fascist greeting to celebrate a football victory", we encouraged the high school students to both experience their own investigation and to grasp more knowledge, and also, by producing a reaction and a comment, to transform that knowledge through reflection. Moreover, we drew on the idea of historical empathy as a capacity that demands knowledge of the past, ability to recognise other perspectives and emotional engagement, or "care", which is crucial both in motivating the students to really enquire and in enabling them to actually reflect about and evaluate actions of the past. We were trying to foster the students' recognition of different perspectives by using examples from a less familiar region and talk about issues that are not common in the Danish high school. Thus we created an experience of investigating and discovering something new.

In the final part of our events, we intended to push them to somehow take a stand, or at least think about what types of positions could be relevant, by demanding they actively contributed by making their statement as a product. The idea of the product can be a helpful way to make audience participate and engage themselves. It is widely used also in Danish schools, and in our case it was actually inspired by advice from the teachers at Niels Brock high school. Yet, it only works if the production process involves thinking about the message and not only the technical skills involved in applying the medium. The Niels Brock students were brilliant and very quick at creating technically perfect memes, but they were not quite sure what they were saying, or why they wanted to say it. The discussion of the products was essential to make them start thinking about their positions.

Thus, in the end, it seems the truly transformative experience lay in the human factor: meeting the high school students mattered. When we succeeded in making high school students and university students actually share reflections, really thinking about history and what we can learn from it, we were probably closest to creating what we had hoped for. Some of the thoughtful memes produced by these students testify to that, we think. Moreover, as a bonus, the events turned out to be a process of experiential learning not only for the high school students, but also for the university students involved as well as us, the facilitators.

Note

1 Many thanks to Anne Stadager and Karen Steller Bjerregaard at Hvidovre Gymnasium, Ismar Dedović and Lauritz Schultz at Niels Brock Innovationsgymnasium, to the pupils at both high schools, and to our students Marija Krgović, Arzemina Bijedić, Emma Krainert, Pernille Mie Jørgensen, and Mila Kovalj.

References

Anon (2018) Slava Srpskom Vukovaru: Delije Odale Počast Borcima za Ovaj Grad!, *Telegraf*, 21 November, https://www.telegraf.rs/sport/navijaci/3009345-slava-srpskom-vukovaru-navijaci-zvezde-odali-pocast-borcima-za-ovaj-grad-foto (Accessed 10 January 2019).

Assmann, J. (2010) Communicative and Cultural Memory. In A. Erll & A. Nünning, eds. *A Companion to Cultural Memory Studies*. Berlin: De Gruyter: 109–118.

Bates, S. (2018) Serbia boss Mladen Krstajic faces World Cup ban after astonishing "war crimes" rant, *Mirror*, 24 June, https://www.mirror.co.uk/sport/football/news/serbia-boss-mladen-krstajic-faces-12784198 (Accessed 10 January 2019).

Barton, K. C. & Levstik, L. S. (2004) *Teaching History for the Common Good*. London: Routledge.

Beard, C. & Wilson J. P. (2018) *Experiential Learning: A Practical Guide for Training, Coaching and Education*, 4th ed. London, England: Kogan Page, Limited.

Boffey, D. (2019) Danish far-right party calling for Muslim deportation to stand in election, *Guardian*, 5 May, https://www.theguardian.com/world/2019/may/05/danish-far-right-party-stram-kurs-calling-for-muslim-deportation-to-stand-in-election (Accessed 10 August 2019).

Brentin, D. (2016) Ready for the Homeland? Ritual, Remembrance, and Political Extremism in Croatian Football, *Nationalities Papers*, 44 (6): 860–876.

Brooks, S. (2011) Historical Empathy as Perspective Recognition and Care in One Secondary Social Studies Classroom, *Theory & Research in Social Education*, 39 (2): 166–202.

Børne- og Undervisningsministeriet (2017) *STX-læreplaner*, Webpage: https://www.uvm.dk/gymnasiale-uddannelser/fag-og-laereplaner/laereplaner-2017/stx-laereplaner-2017 (Accessed 11 August 2019).

Center for Vild Analyse (2014) Madagaskar. Hvor kort er afstanden fra karneval til alvor i dansk politik?, *Information*, 1 November, https://www.information.dk/moti/2014/10/madagaskar (Accessed 11 August 2019).

Connerton, P. (1989) *How Societies Remember*. Cambridge: Cambridge University Press.

Danas online (2018) Krstajić: Nekada prokleti Hag, a danas u fudbalu VAR, *Danas*, 23 June, https://www.danas.rs/sport/krstajic-nekada-prokleti-hag-danas-var/ (Accessed 10 January 2019).

Endacott, J. L. (2014) Negotiating the Process of Historical Empathy, *Theory & Research in Social Education*, 42 (1): 4–34.

Engelbreth, R. (2009) Nazi-kortet-kortet igen-igen, *Politiken*, 5 October, https://politiken.dk/debat/arkiv_debattoerer/engelbreth/art5045657/Nazi-kortet-kortet-igen-igen (Accessed 11 August 2019).

Erll, A. (2010) Cultural Memory Studies: An introduction. In A. Erll & A. Nünning, eds. *A Companion to Cultural Memory Studies*. Berlin: De Gruyter: 1–15.

Gillis, J. R. (1994) Memory and Identity: The History of a Relationship. In John R. Gillis, ed. *Commeorations. The Politics of National Identity*. Princeton: Princeton University Press.

Hedegaard, K. (2011) Rohde: historisk lavpunkt af Pia K, *TV2 Nyheder*, 18 June, https://nyheder.tv2.dk/article.php/id-40917754.html?rss= (Accessed 11 August2019).

Hvilsom, F. (2019) Rasmus Paludan erkender valgnederlag, *Politiken*, 5 June, https://politiken.dk/indland/politik/FV19/art7241985/Rasmus-Paludan-erkender-valgnederlag (Accessed 10 August 2019).

Iljukić N. (2018) KRSTAJIĆ SA SRPSKIM IZVEŠTACIMA: Briha bih poslao u Hag!, *Novosti*, 23 June, http://www.novosti.rs/vesti/sport.697.html:734624-KRSTAJIC-SA-SRPSKIM-IZVESTACIMA-Briha-bih-poslao-u-Hag (Accessed 10 January 2019).

Imgflip (undated) I don't know what's happening, *Imgflip Webpage*, https://imgflip.com/i/3iu111 (Accessed 29 February 2020).
Karlsson, K. G. (2003) The Holocaust as a Problem of Historical Culture. In K. Karlsson & U. Zander, eds. *Echoes of the Holocaust. Historical Cultures in Contemporary Europe*. Lund: Nordic Academic Press: 9–57.
Kolb, D. A. (1984) *Experiential Learning. Experience as the Source of Learning and Development*. New Jersey: Prentice Hall.
Kolb, A. Y. & Kolb D. A. (2009) The Learning Way. Meta-cognitive Aspects of Experiential Learning, *Simulation & Gaming*, 40 (3): 297–327.
Krasnik, M. (2019) Valget, *Weekendavisen*, 3 May, https://www.weekendavisen.dk/2019-18/samfund/valget (Accessed 10 August 2019).
Larsen, J. V. (2019) Paludan svarer igen på Nazikritik: "hank an selv være nazist", *BT*, 3 May, https://www.bt.dk/politik/paludan-svarer-igen-paa-nazi-kritik-han-kan-selv-vaere-nazist (Accessed 10 August 2019).
MČ (2017) Sramotna poruka Delija povodom obljetnice vukovarske tragedije, *gol.hr*, 20 November, https://gol.dnevnik.hr/clanak/nogomet/sramotna-poruka-delija-povodom-obljetnice-vukovarske-tragedije---496841.html (Accessed 10 January 2019).
Mills, R. (2009) It All Ended in an Unsporting Way': Serbian Football and the Disintegration of Yugoslavia, 1989–2006, *The International Journal of the History of Sport*, 26 (9): 1187–1217.
Ringberg, J. & Kristiansen A. L. (2019) Youtube-fænomenet, der pludselig fik medvind og kom på stemmesedlen, *DR*, May, https://www.dr.dk/nyheder/webfeature/stram-kurs (Accessed 10 August 2019).
Ringgaard, A. (2019) Historikere: Nej Rasmus Paludan er ikke nazist, *Videnskab.dk*, 8 May, https://videnskab.dk/kultur-samfund/historikere-nej-rasmus-paludan-er-ikke-nazist (Accessed 10 August 2019).
Rüsen, J. (2008) *History. Narration, Interpretation, Orientation*. New York: Berghahn.
Schwartz, M. (2012) *Best practices in Experiential Learning*. Ryerson University (https://www.ryerson.ca/content/dam/lt/resources/handouts/ExperientialLearningReport.pdf).
Sindbæk Andersen, T. (2016) Football and Memories of Croatian Fascism on Facebook. In B. Törnquist-Plewa & T. S. Andersen, eds. *Disputed Memory. Emotions and Memory Politics in Central, Eastern and South-Eastern Europe*. Berlin: De Gruyter: 297–317
Smith, A. (1991) *National Identity*. London: Penguin.
Stram Kurs (undated) Udlændinge, *Stram Kurs Webpage*, https://stramkurs.dk/vores-politik/udlaendinge/ (Accessed 10 August 2019).
Vistisen, A. (2016) Ja, det minder om Muhammed, *Jyllandsposten*, 29 January, https://jyllands-posten.dk/debat/blogs/andersvistisen/ECE8403470/ja-det-minder-om-muhammed/ (Accessed 11 August 2019).

2 Breaking the nationalistic master-narrative: the case of teaching history in contemporary Croatia

Stevo Đurašković

Introduction

The historical culture[1] of present-day Croatia – as elsewhere in the post-communist Central and Eastern Europe – has been encapsulated by the nationalistic master-narrative conceptualising the history as a kind of a fairy-tale like Manichean struggle of heroes and villains for a metaphysical body of a nation representing an everlasting victim of external and internal others (Judt 2002). In the case of Croatia, the legacy of the 1991–1995 war for independence (called in Croatia the Homeland War) additionally fostered this nationalistic meaning of the history. Ever since the history turned to a kind of political battlefield; the trend even increasing in the last years due to the contemporaneous rise of the revisionist radical right (Jušić & Đurašković 2018; Cipek 2017).

Croatian history teaching curricula has been charged with the task of supporting the process of nation and state-building from ethnocentric and self-contained perspective lacking a wider regional, European, and world context. Besides, the curricula are enforced with obsolete pedagogy stressing names, dates, and memorialisation, thus completely lacking any comprehension of historical events.[2] Although some experts argue in favour of the multiperspectivity in history teaching as a tool to foster civic values (Koren 2012), I assume that multiperspectivity cannot bring the intended outcomes history teaching in the present-day Croatia. Assuming the multiperspectivity as "a strategy of understanding", in which we consider another's perspective (or others' perspectives) in addition to our own (Stradling 2003, 13–14), the prior question comes to my mind: how to exercise the multiperspectivity with the undergraduates entering studies with almost no comprehensive historical knowledge due to the above-exposed state of the school history teaching in Croatia?

Since deep and sound intellectual grounding is required prior to student civic engagement in community (Harkavy & Donovan 2000, 1), in this chapter I argue that the nationalistic understanding of history in case of society such as the Croatian can be much successfully broken by introducing students to complexity and contingency of history rather than forcing them to deal with various, usually antagonistic perspectives and interpretations. In my opinion, if students manage to reflect upon the complexity of historical structures and agencies, they would eventually consider another's perspective simply because they would become suspicious towards any kind of historical teleology, regardless to political orientation one inevitably has.

In this chapter I show how I attempt to break the nationalistic narrative in my course of the Modern Croatian Political History, which I have been delivering since the academic year 2016/2017 to the first-year undergraduate students in Political Science at the Faculty of Political Sciences in Zagreb. The course has been taught in the Croatian language and it delivers a synthetic overview on the 19th – and the 20th – century Croatian political history. Thus, the course objectives are to understand the complexity of processes, structures, and agencies, with special emphasis on the contextualisation in the regional, European, or global history, respectively. Since this is one of the core courses in the first-year Fall semester, around a hundred students typically enrol. While the class participation is assigned on a voluntary basis, all students have to pass a final written exam and to attend certain number of classes. I leave the room for the volunteers willing to read assigned texts and to take an active role in class discussions. Out of approximately 100 students, I usually have some 10 to 15 students actively participating in the classes and I reward them by an extra grade. Throughout the years, I have noticed that for most of the students, history courses appear unappealing, and this is due to the disengaging pedagogic methods they are exposed to in the earlier years of schooling. Therefore, I have to use inevitably some forms of ex-cathedra teaching to provide students with the basics in history knowledge, which is necessary for participation in any thought-provoking discussion later on in the process. In order to boost student's interest in the subject, I perform lecturing as much as storytelling.[3] To keep students engaged and present I usually break the lecturing part by posing some questions.

In seminars I facilitate discussions based upon assigned readings by introducing a cause-effect way of thinking. I approach the subject in a way to break perception on history as a kind of (detached) epic drama. Instead, I offer to my students a perspective on history as a complex set of phenomena and eventually as an engaged "past presence" by highlighting how the present problems have been shaped by past events and experiences.

The course content is devoted to the three historical periods: to the history of Croatia in the 19th-century Habsburg Empire; to the history of Croatia in the Interwar Yugoslavia; and finally, to the history of the Socialist Croatia and the Socialist Yugoslavia. In the following section, I will present the methods used during my course upon the selected examples in order to showcase as much the student coursework.

Teaching the Croatian history in the Habsburg Empire

I devote all together the four classes to the Habsburg Empire. Every class is composed of a two teaching hours lecture and consecutive two teaching hours seminar discussion per week. The introductory class is devoted to the general history of the Habsburg Monarchy, while subsequent three classes are devoted to the modern history of the Habsburg-time Croatia.[4]

I start my introductory lecture with the question of what they know about the Habsburg Monarchy. If anyone is willing to participate (at the beginning of the course students show some hesitation, and only in the flow of the course they gradually increase their performance), one usually reproduces the popular nationalistic narrative. Assuming the lack of comprehensive understanding of the history by my students, I gradually come to the point where we discuss the potential arguments why the "Habsburg" Croatia enjoyed a large-scale autonomy in internal affairs – the historical fact otherwise commonly employed by the nationalist master-narrative to boast the Croatian historical statehood pride. I usually get no answer to this question. Hence at the very beginning of the course, I try to encourage students to participate in seminar discussion by stressing how I would like them to share their thoughts and opinions, and that they should forget that something as "wrong" answer even exists.

Therefore, at the very beginning of the course I introduce students to the general context of the 19th-century history of the Habsburg Empire, most notably through the clash between the Habsburgs and the newly emerged national movements. Aiming to challenge the students in this early stage of the course, I ask them to comment on who and why would present a highest danger to the Habsburgs. It takes some time until I get an answer that Austrian – German and respective Hungarian national movements would present a highest danger since they were the strongest. Then I ask them to explain how the Habsburgs could be the bearers of the pan-Germanism – as claimed in the Croatian nationalistic narrative – if the (pan) German nationalism represented one of the biggest dangers to the Habsburg strife for power.[5] Confronting students with such question as an example of absence of any logic in the uncomprehending (nationalistic) claims, I aim to introduce students to the cause-effect way of thinking. I use this method throughout the course and here I will show it with the example of the seminar discussion on the 1850s Habsburg New Absolutism.

The assigned 20-page text gives to students a good summary on the character of New Absolutism, particularly in Croatia (Horvat 2009, 321–338). Initially, I ask students to share what they know about the New Absolutism prior reading the text. If I get any response, it is usually about how the Absolutism enforced the anti-Croatian authoritarian control over Croatia, thus abolishing achievements of so-called national-awakening movement from 1848. Then I ask students to comment upon what the text argues to be the socio-economic reforms the New Absolutism implemented in Croatia.

As the students speak, I write down their answers as short entries on a blackboard. When we finish exchanging the comments, I call them to relate the outcome of the New Absolutism to the 1848 National-awakeners' demands. I give them some time to think about, and to go through their notes from previous lectures etc. I wait until I eventually get a few vocal objections how the New Absolutism executed the most of the National-awakeners' demands. Then I ask them to help me to impair the 1848 demands and the New Absolutism outputs. Here I start by drawing a kind of table with two columns on the blackboard, the one column being devoted to features of the Absolutism and the other to the features of the 1848 Croatian national demands. As they speak, I write down their comments on the blackboard in a form of notes (see Figure 2.1).

I call this "blackboard method", which I use to make the seminar work intelligible as much to the students, as well to try to invite into the discussion at least some of the students who do not read the text prior the class.

Finally, I move one step forward by asking the students to discuss how come that the New Absolutism eventually accomplished most of the demands of the 1848 Croatian national movement and I let them start to speak as they want. Then I direct the discussion towards clarifying political goals of the Habsburgs and of the Croatian national movement, until we eventually conclude that sometimes the Habsburg and the Croat political goals were coinciding and sometimes were confronting, depending on a particular political context. With this example, students can learn and observe the multilayered and complex narrative of the historical events as opposed to the simplified versions applied and used in the nationalistic discourse.

Then I ask students to comment on the New Absolutism case in relation to the present day. My aim is to draw the parallels between the Habsburg Monarchy and the European Union. Students attend the courses "Political System of the EU", "EU Enlargement and Europeanization of Croatia", and "Political Economy of the EU" only in the third year of undergraduate

Assumption: The New Absolutism as (German) hegemony over Croatia	
The New Absolutism reforms	Demands of the 1848 Croatian National- Awakeners
- Modern Civil administration and the civil code - Modern public-school system - Croatian as official language - Modern market economy - Compensation to the landlords	- Introduction of the parliamentary government - Modern public administration - Modern schools in Croatian as official language - Abolishment of serfdom, introduction of modern market economy o Not having resources to pay the compensation to the landlords

Figure 2.1 Blackboard notes, example 1: New Absolutism.

studies, which makes this discussion challenging. However, in the academic year 2018/19 the question raised some discussion triggered by one student, who commented how the New Absolutism is like the EU: giving money for the reforms while simultaneously derogating the national sovereignty. The comment was immediately followed by objections from few students, for instance, how foreign centres of power have been exercising crucial reforms in Croatia both in the past and in the present since we – i.e. Croatian citizens – have not been capable to do reforms on our own etc. I did not intervene into the discussion, but rather observed how they relate the past to the present, eventually realising how history can be related to a present-day life.

Teaching the Croatian history in the interwar Yugoslavia

When we come to the history of Yugoslavia, the nationalistic masternarrative impacts the students even more, since the history of Yugoslavia has direct bearing to the Croatian contemporary national identity-building. The popular narrative portrays the interwar Kingdom of Yugoslavia exclusively as the greater-Serbian hegemony oppressing the Croatian national identity as well economically exploiting Croatia to an utmost extent (Najbar Agičić & Agičić 2009). Although this claim is not entirely false, it is rather distorted due to the reduction of the entire history of the interwar Yugoslavia on the Croatian national question.

I devote to the history of the interwar Yugoslavia two classes: the first one deals with the 1920s escalation of the conflicts between the Croatian and the respective Serb politics; while the second class deals with the 1930s Royal dictatorship. Here I approach the initial deconstruction of the nationalist narrative by discussing the case of the 1920 currency conversion when the new state introduced the Yugoslav Dinar to replace the Austro–Hungarian Crown and Serbian Dinar.[6]

The assigned text (Matković 1998, 140–149) to read is the very short piece focusing on the economic policy in the interwar Yugoslavia, and also includes the 1920 currency exchange issue. The text is focused on the economic exploitation of Croatia by the royalist regime. I start discussion by inviting students to share the main statements of the text on the currency conversion. While they speak, I write down on the blackboard in the successive rows "the Austro – Hungarian Crown – Yugoslav Dinar exchange rate: 4 = 1", "the Serbian Dinar – Yugoslav Dinar exchange rate: 1 = 1", and "Serbian Dinar – Austro – Hungarian Crown rate before the 1918: 1 = 1." Then I ask them to summarise who eventually ended up with the financial at loss by the currency conversion. I get a few immediate responses that it was "the Croats", only sometimes someone would add "the Slovenes also." Instead of responding to their comments, I project the map as shown in Figure 2.2, side by side to the blackboard notes.

Then I ask the students to name the provinces which were previously in the Austro–Hungarian Empire. After we all hear "Slovenia, Croatia,

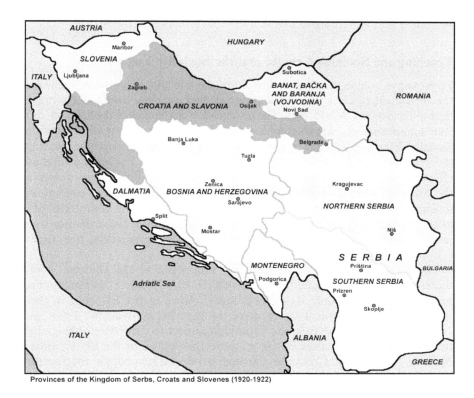

Provinces of the Kingdom of Serbs, Croats and Slovenes (1920-1922)

Figure 2.2 Blackboard notes, example 2: Austro-Hungarian Empire.

Bosnia, Vojvodina", I ask them to name the nationalities living at these territories. With this, we soon add that the currency conversion was unfair not only to the Croats and the Slovenes but also to the Serbs outside the Serbia proper ("Uža Srbija"). I use this short exercise as a kind of an initial striking example, mirroring how the history of the Interwar Yugoslavia has been distorted by the nationalist narrative, as is outlined in the introductory paragraph of this section.

In the course session on the 1930s royal dictatorship, I discuss with the students the 1937 Manifesto written by the Croatian and the respective Serbian political Parties against the regime and I ask the students to discuss what they find as the most important in this one-page long piece of text (Petranović & Zečević 1988, 367–368).[7] Usually the objections from the students consider how the Manifesto emphasises the injustices done to the Croats, how it calls upon the abolishment of the dictatorship and subsequent reconstitution of the state in respect to carry out the equality of the nations. With this, I start a free conversation where I use the example of the Manifesto to remind them again how the interwar history was more complex than the simplified national antagonisms between the Croats and the Serbs.

Teaching the Socialist Croatia and the Socialist Yugoslavia

I devote five course meetings to history of the Socialist Yugoslavia, including the introductory class on the communist lead partisan antifascist struggle during the Second World War. The present-day challenges of the Croatia, as a state and the society, are to a great extent shaped by misinterpretations of the Socialist Yugoslavia, aired by the mainstream public narrative rather than by the very legacies of the socialist past. For this reason, I invest an ultimate effort to discuss with students the complexity of the political processes in the Socialist Yugoslavia. It is challenging to make the course content intelligible to students and at the same time not reducing the complexity of a historical process. Students would often complain how the socialism as a political and economic system is so far distant to their present-day lives that it is even hard to imagine it.

The way to bring closer the socialist Yugoslavia to the students would therefore be to make the comparison with the EU. However, as I mentioned previously, students only have the courses related to the EU later in their studies. For this reason, I try to drive the parallels between the 1960s and 1970s grievances of Slovenia and Croatia in respect to the federal subsidies to the present-day complaints by Germany to the politics of the EU subsidies. Namely, Slovenia and Croatia as the most developed republics in the Socialist Yugoslavia complained in respect to the subsides to the underdeveloped republics of Macedonia, Montenegro, Bosnia-Herzegovina with very similar arguments to contemporary used by Germany in respect to the transfers to the EU Cohesion Fund consumed by the ex-communist East-European underdeveloped EU member states. Eventually at least few students would be able to see some similarities between the complex political relations in the Yugoslavia and the EU, and thus to grasp how the history of the Socialist Yugoslavia could present an interactive part of their present lives.

Yet, the goal of the course is to counter the popular nationalistic masternarrative. Even more than during the previous classes, I tend to deconstruct the nationalist narrative in a similar manner as in the before exposed case of the currency exchange. Here I will elaborate two cases only.

The first case is a seminar discussion on the overrepresentation of the Serbs in the ranks of the state administration and the civil services in the Socialist Croatia. The assigned reading for this seminar is the text comprehending how the communists dealt with the national identity and respective relations between the constituent nations (Radelić 2006, 242–268). The text downplays the popular nationalistic claim that the Croatian Serbs represented between 60% and 80% in the ranks of the state and civil servants in the Socialist Croatia. Instead, it brings data showing the proportion of

Breaking the nationalistic master-narrative 39

around 28% of the Serbs in the state and civil service in the Socialist Croatia (Serbs represented an average of the 15% of the population of the Socialist Croatia). However, the text does not explain the reasons for the over-representations of the Serbs.

To understand this issue, I use my blackboard notes in a similar manner as in the previously presented cases. I start the seminar by writing on the blackboard the two note entries: 1. Historical causes in favour of the overrepresentation; 2. Social causes in favour of the overrepresentations. Then I ask students to help me to fill up each column. At the end, the blackboard looks like following (Figure 2.3):

If my call for a help in filling the columns is met by the students' silence, I try to motivate them to participate by asking to relate the historical causes column to the events during the Second World War, the topic we processed in one of the previous classes. Eventually at least few students respond on how the Croatian Serbs almost entirely sided the anti-fascist Partisans, while the ethnic Croats were siding the partisans and the fascist Ustasha respectively. I write down on the blackboard their comments in a form of the entries, as shown in the picture below. Subsequently I undertake a short discussion on the reasons making the Croatian Serbs to side the partisans unanimously, and on the reasons making the ethnic Croats to split their support between the Partisans and the Ustasha.

When we discuss the social causes, I have to encourage the students a little bit more. I try to initiate brainstorming by asking them to recall what they can see in the Hollywood blockbuster movies about joining the army

---

The Overrepresentation of the Croatian Serbs

1. Historical causes

        The Croatian Serbs – sided partisans during the Second World War to a greatest extent

        The Croats – split between support to the fascist Ustasha and the antifascist Partisans (fifty-fifty)

2. Social causes

        The Croatian Serbs – the most backward regions

        -The Military frontier historical legacy

        The Croat backward regions – siding the Ustaša

Figure 2.3 Blackboard notes, example 3: Representation of Croatian Serbs in Socialist Croatia.

or the police. Students would usually respond how in most cases we can see people of colour or lower-class people joining the army. Then I ask them to draw correlations between the two cases. With a little help from my side, we eventually come to the conclusions that the overrepresentation of the Croatian Serbs in the police force ranks turned to be expected since the Croatian provinces populated by the Serbs had been the most backward parts of country, plus the Serbs were siding partisans during the War. Then we move our discussion to the low representation of the ethnic Croats in the police, eventually coming to the conclusion how the backward provinces dominated by the ethnic Croats were predominantly siding the Ustasha during the Second World War. I invite them to recall some additional arguments which could be also related to the overrepresentation of the Croatian Serbs in the ranks of police and military. This finally leads us to the long-standing history of the Croatian Serb service in the Habsburg Army which we dealt with during the classes on the Habsburg history. By leading students step by step in discussing the overrepresentation of the Serbs in the ranks of the state administration and the civil services in the Socialist Croatia, I aim to train students in cause-effect way of thinking. Simultaneously, this step by step seminar discussion serves better the aim of deconstructing the popular nationalist narrative as oppose to simple lecturing on the causes of the overrepresentation.

The second example on teaching the Socialist history is the closing discussion on the regime's relation to the Croatian and Serb nationalism. This discussion serves somehow different purpose than the former one. It aims to puzzle the students' perspectives rather than leading them to the firm concluding remarks. The assigned reading for this last seminar session is the excerpt from the Memorandum of the Serbian Academy of Sciences and Arts from the (Memorandum 1986, 7–13, 18–27). Most of the students are at least acquainted with the fact that the Memorandum 1986 has been widely considered as the key moment of unleashing the contemporaneous Serbian nationalism which caused a dissolution of Yugoslavia to a great extent. This is why the Memorandum presents good material for the discussion.

I use again my blackboard notes as a method of comprehension. I ask the students to elaborate the most significant points in the Memorandum. I write down on the blackboard their ideas in a form of note entries. Afterwards, I ask students to impair the notes on the Memorandum with the main claims of the Croatian Spring: the late 1960s political movement that called, inter alia, for more national rights for the Croats in Yugoslavia. The eventual outcome is presented in the following Figure 2.4.

After we finish, I ask them to comment in respect to the table drawn on the blackboard. My intention is to see their prospective reactions to impairing historical agents labelled in Croatia as very negative and very positive. When I did the "Memorandum" and the "Spring" impairing in the first generation of my teaching in the year of 2016/2017, I thought that

The Memorandum	The Croatian Spring
- Slovenia and Croatia economically exploiting Serbia	- The centralist Yugoslav state is economically exploiting Croatia
- Leading Communists = Croat Tito and Slovene Kardelj	- The overrepresentation of the Serbs
- Serbia and Serbs = victim of the SFRY	- Croats and Croatia = victim of the SFRY
o Discrimination against Serbs in Kosovo and against Serbs in Croatia	o Croatian national identity jeopardized by the Serbs
o Serbian national identity is discriminated due to the alleged greater - Serbian legacy	o Croatian national identity is discriminated due to the fascist Ustasha legacy
- Demand to full political unity of the Serb people of Yugoslavia	- Demand to full political unity of the Croat people in Yugoslavia

Figure 2.4 Blackboard notes, example 4: Socialist history and Croatian and Serbian Nationalism.

students would object immediately. I was astonished to being met with complete silence in the classroom; yet the same pattern has been repeated in the following years. This silence made me think how even the historical phenomena debated from time to time all over in the media, like the Croatian Spring, have been something unknown to the students, probably due to the "names & dates & memorization", i.e. due to the factual pedagogy they go through the years of schoolings. I try to break this silence by encouraging students to shout out whatever comes to their mind in respect to the socialist Yugoslavia. While today I hear mumbling, in the previous years, some students shared how they were not aware that the Serbs also complained about the Socialist Yugoslavia. However, this year, 2019, the most talkative student in the course, the L.P., commented how the Socialist Yugoslavia seemed to her as a kind of a complete mess. She wondered how everyone complained to be discriminated by others: the Serbs complained to be discriminated by the Croats and vice versa etc. In her words, she kept asking herself how the state existed at all if everyone felt discriminated. My closing remark to this final session has been to call the students to think about the Socialist Yugoslavia as being a kind of "historical fifty shades of grey", and not as a simple black and white picture. Most of them laughed at my remark; of course, I used the title of the famous movie to get their attention.

Concluding remarks

No matter how much I invest in preparing and delivering classes, the predominant part of the students unfortunately remains passive. I could only speculate about the reasons: as political science students, they are perhaps primarily interested in the presence, not in the past; the rooted perception of the history as ultimately boring subject; the long-term legacy of limited teaching approaches in the schools which cannot be deconstructed by one semester of comprehensive course work etc. Or maybe, the reason of their passive presence in the classroom can be simply found in a more general trend of students being apolitical and passive towards the world surrounding them – the fact that my teaching colleagues also keep stressing.

However, it seems that my classes offer a kind of a reward, at least to the students actively participating in it. I often talk to those active students also during the breaks, especially because they speak more freely when eye-to-eye than in a plenary in the classroom. Besides further questions on the content, they usually comment how my course opened their eyes to the "real history." Already mentioned student L.P. told me how my course made her to consider reading some history books for fun; something she said she would not even think about before. I.P., another last semester and a very active student, told that he thought that much more pupils would like history as a subject if it would be thought in schools as it was thought in my course.

In terms of my classes in general, I observe students stop blaming others for the political hardships in the history of the country. The last year student, whom I presumed upon his comments to be a right-wing sympathiser, told me in one seminar, dealing with the Habsburg history, that incompetent national elites were to be blamed for the hardships, and not the Habsburgs, or the Germans, or the Hungarians. Although the comment cannot be labelled to go in line with the goals of the course, at least he stopped blaming others. To me, this proves that the intended outcome of breaking the nationalistic master-narrative is better to be an unspoken goal of the course then the one announced openly by me, and visible directly from my teaching.

Finally, I think that my efforts in helping students to grasp a history as complex and usually as a contingent process, present the assuming step into coming to terms with the past. By aiming to break the nationalistic Manichean historical narrative, I think that my classes contribute to break the image of the nation as eternal victim of others, especially in respect to the legacy of the war for independence that Croatia relatively recently went through. However, at the end of the day, I believe we cannot convince people to change their opinions; we can only expose them to an experience which would give them an impetuous to reconsider and change prospectively.

Notes

1 The term of historical culture (Geschichtskultur) is described by Jörn Rüsen as an articulation of the historical consciousness in particular society providing its present self-definition as well as its projections for the future. (Carr 2006).
2 Although in the last 20 years the multiple history textbooks exist, even the textbooks encouraging critical thinking and individual conclusions on the part of students are very contained by the curriculum discouraging any creativity by the teacher (Koren and Baranović 2009). In 2018 the new curriculum has been passed, however, being very similar to the previous one passed in the mid-1990s. The curriculum has been one of the most publicly debated issues in the last few years. For the course of the debate, see the web-page *Historiografija.hr* (2019). To what extent the historical consciousness of the young generations has been distorted was highlighted by the recent research showing that the half of the Croatian final grade secondary education pupils were uncertain whether the Second World War Croatian Nazi-Puppet state was fascist at all (Kovačić and Horvat 2016, 251).
3 Sometimes I even tell anecdotes about peculiarities of famous historical persons in a way to show students how the national heroes were "flesh and blood" human beings. For example, I tell them how the leader of the early 19th Century so-called Croatian National Awakening Movement was ardent gambler; the fact which jeopardised his political career eventually. I do that to present a "national heroes" as flesh-and-blood human beings similar to us.
4 My teaching on the general history of the Habsburg Monarchy is based upon *The Habsburg Monarchy 1809–1918* by A.J.P. Taylor (originally published in 1941), and *The Habsburg Empire: A New History* by Pieter M. Judson (2016). The modern history of the Habsburg-time Croatia is thought upon the book *Povijest i kultura Hrvata kroz 1000 godina: gospodarski i društveni razvitak u 18. i 19.st*, by Josip Horvat. Originally published in 1938, this book still presents the most nuanced synthesis of the history of Croatia in the Habsburg times. The book's author, Josip Horvat, was one of the most outstanding interwar liberal journalists in Croatia, so the book is easy to read; unlike most of the works by the Croatian professional historians.
5 Here I also use one simple case to stress on the multinational character of the Habsburg Empire I am teaching about. Namely, I ask students to name commanding Habsburg generals cracking down on the 1848 national revolutions in the Monarchy. As the students spell out their names, I write them on a blackboard as follows: Alfred Windischgrätz, Josef Radecký, Josip Jelačić. Then I ask the students to comment upon their prospective nationality. Off course, we come immediately that Windischgrätz was an (Austrian) German, that Radecký was a Czech while Jelačić was a Croat.
6 The newly founded Yugoslav state was composed of the provinces previously belonging to the Austro Hungary – Slovenia, Croatia, Bosnia-Herzegovina, and Vojvodina – and from previously independent Kingdom of Serbia and Kingdom of Montenegro. The state was originally founded in the 1918 as the Kingdom of Serbs, Croats and Slovenes, to be renamed in Kingdom of Yugoslavia by the proclamation of the royal dictatorship in the 1929. For the purpose of clarity, I use the word Yugoslavia in this paper. For the best comprehensive account on politics in the Interwar Yugoslavia, see Dejan Djokic, *Elusive Compromise: A History of Interwar Yugoslavia*, New York and London: Columbia University Press, 2007.
7 When I started teaching the course in the year 2016/2017, I was so ambitious to assign some primary sources, like speeches of some politicians or excerpts from papers of some intellectuals etc. However, I faced that only two or three students were able to discuss about the assigned texts. Other complained how the primary sources were too complicated to grasp. The texts were in fact not so complicated,

but rather – as I stated previously – the students in general have a such a poor grounding that they can't find any comprehensive meaning in primary sources. So later I dropped these excerpts out, and instead gave them to read some page long pieces during classes.

References

Carr, D. (2006) History as Orientation: Rüsen on Historical Culture and Narration, *History and Theory*, 45 (3): 229–243.

Cipek, T. (2017) The Specter of Communism is haunting Croatia. The Croatian Right's Image of the Enemy, *Politička Misao*, 54 (1–2): 150–169.

Harkavy, I. & Donovan, B. M. (2000) Introduction. In I. Harkavy & B. M. Donovan, eds. *Connecting Past and Present: Concepts and Models for Service-Learning in History*. Washington, DC: American Association for Higher Education: 1–11.

Historiografija.hr (2019) *O obrisima novog kurikuluma povijesti*. Available at: http://www.historiografija.hr/?p=14076 (Accessed 22 July 2019).

Horvat, J. (2009) *Povijest i kultura Hrvata kroz 1000 godina: gospodarski i društveni razvitak u 18. i 19.st.* Split: Marjan knjiga.

Judt, T. (2002) The Past is Another Country: Myth and Memory in Post-War Europe. In J. W. Müller, ed. *Memory & Power in Post-War Europe: Studies in the Presence of the Past*. Cambridge: Cambridge University Press: 157–184.

Jušić, L. & Đurašković, S. (2018) Politike povijesti u Estoniji i Hrvatskoj: Drugi svjetski rat kao "prošlost koja nikad neće proći"?, *Anali Hrvatskog Politološkog Društva 2017*, 14: 125–143.

Koren, S. (2012) Poučavanje o Interpretacijama, *Povijest u nastavi*, 10 (2): 185–217.

Koren, S. & Baranović, B. (2009) What Kind of History Education Do We Have after Eighteen Years of Democracy in Croatia? Transition, Intervention, and History Education Politics 1990–2008. In A. Dimou, ed. *Transition and the Politic of History Education in Southeast Europe*. Gottingen: V&R University Press: 91–140.

Kovačić, M. & Horvat, M. (2016) *Od podanika do građana: razvoj građanske kompetencije mladih*. Zagreb: Institut za društvena istraživanja u Zagrebu – GONG.

Matković, H. (1998) *Povijest Jugoslavije, 1918–1991 – Hrvatski Pogled*. Zagreb: Naklada Pavičić.

Memorandum Srpske akademije nauka i umetnosti (nacrt), Jesen 1986. Available at: https://www.helsinki.org.rs/serbian/doc/memorandum%20sanu.pdf (Accessed 31 March 2020).

Najbar Agičić, M. & Agičić D. (2009) The Use and Misuse of History Teaching in 1990s Croatia. In S. P. Ramet & D. Matić, eds. *Democratic Transition in Croatia: Value Transformation, Education & Media*. TAMU, College Station Texas: Texas A&M University Press: 193–223.

Petranović, B. & Zečević M. (eds.) (1988) *Jugoslavija 1918–1988: tematska zbirka dokumenata*. Beograd: Rad.

Radelić, Z. (2006) *Hrvatska u Jugoslaviji: 1945. – 1991.: od zajedništva do razlaza*. Zagreb: Školska knjiga.

Stradling, R. (2003) *Multiperspectivity in History Teaching: A Guide for Teachers*. Strasbourg: Council of Europe Press.

3 Fictional family tree: storytelling and short film project

Taina Kilpelä and Elina Mäkilä

Background

We all are born in a certain time and place as members of particular families and become marked by the people and relationships that precede us. Each of us carries past generations in us in the form of burdens, potentials, and positive resources. By exploring and sharing these intergenerational experiences, we can better understand others and ourselves. This was the premise of the Fictional Family Tree project. We are interested in the invisible stories and intergenerational knowledge that we carry and transfer to future generations. *Taakkasiirtymä* (*transfer of burden*), a concept created by psychotherapist Martti Siirala in the 1960s, refer to burdens of previous generations that we carry and pass on unless the burdens are recognised and relieved. "What is not commonly shared will become a burden of someone to carry." Siirala (Siltala 2016, 7). Nowadays the same phenomenon is described as intergenerational trauma.

The project explored real and fictional family trees created collectively with experiential methods of storytelling and filmmaking. It was organised as a workshop course in spring 2019 in collaboration with the Universities of Applied Science Metropolia and Diak for students of social work.

The course consisted of seven three-hour meetings, course readings, a learning diary, and an essay. Students got five credits for the course as part of their elective studies. We had an international group of seven students of social work with participants from Finland, Israel, USA, Poland, Sri Lanka, France, and Bulgaria. Course was held for students of social fields. We thought understanding their own personal backgrounds through the course might help the students to work with other people and their problems in social work. Good self-knowledge helps to recognise how people's backgrounds affect their present situation and the way they act. It also increases understanding of one's own reactions in different situations. Both authors have background in anthropology but in the article we approach the project as facilitators and art educators.

Collective sharing

The focus of our project was on sharing intergenerational experiences. We tried to identify commonly shared burdens as well as positive potentials by exploring everyone's own family trees and by creating a fictional story built on shared experiences. Aim of the project was to create a participatory film that would tell a story of generational continuation.

Experiences are carried in the minds of individuals as well as in collective memories. Some of the collective memories are traumatic. Sharing and talking publicly about them can be difficult. According to Siirala, unrelieved burdens of traumatic memories can transfer from generation to generation without recognition or understanding that certain issues might be reflections of past traumatic events. For example, in Finland, the traumas experienced by men in the Winter War (1939–1940), The Continuation War (1941–1944), and The Lapland War (1944–1945) were not discussed in public. Culturally men were not allowed to express their anxieties resulting in mental health problems, alcoholism, and violence (Kivimäki 2013). Social sharing is an important link in relieving and healing traumas and in recognising painful as well as positive heritage we carry across generations. By sharing, recognising, and working with our past we can widen our understanding, grow empathy towards each other, and break the chains of transmission of traumatic pasts. In this chapter, we will present and analyse our course process. We revise its benefits and challenges as a tool of experiential learning and discuss how it could be applied.

Methods: family tree, ethnofiction, and participatory filmmaking

Ethnofiction as an inspiration

In the course we combined family tree technique with elements of ethnofiction filmmaking. Family tree technique means that students create their own family tree focusing on burdens and potentials running in their family. Ethnofiction is usually used in ethnographic filmmaking. Initially, ethnofiction was based on the genre of *cinéma vérité* founded by a French filmmaker and anthropologist Jean Rouch. Ethnofiction combines documentary and fiction and gives the participants a creative tool for handling challenging and often silenced and invisible issues. In his work Rouch used projective improvisation. Rouch asked his informants to improvise their experiences in front of the camera assuming that this method would reveal aspects of culture that conventional ethnography might fail to grasp. By reflecting on their experiences through fiction and drama, the protagonists would, according to Rouch, reveal "the hidden truths" of culture.

In ethnofiction the role protects the actor. Playing a role offers a chance to describe reality. It allows the actor to hide behind the role and to say, "It is not me." Through the process protagonists start to think and express their own problems and who they are (Blue 1967, 84–85). Ethnofiction inspired us to work on our own experimental method of studying intergenerational transmission. In our project, we did not do research on informants. Our understanding of ethnofiction was informed by Augusto Boal's (1979) notion of learning as dialogue where teacher and student encounter each other as equals in two-way communication that happens in a spirit of cooperation (Sjöberg 2009, 185–186). We wanted to create and explore our backgrounds and realities together with the students. We combined exploration of our own family backgrounds with participatory and ethnofiction filmmaking.

Participatory filmmaking

Creation of the short film in the project was participatory. Participatory filmmaking gives the power of creation to the participants. Decisions usually done by film director and/or producers were made democratically within the group. Ethnofiction was applied as the fictional story used reality as its raw material. The creation of the film made it possible for the participants to explore, express, and even change their personal views on topics that might have been difficult to discuss openly. Feelings could be written into the story of the film's fictional characters. Participatory filmmaking focuses on process and meaning rather than the final product. Below we describe this process and our main observations more closely.

Process – course structure and content

Main task of the workshop was to create a participatory fictional short film during seven sessions. Students were encouraged to prepare for the course by collecting background information about their family so they could draw their family tree in our first session. During the course students kept learning diaries on every session.

In the first session we wanted to create a safe space and group spirit for students. This was the most important session in the workshop process as we wanted to inspire the group to share on quite sensitive issues. We started by introducing ourselves and the idea of the workshop. We discussed theories, ideas, and inspirations behind the project. Students were told that this was a pilot workshop and we encouraged them to participate as co-creators by giving us feedback and reflections during the process. Next the students created personal family trees using collage technique. At the end, we discussed the family histories, burdens and potentials illustrated in the collages.

Creating safe space and responsibility of the facilitator

We knew that asking students to create their own family tree and to share it with a group of new people could be sensitive and challenging. We put a lot of effort into creating a safe space for the participants. This was done by telling about the tasks in the course, by underlining that participation was voluntary and how everyone could share as much as they felt comfortable with. We had also made our own family trees and introduced them to the students indicating that we too were part of this process.

We discussed how the method could affect participants and especially about protecting them in case the process would become too personal and start to have negative effects on the participants psychologically. We talked about setting boundaries, voluntarism, and using fiction as a shield with the most vulnerable issues. Students were repeatedly told that they should set their boundaries on what and how much they wanted to share. We stressed that it was crucial to keep the limits between reality and fiction and that students themselves would draw the limits of revealing personal data.

It is crucial for facilitators to know the group. We worked with students of social work who were aware of such issues. If the process would be done with a group children or people with challenging issues, facilitators should consider including a counsellor in the group or place more emphasis on fiction and potentials. This type of working process requires careful facilitation and instruction so that participants feel safe sharing their personal stories. This cannot be emphasised too much as sharing is the backbone of the whole process.

Creating family tree

We asked students to create their family trees, to add in important persons and their characteristics and to think of the burdens and potentials they saw running in their family. We also urged them to add historical events that took place in different times on their family tree. Family trees were done with collage technique where students could use magazine photos, texts, paints, pencils, and the like. By using collage we wanted to give students freedom to express themselves creatively. These tools helped to think "emotionally" and to express difficult things indirectly (Figure 3.1):

> I have been focusing on an aesthetic aspect of my work instead of its deeper meaning. And now, during the session, I did not need to think "aesthetically" but rather "emotionally". Thus, drawing my own family tree as a small act of creating art gave me an opportunity for the new experience of practicing art. – Student diary

Sharing

At the end of the session everyone, including the facilitators, told about their family tree. To have done the process yourself before asking people to contribute was important. Everyone shared as much as they liked.

We were surprised how bravely the students shared about their families. They had made interesting notes and analysis on their discoveries during the

Fictional family tree 49

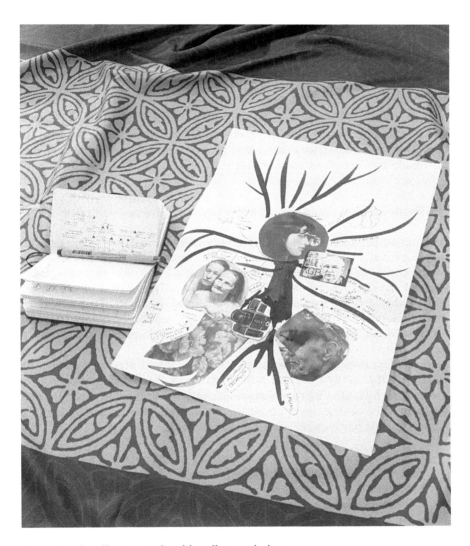

Figure 3.1 Family tree made with collage technique.

process. International background of our group meant that family roots of the participants were spread all over the world. Some of the students felt at ease because of the group size and heterogeneous background.

> Perhaps the diversity of our group also helped to share our stories – it became a kind of a filter, which changes the dynamic of session.
> – Student diary

Backgrounds and stories were obviously different but there were surprisingly many similarities in family histories.

> It was revealing that that the same themes repeat itself globally but it would be also interesting to do the same process with the people of same culture. – Student diary

This first session of the process was the most challenging as it required trust and a feeling of being in safe environment. One of the students wrote in the diary that he did not trust other group members and did not go as deep into his family tree details as some others:

> I don't trust the participants of the group to be able to really tell my family story in detail. I kept my presentation formal. – Student diary

Amount of personal details in the family trees varied. We were surprised how personal things students were able to share even in the first session when people really did not know each other at all. It would be interesting to know if the outcome would be similar with a different kind of group. We assume that it could produce even more fruitful outcomes if we would use more time on group formation and on the elaboration of family trees. On the other hand, we tried to make it flexible and light so people would not feel too obligated to share either.

In the next session, we concentrated on the content produced during our work with the family trees and how to elaborate it into fiction. We started the meeting by collecting thoughts and feelings about the first session. There was also a lot of discussion about the method and the negative feelings it might evoke if participants used it in social work.

> I was concerned about the consequences on the client(s), if we let them deal with their emotions raising from the workshop/re-enactment. I realized that, as facilitators, we need to provide them a safe space where they can express their feelings and let go, as well as feel heard. – Student's diary

We discussed how the method could be directed to positive resources. Some students felt we might have included too many heavy issues for such a short process. The discussion shifted to therapeutic aspects and the willingness to address one's own family background as well as the self-regulation in the process. Not everyone was ready to deal with everything. It must be accepted that people take part in the process at their own stage.

We moved on to do drama games so the group members could get to know each other better and to relax. Next we collected on post-it notes themes that arose from the family tree presentations. The group members wrote down and organised the themes in consensus. Family trees brought up

Fictional family tree 51

many topics dealing with issues of historical trauma and intergenerational transmission. Many were common for different students. This led to a discussion about how common the symptoms and burdens affecting families were despite their origins (Figure 3.2).

> Despite various places of origin and different backgrounds, our family stories had a lot of elements in common. Whether it was in Asia or Europe, our families have been experiencing traumas and tabus. Each of us could tell the stories related to war, addictions, unspoken and unsolved conflicts, difficult relationships, etc. It was especially visible when during the second session we recalled and wrote down all issues and matters that we had shared while telling the stories of our families.
> – Student's diary

The themes for our story were selected from the grouping task. We inspired students to create a storyline as a group and to invent main characters. We worked on characters, for example, with an improvisational task "hot chair" where one of the students was a character and others asked him/her questions about the character's life, past, and background. By doing this we gave characters background and motives for their actions so they would be real and credible people in the story, not just caricatures. Students were encouraged to draw inspiration from their family trees but still work on fictional characters to create a fictional story. Working on storyline and content was very intense. The short course did not allow students too much time to deepen the characters. The result was a quite straightforward story

Figure 3.2 Students grouping themes that came up from the family trees.

with two characters, Charlotte and John. Here are some reflections from a student:

> Collecting our family issues helped us to build the basis for the story for the short film. This was the moment where we started transforming the realities of our families into fiction – or, in other words, where we started constructing the ethnofiction story. – Student diary

The group created a fictional family tree for the characters as well as a plot for the film. The plot did not directly become a burden defined by generations, but the story had excellent ingredients for the film and we were guided by the idea that previous generations would somehow appear in the film.

The group worked very well and everyone participated quite actively. As instructors, we did not participate but rather tried to assist students in the tasks when they needed help and instructions. Limited time did not allow us to deepen characters or to connect the stories even more to larger historical events, as present in the family trees. During this session we went through the basics of filming and filmmaking and started working on our fictional story. We introduced students with the drama structures and basic elements of storytelling by using short film examples and hands-on tasks.

In the third session we concentrated on creating our fictional story by working further on the characters, getting to know the basic elements of filmmaking, drawing storyboards, and planning the shooting. If the previous session was about analysing, this session was about creating, doing, and making the storyboard and script in preparation for the shooting. Time pressure directed the process in productive direction and we were surprised how well the group worked together. We also noted how the content, plot, and choices made by students reflected ethnofiction process even better than we expected.

How it all turned into fiction?

The outcome of the first three sessions was a short film script, Heavy Bags. Group decided that the film would be in black and white. The story was about Charlotte and John who participate in an entrance exam while struggling with their inner difficult feelings. These feelings seem as echoes form their past, burdens they got from parents and now carry in heavy bags.

Characters of the short film depicted the world of the students in a straightforward manner. Students picked an environment and topics that were close to their real life. The main burdens that came up in family tree session were present in a modified manner in the short film. In addition, the closing scene addresses the ideas of sharing and becoming visible as keys in resolving intergenerational burdens. The main characters carry burdens in their heavy bags and on their skin. In the last scene, they see each other's pain and burdens. By connecting, they leave their heavy bags and burdens behind.

Students used the central tools of film-making creatively to deal with topics and issues we had discussed in the first session. The plot projected the elements of the personal family trees through fiction, weaving personal stories into a fictional film with a positive ending. This made us feel that ethnofiction and the objectives of our workshop worked quite perfectly. At the end of the third session, we decided the roles for shooting and prepared the schedule for next two sessions.

Filming

In the next two sessions we filmed our short film according to the storyboard. We shared roles between students. Everyone had a role that fitted their skills or interests. These decisions were quite effortless and everyone seemed happy with their part (Figure 3.3).

> It was my first experience in filmmaking. (...) I could see that the team members have been getting better in what they have been doing throughout the day, the camera men, producer, director and coordinator as well as my fellow actor were learning and improving their skills with the progression of the session. – Student diary

During the filming we as facilitators were almost jobless and only assisted when students needed help.

Figure 3.3 Students filming scenes outside University of Applied Science of Metropolia.

> I believe that the dynamics between the group members and the facilitators are also changed from the starting session to where it is now. The facilitators ability to understand what type of help we need to continue our progress in the creation of the movie is increasing all the time. – Student diary

At the end of the fifth session, we also managed to start editing with WeVideo online editor.

Editing

With editing, one of the most important parts in filmmaking, our goal was to make the students work together. In the participatory method it was important that everyone took part in finalising the film. For this purpose we used WeVideo online editors that enabled work online with several simultaneous timelines.

> All in all, filming and editing process combined both learning and having fun. It became a kind of passage from the reflections on family stories towards the expression of these reflections. It was a tool that gave us a voice and a chance to process difficult issues. I would name it as a jump from reality into fiction that can help to create a new and positive perspective on family matters. – Student diary

In the end, we succeeded in putting together a quite balanced film without it becoming a one-person effort. Had we had more time for editing we could have reflected more on each other's work and choices during the process and could have talked more about choices in music and style. On the other hand, we managed to bring different visions together in a way that allowed the students to feel their own handwriting in the film. This made the film shared and participatory. By concretely working together on the film, the students also shared the burden of its content. In the process we made room for sharing to happen on every level from the start until the end of the course in the screening.

Screenings and feedback session

In the seventh and last workshop session we concentrated on editing and finalising the film, screening it and having a feedback session. We ran a bit out of time and decided to organise a separate screening for teachers and other students. We did not have enough time for a proper feedback session with the students after the screening. In our feedback session, we collected feedback on the students' experience of the course and not how they individually felt about the content. One of the students noted that if the session would have been made with clients the reflections session would have been important and should have been done from the perspective of the individual's process. This is something we should work on in the future. It is important that we give enough time to feedback and talk about the process.

We invited all students and teachers for the extra screening. During this time of semester students were out doing their internships and not too many people came. Participants actively organised the screening and even created a poster for the film. Two responsible teachers came to the screening and were fairly impressed with the outcome. The film was later shown in a teachers meeting.

Reflection: fictional family tree as experiential learning

> First of all, having the discussion about strengths and weaknesses and using the family tree format to generate ideas for the discussion I think amongst our group really humanized the idea of shame or vulnerability and to me it seemed like it was such a healthy space to talk about those things, even when they weren't very positive. (…) In the end, I think within our group, everyone had these similar life experiences within their family, so it wasn't in my mind particularly embarrassing for any individual. – Student essay.

This comment describes the outcome of our process. We met our goals much better than we expected.

Ethnofiction at work

In the above the student reflects on the use of ethnofiction and on how it works to portray reality with fiction by giving participants the chance to use their imagination and voice. With the method we managed to use fiction to project some issues that might have otherwise been difficult to handle in a group.

> Super interesting part of this process was the idea when you offer space in an imaginary realm to a participant, and the freedom to improvise or create something new or fictional, that they may reveal values or feelings that they otherwise might not express. – Student essay

Interestingly the students wanted to place the story in a study context that represented their real life. This reflects ethnofiction better than we ever expected. One student reflected on this further in his essay:

> I think it makes sense that we used the campus to film and used components about school because we're all students and academic achievement is on all of our plates at the moment but we had all the freedom in the world to talk about. – Student essay.

References to historical events were not as obvious as we concentrated more on the story and its intimate details. Broader historical contexts were discussed in the beginning of the session. As students were from different parts of the world we could not reflect on the same events. Maybe this is the reason why school and immediate family histories became the focus.

Shared experiences – shared learning

Storytelling, participatory film-making, and experiential learning process as a whole increased understanding of generational transmission in several ways. A participant's point of view:

> We have been getting to a point that perhaps the facilitators and the group members are in many ways equal coworker in the project, but on the same time they manage to still affirm themselves as the project directors. I am pleased with the amount of help and effort they can offer us. Without them this project would have never gotten to the stage it is in right now. – Student's diary

Collective process was at the core of all teamwork. Every step was a learning process that encouraged dialogue, negotiation, creativity, sharing, and active participation among every member of the group, including instructors. In the film-making process everyone could use their strengths and learn from others. Together we found an interesting way to depict transmission processes over generations. Including personal aspects, creating script, and learning basic techniques of film-making made the course experiential and participatory. Methods of experiential learning helped to explore transmissions between generations and relationships between individuals, culture, and history. During the course, students also learned basic filmmaking skills.

> A group of strangers have managed to create a real product inside the barriers of the method. Something is working in the method. I think that the group work was the key here. The group seemed to be working even better under time pressure. I was sceptic before we started the process but now I see it is possible. – Student's diary

This method has a lot to offer if the process is given enough time. Sharing, group formation, building trust, and creating a safe space demand time and effort, but once these elements are in place results can be very rewarding.

Application – where and how does it work?

Metropolia students' film told an intergenerational story about challenges that had been transmitted as heritage from previous generations. The most important thing was not to make a great movie, but the process itself where participants were sharing and discovering different meanings of family history and how it affected the present. Learning about the process of filmmaking was also important. This method is variable for different kind of groups with different emphasis. It is important to clarify what is the goal and focus in the process.

Two things were highlighted at the end of the course and at the Never Again symposium: the importance to frame carefully what kind of group participates in the course; and effects on the participants. When we cannot assure that students can draw the limits themselves, how to deal with situations where the experience becomes too traumatic?

> I do question the idea of trauma transmission when a participant has a very heavy experience that they feel they are ready to share (...) what if it's too much for them and they don't realize it ahead of time? What if it's too much for the group? How uncomfortable is too uncomfortable and what happens when someone insists on sharing really difficult experiences? Coffee break? – Student essay

The Fictional Family Tree concept should always be modified for the particular group and emphasis laid on different things depending on the goal of the process. During the course in the Metropolia, we concentrated more on challenges in family histories which were portrayed in the short film as well. The process could also be adapted and facilitated from the perspective of potentials and coping strategies.

Our group consisted of adults who had already studied some years of social work. They had the capacity to explore their family roots and felt it was important from a professional perspective. If severe personal and traumatic experiences or feelings should rise up in any kind of art processes, participants should be guided to talk with professionals. Empowering and therapeutic elements are a great power in art processes but it is also important for facilitators to be sensitive and to listen to all the group members carefully. Participants should write a working diary during the course to better recognise their own reactions and feelings. This way the process is under good guidance.

Using this method or parts of it can give participants many tools to observe and work with their reality and to explore personal as well as broader historical and social issues in the classroom and further work. One student of social work understood this quite clearly:

> In closing I would say that coursework and the readings and media examples have provided a thorough understanding of ethnofiction and experiential learning. I think the time spent in the course allowed me to sharpen my own perspective with regard to identity and forced me to reimagine what social services can be rather than what it should be.
> – Student's essay

References

Blue, J. (1967) Jean Rouch in Conversation with James Blue, *Film Comment*, 2–3 (4): 84–86.

Boal, A. (1979) *Theater of the Oppressed*. London: Pluto Press.

Kivimäki, V. (2013) *Murtuneet mielet. Taistelu suomalaissotilaiden hermoista 1939–1945*. Helsinki: WSOY.

Siltala, P. (2016) *Taakkasiirtymä. Trauman siirto yli sukupolvien*. Helsinki: Therapeia-säätiö.

Sjöberg, J. (2009) *Ethnofiction and Beyond: The Legacy of Projective Improvisation in Ethnographic Filmmaking*. Paper presented at the international conference "A Knowledge Beyond Text" at Centre Pompidou in Paris, November 2009.

4 From traditional to the moving classroom: empathy as a key component of the classroom teaching

Alma Jeftić

Introduction

A year after the atomic bombs were dropped on Hiroshima and Nagasaki, John Hersey, a reporter for the New Yorker, was assigned to interview and write the memories of six hibakushas (Srikanth 2012). At the last minute, the New Yorker Editor decided to turn that report into a single issue believing that it had helped to humanise the destruction and show the American public faces under the mushroom cloud (Srikanth 2012, 64). Even though copies sold rapidly and people read eagerly, no one actually went out and protested against bombing of civilians. That issue brought glory to the Editor and the newspaper in general, as it was the first attempt to humanise the civil victims of atomic bombing; however, it somehow failed to contribute to the dialogue on bombing and war by themselves, on different perspectives and justification for such actions.

How can one write an article on war atrocities in a way to educate and motivate people to think and analyse from different angles and perspectives? This question reflects one of the goals of this chapter that deals with education in post-conflict societies, Bosnia-Herzegovina, particularly while taking into consideration that both teachers and students either directly or indirectly survived the war and suffer from its consequences. It is important to emphasise that the primary objective was to test three experiential learning games during two workshops with teachers and pedagogues from primary schools in the Herzegovina-Neretva Canton in Bosnia-Herzegovina. Workshops were organised from 18th to 19th December 2018 in the premises of the Fourth Primary School in Mostar. They were attended by 40 teachers and pedagogues from Herzegovina region. Workshops were organised with the help of Ministry of Education, Science, Culture and Sport of Herzegovina Canton, whose representatives actively participated during both events. All three tools are based on the premise that empathy can turn a traditional classroom into a *moving* classroom that connects ordinary teaching activities to art, theatre, and museum industry.

The aim is therefore not to provide a method and technique that can be used in the classroom to ultimately ensure better working conditions to both teachers and students, and to lead to reconciliation of narratives and healing of wounds. It would be simply too ambitious to claim that a tool to address the complexity of trauma could be produced from just one single workshop but such activity provides deeper insights into trauma management in the classroom.

Teaching difficult history in post-conflict society: toward the moving classroom

Education contributes significantly to the process of dealing with the trauma; however, both teachers and pedagogues have to be trained to recognise the danger of trauma and its rhetoric in the classroom. According to Kaplan (2005) trauma can never be healed in the sense of a return to how things were before the traumatic event took place, or before one witnessed such an event. However, its impact can be worked through both individually and collectively. This is what Zemblyas (2008) meant when he coined the term *translating trauma* which refers to finding new ways to make meaning out of traumatic experiences of the past. Such process can be achieved through reflection on personal narratives of the traumatic past, but only if it occurs in a safe environment. Psychosocial research has shown (Albeck et al. 2002) that using personal narratives can help move Germans and Jews, and Israelis and Palestinians, closer to reconciliation, especially when these narratives take place in a "safe space" that encourages active listening and honest dialogue and reflection (Chaitin & Steinberg 2014). Safe environment refers to a judgement-free place where both groups can sit together and express their views of the past; therefore teachers have to be well trained to respond to such situations. History-teaching projects can occur in two different formats: as an attempt to produce a shared memory, or as an initiative to have each group acknowledge the other's narrative (Bilali & Ross 2012). The question if groups should acknowledge diverse memories or if they should strive to form one mutual narrative remains unanswered. For instance, in Israel, social psychologists have worked with Palestinian and Israeli teachers to develop a joint history textbook, which depicts both groups' historical narratives and one empty sheet which is supposed to be used for one common narrative teacher and students will write together (Albeck et al. 2002). Similar activities are underway in Bosnia-Herzegovina, where (mainly history) teachers have been undergoing training through EUROCLIO project on how to talk about sensitive and difficult events from distant and recent past. However, both of these two projects strive at achieving one mutual narrative that will satisfy all involved sides. Assuming there are two sides in the conflict, it is hard to achieve one narrative that will be in line with both group's needs and memories. One of the influential models that are commonly used when addressing trauma and violence is needs-based model developed by Shnabel and Nadler

From traditional to the moving classroom 61

(2008). Model suggests that victims need to restore their lost power and status, while perpetrators need to restore their positive identity (Shnabel & Nadler 2008). However, empathy is required to understand needs of the other person, therefore an important question is how to organise classroom activities in a way that can potentially teach both student and teacher to respect each other's opinion and to analyse why certain events from the past should never happen again. How important all these elements are is given in Figure 4.1.

Figure 4.1 is grounded on the analysis of difficult memories and education conducted between 2016 and 2019 in Bosnia-Herzegovina (Jeftić 2019). Both generation who survived the war and the second generation born after the war have been affected by its consequences. While teachers have direct (they lived in Bosnia-Herzegovina during the 1992–1995 war) or indirect (they were outside of the country) experiences of the war, students (the second generation) have to deal with the transgenerationally transmitted memories and traumas. According to Chaitin and Steinberg (2014), the descendants of the war trauma survivors hold images and "memories" in their heads, and feel them in their hearts and bodies, the phenomenon they called my-their memories. Such memories are the second generation's understandings of "what has happened." Hoffman (2004) assumes that by understanding the formation and existence of my-their memories one can gain insight into the ways in which we are living connections to the traumatic past. Hence we can assume that students bring to the classroom "my-their" memories which stand between autobiographical memories of the direct victims, and the collective memories of the new generations. Such recollections can elicit certain traumatic memories from the past in situations when indications for such events

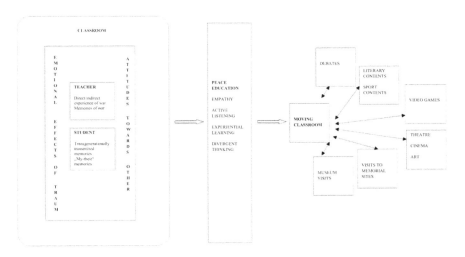

Figure 4.1 Moving classroom.

exist (for instance, during history class), therefore it is important to transform the classroom into a safe environment in which teacher and students can feel respected. In contemporary Bosnia-Herzegovina that is a pretty difficult task, considering different memories of war (Jeftić 2019). The biggest challenge is to teach history, literature, art, and geography as these courses come with certain emotional baggage and different interpretations of the same facts. Such interpretations and analysis largely depend on different ethnic background (Bosniak, Serb, Croat, Other), different textbooks in use in different areas (Federation Bosnia-Herzegovina, Republic of Srpska, District Brčko and cantons that utilise Croatian teaching curricula), and attitudes toward different ethnicity. Even though multiperspectivity refers to interpretation of the past in a way it is being perceived from *our* perspective but also from the perspective of *Other*, it has not been applied yet as the agreement on how to teach about 1992–1995 war has not been reached. As presented in Figure 4.1, it is important to give voice to everyone in the classroom; however, it is even more crucial to teach teachers and students how to do it. This is where the concept of empathy as "an affective response more appropriate to another's situation than one's own" (Hoffman 2012, 4) finds it place. According to Zembylas (2007, 207), the ideals of empathy and reconciliation are examined through the lens of emotion; while the emotional effects of trauma narratives raise a question that has been largely ignored in the peace education literature. Peace education is defined as a series of teaching encounters that draw from people their desire for peace, non-violent alternatives for managing conflict, and skills for critical analysis of structural arrangements that produce and legitimise injustice and inequality (Harris & Synott 2002). Hence, scholars engaged into peace-building and education need to consider how to develop strategies that will contribute to the implementation of teaching curricula that combines theory and practice. Education for Peace was introduced into schools in Bosnia-Herzegovina in 2002, and it was based on the notion that peace is inherent capacity of humans (Clarke-Habibi 2005). Its strength can never be underestimated; however, it failed to provide the solution for both divided schools and curricula, which has not been found yet (Jeftić & Joksimović 2014).

In this chapter, peace education is understood as the ability of both teacher and student to respect and discuss different perspectives, and to combine classroom setting and experiential learning. As presented in Figure 4.1, teacher is supposed to combine different techniques in order to transform the traditional classroom into the moving classroom which combines debates, museum and memorial visits, theatre plays, literary and sports contents, and videogames. As such, the classroom becomes a place where one can learn, perform, analyse, express, and discuss without fear of being judged and discriminated. Therefore, teachers should be trained to use experiential learning techniques and empathy that will together enhance divergent thinking which correspond to the thought process or method that leads to creative solutions.

Empathy as a methodological component in the classroom

The discourses of empathy and reconciliation in curriculum and pedagogy are critical components of the re-formation of peace education goals in a conflict-ridden society (Zembylas 2007, 207). Nevertheless, ability to listen to someone actively is crucial for further understanding of person's feelings and emotions. Hence teachers and students should be trained the active listening skill that includes paying attention to the speaker, showing patience and understanding, providing feedback while avoiding judgment and discrimination and finding the most appropriate response. Active listening means, as its name says, to listen to someone actively. That includes specific nonverbal communication (nodding, leaning forward, eye contact), and specific verbal affirmations ("Sure", "Of course", "I understand", etc.). It requires full concentration, paraphrasing, developing trust, and showing concern. When combined with empathy, the active listening skill becomes a powerful method that transforms the ordinary classroom into the moving laboratory that teaches about difficult past in a safe environment full of support and understanding. Even though neglected in literature and sometimes taken for granted, active listening enhances empathy and supports the establishment of a safe environment which makes it an important part of peace education.

The major benefit of active listening and empathy in such setting is that they can ensure safe space for discussion and reflection – all of which would have been impossible otherwise. The major benefits of moving classroom are in its flexibility and openness towards experience which does not correspond and definitively does not equal to "stepping into perpetrator's shoes." The role of active listening and empathy is to provide safe space for both sides to talk, listen to and understand what is being listened. It prevents all sorts of judgements and comments, both positive and negative. Through such method one can establish moving classroom: one that connects the opposing views and makes space for their distribution, analysis, and integration. Assuming history class that would include not only lectures, but movies, theatre, debates, and visits to memorials and museums, one comes to the analysis of relatively new concept of historical empathy.

Historical empathy highlights the interaction of the cognitive and affective dimensions of empathy and as such is the basis for understanding the processes through which learning history through textbooks and museums influences a change of consciousness about particular events (Jeftić 2019). It is developed through the methodology of history teaching, focusing on the dialogue between teaching about historical characters and facts as well as reconstructing the evidence-based perspective that provides a useful operationalisation for the analysis of cognitive and affective dimensions (Savenije & de Bruijn 2017, 833). It implies a perspective that the individual takes up through knowledge and understanding of the broader historical concepts, the actors in these actions, as well as the motives, beliefs, and emotions that led them (Endacott & Brooks 2013). History classes can enhance development of historical empathy inasmuch teachers demonstrate active listening, respect of different perspectives and enable students' divergent thinking. The aim is to enable teachers and students to provide safe environment for each other, to move classroom walls and go out: to the playground, to the theatre, museum, and memorial site. While confronting narratives and meeting new thoughts and ideas, both students and teachers will satisfy their needs to be listened and understood, which is in line with the needs-based model. Also, that will support the overall climate in the classroom and help students think "out of the box", analyse more ideas and find more creative solution. Therefore, the overall goal of moving classroom is its connection to the space outside of it, process that represents bond between people and historical places. According to psychological research, the cognitive and affective aspects of empathy are mutually dependent, and the very definition of empathy is reduced to the process of understanding and the emotional response to the thoughts and feelings of another person (Hoffman 2012). Also, this perspective is in line with research in the field of museology that suggests a mutual relationship between reason and emotions and the fact that emotional responses shaped by our culture should be emphasised (Watson 2015). Empathy can be learnt through contact with people and events they can transmit, and as such this is the first step towards breaking prejudices and changing the attitudes – all of which would not be possible in an ordinary classroom. In this process, museums play a key role as they are equipped in a unique way that encourages visitors to imagine, explore, and feel a rich human heritage, therefore they have the ability to connect art, technology, science and literature, develop empathy, and show the way in which all human beings are interconnected (Jeftić 2019). Moving classroom can be used as a connecting line between conventional education and museum industry.

"Let me listen to your perspective": interactive workshop with teachers and pedagogues from Bosnia-Herzegovina

Based on the previously described research and theories of difficult memories, trauma, and empathy, interactive workshop for 40 teachers and pedagogues from Herzegovina Neretva Canton in Federation Bosnia-Herzegovina was designed. The aim was to test three experiential learning tools that were supposed to enhance empathy and further contribute to teachers' understanding of peace education and importance of experiential learning when dealing with trauma.

Workshop was organised in the premises of an elementary school in the city of Mostar and teachers were randomly divided into two groups. Both groups attended the same workshop but on two different days, and the main reason was to make it easier for facilitator; 20 participants per group was more than enough for experiential learning workshop. Both groups were quite diverse in terms of religion and ethnicity of participants, but also their work experiences: the group consisted of teachers and pedagogues with more than 20 years of teaching experience and those with less than ten years. Teachers came from various disciplines including history, education, biology, art, foreign language, and religion. However, it was impossible to achieve gender balance as majority of teachers in Bosnia-Herzegovina are females, therefore only five males attended the workshop.

Workshop was designed to include interactive exercises and discussion, avoiding frontal lecturing as much as possible. It was divided into three parts, and each one was followed by discussion between participants and facilitator:

1. perspective taking exercise;
2. let's define! (interactive game);
3. debate.

In the first part, all participants were asked to complete the following sentence: "When it comes to this workshop, I am mostly worried about ..." Upon the completion of that task, facilitators collected all responses and then distributed them randomly to participants. Their task was to read the sentence and describe it as if it was their own worry or concern.

That was a very good warming-up exercise that helped participants to get a glimpse of the main aim of the workshop, but also get ready for further empathy training. It also helped to open up a discussion into pros and cons of empathy, which continued into further analyses of advantages and disadvantages of being an emphatic person.

In the second part of the workshop, participants were divided into pairs and given a list of four words: victim, perpetrator, nationalism, and patriotism. Participants' task was to define these words among each other first, and then to define them in the context of the 1992–1995 war in Bosnia-Herzegovina. While the first task was very easy for the participants, they struggled during the second part. All of them experienced the 1992–1995 war in Bosnia-Herzegovina and the idea of putting sensitive terms into that context was not very welcomed. Some of them complained of the exercise being off-topic as they wanted to talk about heavy workload more; while some reported that it was not easy to define these words within war concept. They underlined the importance of listening and, as they called it "monitoring" other person's reactions while they were giving definitions and explanations, because they did not want to upset him/her or to make him/her feel uncomfortable. The fact that they recognised the importance of empathy at the very beginning was extremely important for the last exercise; however, it took some time for them to go through their own feelings at the end of this game and most of them asked for a short break.

Even though widely used as a tool, this exercise provoked different responses and emotions, causing certain degree of uneasiness. During discussion participants described their inability to talk about the war even if it included four sentences. The first reason for that was their trauma and feeling of being overwhelmed by emotions; while the second reason was related to the feelings of uneasiness to talk in front of someone whose opinions and past experience was unknown to them. When we put it into the classroom setting, they reported how sensitive topics had usually been avoided (mostly due to the fact that they cannot teach about the 1992–1995 war and that it has not been covered in their textbooks). Also, they were more prone to discuss topics related to their personal burnout caused by large workload and large number of students, as well as high rate of peer- and gender-based violence. Interestingly, the older generation of teachers and pedagogues did not attribute those problems to the possible transgenerational transmission of trauma and the fact that their students were raised by people who survived the war. However, few teachers of younger generation were first to recognise this connection and to report it. They also added that such exercises have power to facilitate thinking and discussion.

In the last part of the workshop participants were organised as two debate teams (affirmative and negative), with the chairperson and the audience. The topic was: "1992–1995 War in Bosnia and Herzegovina should (not) be included into History Textbooks." All participants were first acquainted with the basic rules of debate and were given additional time to prepare. Having in mind these rules, we decided to have three groups: one supporting a topic (affirmative team), one opposing the topic (opposing team), and those who are judging the quality of the evidence, arguments and the performance in the debate. In addition to the three specific groups, there was an audience that was not involved in the formal debate. After the rules were established, the affirmative team opened the debate that lasted for an hour. Most teachers reported how they practice the same exercise in their classes (for example, history teacher said that she usually organises debates), therefore they were well prepared for it. We put the emphasis on teachers' ability to follow and actively listen to the opposing side, as well as to understand and respect their comments and arguments. However, they reported that they had fun during the debate, even though the topic was quite sensitive and provoked different arguments. In the discussion afterwards, some teachers expressed their disappointment for not being listened to and empathised more during their everyday work which they described as very stressful. History teachers said that tools and interactive games provided to them by EUROCLIO project leaders helped them to organise classes in an interesting way. One teacher said that students were very satisfied by short movies and debates that were part of the history class and that this helped them to learn the history better. Even though they did not know a lot about experiential learning, its methods and benefits, majority was using and applying some experiential tools in their classes (movies, debates, literary works, etc). However, lack of time and large workload hinders the whole processes and forces them to focus on the textbooks and tests. They reported a need for a space for such activities, but also a need for some anti-stress workshops for them. Majority said that no one wants to talk to them about their problems, and no one wants to listen to their problems and to empathise with them about the workload stress. On the similar note, they concluded that regardless of the type of the content, textbooks should be written for children, not for nationalists and their ideals. Given the time and efforts invested into this workshop they were not ready for deeper reflection, but concluded that we had to invent the classroom in which opinions that differ from dominant narrative would be respected and heard.

Conclusion

It has become evident that conventional education cannot answer to question on how to teach sensitive topics such as war. Many programs have been established in order to help teachers and students deal with their traumas; however, it is still unknown how to organise classroom activities in situations when sides who were in conflict at some point have to cooperate and learn together. The workshop described in this chapter did not elicit one single response and/or one single tool that can efficiently solve this problem, however, it tested some well-known practices and produced important conclusion: what teachers and students are studying in classroom is less important than how they study it.

Throughout the workshop it was obvious that teachers were neither ready nor willing to talk about war (or to discuss the provided concepts in line with war events). That can be explained by the overwhelming feeling of fear to talk openly in front of people one is not closed with. However, the good thing is that while progressing through three games they became more relaxed, opened, and ready to communicate (and tell jokes). Those moment of recognising the human pain and empathising with each other's suffering are what Zembylas (2007) called small openings. As such, they constitute possibilities for cultivating an alternative political consciousness and criticism against fixed categorisations of the past (Zembylas 2007). Even though this does not imply huge transformations and success of the workshop, it sheds some light on the experiential learning techniques and possibilities they can provide in teaching practice. The concept of moving classroom developed through this research yields one new perspective on education process – teaching cannot be restricted to one person and textbook. In conflict and post-conflict societies, teachers are expected to provide explanation and define sensitive terms such as war, battle, nationalism, victim, perpetrator, and patriotism. While doing that, they are expanding the walls around these classrooms and opening up towards new solutions and ideas.

References

Albeck, J. H., Adwan, S. & Bar-On, D. (2002) Dialogue Groups: TRT's Guidelines for Working through Intractable Conflicts by Personal Storytelling. *Peace and Conflict: Journal of Peace Psychology*, 8 (4): 301–322. https://doi.org/10.1207/S15327949PAC0804_01

Bilali, R. & Ross, M. (2012) Remembering Intergroup Conflict. In L. Tropp, ed. *The Oxford Handbook of Intergroup Conflict*. Oxford: Oxford University Press: 123–135.

Chaitin, J. & Steinberg, S. (2014) "I Can Almost Remember It Now": Between Personal and Collective Memories of Massive Social Trauma. *Journal of Adult Development*, 21 (1): 30–42. https://doi.org/10.1007/s10804-013-9176-4

Clarke-Habibi, S. (2005) Transforming Worldviews, *Journal of Transformative Education*, 3 (1): 33–56.

Endacott, J. & Brooks, S. (2013) An Updated Theoretical and Practical Model for Promoting Historical Empathy. *Social Studies Research and Practice*, 8: 41–58.

Harris, I. & Synott, J. (2002) Peace Education for a New Century, *Social Alternatives*, 21 (1): 3–6.

Hoffman, E. (2004) *After Such Knowledge: Memory, History, and the Legacy of the Holocaust*. New York: Public Affairs.

Hoffman, M. L. (2012) *Empathy and Moral Development. Implications for Caring and Justice*. UK: Cambridge University Press.

Jeftić, A. (2019) *Social Aspects of Memory. Stories of Victims and Perpetrators from Bosnia and Herzegovina*. Abington: Routledge.

Jeftić, A. & Joksimović, J. (2014) Divided Presentations in History Textbooks in Three ex Yugoslav States: Discussing Implications for Identity Development. *The European Conference on Psychology and Behavioral Sciences*. IAFOR, Brighton, UK, 12–14 July 2014.

Kaplan, A. E. (2005) *Trauma Culture: The Politics of Terror and Loss in Media and Literature*. Rudgers University Press.

Savenije, G. M. & de Bruijn, P. (2017) Historical Empathy in a Museum: Uniting Contextualisation and Emotional Engagement. *International Journal of Heritage Studies*, 23 (9): 832–845. https://doi.org/10.1080/13527258.2017.1339108

Shnabel, N. & Nadler, A. (2008) A Needs-based Model of Reconciliation: Satisfying the Differential Emotional Needs of Victim and Perpetrator as a Key to Promoting Reconciliation. *Journal of Personality and Social Psychology*, 94 (1): 116–132.

Srikanth, R. (2012) *Constructing the Enemy. Empathy/Antipathy in US Literature and Law*. Temple University Press.

Watson, S. (2015) Emotions in the History Museum. In K. Message & A. Witcomb, eds. *The International Handbooks of Museums Studies. Volume 1: Museum Theory*, Oxford: John Wiley & Sons: 283–301.

Zemblyas, M. (2008) *The Politics of Trauma in Education*. New York: Palgrave McMillan.

Zembylas, M. (2007) The Politics of Trauma: Empathy, Reconciliation and Education. *Journal of Peace Education*, 4 (2): 207–224.

Part II
Places of pain as sites of critical knowledge production

5 The last ones: Serbian and Russian prisoners on the Alpine front

Niccolò Caranti, Luisa Chiodi, and Marco Abram

Introduction: choosing the topic

Osservatorio Balcani Caucaso Transeuropa or OBCT's contribution to the *#Never Again Teaching Transmission of Trauma and Remembrance through Experiential Learning* project focuses on the First World War as the deepest trauma of the region where OBCT is located. OBCT is a think tank, an online media outlet, and an operational unit of the International Cooperation Centre (ICC), an institution based in Trento, Trentino-Alto Adige/Südtirol. In this contested European borderland, over the last four decades, the local scholarly community has carried out outstanding research on the social history of war, trying to offer a new contribution to the public understanding of this conflict.

The specific angle of the experience of Serbian and Russian prisoners on the Alpine front was chosen because of wanting OBCT's focus on Southeastern Europe wanting to contribute to the still under-researched topic of the wider experience of war prisoners, which emerged in Italy almost three decades ago with the first academic studies (Procacci 1993). We also seek to overcome a narrative of victimhood by recognising the historical responsibilities of the community living in the territory where our Centre operates. OBCT's work has been stressing for years the need to elaborate past trauma through taking responsibility, showing empathy with the suffering of the "Other", and unconditionally condemning violence (Chiodi & Vanoni 2008).

The first step we took was to involve the main local stakeholders in the definition of our project, starting with historical museums and historians that had been extensively working on the topic. Initially we considered using role play to help participants to develop a degree of empathy with war prisoners, but we concluded at the end that it was not an appropriate strategy, as it is almost impossible to reproduce – and to do it ethically – those physical and emotional conditions of fear, hunger, cold, etc. The discussions with the historians involved in the project confirmed and increased our concerns. In addition to the risk of producing a parody of the trauma we wished to address, there was also the need to offer an experience respectful of the victims' memories. Furthermore, historians shared the awareness that most places where the First World War took place have profoundly changed. Unlike other sites of the 20th century's most tragic episodes, where the following processes of memorialisation have often been aimed at preserving the physical traces of violence and destruction (e.g. Farmer 1999), in Trentino-Alto Adige/Südtirol many of these places are beautiful locations where nature is regaining its space over history. Even the trenches, cleaned by local authorities on the occasion of the 100th anniversary of the Great War, are aseptic, silent, pleasant places that can hardly evoke the dramatic experiences of the past. The choice we made was to devise a twofold programme including first a guided visit on the experience of war prisoners in Trentino for the local community, and then a Wikipedia workshop for school students.

History and memory of the First World War in a border region: the forgotten prisoners

Today an Italian region, until 1919 Trentino-Alto Adige/Südtirol was part of the Austro-Hungarian Empire. For a long time, the irredentist narrative about the First World War was hegemonic in the public space: celebrating the "reunification" of the cities of Trento and Trieste with the "Italian motherland" and the martyrs of irredentism such as Cesare Battisti, a member of the Italian-speaking community in Austria-Hungary who fought for the Italian army, was captured, and executed as a traitor (Antonelli 2018).

This very partial, nation-oriented narrative was mainly focused on the experience of the few hundreds of people from Trentino who chose to cross the border and join the Italian Army. Then, a careful local historiography began to address the complexities of a ravaging war: the buried memory of the local civil population, the refugees in the Habsburg and Italian territories (75,000 and 35,000 respectively), but also the memory of the men from Trentino who died wearing Austro-Hungarian uniforms (around 11,000). Only in 2008 did the municipality of Trento dedicate a plaque to its 1,000 soldiers who died in the Habsburg army, and in 2018 another one to commemorate the experience of the displaced population. As shown by the debates on the centenary of the war, divergences in the interpretation of the events still remain, and political agendas still influence them, as highlighted by the use by Italian far-right parties of the century-old Piave's patriotic song "the foreigner shall not pass" in order to invoke a new "defense of borders" against today's migrants seeking to reach Italian territory (Zagni 2015).

Despite the deeper scrutiny, little space has been devoted to those foreigners who were dragged by war to this border region. This is true for the soldiers who came from the different regions of the Habsburg Empire to fight on the frontline, but especially for those who were already defeated: the thousands of prisoners of war – especially Serbs and Russians – captured on the Eastern and the Balkan fronts and dragged to Tyrol as forced labourers. Relevant traces of their presence remain in the writings of local population, as witnessed by the work of mountaineer and writer Dante Ongari (1965):

> Columns of women, kids, and elderly men, pushed by the need for a loaf of bread, travelled every morning back and forth between Borzago and Malga Coel, loaded with wood or other materials. The resumption of the exhausting journey from Coel to the Caré Alto shelter was enabled by the forced labour of Serbian and Russian prisoners of war, guarded by Bosnian, Croatian, and Czechoslovak guards, who somehow managed to understand each other in their various languages. The Serbs, of a more rebellious nature, were the pariahs of the nascent organization, while Russians enjoyed more leniency as more docile and skilled wood craftsmen – for their work, two Venetian sawmills had been put into operation in Baùt and Pian della Sega. The prisoners lived packed in the barns of the Valaverta and Cornicli haylofts, while a hut in front of Solan had been built for the Bosnians along the Coel mule track.

Academic work on the topic is still rare, and only some pioneering studies have been published. We still lack a thorough estimate of their number: according to some information there were 27,000 Prisoners of War (POWs) in Tyrol in 1915, and their numbers continued to grow until the end of the war (Leoni 2015, 337). Other research reveals that the following year, at the South of the Brenner pass (the present border between Italy and Austria), there were around 47,770 POWs, mostly – if not all – Russians and Serbs. The use of Italian prisoners was generally considered too problematic on this frontline, where the risk of escape was higher (Zangerl 2019, 128–130).

During the First World War, the number of prisoners rapidly grew, making it difficult for the belligerent countries to provide them with the necessary care. Later information estimates that Austria-Hungary captured between 1.86 and 2.3 million POWs during the war. Most of them were crammed together in camps where the living conditions were particularly hard (Moritz & Walleczek-Fritz 2014). In Spring 1915 the authorities started using the prisoners also as forced labourers, first in the rears and later even on the frontline. This was a violation of the IV Hague Convention that resulted from the quick turning of the conflict into a "total war", as Art. 6 of the Annex establishes that: "the State may utilize the labor of prisoners of war according to their rank and aptitude, officers excepted. The tasks shall not be excessive and shall have no connection with the operations of the war."[1]

In Trentino, the POWs were used to build many infrastructures, some of which are still in use today. That deeply contributed to shaping the Alpine landscape: forts, trenches, railways in Val Gardena, Val di Fiemme, state roads in Val Badia and Valsugana. Several traces can also be found in local toponyms such as the "path of the Serbs" in Vallagarina, the "road of the Russians" in Val S. Nicolò and on Mount Misone, and the so-called "blood road" in Val d'Adige.

As peasants were forced to become soldiers and farms had been left to old people, women, and children (those who had not been deported), POWs became indispensable also to help the work in the fields. As the war went on, food became scarce, even for the local population. Exploited for the heaviest tasks, prisoners often starved to death. While the Austro-Hungarian propaganda denigrated the prisoners, and even talking to them was often forbidden, there are records of many episodes of solidarity by the local population (Leoni 2015, 341–342, Zangerl 2019, 133–134). The presence of those who came from afar and experienced the war on the Alpine Front has re-emerged publicly only on a few occasions, mainly in the case of celebration of those who fell on the battlefields. Yet, it is more complicated to shed light on "those under", those who did not die fighting, but of hardship and exploitation.

Memory is often a political act, influenced by the commitment of multiple subjects, active at multiple levels. In recent years, the memory of Russian prisoners of war has been partially reaffirmed, especially in Alto-Adige/Südtirol, by the initiatives of the Borodina Russian Centre in Merano, which organised lectures and expeditions to places particularly significant for the Russian experience. The first public commemorations and religious ceremonies were held in Carè Alto, where a wooden church built by Russian prisoners still stands (Figure 5.1), and in some military cemeteries of South Tyrol, with the presence of local authorities, Russian representatives, and the Russian Orthodox Church.[2]

On the other hand, the memory of Serbian prisoners of war remains totally marginalised. Various testimonies convey divergent perceptions already at the time of the conflict, with greater aversion towards them, perhaps linked to stereotypes and the idea that the Serbs could be considered guilty for the outbreak of war (Leoni 2015, 341). Anyway, not even Serbian historiography – which has resumed the topic of First World War after marginalising it in the socialist era – has devoted insights to this specific experience on the Alpine front. Research has instead focused on the large camps established in the rest of Austria-Hungary, where tens of thousands of Serbian soldiers and civilians were imprisoned, with a huge number of victims (Vemić 2014).

Today, after the centenary of the First World War, the history of POWs remains little integrated in the overall representation of the events of the conflict in this Alpine border region. An important exception lies in the exhibition *Cosa videro quegli occhi!* (What those eyes saw!), organised in the town of Rovereto by the local organisation *Laboratorio di Storia* (History Lab) in 2018, which, while focusing on the experience of men and women from Trentino in the conflict, highlighted also the destiny of the Russians and Serbs dragged to the Alps. This is a useful way to understand the depth of the conflict and add a perspective outside the usual patterns: that of thousands of people who arrived

Figure 5.1 The church on Carè Alto build by Russian prisoners in 1917 (photo by Marco Abram).

in Trentino and South Tyrol after being uprooted from their homeland, carriers of different languages and religions, exploited to support the war economy, separated from local communities, with which they developed a complex, but also very human relationship, and who died in anonymity and forgotten, a fate parallel to that of many Trentino prisoners in Russia, which invites us to look at local events without losing sight of the transnational, European, and global dimension Figure 5.1.

A guided tour and a conference

As there are no officially marked commemorative sites of the First World War devoted to the experience of Serbian and Russian prisoners of war in Trentino, we identified an interesting location for the event in the Castle of Castellano, a manor house built around the year 1000, located in the village of Castellano, in the municipality of Villa Lagarina, Trentino. There, around 300 Serbian prisoners were held captive in the dungeons during the First World War. With the local historians that we involved in our initiative, we agreed that some readings, to be carried out where the historical events took place, were the closest to an experiential learning we could offer.

Figure 5.2 Participants at the Castle of Castellano (photo by Paolo Martino).

The event took place on 24 March 2019 (Figure 5.2) and started with an introduction to the history of the castle built in the 11th or 12th century given by Gianluca Pederzini, a member of the local association *Sezione Culturale Don Zanolli* (Don Zanolli cultural section). Since 1266, the castle had been owned by the Castelbarco family. In 1456 it was conquered by the Lodron family, under the auspices of the prince-bishop of Trent. In 1924, the Lodron family put it up for auction, and it was bought by the Miorandi family, who still owns the property and kindly opened it to the public for the event. At the castle Quinto Antonelli, head of the *Archivio della scrittura popolare della Fondazione Museo storico del Trentino* (Archive of popular writing of the History Museum of Trentino Foundation), introduced the topic of the prisoners of war and read some excerpts from diaries written by the witnesses of the time. Among others, Antonelli read the diary of Luigia Miorandi, a woman who worked in the castle and in her memoirs described with compassion the tragic conditions of Serbian war prisoners. The relationship between the local population and the war prisoners was a deeply ambivalent one: under extreme conditions for everyone and the constant pressure of war propaganda, a prisoner was an enemy in the struggle for survival. At the same time, many diaries show how women saw in these foreign prisoners the experience of their own brothers and husbands imprisoned in enemy countries. The compassion present in many of the documents retrieved shows how empathy exists even in the worst conditions.

As we expected, the beauty of the place contrasted with the tragedies narrated by the readings. At the same time, the historical documents collected and presented by local historians had a powerful effect on all the attendees. Then we left the Castle, and after a coffee break offered by the *Pro Loco Castellano-Cei* (a grass-roots organisation that seeks to promote local culture and tourism), we moved to the Municipal Theatre. After an introduction by OBCT director Luisa Chiodi, Quinto Antonelli gave a presentation titled "The First World War between yesterday and today: memories and forgetting", trying to explore the evolution of the collective memories of the First World War and to explain why the experience of the POWs, the "foreigners", went completely forgotten. Then, Diego Leoni went into the core of the subject of our event talking about "The experience of Serbian and Russian prisoners of war on the Alpine front", and offering some more data about their presence and their role in the warfare. The guided tour and the conference had a positive turnout, as nearly 50 people participated in the afternoon's activities. The involvement of the local community was successful, and the local media positively responded to our initiative by publishing a number of dedicated articles that helped increase the impact the initiative had on the public debate on the past.

Our hope is that the public memory of the First World War will gradually incorporate the experience of *gli ultimi,* the last ones that we came to identify as victims of 20th-century history. In Diego Leoni's words, our hope is that "the history of the forgotten Serbian and Russian prisoners creeps into the history of Trentino." The renewed commitment of local historians to intensify the research agenda in this direction is a guarantee that more light will be shed on their experience. The fact that their pioneering work receives some international attention is also an important outcome of this project.

A downside of the selected location is that the Castle had been largely rebuilt in the last century, so people were not able to see the actual rooms in which prisoners were kept. We had considered taking a walk on the nearby *Sentiero dei Serbi* (Path of the Serbs), built by war prisoners. However, as the path is recommended only for expert hikers, this choice would have implied limited accessibility to the event and excluded people with disabilities. In addition, it would not have been feasible in case of bad weather, and we would have had to cancel our event (at least for that part) at the last moment. Figure 5.2

A Wikipedia workshop

The second initiative promoted within the project was a Wikipedia workshop for school students (Figure 5.3), aimed at dealing with local First

Figure 5.3 The Wikipedia workshop (photo by Paolo Martino).

World War histories of violence and exploitation. Wikipedia is an online encyclopedia with 301 language editions. It is the 5th website on the global Alexa ranking, based on a combination of average daily visitors and pageviews (Alexa Top sites n.d.). Wikipedia is written by a community of volunteers based on loose collaboration and conflict, dissent and disagreement (Jemielniak 2014, 59–84). It has no editorial board and contributions are immediately published without revision. Registration is not compulsory in order to contribute, nor is giving a real name necessary, as it is possible to register using a nickname. Contributions must be based on reliable sources, original research is forbidden, and personal knowledge is not recognised (Ross & Nguyen 2016). OBCT has been involved with Wikipedia since 2015, working on several international projects aimed at exploring new ways to develop a collaborative approach in different fields of knowledge.

While school and university papers usually risk ending up in a drawer (or in a virtual folder), writing on Wikipedia means making the content available for everyone to read and edit. This makes things more complicated as educators cannot provide their own guidelines, but have to follow Wikipedia's. Using Wikipedia, however, also means that, even if what the students write is not perfect, someone else can improve it later. Wikipedia has been used as a teaching tool in schools for a long time, in Italy ("Fare didattica con i progetti Wikimedia" 2017) and worldwide ("Wikipedia: School and university projects" n.d.). While it is often used by students who just copy-paste articles in their papers, Wikipedia offers more educational opportunities: it can be used to find basic information on a topic and reliable sources (which entries cite). Most importantly, students can contribute to Wikipedia as a part of a workshop or an assignment. This is useful to develop media and information literacy, including the skill to recognise "fake news." As Omer Benjakob pointed out, "Wikipedia offers greater transparency and a much better model for fighting disinformation than any social media platform has yet to do, simply by building a community of fact-checkers dedicated to keeping the site accurate" (Benjakob 2020). The work of a Wikipedia contributor recalls the work of a historian: in both cases you need to search for sources and evaluate them, although there are also differences, as Wikipedia articles cannot be based on primary sources. This is mainly to avoid editors misinterpreting them: as Wikipedia is not necessarily written by experts, it is based on expert sources being reliable and verifiable. History-related projects on Wikipedia are becoming more common in Italy. For example, the workshops organised by Istoreto, a Turin-based research centre on the Italian resistance, led students to write articles such as *Pietre d'inciampo*, the *Stolpersteine* honoring victims of Nazism (Vayola 2017). Our project was inspired by previous experiences but also adapted according to our expertise and interests.

To start, we prepared a list of articles to be created or edited and a list of sources, in order to make the students' task easier. We wanted to avoid the creation of articles that the Wikipedia community could deem as non "notable" ("Wikipedia:Notability") and thus would risk being deleted (e.g. an article specifically about "Russian prisoners in Trentino" would have probably been deemed too specific and so it would have risked being deleted from Italian Wikipedia). We also wanted to make sure they had the necessary sources to write the articles, and to prevent them from engaging with articles already of good quality that it would have been difficult to improve.

OBCT has a solid experience in contributing to both English and Italian Wikipedia. In this project, however, we engaged with Italian Wikipedia in order to avoid language difficulties for the students. The Wikipedia workshop involved a group of 22 students from the 4th and 5th grades at the high school "Lorenzo Guetti" in Tione, coordinated by teacher Cristian Mosca. The students, coming from different classes, volunteered to participate. We had our first two-hour meeting on 26 February 2019. First, Tommaso Baldo (Fondazione Museo storico del Trentino) introduced the students to the experience of the prisoners of war as discussed during the first phase of the project. Since most of the students were from the fourth year and had not discussed the First World War yet (it is usually part of the curriculum of the beginning of the 5th year), Baldo's introduction had to provide also a wide context of the war. OBCT's Wikipedia expert Niccolò Caranti gave a short theoretical introduction to Wikipedia, highlighting its fundamental principles ("the five pillars"):

1. Wikipedia is an encyclopedia;
2. it is written from a neutral point of view;
3. it is free content;
4. editors should treat each other with respect and civility;
5. it has no (other) firm rules.

He then conducted a practical workshop to teach students how to edit Wikipedia: using their personal "sandboxes" (pages which are specifically designed for users to experiment), they learned how to create an article, how to save it, how to add sections, internal links and references, etc. At the end of the workshop, students received some materials to be used as sources for the Wikipedia articles we assigned them, and namely:

- a new article about the *Sentiero dei Serbi*, a mountain trail built by Serbian POWs;
- a new article about the *Frana di Venzan*, a landslide that killed 55 Russian POWs (a memorial is pictured in Figure 5.4);
- a new article about Prisoners of war in the First World War (*Prigionieri di guerra nella prima guerra mondiale*);
- a new section about prisoners of war in the already existing article *Guerra Bianca*, the White War, the war on the Alpine front;
- an addition about prisoners of war in the already existing article about the History of Trentino (*Storia del Trentino*);
- a rewriting of the article "Prisoner of War" (*Prigioniero di guerra*).

The students worked in groups to prepare the drafts. Then, on our second (and last) meeting on 21 March 2019, we helped them revise their texts and publish them on Wikipedia. *Sentiero dei Serbi*, *Frana di Venzan*, and the new paragraphs in *Guerra Bianca* and *Storia del Trentino* were published that day. Two articles could not be published at that time as the source texts had not been reworded enough, so the rewriting of *Prigioniero di guerra* was published later.

Assets, obstacles, and feedback

The timing of the project made it difficult for us to find a class interested in the workshop. Some history professors showed their interest, but they wished to schedule the project in autumn, when they teach the First World War, and it was not possible to arrange the logistics in a short notice. Schools receive a lot of proposals, and they arrange the programme of the initiatives early in the school year, or even at the end of the previous one. Some of the students participating in the project could not attend our first meeting because of conflicting schedules, so they missed the background. Originally, the project included the guided tour and the conference in the educational programme for the students, but it was not possible to make it a compulsory part of the

The last ones 81

Figure 5.4 Memorial of the victims of the Venzan landslide (photo by Niccolò Caranti).

workshop, and the considerable distance between Tione and Castellano discouraged students from joining the event on their own.

In order to test the students' appreciation of the project we administered an anonymous questionnaire, which was undertaken by 19 of them. On a 1–5 scale (where 1 was the minimum and 5 was the maximum), three students said they did not like the workshop (1 or 2) and nine students did (4 or 5), while seven students put themselves in the middle (3). The historical introduction by Baldo was highly appreciated with 11 students giving a 4 or 5 rating, and five students giving lower ones (1–2–3). On average, the appreciation for the introduction to Wikipedia was lower, with most students (14) giving 2, 3, or 4. Most students (13) appreciated the autonomous work on Wikipedia. The choice of the topic might have played a role here: when asked if they found it interesting, eight students gave 4 or 5, while nine gave a 3. Nearly all of them found that the help of the experts during the second meeting was adequate, as was communication with the experts and the teacher in general. They appreciated that the activity was offered not to a class, but to a group. Most said that time was sufficient, but some would have asked for more time to carry out the tasks. Fifteen thought the project was useful and would like the school to repeat it, maybe examining various local history topics.

We then conducted more in-depth interviews with some of the students, in which they said that they had appreciated the workshop, highlighting the importance of direct experience and of feeling protagonists of a dissemination activity. For instance, Lisa told us about her fear of publishing online and the pride she took in her work. She had always thought that contributing to Wikipedia would be more difficult than she discovered, and expressed her belief in the importance of spreading knowledge of the First World War to avoid events to repeat.

Daria showed considerable self-reflexivity when analysing why war prisoners were the last ones to be commemorated: "maybe we are ashamed of how we treated them. When discussing prisoners of war we think of those from Trentino who were prisoners in Galicia, not those that were here. It was a waste of human lives, and a loss of human dignity." She also stressed that many people visiting places of the First World War are not interested in what happened, while it is important to think of the conditions, such as cold and snow, endured by people there; you need to be prepared, or to go with someone who is, in order to learn something from the visit.

Daniele joined the seminar as he was strongly interested in learning how Wikipedia works. He appreciated the emphasis on references. He stressed his pride for the result and hopes that someone will read the work of his group, since he considers the history of the POWs a facet of the First World War which is little known. He liked the experience and was excited that people doing online searches will find what he wrote. He found other articles that needed improvement and underlined the importance of remembering history to understand the past. He also revealed that where he comes from there are many barracks and trenches from the First World War and he finds it touching to visit them; they are silent places where you can spend time and reflect on what happened.

The seminar gave students the possibility to experiment with an instrument they use every day, but often without knowing how it works. It was also a media literacy experience: working with Wikipedia showed them its pros and cons, and enabled them to appreciate the importance of reliable sources in the building of knowledge. By giving students the opportunity to feel like the protagonists of dissemination, the project encouraged them to adopt a participative, self-aware, and creative approach to learning Figure 5.4.

Conclusion

OBCT has addressed some of the most tragic memories of the 20th century for the local community, trying to offer a new perspective aimed at challenging a self-centred narrative on the past. Discovering the places of the exploitation of the prisoners of war and the testimonies of the time has been a crucial practice in reviving and understanding the past, but also the direct experience of going through different sources and recreating the reality of the war on the pages of Wikipedia has proven the strength of these participatory forms of knowledge creation.

One of the project's merits and reasons for success was the creation of a network of local stakeholders active in the local community that were interested in addressing this traumatic local history from different angles: we as OBCT were interested in Serbian and Russian prisoners because of our focus on the Balkans and the Caucasus, the *Fondazione Museo storico del Trentino* (Trentino History Museum Foundation) and the *Laboratorio di storia di Rovereto* (Rovereto History Lab) for their strong record on the social history of the province. The cooperation between institutions at the forefront in the territory made it possible to give publicity to the project's topic in the local media and achieve wide public involvement. In addition, the municipality of Villa Lagarina, the *Pro Loco Castellano-Cei*, and the *Sezione Culturale Don Zanolli* were interested in the history of the place we chose to focus on, and the Lorenzo Guetti institute was interested in offering a workshop to its students. This wide synergy was particularly important in building for the first time public consciousness of "the last ones."

Finally, it is worth stressing that the local media reacted positively by publishing several articles on the initiatives, and OBCT used its website and social media to disseminate knowledge on these neglected historical events and on the experiential initiatives, so as to foster interest on the issue in the wider European public sphere. Last but not least, the video by professional film-maker Paolo Martino is a further important asset for the project, as it will favor the circulation of the experience for a much wider audience in the months to come.

Once again, with this project, OBCT confirms its commitment to foster the elaboration of the tragic European past and highlights the importance of overcoming a victimisation narrative of the past, integrating it with facing the responsibilities of one's own side, empathising with the Other's sufferings, and condemning violence unconditionally.

Notes

1 The text of the Convention is available on the website of the Yale Law School: http://avalon.law.yale.edu/20th_century/hague04.asp#art6 URL consulted on 27 February 2020.
2 The history of the Russian presence in Merano dates back to the end of the 19th century. The Borodina Centre was established in June 2009 to promote cultural and economic relations between Russia and Alto-Adige/Südtirol, with the support of local administrations and the Russian Embassy in Rome. For an overview of the activities, see URL: https://www.facebook.com/Borodinamerano/

References

Alexa Top sites (n.d.) Available at: https://www.alexa.com/topsites (Accessed 28 February 2020).
Antonelli, Q. (2018) *Cento anni di Grande Guerra: Cerimonie, Monumenti, Memorie e Contromemorie*. Rome: Donzelli editore.
Benjakob, O. (2020) *Why Wikipedia Is Much More Effective Than Facebook at Fighting Fake News*, Haaretz, 9 Jan. Available at: https://www.haaretz.com/us-news/.premium-why-wikipedia-is-much-more-effective-than-facebook-at-fighting-fake-news-1.8378622 (Accessed 10 February 2020).
Chiodi, L. & Vanoni, F. (2008) Dealing with the Past and Reconciliation with the Balkans, *Osservatorio Balcani e Caucaso Transeuropa*, 2 December. Available at: https://www.balcanicaucaso.org/eng/Areas/Italy/Dealing-with-the-Past-and-Reconciliation-with-the-Balkans-43963 (Accessed 11 February 2020).
Fare didattica con i progetti Wikimedia (2017), *Bricks*. Available at: http://www.rivistabricks.it/2017/12/19/n-4-2017-fare-didattica-con-i-progetti-wikimedia/ (Accessed 28 February 2020).
Farmer, S. B. (1999) *Martyred Village: Commemorating the 1944 Massacre at Oradour-sur-Glane*. University of California Press.
Frana di Venzan, *Wikipedia*, n.d. Available at: https://it.wikipedia.org/wiki/Frana_di_Venzan (Accessed 27 February 2020).
Guerra B., *Wikipedia*, n.d. Available at: https://it.wikipedia.org/wiki/Guerra_Bianca (Accessed 27 February 2020).
Jemielniak, D. (2014) *Common Knowledge? An Ethnography of Wikipedia*. Stanford University Press: 59–84.
Leoni, D. (2015) *La guerra verticale. Uomini, animali e macchine sul fronte di montagna 1915–1918*. Einaudi.
Moritz, V. & Walleczek-Fritz, J. (2014) Prisoners of War (Austria-Hungary). In U. Daniel, P. Gatrell, O. Janz, H. Jones, J. Keene, A. Kramer, & B. Nasson, eds. *1914–1918-online. International Encyclopedia of the First World War*, issued by Freie Universität Berlin, Berlin, 8 October. https://doi.org/10.15463/ie1418.10374. Available at: https://encyclopedia.1914-1918-online.net/article/prisoners_of_war_austria-hungary/2014-10-08 (Accessed 28 February 2020).

Ongari, D. (1965) La valle di Borzago, caposaldo di guerra austriaco, "Bollettino della Società Alpinisti Tridentini", Anno XXVIII, (2): 4
Prigioniero di Guerra, *Wikipedia*, n.d. Available at: https://it.wikipedia.org/wiki/Prigioniero_di_guerra (Accessed 27 February 2020).
Procacci, G. (1993) *Soldati e prigionieri italiani nella Grande Guerra: con una raccolta di lettere inedite*. Roma: Editori Riuniti.
Ross, R. & Nguyen, C. (2016) Authoring the Neighbourhood in Wikipedia. In B. Campkin & G. Duijzings, eds. *Engaged Urbanism: Cities & Methodologies*. I.B. Tauris: 83–86.
Sentiero dei Serbi, *Wikipedia*, n.d. Available at: https://it.wikipedia.org/wiki/Sentiero_dei_Serbi (Accessed 27 February 2020).
Storia del Trentino, *Wikipedia*, n.d. Available at: https://it.wikipedia.org/wiki/Storia_del_Trentino (Accessed 27 February 2020).
Vayola, P. (2017) Scrivere di storia contemporanea a scuola: un percorso su e per Wikipedia sviluppato dall'Istoreto di Torino, *Bricks*, (4). Available at: http://www.rivistabricks.it/wp-content/uploads/2017/12/2017_4_05_Vayola.pdf (Accessed 11 February 2020).
Vemić, M. (2014) Pomor srba ratnih zarobljenika i interniranih civila u austrougarskim logorima za vreme prvog svetskog rata 1914–1918. Zbornik Matice Srpske za Društvene Nauke, 147: 205–225
Wikipedia:Notability, *Wikipedia*, n.d. Available at: https://en.wikipedia.org/wiki/Wikipedia:Notability (Accessed 27 February 2020).
Wikipedia: School and university projects, *Wikipedia*, n.d. Available at: https://en.wikipedia.org/wiki/Wikipedia:School_and_university_projects (Accessed 28 February 2020).
Zagni, G., Il 24 maggio «non passa lo straniero»? No, eravamo noi ad attaccare, *Linkiesta*. Available at: https://www.linkiesta.it/it/article/2015/05/21/il-24-maggio-non-passa-lo-straniero-no-eravamo-noi-ad-attaccare/25999/ (Accessed 28 February 2020).
Zangerl, C. (2019) I prigionieri russi e serbi nel Tirolo meridionale. In *Cosa videro quegli occhi! Uomini e donne in guerra (1913–1920)*, 2. Rovereto: Comune di Rovereto: 123–138.

6 #Never Forget: teaching trauma experience at historical places

Neringa Latvytė

Theoretical insights

In the aftermath of the Second World War, Lithuanian Jews who had survived the Holocaust felt the need to mark and commemorate the fateful loss of community members, as well as the cultural and spiritual losses suffered by the Jewish community. This was the only way for them to sustain both their existence as a community and do justice to their traumatic experiences. Right after the war ended, however, the annihilated Jewish community also was confronted with a policy of suppression of this memory, on the part of the Soviet Lithuanian authorities: they were faced with various forms of denial of their own fate of mass destruction, including the levelling of the Jewish victims by assigning them to (and absorbing them into) the category of "peaceful Soviet citizens." At the time, this framed the discourse of the traumatic experience of the Holocaust and helped to mobilise society, as the Soviet occupiers tried to suppress the plurality in ways of communicating the experiences of the Second World War chosen by the different communities, which they considered unhelpful in terms of establishing a legitimate presence on the territory of Lithuania. According to Alvydas Nikžentaitis, plots from the past are indeed frequently crafted, emphasised and communicated 'from the top', to create and consolidate a society's self-consciousness and identity, whereby a politicised remembrance culture may help to overcome particular historical traumas (Nikžentaitis 2010, 17–18). However, it renders them unstable, making them vulnerable, at the same time, to radical transformations or manipulations. With the changes in the geopolitical situation, military battles are then followed by memory battles.

The memory constructed during Soviet times was inevitably influenced by the prevailing ideological norms. The recent past was presented as an argument to justify the ongoing Soviet modernisation, industrialisation and urbanisation, and also legitimise the myth of the Red Army being the winner of the Second World War. As the German historian Jörn Rüsen (2007) has claimed, a political regime or a system can only consolidate itself when it is perceived as legitimate in the memory of a certain community. Collective memory has everything to do also with power relations, as the French sociologist Maurice Halbwachs (1997) argued, because it is being constructed in the present and is selective, that is, it tends to emphasise only the things that match the expectations of a particular society or regime. When used for political reasons, memory provides numerous opportunities for political manipulations and the reformulation of history. This was exactly what the Soviet government was aiming for when it gave its permission to mark the sites of the mass killings of Jews. In the meantime, for the Jewish survivors of the Holocaust, it was important to give meaning to their traumatic experiences and express this in a material form *in situ*, which, according to James E. Young (1993), would help to consolidate the practice of mourning and turn it into a ritual, at the same time sustaining the memory of society. Rüsen (2007) has also argued that various collective memory points in their entirety contribute to giving meaning to a memory. It is focusing on the past as a present experience, which is rendered meaningful and familiar through interpretation, turning history into a present-day experience. Rüsen suggests three concrete strategies of rendering the Holocaust meaningful, which all three allow us to make the past visible in the present: a museum as a site of memory, enabling to actually see history (Rüsen 2007, 365); a monument that invigorates historical memory (Rüsen 2007, 368); and a cemetery or a memorable site where particular objects serve as genuine proof of what happened there and guarantee authenticity (Rüsen 2007, 387, 391–398).

According to sociologist Irena Šutinienė (2003), certain events, such as traumatic ones, have a continuation in the present, and as such they are remembered by society the longest. The continuation of the collective memory of Litvak culture, interrupted by the Second World War and censored during the years of the second Soviet occupation, is accomplished through symbolic sites, which also tend to bear witness to the fear of losing memory alltogether, in addition to promote perception and emotional connection or simply evoke the ambience of a particular site. As French historian Pierre Nora (1989) argued, the dialogue between community memory and history is an important factor ensuring the existence of such sites of memory: they appear and continue to exist not as a result of spontaneous memory only. Their sustained importance depends on their material function and commodification, which is at the same time also inseparable from immaterial signs and forms of heritage (rituals, community practices, celebrations, ceremonies, and traditions), giving sites of memory their symbolic aura (Nora 1989, 7–241). Authentic sites of traumatic heritage are sites of exceptional importance, *genius loci* of a kind. The concept of *genius loci* has indeed been used in this context by several Lithuanian scientists, receiving less attention from foreign authors. Rūta Šermukšnytė (2014, 119) says that "the metaphor *genius loci* is used to describe all what is alive, dynamic and functioning as part of the world that a particular community inhabits." Rasa Čepaitienė (2014, 23, 61–63) defines "the spirit of a site" as the outcome of a relationship between a community and a particular site, influenced by its architectural and historical heritage, the historical-geographical context, the psychological states it triggers, and the cultural sensitivity it demands. British anthropologist Paul Connerton similarly defines a *locus* as a type of memory site, as an urbanistic and mnemonic object, where memory revolves around collective activities. These activities create a story, encourage the community to share its oral history, and create added value by giving new functions to the *locus* itself (Connerton 2009, 11–13). The International Council of Monuments and Sites (ICOMOS) Quebec Declaration (2008) states that material heritage, such as buildings, landscapes, and urban ensembles, as well as immaterial elements, such as memories, stories, traditions, celebrations, written sources, colours, smells, etc., all constitute a single whole. The added value of the heritage site is created by people, by communities who live in that particular area and are committed to the preservation and continuation of a site's memory. A community may promote a collective memory and thereby establish a shared cultural memory. All these factors contribute to the formation of a site's ambience or *genius loci*. In its own turn, getting to know the ambience of a site is an important component in the process of building a stronger society and providing an opportunity for local inhabitants to develop a sense of responsibility for the site's preservation.[1] In her article *Reception of Jewish Heritage in Modern Lithuanian Society: the Case of Vilnius,* Jurgita Šiaučiūnaitė-Verbickienė (2015) also uses the term *genius loci,* the exceptional nature of which is defined through strong emotions, elevated categories, and mythologised plots which often have no direct material expression (Šiaučiūnaitė-Verbickienė 2015, 336). It is quite obvious that the immaterial quality of the *genius loci* is again being emphasised here. Is this really the only way to express the exceptional nature of a site? One may disagree, because mass killing sites of Jews are these special – *in situ* – places that have become unique spaces invoking empathy only after they were attributed importance, put into operation and subjected to heritisation, and only after, that emotional closeness resulting from practice and rituals appears.

The largest mass killing site in Paneriai always possessed that peculiar *genius loci*: the community and survivors have been giving meaning to the place in both the material and spiritual sense of the word, inciting emotions, providing a sanctuary and promoting dialogue. Nowadays, the perception of the site's authenticity and its heritisation is an important factor, which, according to Romualdas Juzefovičius (2015, 15), makes an important contribution "not only in terms of cultural expression, but also in terms of consolidating the ideology of statehood continuity" (Juzefovičius 2015, 15).

Not only Paneriai but Lithuania as a whole is dealing with the legacies of the so-called "Holocaust by Bullets" (through massacres instead of death camps), where mass extermination pits physically exist in the proximity of nearly every larger town, and the ghosts of those killed on these sites are haunting the living. These places are marked by a crime, which was committed with the help of local people. They continue to emanate an atmosphere of brutality, violence and helplessness until the present day: the pits unmistakenly evoke the dark power of the place, the criminal involvement of the neighbours, the pain of the victims, the anger, shame, confusion, and even the fear of the visitors that visit the place now. Victor Counted refers in this specific context to the three separate dimensions of place, as proposed by David Seamon (2016), who pointed at the interaction between a spatial ensemble, the people who visit, inhabit and enliven it with their activities, actions, intentions and experiences, and the ambience of a place that arises from presences and absences, as something that is ephemeral, sensuous, and impalpable, and difficult to identify exactly (Counted 2016, 7–32).

Paneriai

Among the more than 227 mass killing sites of Jews in Lithuania,[2] Paneriai is the largest, where the killings were organised and perpetrated by the Nazi regime and their local helpers. Before the Second World War, the Paneriai forest, located 12 km from Vilnius, was a very popular recreational destination for the city's residents. During the Soviet occupation in 1940–1941, a liquid fuel depot was set up in Paneriai; when the Germans occupied Vilnius on 24 June 1941, they discovered the unfinished depot in the Paneriai forest, where already dozens of pits had been dug. The Nazis decided to use them for mass executions. The site's location enabled those doomed people from nearby Vilnius to be herded or brought from other places to the killing site, on foot, by truck or train. In 1944, the Vilnius Special Squad, consisting of around 100 Lithuanian volunteers (Bubnys 2019; Bubnys 1995), formed by the German occupational government and subordinated to the Einsatzkommando 9, and later to the Sicherheitsdienst (SD) and Sicherheitspolizei (Sipo), shot between 50,000 and 70,000 people here. The overwhelming majority of the victims were Jews from Vilnius and the Vilnius region. However, among the victims were also Polish underground fighters, Soviet prisoners of war, a group of soldiers of the Lithuanian Territorial Defence Force, a group of Roma, and other local residents. The first mass exterminations started in July 1941, and continued till July 1944. Between November 1943 and April 1944, the Sonderkommando 1005A, which consisted of 80 (mostly Jewish) detainees, was imprisoned in Paneriai with the task to exhume and burn the corpses of the victims (Šuras 1997).[3]

Paneriai was the first large-scale massacre site discovered by the Soviets in former Nazi-occupied Lithuania when the Red Army entered Vilnius on 13 July 1944. It was also the first location where between 15 and 23 August 1944 the Soviet Extraordinary Commission began exhuming the victims, interpreting the findings of these exhumations through the lenses of Soviet ideology.[4] On 23 August 1944, Holocaust survivors and the Communist authorities of Soviet Lithuania organised a rally there in which Paneriai was presented as the largest extermination site of Soviet citizens, constituting a "brotherhood burial ground."[5] Until 1947, the Lithuanian Soviet authorities allowed Holocaust survivors to officially commemorate Jewish victims, but only upon prior request.[6] Attempts to gather at the mass extermination site during Jewish religious holidays were not permitted because religious commemorations were at odds with Soviet ideology. Nevertheless, in 1948, due to efforts and funding provided by the Vilnius Jewish community, one of the first monuments in the Soviet Union in memory of the Jews who were killed by the Nazi regime was erected close to the largest pit.

Alongside the monument dedicated to the exterminated Jews, the Polish residents of Vilnius built a wooden cross with an image of the suffering Mother God's (the Virgin Mary), in memory of killed compatriots. After 1952, however, the wooden cross was removed by the Soviet authorities (Sosnowski 1990, 3).

In 1960, the Soviet Lithuanian authorities established the Memorial Museum for the "Victims of Fascism" at the site of the mass killings, to emphasise the victory of the Red Army and commemorate the "peaceful Soviet people" who had fallen victim and had been exterminated, supposedly because of being Soviet citizens. The Memorial Museum of Paneriai was a subsidiary of the Vilnius Regional Research Museum. In 1962, the museum became a branch of the LSSR History and Revolution Museum. In 1977, the memorial park was officially renamed into the Paneriai Memorial. In 1985, the area was rearranged, based on a design by architect Jaunutis Makariūnas, acquiring the current shape.

In 1991, the museum building with the exhibition was handed over to the Vilna Gaon Jewish History Museum. In 2014, the complete area of the memorial was then also handed over to the latter and this again led to a comprehensive re-arrangement of the entire site. In 2015–2017, in cooperation with scientists from other institutions (the Lithuanian Institute of History amongst others), the museum carried out new research, in three consecutive stages, which resulted in an entirely different perception of the mass killing site in Paneriai. In the course of its explorations, a number of new sites and objects were identified and located: killing sites, trenches for inmates, places of former buildings, etc. It also became clear that the territory of the site was much larger than originally thought, covering an area of up to 72 hectares. Now that the investigations are completed, attempts are being made to find the best solution to mark and arrange the former mass killing site in Paneriai and present this complicated period in history to visitors.

Commemoration

The first official commemoration event at the end of the war was held in Paneriai on 23 August 1944. At the time, officials of Soviet Lithuania referred to the victims of the Paneriai killings as "residents of Vilnius," "residents of Lithuania," and "Soviet citizens," thus levelling all the Jewish victims with the rest of the victims that had perished there. Even though the monument to Jewish victims mentioned earlier was erected with the consent of the government of the Soviet Socialist Republic of Lithuania, it was pulled down as a result of the rise of an anti-Semitic campaign triggered by Moscow between 1948 and 1952. It is highly probable that in the 1950s, the old foundation of the monument was used to build a temporary obelisk with a five-pointed star, bearing the standard inscription, in Lithuanian and Russian: "In memory of the victims of Fascist Terror 1941–1944", thus omitting the fact that the large majority of victims in Paneriai were Jews.

The narrative of "Soviet citizens" killed by Fascists, which was introduced very soon after the Red Army had entered and occupied the country, continued to be supported by the memorial museum which was established in Paneriai in 1960. As part of the museum, also a first information infrastructure was created at the memorial site: metal information stands in Lithuanian and Russian were erected, at the entrance and at the killing sites. Jewish victims were not mentioned at all. Although they completely vanished from the (local) official narrative they were silently retained in the collective memory of the survivors:

> Every day passing by at the site going to my working place, I used to see flowers in the mass killing pits. It didn't look as if somebody wanted to honor the victims. The flowers were just lying in the pits. But I knew the real intention of this. This was a secret commemoration, which we tried to hide from the Soviet authorities ... (interview with Jewish dissident Natan Finkestein by Neringa Latvytė, 2015).

After the site was re-designed in 1985, five commemoration stones, with the inscriptions (in Lithuanian and Russian) "Corpses exhumed from mass killing sites were burned here", were erected in the five mass killing pits. The inscription is not quite accurate, because as of the end of 1943, bodies were burnt at special sites next to each pit designated for that purpose. In front of the entrance to the memorial a two-piece installation was erected, with inscriptions in Lithuanian and Russian, saying that "more than 100,000 Soviet people" were shot to death in Paneriai. In 1989, on the initiative of the reviving Lithuanian Jewish Community, a vertical black granite stone was inserted between the two original commemorative granite blocks, with an inscription in Hebrew, Yiddish, Lithuanian and Russian, saying that "among the victims killed in the Paneriai forest were 70,000 Jews: men, women and children." Only in 2004, marble plaques were fixed to the two original blocks of the monument, covering the inscription "Soviet citizens," which had merely pointed out that "one hundred thousand people" had been killed in Paneriai. For decades, the largest Jewish mass extermination site in Lithuania had been ignored and forgotten, overwritten by the dominant Soviet narrative that simply talked about exterminated Soviet citizens.

In 2009, for the fiftieth anniversary of the Vilna Gaon Jewish History Museum, parts of the Paneriai Memorial exhibition were renovated. The exhibition showed documents and reports issued by the Nazis and their local collaborators, personal belongings of victims found in the area of the massacres, and other objects such as a sieve used to sift the ashes of burnt corpses for gold, a hook used to drag the corpses out of the pits, chains used on prisoners who had burnt corpses, and the clothes of the escape leader Yuri Farber, all excavated at Paneriai in 1964, 1973, and 2004.

In 2018, the Paneriai Memorial Museum was renamed into the Paneriai Memorial Visitors Information Centre: a new exhibition was opened, presenting the findings of recent archaeological and geophysical surveys that had taken place in the memorial site. Nineteen additional information panels in Lithuanian, English, Polish, and Hebrew were installed in October 2018. Currently, the panels provide visitors with brief information about the different objects to be found on the site: mass killing pits, trenches, and monuments to the various categories of victims. This allows visitors to read the information individually, without help of a guide. The updated exhibition and the information panels in the area of the memorial present the site not only in its historical context, but also how it has been retained in collective memory.

Nowadays the Paneriai Memorial with the exhibition in the Visitors Information Centre has a two-fold function in Lithuania's commemorative culture: it is a symbol of the Holocaust and a commemoration site for the victims of the Second World War. Various Lithuanian and foreign institutions, including non-governmental organisations, hold major commemoration events there each year, such as:

1. International Holocaust Remembrance Day (on 27 January)
2. Yom HaShoah or Shoah Remembrance Day (in April)
3. The end of the Second World War (on 8–9 May)
4. The remembrance of the soldiers of the Lithuanian Local Squad killed in Paneriai (in May)
5. The International Roma Holocaust Remembrance Day (on 2 August)
6. The *Rodzina Ponarska* commemoration paying tribute to the Poles killed in Paneriai (in September)
7. The National Day of Remembrance of the Genocide of the Jews of Lithuania (on 23 September).

Competing memories

The Paneriai Memorial is an example of how traumatic memories in Eastern Europe (and beyond) are (re)presented, interpreted, collectively remembered, instrumentalised, but also silenced and forgotten. For decades, the different victim groups were, if at all, commemorated separately, but recently the trend is to light a candle at each of the monuments during the seven major commemorations that happen at the site, which has been encouraged by the historians of the Vilna Gaon Jewish History Museum.

Commemoration of Polish victims

In 1990, a wooden cross and an altar tombstone were erected in Paneriai to commemorate the Poles who were killed here. This happened on the initiative of a former member of the Polish underground in Vilnius, Helena Pasierbska (1921–2010), with the support of the Lithuanian Polish Union. A monument specifically designed for this site (by architect Jaunutis Makariūnas) was unveiled in 2000. Annual commemorative events have been organised by the organisation *Rodzina Ponarska* and The House of Polish Culture in Vilnius.

Commemoration of Lithuanian victims

In 2004, a statue was erected in memory of 86 soldiers of the Lithuanian Local Squad. In February 1944, with the permission of the German SS and police headquarters, General Povilas Plechavičius started forming a military unit to fight Soviet and Polish partisans. Between 17 and 21 May 1944, following a conflict between the Lithuanians and Germans over the military unit's subordination and areas of operation, the Nazis arrested 86 soldiers of the defence force and shot them to death in Paneriai. Annual commemorations are being organised in May by the Genocide and Resistance Research Centre of Lithuania and the Ministry of National Defense of the Republic of Lithuania.

In 1996, on the initiative of the then head of the Paneriai Memorial exposition, Algis Karosas, a commemoration stone (designed by architect Julius Masalskas and sculptor Gintas Šuminas) was erected in memory of Enzis Jagomastas. He and his family were killed in Paneriai between 21 and 23 August 1941 by the Nazi security police. Enzis Jagomastas (1870–1941) was a public figure in Lithuania Minor, a bibliophile, book smuggler, publisher, and owner of a printing house. He had been persecuted by the German government for a number of years for defending the rights of the Lithuanians before being finally exiled together with his family. From March 1941 he lived in Vilnius, where he and his family members were caught by the Gestapo and killed in Paneriai.

A monument with a cross bearing the inscription "In memory of the Lithuanians killed by the occupiers in 1941" was already erected in 1992. Most probably, the monument was to be devoted to the soldiers of the Lithuanian Territorial Defense Force, the Jagomastas family and the Lithuanian communists executed in Paneriai in 1941.

Commemoration of Jewish victims

In June 1991, a monument was erected bearing inscriptions in Yiddish, Hebrew, Lithuanian, English and Russian, to commemorate the Jews that had been killed in Paneriai. It was erected on the initiative of Shaya Epstein, chairman of the Vilnius Committee in Israel, together with the Lithuanian Jewish Community and the Republic of Lithuania. Architect Jaunutis Makariūnas, who designed the monument, based his work on the initial monument that had been part of the Paneriai Memorial from 1948 to 1952.

In 1999, Rachilė Margolis (1921–2015), a former inmate of the Vilna Ghetto and member of the underground ghetto resistance organisation and long-standing employee of the Vilna Gaon Jewish History Museum, initiated and personally financed the erection of a memorial stone to pay tribute to the inmates of the *Kailis* and *HKP* forced labour camps, as well as to the Jewish doctors from the Military Hospital in Vilnius, who had been killed in Paneriai at the beginning of July 1944.

In 2000, a monument was erected in memory of medical doctor Hilaris Feigus (1888–1944), whose body had been identified by the Special Soviet Commission in 1944. The monument bears the inscription: "Here rests doctor Hilaris Feigus (1888–1944), the one and only of the 100,000 victims of Paneriai who has his own grave." Also this monument was erected on the initiative of Rachilė Margolis.

Commemoration of Soviet prisoners of war

With the Independence of Lithuania in the 1990s, the victims amongst the Soviet prisoners of war, killed in 1941, remained silenced as they are considered as no one's victims, although a monument was nonetheless established on the initiative of the veterans of the Second World War II in 1998. The inscription on the monument states that "In 1941, in this trench, 7,514 Red Army prisoners of war of various nationalities died of disease and hunger."

In fact, this information is not accurate, because the actual number of victims remains unknown. It is assumed that some 5,000 prisoners of war may have been killed here, but due to the lack of archival sources, the number has not been confirmed. With the war in Ukraine, this monument has triggered controversial discussions about how to commemorate the victims amongst the former Soviet occupiers.

Commemoration of Roma victims

The extermination of Roma in Paneriai is hardly documented and the material which is available is quite fragmented. The earliest data are from 1942, and concern the first four Roma victims exterminated in Paneriai (Erslavaitė 1965, 40). A member of the Sonderkommando 1005A, Konstantin Potanin, testified about a second group of 87 Roma and 15 Polish victims, who were brought by train to be massacred in Paneriai at the end of March 1944. He remembered that they were all shot, one by one, in the so-called Kaunas pit: "a shot and a scream was heard, then again a shot and a scream," he declared. The huge pit was near the Grodno road and consisted of a 560 cubic meter pit and a 628 cubic meter trench.[7]

Another member of the Sonderkommando 1005A, Yuliy Farber, mentioned in his memoirs that in early April 1944, he along with other members of Sonderkommando 1005A were taken to the end of the railway branch, where 50 Gypsy corpses lay on the ground, probably an entire camp of Gypsies brought here the previous evening and shot immediately. Most likely they were trying to escape as the bodies were scattered on all sides. Some of them managed to run 60 steps. One girl seemed to be still alive. Among the victims were indeed women and children. The members of Sonderkommando 1005A were told to undress the victims (the Roma men were wearing short fur coats), to collect the bodies and create a pile of corpses and set them on fire. Farber mentioned that in March, along with 450 Jews and 15 Poles, 50 Gypsies (five men, and the rest women and children) had been liquidated.[8] The daily newspaper *Tiesa* reported in August 1944 about the exhumation in Paneriai: "In this same year (1944) dozens of Gypsies were brought in and dozens of Lithuanian soldiers were shot in the so-called Kaunas pit."[9]

A priest and chaplain of the Lukiškės prison, Juozas Baltramonaitis, mentions in his diary that on 12 April 1944, just before Easter, "46 Gypsies and one Russian were taken away for a *final decision*, which completely spoiled the mood on Good Saturday. Gypsies were taken away with small children. 26 Gypsies (all adults) made a confession and accepted communion. I baptized three Gypsy children" (Aliulis 2003, 590).

Based on the archival documents, it can be assumed that up to 100 Lithuanian Roma were killed in Paneriai, the largest massacre site of Roma in Lithuania (Latvytė 2020, 52).

Commemorations of the Roma victims in Paneriai started with the local initiative of the Vilnius Roma Community in 2001. A circle of stones in memory of the Roma who perished here was laid out in August 2015 by the pupils of the Vilnius Roma Community, together with the historians of the Vilna Gaon Jewish History Museum, on the occasion of International Roma Holocaust Remembrance Day.

Practical activities. #Never Forget: teaching trauma experiences at historical places

It is clear that one should not ignore the actual locations where traumatic events took place when teaching people about historical trauma and memory transmission. Such physical places abound: monuments dedicated to victims are erected by different memory groups and annual ceremonies are organised to commemorate these events. In spite of this, some trauma locations still remain forgotten and excluded from local narratives. With the event that we organised in Vilnius we wanted to impart theoretical and practical background knowledge to teachers, educators, librarians, and memory institution specialists, who are memory agents and often work with the younger generations. The event organised by the Faculty of Communication of Vilnius University was the first in its kind where academics were invited to share there views on how to teach young people about these traumatic events at the places where they occured, and how to introduce place-based remembrance education into the curriculum. The two partner organisations in this project, the Vilna Gaon Jewish History Museum and the International Commission for the Evaluation of Nazi and Soviet Occupation Regimes in Lithuania, were not accidentally chosen. They both work directly with teachers and together organise seminars and workshops for this target group on a regular basis. Since the Panerai forest, the largest mass extermination site in Lithuania, is a branch of the museum, the participants also were provided with the possibility to be shown around at the site by a guide, having an opportunity to visit the museum which is usually closed from October to April.

Although the Vilna Gaon Jewish History Museum has experience working with teachers, bringing together participants for one whole week was quite a challenge. Our partner, the International Commission for the Evaluation of Nazi and Soviet Occupation Regimes in Lithuania, assisted us: its activities are usually welcomed by teachers, who broadly trust the Commission. In the end, 50 participants (mostly teachers) registered online over the course of four days. We also invited librarians because they are able to help teachers by recommending materials that can be used when teaching about past trauma. In the future, librarians can indeed become instrumental in partnering up with teachers and memory institution staff in joint projects.

For us, it was important to encourage teachers, educators, librarians, and memory institution specialists to step out of their usual comfort zone (like the classroom), drawing on experiential learning methods: to explore authentic sites with the aim to overcome the stereotypical framing of the traumatic past, to discuss silenced memory topics, and raise moral responsibility and awareness. Our four main objectives were: to integrate historical places, where traumatic events occured, into the teaching about trauma and its memory transmission; to project knowledge into a place; to take advantage of a place to create honest, meaningful, and engaging learning experiences; and to help a student or visitor to understand their own role in this particular environment, landscape, social circle, and historic moment.

The activities that we offered for the participants, tasked to bring together theory and practice, were the following: two auditorium lectures on trauma heritage by professors of the Faculty of Communication from Vilnius University (Rimvydas Laužikas gave a presentation with the title *Communication of Heritage: from Knowledge and Artefacts to Messages, from the Messages to Historical Memory*, while Arvydas Pacevičius talked about *Trauma Experience Testimonies in Ego Documents*), as well as a practical tour to the authentic site with the museum staff.

The theoretical part took place at the Faculty of Communication of Vilnius University and started in the morning with the registration of the participants. During the registration, staff members of the faculty introduced the activities of the faculty, while partner institutions distributed information packages with material concerning their own activities. The participants had also an opportunity to get more information about each other before the event.

The presentations encouraged the participants not only to be passive listeners, but also to share challenges they are facing while teaching about the traumatic past. Afterwards, one of the participants provided the following very positive feedback: "the lectures had a heart-to-heart style". It shows that teachers and educators, as well as librarians, often feel ignored or excluded as constituting somehow a "lower" and less important echelon of the Lithuanian education system. Their efforts in developing field skills are never taken into account in academia, and their innovative ideas are implemented only partially due to the lack of theoretical knowledge and moral support from academics. The discussions with the presenters continued in an informal manner during lunchtime at the Faculty's canteen, and this was a great opportunity for the participants to feel welcome and appreciated.

The site-specific practical part took place in Paneriai, where the participants were brought by bus. During the 40 minutes trip from the Faculty of Communication to Paneriai, the participants were provided with information about the history of the place, how the former resort was transformed into the largest mass extermination site, and how it was then, after the war, faced with the challenges of commemorating the victims. Based on the questions that were asked during the trip, it was obvious that teachers and educators not only lack historical information, they also have difficulties talking about the memory and meaning of such a traumatic place today, being reluctant even to bring pupils to these authentic sites. As place-based or *in situ* remembrance education refers to forms of education where learners engage with such places, and learn by visiting the sites themselves, emotions and overall embodied experiences play a central role. Our aim was indeed to together explore, read, and map a place where the mass atrocities were committed, to meet and discuss with the staff of the Vilna Gaon Jewish

History Museum, learn about services provided to visitors, discuss the spirit of the place (the *genius loci*) and learn by doing.

After visiting the site and seeing a small exhibition in the local museum, we discussed the topic of good and bad teaching practices and *in situ* learning with the participants. We talked about problem-orientated rather than fact-orientated teaching, the use of various new resources, and so forth. Usually, visits to trauma sites tend to include presentations of the 'facts' (when, what year, what month, what day) and statistics (how many victims, perpetrators, mass extermination pits, corpses, monuments, commemoration events, etc.), and indeed, such fact-oriented guided tours are routinely offered by the Paneriai Memorial Visitors Information Centre. While this is important, it fails to present the broader perspective or promote a deeper understanding of what happened, what participants should 'take away' from their visit, and what and why we should remember. James Young claims that visitors bring their own knowledge and perception to a Holocaust site (Young 1993, 70–71), but the impact of the place offers a far more valuable educational tool if we observe the obligation to "never forget" and cultivate an empathic attitude towards the victims and their suffering. Very often these two components are forgotten due to the conventional focus on the facts and figures.

The event also showed that traumatic events and memories are not talked about easily and that it can be scary to do so. The majority of the participants indeed felt that bringing pupils to a mass killing site was the same as giving them an introductory class to the Holocaust. It is not imperative that pupils know where they are or what has happened at the location, for teachers and educators never attain the results they expect, even when pupils are prepared and understand the chronology of the Holocaust.

Another important finding was that, although the teachers and educators understand how to work with sources, they lack the methodology to work in actual trauma locations. So, with that in mind, the seminar participants discussed how to include the diaries of those who witnessed the mass exterminations at Paneriai in the curriculum. We talked about how to analyse such sources and the importance of not only reading extracts but also trying to find out about the experiences of bystanders who witnessed such crimes. Instead of speaking about collaboration, it may be better to discuss the choices that perpetrators, victims, and bystanders faced. This could include the study of new ego documents (the protocols of trials involving collaborators and perpetrators, for example) in order to further explore the various forms and aspects of trauma.

Having noticed some anxiety in speaking about the Roma Holocaust, we recommended that teachers visit the alternative memorial site in Paneriai, which commemorates the Roma victims. We asked them to talk about why a circle of stones was made, whose idea it was, why there is just a sign and not a proper monument, why the site has an information panel and who initiated the sign's installation. If it is difficult to speak about the past itself, then we should try to speak about the present – pinning down exactly what hurts and the issues we face in terms of stereotypes, prejudice, lack of knowledge, and, perhaps, fear of future trauma.

In the course of the workshop, I noticed that, in terms of general Holocaust education, teaching about the Roma Holocaust creates additional challenges. Often, teachers do not want to hear about the Roma community: this is a controversial issue being perpetuated in Lithuania, where "never again" somehow seems to have failed when it comes to the Roma. Anti-Gypsyism is experienced on a daily basis, and teachers are ill-prepared to fight it. One teacher shared the experience of a Roma child being called "Chinese" because the word Roma was seen as too dirty to be uttered by an ethnic Lithuanian. In everyday communication, the Lithuanian words *cygan*, *tzygan*, and *čigonas*, although commonly used, are still extremely stigmatising.

Facing challenges

"Never again" education tries to develop new formats of teaching about a difficult past, introducing new transformative tools that go beyond the classroom, not only drawing from textbooks but sharing information *in situ* as well. For this to succeed, a strong motivation, practical skills and courage are needed, while understanding and keeping in mind the challenges. The key challenges that we faced in the practical part of the project were, amongst other things:

1. Breaking down the barriers between teachers, educators, and academics. This was the first time that the Faculty of Communication had organised such a seminar for teachers, librarians, and museum specialists. It was challenging because academics quite often feel superior to teachers and educators. By holding the event, we broke down these barriers and connected the two sectors. We all learned that teachers and educators need help with developing methodological tools, especially in terms of how to communicate trauma heritage, how to explore trauma sites, and so on.
2. Leaving the classroom and explore a place, not only to speak about the past but also to talk about the present – pin down exactly what hurts: speaking about the Roma Holocaust, or the Soviet prisoners of war, or the Polish victims for that matter. Exploring what are the sources of these anxieties: stereotypical attitudes, prejudice, lack of knowledge, or maybe, fear of future trauma and the inability to face the open wounds of an unspoken past?
3. Introducing and exploring new teaching material. The majority of the teachers felt that bringing pupils to a mass killing site was equal to

teaching them a class on the Holocaust, effectively saying that most pupils are not prepared for the visit (they do not know where they are or what has happened at the location). Inappropriate methodological preparation does not allow teachers and educators to attain the results they expect.

4. Discussing silenced topics. With that in mind, seminar participants discussed how to include new materials in the curriculum: for example, the diaries of those who witnessed the mass exterminations at Paneriai, which could help to build up empathy and emotional contact with the site.

5. Giving an idea for museum specialists, guides and historians, what should be included on the exhibition panels or in the guided tours for a better understanding and perception of the site, for promoting awareness and making the traumatic past our concern, so that we can in the end help to fulfill our "Never Again" pledge.

Notes

1 Quebec Declaration on the Preservation of the Spirit of Place (4 October 2008), see: http://www.international.icomos.org/quebec2008/quebec_declaration/pdf/GA16_Quebec_Declaration_Final_EN.pdf (last accessed on 2 June 2016).
2 Paradoxically they remain forgotten and excluded from the local discourse, due to a lacking collective memory, despite having the status of protection of immovable cultural heritage of Lithuania and being marked as monuments and maintained by the local municipalities.
3 See also: Заявление Потанина Константина в Государственную Черезвучайную комиссию ЦК партии. 1944 08 13. Государственный архив Российской Федерации (ГАРФ), ф. 7021, оп. 94, д. 1, л. 12, 35. Фарбер, Ю. (1997) 'Мы несдавались', Дружба народов (5), 186.
4 Ypatingosios komisijos aktas. 1944 08 26. Lietuvos ypatingasis archyvas (LYA), fond K-1, description 46, file 4911, volume 8, page 21.
5 J. Paleckis, Kelkime aikštėn vokiškųjų fašistų nusikaltimus (typeprint). Lietuvos ypatingasis archyvas (LYA), fond. 17541, description 1, file 33, pages 6–7A; Kerštas žmonių žudikams hitlerininkams!. 1944; 'Vokiškieji piktadariai turi atsakyti už savo nusikaltimus' (1944). *Tiesa* 41 (102), 24 August, 3; Venclova (1944) 'Žudynių laukai Paneriuose'. *Tiesa* 42 (103), 2; 'Prie didvyrių ir kankinių kapų' (1944). *Tiesa* 47 (108), 2; photo collection of the Vilna Gaon Jewish History Museum.
6 1946 m. kovo 16 d. Religinių kultų reikalų tarybos prie SSRS Liaudies komisarų tarybos įgaliotinio raštas LSSR Liaudies komisarų tarybos pirmininko pavaduotojui drg. Gregorauskui, Lietuvos centrinis valstybės archyvas (LCVA), fond K-181, description 1, file 10, page 39.
7 Заявление Потанина Константина в Государственную Черезвучайную комиссию ЦК партии. 1944 08 13. Государственный архив Российской Федерации (ГАРФ), ф. 7021, оп. 94, д. 1, л. 35; Petrauskas, J. Paneriuose. 1944. *Tiesa* 40 (101), 3; *План лагерей в Понарах, где немцы уничтожавали мирное население*. 1946 08 31. Lietuvos ypatingasis archyvas (LYA), fond. K-1, description 46, file 4911, page 14-8.

8 Розин, Б., Фарбер, Ю. 2011. Яма. Независимый альманах *«Лебедь».* Но. 636:10–11. http://lebed.com/2011/art5860.htm. (accessed March 31 2019); Фарбер, Ю. 1997. Мы несдавались. *Дружба народов* 5:186.
9 Petrauskas, J. (1944) 'Paneriuose'. *Tiesa* 40 (101), 23 August, 3.

References

Aliulis, V. (2003) Kalėjimo Kapeliono Juozo Baltramonaičio Dienoraštį (1942–1944) suradus, *Lietuvių Katalikų Mokslo Akademijos Metraštis*, 22: 590.
Ashplant, G. T., Dawson, G., & Roper, M. (2000) The Politics of War Memory and Commemoration. Context, Structures and Dynamics. In G. T. Ashplant, G. Dawson, & M.Roper, eds. *The Politics of War Memory and Commemoration.* London: Routledge.
Bubnys, A. (1995) Vokiečių Saugumo Policijos ir SD Ypatingasis Būrys Vilniuje (1941–1944). In E. Zingeris, ed. *Atminties Dienos.* Vilnius: Baltos lankos: 181–184.
Bubnys, A. (2019) *Vokiečių saugumo policijos ir SD Vilniaus ypatingasis būrys, 1941–1944 m.* Vilnius: LGGRTC.
Čepaitienė, R. (2014) Vietos Dvasia: Prijaukinimas ar Medžioklė?. In R. Čepaitienė, ed. *Vietos Dvasios Beieškant.* Vilnius: Lietuvos istorijos institutas.
Connerton, P. (2009) *How Modernity Forgets.* Cambridge: Cambridge University Press.
Counted, V. (2016) Making Sence of Place Attachment: Towards a Holistic Understanding of People-Place Relationships and Experiences, *Environment, Space, Place*, 8 (1): 7–32.
Erslavaitė, G. (ed.) (1965) *Masinės žudynės Lietuvoje 1.* Vilnius: Mintis.
Halbwachs, M. (1997) *Mémoires Collective.* Paris: Presses Universitaires de France.
Juzefovičius, R. (2015) Istorinė Atmintis ir Lietuvos Kultūros Rinkodara, *Sovijus*, 3: 15.
Kerštas žmonių žudikams hitlerininkams! (1944) *Tiesa*, 41 (102), 24 August: 3.
Latvytė, N. (2020) Paneriai – Didžiausia Aukų Sušaudymo Vieta. In A. Jutelytė, ed. *Užmirštas Genocidas. Lietuvos Romai Okupacijos Metais.* Vilnius: Petro ofsetas.
Nikžentaitis, A. (2010) Katyne ir Jogailaiciu Ideja: Atminties ir Atminimo Kulturos Modeliai Vidurio ir Rytu Europoje. In *Šiuolaikiniai istorines samones formavimo budai: prielaidos, galimybes ir ribos.* Vilnius: Vilniaus Universiteto Leidykla.
Norkus, Z. (2007) Istorika ir Istorijos Kultūros Studijos: Jörno Rüseno Idėjų Bruožai. In Z. Norkus, ed. *J. Rüsen. Istorika: istorikos darbų rinktinė.* Vilnius: Margi raštai.
Norkus, Z. (ed.) (2007) *J. Rüsen. Istorika: istorikos darbų rinktinė.* Vilnius: Margi raštai.
Nora, P. (1989) Between Memory and History: Les Lieux de Mémoire, *Representations*, 26: 7–24.
Розин, Б., Фарбер, Ю. (2011) Яма, Независимый альманах «Лебедь» (636) [online]. Available at: http://lebed.com/2011/art5860.htm. (Accessed 6 March 2019).
Quebec Declaration on the Preservation of the Spirit of the Place (2008), Available at: http://www.international.icomos.org/quebec2008/quebec_declaration/pdf/GA16_ Quebec_ Declaration_Final_EN.pdf (Accessed 2 June 2016).

Šermukšnytė, R. (2014) Muziejus ir Genius Loci: Sąveikos įvairovė. In R. Čepaitienė, ed. *Vietos Dvasios Beieškant*. Vilnius: Lietuvos istorijos institutas.

Šiaučiūnaitė-Verbickienė, J. (2015) Žydų Paveldo Recepcija šiandienos Lietuvos Sisuomenėje: Vilniaus Atvejis. In A. Nikžentaitis & M. Kopczyński, eds. *Atminties Kultūrų Dialogai Ukrainos, Lietuvos, Baltarusijos (ULB) Erdvėje*. Vilnius: Lietuvos istorijos institutas.

Sosnowski, H. (1990) Pomnik Ponarski, *Kurier Wilenski*, 226: 3.

Šuras, G. (1997) *Vilniaus Geto Kronika 1941–1944*. Vilnius: Era.

Šutinienė, I. (2003) Įvadas. In *Socialinė Atmintis: Minėjimai ir Užmarštys*. Vilnius: Eugrimas.

Young, E. J. (1993) *The Texture of Memory: Holocaust Memorials and Meaning*. New Haven and London: Yale University Press.

7 Exploring the 1991 Battle of Vukovar through experiential learning

Sandra Cvikić

Introduction

Transitional faith of Croatian traumatised communities is for more than 20 years under the scrutiny of transitional justice[1] policies implemented by all respective governments (Cvikić 2019). Its management inside newly acquired liberal democracy thus renders transgenerational transmission of trauma and remembering as a crucial issue that contemporary society must overcome in order to become a functional and sustainable peaceful society.[2] This chapter, therefore, introduces sociological research and provides an analysis of its impact on the post-communist/post-war traumatised Croatian society, based on the Vukovar case. My case is a government-sponsored national educational project implemented in the city of Vukovar (2016–2017) which includes a mandatory field trip to memorial sites and systematic experiential learning[3] as integral part of students' history classes about the Croatian liberation war[4] and the 1991 Vukovar Battle. Students' active participation in lectures about the 1991 Vukovar Battle are hereby coupled with engaged dialogue developed inside the School of Peace organised by the Memorial Centre of the Homeland War Vukovar. Based on the surveyed narrations created by students and teachers in the aftermath of their field trip, this chapter provides an insight into how history, knowledge and experience is developed through systematic experiential learning about the recent traumatic past.

The Memorial Centre of Homeland War Vukovar established by the Croatian Government in 2013 represents an institutionalised effort to provide post-war generations of Croatian students (and the public in general) with factual truths about the war, destruction and violence through education, scientific research and information distribution.[5] Since 2014 however, the primary activity of the Memorial Centre is to cater for the government-sponsored compulsory field trip to Vukovar for all Croatian Eighth Graders. Namely, in the School Year 2014/2015 the first generation of Croatian Eighth Graders from the eastern counties visited memorial sites in Vukovar. Based on their positive feedback, in the School Year 2016/2017, 6,000 Eighth Graders participated in this pilot-project which afterwards became a national educational programme supported by the Croatian Ministry of Veterans' Affairs

104 *Sandra Cvikić*

and supervised by the Ministry of Science and Education. In the School Year 2018/2019 the number ammounted to 40,000 students.

The national educational (two day) programme introduces students to the Homeland War and the 1991 Battle of Vukovar in the framework of two lectures (*An Introduction to the Homeland War* and *The 1991 Battle of Vukovar*)[6] supplemented with visits to 14 interconnected memorial sites,[7] peace education (School of Peace), and a quiz. The lectures are in line with the Eighth Grade National Curriculum for History Classes in Primary School.[8] The first lecture provides facts about the period prior to the Homeland War, namely the aftermath of the Second World War and the former Yugoslav communist regime (1945–1990), followed by the 1990–1996 war and the peaceful reintegration of Eastern Slavonia which ended in January 1998. This lecture also tries to give a brief overview of the main reasons behind socialist Yugoslavia's disintegration in order to ensure students' better understanding of the complex socio-political context of the Homeland War. The 1991 Battle of Vukovar, which is covered in the second lecture, singles out historical events and circumstances deemed important for students' comprehensive understanding of the Vukovar case study based on the influence it had on local community settings in the context of the overall open armed aggression on Croatia by Serbia and Montenegro and the five-year liberation war. At the end of students' stay in Vukovar peace education (and a quiz) completes their educational programme producing a hightened sense of responsibility and understanding along with the awareness of the value of peace that they as individuals and society must strive for. Thereby students leave Vukovar with the knowledge about the value of peace and how important it is to establish mutual trust and respect amongst Croatian citizens and different nations of the world.

The general frame of analysis

The sociological research framework devised to survey narrations – retrospections – created by Croatian students and teachers in the aftermath of their field trip to Vukovar, entails the deconstruction of their socially constructed discourse (Berger & Luckmann 1992) through critical analysis (Klos-Czerwinska 2015) of the vocabulary utilised to express their impressions of memorial sites visits and facts learned about the 1991 Battle of Vukovar and Croatian Homeland War. As indicated before, critical discourse analysis is applied as methodology, which provides a workable framework to acquire more comprehensive knowledge about issues related to cognitive recognition, memory and transmission of collective trauma inside the contemporary Croatian educational system; while the overall theoretical debate on the issues under investigation in this study rests upon Michel Foucault's (Foucault 2007; Klos-Czerwinska 2015) understanding of postmodern European society through his conceptions of knowledge and power – produced by science.[9]

The experiential learning institutionalised in the Croatian educational system is therefore explored through primary data resources, namely e-mail messages received by the Memorial Centre in the aftermath of the Eighth Graders' visit to Vukovar in the School Year 2016/2017.[10] Primary data in received e-mails contain following information: student/teacher name and last name,[11] school name, place, and county,[12] school year, field trip's date, narration (school report/essay). Those e-mail messages were first categorised in two categories: teacher reports and student essays. This type of narration can be called "retrospection". Further on, properties of retrospections are categorised based on the first line of investigation into facts and/or impressions. Namely, the analysis treats this type of narrations – retrospections – as discourse developed by teachers and students alike, bearing in mind population and geographical criteria differences – whether they live in Croatian regions directly affected by the war or indirectly – or whether they live in former occupied Croatian territories or unoccupied Croatian territories (Nazor 2011, 97). Discourse is thereby considered a social action or something that impacts and legitimises it, while statements are social representations of teachers and students facts and/or impressions expressed in their discourse about the 1991 Battle of Vukovar and the Homeland War, thus producing performative effects – they socially construct reality (Austin 1962). As indicated by Austin (1962) to speak means to act. Thereby a developed discourse is not only a description of social practice, but a thing in itself, which requires one to acknowledge the power and ambiguities of words since they create concepts, thus constructing social reality.[13] Based on the post-modernist stand that there is no value-free/neutral (Denzin & Lincoln 1998) and interest-free (Charmaz & Belgrave 2018) science, discourse produced by teachers and students is analysed to improve understanding of the acquired knowledge and gained experience on the level of meaning and rules that constitute social action (Austin 1962) since produced knowledge has profound effects on people's lives and their society (Foucault 2007). Therefore, discourse is understood as a whole, containing both language and non-language practices[14] of experiential learning in Vukovar (Austin 1962). The developed teachers' and students' framework of retrospections can be thus qualified as good, correct, true, and meaningful (Herta 2017) contributing to an improved understanding of contemporary cognitive recognition, memory and transmission of collective trauma inside the Croatian educational system.

Preliminary research results

As previously mentioned, in the School Year 2016/2017, 6000 Eighth Graders from Croatia visited Vukovar.[15] In the aftermath of their field trip, the Memorial Centre received from teachers and students their feedback – 271 e-mails: 161 from teachers and 110 from students (approximately 1% out of 6000).

106 *Sandra Cvikić*

The first line of inquiry into discourse produced by teachers and students indicates that out of 271 received retrospections, 33 were received from schools in the former "war occupied Croatian territories", while the majority – 238 – came from schools in "unoccupied territories" (Nazor 2011, 129). Overall, 208 schools sent their teachers and students to Vukovar, out of which 29 were from former occupied Croatian war territories, while 179 were from unoccupied territories. Out of 271 received retrospections, 161 were produced by teachers while 110 by students. Furthermore, based on their properties, out of 271 retrospections 108 provide largely facts while 163 are personal impressions. Out of 110 retrospections produced by students, the majority was written by female students (75) which were mostly impressions (65). Among the retrospections produced by teachers (161), 124 were also predominantly written by female teachers, but here the majority were facts (75) rather than impressions (49).

However, if one looks into retrospections of teachers and students that came from schools in former war-occupied Croatian territories, then teachers produced more factual reports (17 in total) than impressions about their visit to Vukovar's memorial sites (ten in total). Compared to them, students produced only one factual report while five were impressions of their field trip to Vukovar. It is evident therefore, that based on their properties, retrospections of both students and teachers (33 in total) are mostly impressions (25 in total) rather than factual reports (18 in total).

The analysis of retrospections produced by teachers and students coming from schools in former unoccupied Croatian territories indicate that teachers wrote, like their colleagues from former occupied Croatian war territories, more factual reports (83 in total) than impressions about their field trip to Vukovar (51 in total). However, students produced only seven factual reports while substantially more were impressions of their visit to Vukovar's memorial sites (97 in total). Here, again, based on their properties, retrospections of both students and teachers (238 in total) are mostly impressions (148 in total) rather than factual reports (90 in total).

Within this preliminary research results framework, the next level of analysis provided an insight into the content of the retrospections' discourse produced by teachers and students coming from schools in both, former occupied Croatian territories and unoccupied territories. Thereby, in this case retrospections' discourse is overwhelmingly developed by teachers and students from schools in the former unoccupied Croatian territories. Their discourse is more impressionist than factual. However, the impressionist discourse is largely developed by students (97 in total) while the factual discourse is mostly developed by teachers (83 in total) even though it is evident that out of 134 retrospections produced by teachers, 51 are impressions, while out of 104 retrospections produced by students, only seven are factual. Therefore, teachers (coming from schools in both former occupied and unoccupied Croatian war territories) developed in their official school reports largely factual discourse (100) and to a lesser degree impressionist (61), while students' discourse was more impressionist (102) rather than factual (eight). However, it could be inferred that even though there are more teacher (161) than student (110) retrospections, and teachers' discourse is largely factual, the dominant discourse developed by both teachers and students from former occupied and unoccupied Croatian war territories is largely impressionist (163) rather than factual (108).

Nonetheless, the insights into the content of the retrospections' impressionist and factual discourses based on the third level of critical discourses analysis, enabled the investigation of discursive practices of teachers and students within the conceptual framework shaped by lectures and experiential learning provided in Vukovar. The rational language of the factual discourse and emotional language of the impressionist discourse developed by both teachers and students shows not only how knowledge is disseminated through language appropriated facts about the war events but, more importantly, how experiential learning shapes the minds and hearts of students and teachers alike. The rational language of the factual discourse developed by teachers to a larger degree, and to a lesser degree by students, reflects the conceptual framework of historical factual truths produced by science, disseminated through lectures. Among others, the most frequently used terms developed within the historical conceptual framework of the factual discourse could be ascribed to the following purpose-built sets of vocabulary:

- military concepts: the Homeland War, the Vukovar 1991 Battle, Croatian defenders, Serbian concentration camps Stajićevo and Begejci, 204th Brigade, Vukovar's defense, war participants, war crimes, victims, military barracks, weapons, Croatian defense operations and actions, Vukovar's siege, soldiers, detainees, occupation, captivity, the Yugoslav People's Army, paramilitary forces, three months' struggle, systemic shelling, Croatian Eastern Front;
- memorial sites concepts/symbols: the Water Tower – the symbol of resistance/of war trials/of Vukovar's defense/of war destruction/of the city's suffering and resistance/of victory and a new life/of Croatian unity/of Croatian identity/of resistance to aggression, the Memorial Home Ovčara, the Ovčara Mass Grave, the Memory Site Vukovar Hospital 1991 – one of the symbols of the Homeland War, Vukovar – symbol of the Homeland War/of resistance to Serbian war aggression/of Croatian resistance/of suffering/the city as Croatian guardian;
- historical figures: defenders Blago Zadro and Marko Babić, Siniša Glavašević;
- values/ideas: truth, the values of the Homeland War and the 1991 Battle of Vukovar, Vukovar's sacrifice, homeland's freedom, peace, tolerance, memory, the Greater Serbian idea, Croatian freedom, independence, diversity, coexistence, liberty, free country.

108 *Sandra Cvikić*

Therefore, teacher retrospections as official school reports, and to a lesser degree student essays, utilised this conceptual framework to develop the factual discourse of historical facts, which function as the informative tool supporting the field trip's itinerary content stipulated by the operational (teaching) plan and Eighth Grade Curricula. Since it is not possible to conduct a deeper discourse analysis of lectures' content, one is left to conclude that history teaching in Vukovar, based on teachers' retrospections, fulfil its initial aim of providing knowledge of basic historical facts to students. Even though their retrospections seem technical in nature, its discourse, however, provides an overview of the field trip's itinerary, indicating how important are memory sites visits in Vukovar and to what extent experiential learning contributes to a more comprehensive understanding of the recent violent past, which is visible from students very impressionable retrospections. Nonetheless, it is important to note that almost all teachers retrospections (more than 90%) mention peace education inside the School of Peace, and the values of peace, tolerance and respect of diversity, thereby providing an insight into how this knowledge was internalised by students at the end of their field trip to Vukovar, as is evident not only from the students' narratives, but the teachers' as well.

The emotional language of the impressionist discourse, developed in retrospections to a lesser degree by teachers and to a greater degree by students, reflect the conceptual framework of cognitive liberation providing an insight into how experiential learning impacted their minds and hearts. Inside their statements, the most frequently used terms could be ascribed to the following cognitive purpose-built vocabulary:

- emotions: horrified, weary, empathic, and compassionate, victorious mood, great pain and great pride, great responsibility, impressed, sad, mixed feelings of pride-patriotism-grief, enthusiastic, grateful, happy and satisfied, smitten, angry, furious, scared, thankful, surprised, bitter, in disbelief, resentful and shaken, great love towards the homeland and true dignity and gratitude;
- ideas/ideals: Vukovar – the hero city, heroes of the city, national belonging, the most important thought – never to repeat again, to forgive but never to forget, an independent and sovereign *lijepa naša*,[16] the sacrifice made for the Croatian freedom, our homeland, the truth about the Homeland War, national identity.

The teachers' both factual and impressionist discourse about their field trip to Vukovar with Eighth Grade students is best exemplified by the concluding statements in the reports[17]:

- (Vukovar) "... is a place where new generations are taught in a modern, contemporary and dignified way about the values of the Homeland War ..."

- "... in an objective and peaceful manner, students were provided information along with the message of peace and encouragement ..."
- "... students and teachers alike experienced this trip as necessary and of high quality (...) the knowledge and experiences they gained will remain permanently in their memory..."
- "... students have experienced the Homeland War in a vastly different way ..."
- "... visit to the hero city ... has resulted in greater awareness of students and young people about their own history, which will reinforce their efforts in preventing something like this from ever happening again, and that freedom, independence and the right to life are basic rights for every individual and nation."

Therefore, one can see how experiential learning methods had an impact on students visiting the memorial sites in Vukovar and how lectures about the Vukovar 1991 Battle and the Homeland war were received by children, especially a lecture about peace and tolerance. The students' impressions about their field trip to Vukovar can be best exemplified by following statements:

- "... we returned to our homes enriched by knowledge and filled with emotions ..."
- "... the visit to Vukovar (...) unforgettable experience ..."
- "... before this field trip the war stories were just empty talk ..."
- "... at the end I would like to say: to forgive but never to forget!"
- "... this visit has ignited in us a great love towards the homeland and true dignity and gratitude ..."
- "... by having seen the conditions under which people lived (...) I am grateful to all that was given to me"
- "... seeing photos of the destroyed city, I was overwhelmed by fear and wish that something like that never happens again ..."
- "... one learns about the Homeland War and victims, from history, one reads about it in books, listens to parents and grandparents, but nothing can substitute the emotions and experience of the city at the very place where it happened ..."
- "... listening to the lectures we understood that we cannot say that the war was between Croats and Serbs because some Serbs fought on the Croatian side ..."
- "... disbelief in the cold-heartedness of people ..."
- "disbelief in the human cruelty"
- "... a love for the homeland has conquered all the miseries and pain and helped to gain freedom for Croats ...".

Their feelings and thoughts can be summed up in the slogan "To forgive, but never to forget!" and/or "Never again!"

Debating "experiential learning" in Croatian context

The discursive practices and conceptual frameworks developed over the time by domestic and international TJ scholars and experts have shaped the reconstruction of the Croatian social and political reality, having an upper hand on the knowledge produced about post-war traumatised populations and their histories (Cvikić 2019). The tangible and fragile fabrics of memory and emotions that resonate with the perceived and expected rational confrontation with the violent past has, therefore, reinforced the need to control and manage transgenerational transmission of trauma and grievances (Cvikić 2019). To teach history in such circumstances is, however, extremely challenging as indicated by sociologist Žunec (2007) and numerous Croatian historians (Skenderović et al. 2008; Skenderović 2015; Barić 2005). Nonetheless, domestically produced knowledge disseminated to post-war generations through experiential learning methods in Vukovar so far has proved to be a feasible solution. Developed by both, teachers and students, factual and impressionist discourses studied through a Foucauldian lens indicate to what extent knowledge and emotions can be balanced through experiential learning methods, thus having lasting impact on how students internalise factual truths and nurture positive/healthy feelings about the Homeland War and the 1991 Battle of Vukovar. Both discourses, however, are educational and emotional expressions of the knowledge acquired and feelings developed in Vukovar, thus, resulting in an improved capacity to merge the two presented narratives of war (the national, Croatian and the local, Vukovarian) into a complex historical interpretation of factual truths and comprehensive understanding of historical events. Cognitive recognition detected in both discourses provides evidence to support the ongoing implementation of systematic experiential learning in Vukovar as an integral part of students' Eighth Grade history classes, but with certain limitations.

The preliminary results of this sociological research indicate that female students and teachers in general are more impressionable than their male colleagues. Why is it so, and how and in what way this is related to their place of residence, and where the differences in reception come from, requires additional investigation. Further research could also benefit greatly from an investigation into the reasons and obstacles behind the Serbian minority school students' and teachers' non-participation in this government-sponsored project. Apart from this, it would be worthwhile to determine if students and teachers had negative experiences of their field trip to Vukovar. Nonetheless, despite its limitations, the preliminary results of this sociological study indicate that Croatian Eighth Grade students did not develop negative emotions of hostility, hatred, and nationalism in the aftermath of their field trip to Vukovar. Whether this could be attributed to peace education or the knowledge that students acquired in Vukovar, it is nonetheless clear that experiential learning did contribute to the cognitive liberation of their memory, thus mitigating transgenerational transmission of grievances and trauma inside the

Croatian educational system. However, whether this Croatian experiential learning model can be applied to different historical, geographical, social, and educational contexts remains to be seen, since its implementation in Croatia still requires additional research, practical modification, readjustment and time in order to demonstrate its generalised applicability.

Notes

1 The transitional justice (TJ) definition used in this chapter is the one provided by the UN (2010, 2). Since an overview of the TJ scholarly production will not be provided here, readers are advised to consult the seminal work of Ruti Teitel (2003) related to the field's development.
2 There is still an ongoing scholarly debate in Croatia on how history is to be taught to students, which has over the time created controversial outcomes and divergent points of views. The public debate was initiated by Croatian historian Tvrtko Jakovina in 2007, prompting historians Robert Skenderović, Mario Jareb, and Mato Artuković to join the debate in 2008. There was also an international initiative inviting historians from former Yugoslavia in a joint effort to confront the controversies of the recent violent past led by Charles Ingrao and Emmert (2010).
3 The theory of experiential learning is neither discussed nor applied in this chapter. Thus, the concept is used because it best describes students' learning process inside a government-sponsored project. An excellent example of a critical investigation into the concept's theory and application is provided by Miettinen (2000) and, Ord and Leather (2011), as well as Kolb's (1984) model of experiential learning.
4 For the Homeland War's definition see Nazor (2011, 10–11).
5 For additional information see the Memorial Centre's official web site (https://www.mcdrvu.hr/en/). The e-mail data received by the Memorial Centre were collected by Ivan Fremec (an employee) who also participated in this sociological study conducting the first line of investigation.
6 Based on the Memorial Centre's Management Board meeting in 2017, the literature approved for use in combination with the two lectures is the following: Bekavac and Jareb (2014), Erdelja and Stojaković (2014), Đurić (2014), Koren (2014), Nazor (2011), Radelić (2006), and Marijan (2003, 2016). Lectures are also supplemented with veterans/defenders and eyewitness firsthand accounts and an animated map of the Homeland War provided by the Croatian History Museum (Zagreb).
7 Memorial sites in Vukovar are listed and presented at the official web site of the Memorial Centre.
8 Available at the Education and Teachers Training Agency's official web site: https://www.azoo.hr/images/AZOO/Ravnatelji/RM/Nastavni_plan_i_program_za_osnovnu_skolu_-_MZOS_2006.pdf.
9 It is assumed that most contemporary scholars are familiar with Foucault's and Berger and Luckmann's work, so in this chapter an overview of their developed methodological and theoretical frameworks will not be provided.
10 The content of the received e-mails has been translated from Croatian into English by the author.
11 From which one can discern teacher's/student's gender.
12 From which one can discern whether teachers/students were coming from former occupied or unoccupied Croatian territories during the war.

13 The different theoretical schools and authors that focus on discursive and non-discursive social practices, namely, language, and non-language social practices are left out of the scope of this text.
14 The social reality related to cognitive recognition, memory and transmission of collective trauma inside the Croatian educational system is not only a result of produced discourses. It is profoundly shaped by various circumstances of a non-discursive character such as TJ policies (Cvikić & Živić 2016). Based on the sociological research results presented at the VII. National Congress "Social Cohesion in the Society of Polarization, Conflict and Inequality" (Zagreb, 11–12 April 2019) in her lecture *Transitional Justice and Social Cohesion – City of Vukovar Case Study,* S. Cvikić identified four development periods of Croatia's TJ policy implementation. The first period (1991–1995) is marked by the aggression, war of liberation and national state independence, thus defined by the UN Security Council's Resolutions and EU political decisions. The second period (1996–1998) introduces additional TJ provisions into the post-war Croatian/UN's peaceful reintegration process followed by human and minority rights protection, reparation and reconstruction, conflict-transformation and peacebuilding process. The third period (2000–2013) was defined by the EU Stabilization and Accession Agreement, which stipulated a tailor-made EU accession membership conditionality for Croatia (human and minority rights protection, and cross-border cooperation). The fourth period (2013–2018) was marked by Croatian EU membership and strongly shaped by society's democratic efforts to come to terms with the post-war trauma, violence and war crimes facilitated and promoted by TJ experts, political entrepreneurs and NGO activists (Cvikić 2019).
15 Based on the Memorial Centre's administration records, even though field trips to Vukovar are mandatory for all Croatian Eighth Graders as an integral part of their history classes, this national educational programme was not implemented by some Serbian ethnic minority schools (schools in the villages Negoslavci and Dalj). This was due to invoked parents' rights ensured by the Croatian Constitution and the Primary and High School Education and Upbringing Law. Namely, scholarly research conducted in areas such as Vukovar's, with Serbian ethnic minority schooling, indicates that ethnic distance between children of Croatian and Serbian descent has not decreased since the peaceful reintegration process of Eastern Slavonia (Čorkalo Biruški & Ajduković 2008). Paradoxically, what the liberal constitutional national minority rights law in education for Serbian ethnic communities has helped to accomplish is precisely what the legislation tried to avoid in practice – self-segregation.
16 This phrase denotes national feelings from the Croatian anthem.
17 To ensure their privacy, teachers' and students' selected statements quoted in this chapter are without any reference either to their identity or the school they belong.

References

Austin, J. (1962) *How to do Things with Words. The William James Lectures Delivered at Harvard University in 1955.* Oxford: The Clarendon Press.
Barić, N. (2005) *Srpska Pobuna u Hrvatskoj 1990–1995.* Zagreb: Golden Marketing-Tehnička knjiga.
Bekavac, S. & Jareb, M. (2014) *Povijest 8.* Zagreb: Alfa.
Berger, P. & Luckmann, T. (1992) *Socijalna Konstrukcija Zbilje. Rasprava o Sociologiji Znanja.* Zagreb: Naprijed.

Charmaz, K. & Belgrave, L. L. (2018) Thinking About Data with Grounded Theory, *Qualitative Inquiry*, 25 (8): 743–753.
Cvikić, S. & Živić, D. (2016) In Between Transitional Justice and Genocide – Vukovar 1991 and Srebrenica 1995. In H. Karčić, ed. *Remembering the Bosnian Genocide: Justice, Memory and Denial.* Sarajevo: Institut za islamsku tradiciju Bošnjaka: 313–346.
Cvikić, S. (2019) Deconstruction of "Scientifically Based Injustices": About Post-War Traumatized Populations of "Spoilers" in Croatia, *Sociologija, Časopis za sociologiju, socijalnu psihologiju i socijalnu antropologiju*, 61 (5): 697–717.
Čorkalo Biruški, D. & Ajduković, D. (2008) Stavovi učenika, roditelja i nastavnika prema školovanju: što se promijenilo tijekom šest godina u Vukovaru?, *Medijske i etničke teme*, 24 (3): 189–216.
Denzin, N. K. & Lincoln, Y. S. (1998) *Collecting and Interpreting Qualitative Materials.* Thousand Oaks, CA: Sage Publications.
Đurić, V. (2014) *Vremeplov 8.* Zagreb: Profil.
Erdelja, K. & Stojaković, I. (2014) *Tragom prošlosti 8.* Zagreb: Školska knjiga.
Foucault, M. (2007) *Security, Territory, Population. Lectures at the College de France 1977–78.* New York: Palgrave Macmillan.
Herta, L. (2017) Security as speech act. Discourse construction of the Syrian Refugee Crisis. In: *International Conference RCIC'17. Redefining Community in International Context.* [online] Bari: RCIC, 283–287. Available at: http://www.afahc.ro/ro/rcic/201 7/rcic'17/LSDA/283–287%20Herta.pdf (Accessed 10 January 2020).
Ingrao, C. & Emmert, T. A. (2010) *Confronting the Yugoslav Controversies – A Scholars' Initiative.* Sarajevo: Biblioteka Memorija.
Kolb, D. (1984) *Experiential Learning, Experience as the Source of Learning and Development.* Englewood Cliffs, NJ: Prentice Hall.
Klos-Czerwinska, P. (2015) *Discourse: An Introduction to Van Dijk, Foucault, and Bourdieu.* Wydawnstwo: Wyzszej Szkoloy Filogieznej we Wroclawiu.
Koren, S. (2014) *Povijest 8.* Zagreb: Profil.
Marijan, D. (2003) *Obrana i pad Vukovara.* Zagreb: Hrvatski institute za povijest.
Marijan, D. (2016) *Domovinski rat.* Zagreb: Hrvatski institute za povijest.
Miettinen, R. (2000) The concept of experiential learning and John Dewey's theory of reflective thought and action, *International Journal of Lifelong Education*, 19 (1): 54–72.
Nazor, A. (2011) *Velikosrpska Agresija na Hrvatsku 1990-ih.* Zagreb: Hrvatski memorijalno dokumentacijski centar Domovinskog rata.
Ord, J. & Leather, M. (2011) The Substance Beneath the Labels of Experiential Learning: The Importance of John Dewey for Outdoor Educators, *Journal of Outdoor and Environmental Education*, 15: 13–23.
Radelić, Z. (2006) *Hrvatska u Jugoslaviji 1945. – 1991., od zajedništva do razlaza.* Zagreb: Hrvatski institute za povijest.
Skenderović, R., Jareb, M., & Artuković, M. (2008) *Multiperspektivnost ili relativiziranje?: dodatak udžbenicima za najnoviju povijest i istina o Domovinskom ratu.* Slavonski Brod: Hrvatski institute za povijest, Područnica za povijest Slavonije, Srijema i Baranje.
Skenderović, R. (2015) Great Scholarly Authorities and Small Nations – The Formation of Historical Narratives on Franjo Tuđman and the Homeland War, *Review of Croatian History*, 11 (1): 121–137.

Teitel, R. G. (2003) Transitional Justice genealogy, *Harvard Human Rights Journal*, 16: 69–94.
Tvrtko, J. (2007) *Jedna povijest, više historija. Dodatak udžbenicima s kronikom objavljivanja*. Zagreb: Documenta – Centar za suočavanje s prošlošću.
UN, (2010) *Guidance Note of the Secretary General – United Nations Approach to Transitional Justice* [online]. New York: UN, p. 2. Available at: https://www.un.org/ruleoflaw/files/TJ_Guidance_Note_March_2010FINAL.pdf (Accessed 10 January 2020).
Žunec, O. (2007) *Goli život I. i II. Socijetalne dimenzije pobune Srba u Hrvatskoj.* Zagreb: Demetra.

8 Speak Your Mind But Mind Your Speech

Benedikt Hielscher

Introduction

As partners in the European Commission project #*Never Again: Teaching Transmission of Trauma and Remembrance through Experiential Learning*, the Peace Action, Training and Research Institute of Romania (PATRIR) implemented two activities: a simultaneous public film screening and subsequent video call between participants, and a two-day intensive training course on communication and dialogue titled "Speak Your Mind but Mind Your Speech" (SYMMYS). In this chapter, only the training course will be critically analysed. For further information on the simultaneous screening of the film "*I Do Not Care If We Go Down In History As Barbarians*" by Romanian director Radu Jude (2018), see the contribution "Performative experiential learning strategies: reenacting the historical, enacting the every day" (Duijzings, Lange and Walther, 2021) in chapter 15 of this book.

Unlike the simultaneous film screening, which focused on the role of Romania in the Holocaust, the SYMMYS training course did not address a singular historical event in its history. Instead, it was designed as an intervention facilitating a deep reflective process by combining theoretical elements and practical exercises for experiential learning. The goal of the intervention was to contribute to participants' better understanding of factual knowledge and more effective communication skills, indirectly triggering attitudinal change. On the one hand, knowledge of the reciprocal relationship between the Romanian collective history, participants' individual past, and their individual communication behaviours can result in a greater understanding of the status quo. Practicing effective communication skills equips participants with the ability to have difficult conversations on an interpersonal level. On the other hand, the recognition of these factors simultaneously being cause and effect of the ongoing transmission of an unprocessed collective trauma of Romania's ethnically and culturally diverse society, is instrumental in developing a kinder attitude towards other members of society. The intervention applied a systemic peacebuilding approach with multi-disciplinary theoretical foundations, combining concepts and insights from the fields of political psychology, clinical psychology, psychoanalysis as well as peace and conflict studies.

After the violent overthrow of the regime of dictator Nicolae Ceaușescu in December 1989, restorative efforts in the country were mostly focusing on strengthening the economy and changing the political system. Little attention has been paid to national reconciliation and to repairing the social fabric that was damaged by years of authoritarian rule, thus neglecting a real potential for violence in the country. In March 1990, this potential resulted in violent clashes between ethnic Romanian and ethnic Hungarian citizens of Romania during which several people were killed. Now, almost 30 years later, the potential for direct violence between ethnic Hungarians and Romanians has significantly decreased. But the country is still far from being healed: discrimination against the Roma minority and the LGBTIQ+ community are widespread and can be observed regularly, and gender-based violence and victim-blaming are all too common. In October 2018, a dividing referendum attempting to make gay marriage unconstitutional failed to the great relief of the members and allies of its LGBTIQ+ community. Nonetheless, public discourse had become even more divided than before during the months leading up to the referendum. The referendum also further contributed to the general mistrust of Romania's political system and class, the extend of which is evidenced by regular large-scale protest against what is widely perceived as a corrupt government.

The European Union (EU) and its predecessors are regularly credited as the most important factors contributing to an era of relative peace and stability in Europe. After centuries of armed conflict in the central European mainland peaked in the early and mid-20th century in two devastating world wars, the European project certainly resulted in fewer wars between its member states. As outlined by Hielscher in Schiffers and Habersetzer (2018), defining peace simply as a state characterised by the absence of armed conflict results in a false dichotomy, making it impossible to measure the quality of peace. The concept proposed by Galtung in 1964, and enhanced in 1996, overcomes this limitation by introducing peace as a spectrum ranging from positive to negative. Whereas negative peace is only characterised by the absence of direct violence (that is, any kind of violence visible to the naked eye, including psychological violence), positive peace describes a society characterised by the absence of structural violence (i.e. laws and policies that protect victims/survivors of direct violence) as well as cultural violence (i.e. norms justifying direct violence). For the purpose of this paper, the term "peace" refers to the concept of positive peace unless explicitly stated otherwise. Similarly, the term conflict will not be used synonymously with violent or armed conflict. According to Bar-Tal (2011), "conflicts are defined as situations in which two or more parties perceive that their goals and/or interests are in direct contradiction with one another and decide to act on the basis of this perception." The difference between conflict and violence is therefore that the former is inevitable while the latter is a consciously chosen strategy to enforce a position during a conflict.

In societies across the EU, conflicts caused by social and political polarisation are becoming more frequent. These conflicts cause the formation of factions along sociopolitical fault lines and negatively impact social cohesion within the bloc. This trend is caused, in part, by growing economic inequality, ongoing systemic injustice and political marginalisation of disenfranchised groups. Like many of the new member states from Eastern Europe, Romania carries the additional burden of its largely unprocessed authoritarian past stemming from two brutal dictatorships.

To maintain their power, authoritarian regimes instill terror in their subjects with the intent to demobilise their population. Coercion tactics include harassment, arrests, mass incarceration, raids, forced labour, torture, rape, forced disappearances, targeted assassinations, public executions, mass killings, and collective punishment. Opposition, regardless if real or suspected, is being quelled by a security apparatus whose members enjoy special privileges compared to the rest of the population, and in return are expected to show unwavering loyalty (Nugent 2018). Access to these and other positions of power or leadership is regularly limited to members of a specific group that is defined by an attribute distinguishing it from the rest of the population (e.g. ethnicity, religion, party membership, heritage, social class, political ideology, etc.). Over time, this leads to the establishment of an elite that has a strong interest in maintaining the status quo out of fear for retribution for their complicity in the oppression. More than that, being a member of any group for an extended period of time results in strong identification with it and becomes an integral part of an individual's personal and social identity.

Having a sense of identity is central to human existence, offering an answer to the question "who am I?" and enabling us to establish ourselves as individuals. Social psychology helps to understand why humans are sometimes willing to go to great lengths to protect themselves from threats to their identity. It also provides the theoretical foundation for finding a way to come to terms with collective trauma stemming from intergroup conflict with a significant identity component. Social Identity Theory was first postulated by Tajfel and Turner (1979) in an attempt to provide an explanation for intergroup conflict in contexts that were not characterised by competition over scarce resources. According to their model, a shared social identity is formed by members of any group regardless of size. Three separate cognitive processes are involved: (1) *Social categorization* describes segmentation and classification of humans on the basis of readily available attributes (e.g. gender, age, ethnicity, sexual orientation, etc.). (2) *Social identification* describes the awareness of being a member of a group on the basis of shared social categories and the adoption of the norms and behaviours associated with that group. The perception of what constitutes normative behaviour representing both ingroup and outgroup prototypes are generally shared by members of a group and can (and often does) result in the production of stereotypes. The need for affirmation of maximum differences between in- and outgroup regularly leads to overestimated intragroup similarities and intergroup differences. As a consequence of this ingroup favouritism, individuals tend to be under the impression that their ingroup has a more complex identity resulting in a more context-dependent behaviour than their outgroup is capable of (Rouhana 1999). When groups are in direct conflict with each other the degree of group identification increases as a result (Nugent 2018).

Tajfel and Turner (1979) hypothesise that one of the defining elements of humans is the need to maintain a positive self-image. (3) *Social comparison* is the process of contrasting the ingroup with the outgroup in the expectation that it will compare favourably, elevating the individual's self-esteem. If this is the case, the evaluation of the self in context is a successful strategy to satisfy this need. Groups characterised by stark prototypical differences regarding political ideology or other attributes used as categories usually also display normative differences in their evaluation framework. To maintain a positive perception, differences with the outgroup can be framed as normative virtues that intrinsically offer grounds for success simply by existing. If positive evaluation is not possible or the outgroup is perceived as a threat to their self-esteem (e.g. by challenging their social status), it may serve as a motivation to take action to counter the threat.

Social identity is not one fixed concept. Every individual has a multitude of different social identities that are activated whenever the social context requires it and sometimes conflict with each other. The cognitive processes summarised above are neither taking place in isolation nor do they conclude at a certain point. They interact and continue to produce new information. Social Identity Theory holds that the stronger a social identity is, the more we are likely to participate in actions that are oriented towards the ingroup (Tajfel & Turner 1979).

Several implications can be drawn for social identity derived from membership in an elite group in a repressive regime. On the one hand, the cautious behaviour of the outgroup out of fear for retribution serves as an omnipresent reminder of the omnipresent conflict. When the social identity is threatened by non-compliance, the resulting affirmation of normative ingroup behaviour can result in acts of violence. The violent behaviour will be rationalised as a justified response and result in an even stronger sense of identity and identification with the regime. The social identity of the victims of violence on the other hand will also be enhanced, centred around the experience of powerlessness. The resulting polarisation of the society plays directly into the hand of the regime because a fragmented society with low levels of intergroup trust is easier to rule.

The fascist and communist regimes that ruled Romania prior to the 1989 revolution were generally characterised by the normalised use of extreme violence in the pursuit of their ideological goals. During the fascist regime of Antonescu, terror and violence concentrated almost exclusively on Romania's

Jewish and Roma population as well as political opponents. After his removal from power, the Soviet Union established a communist dictatorship that was ruthless in its persecution of political opponents and enforcement of compliance. Suddenly every Romanian citizen regardless of ethnicity became a potential target of the terror of the nefarious secret police. After Ceauşescu assumed power in 1965, the violence was significantly reduced as a result of changed policing tactics and terror gave way to fear (Deletant 2001). Nonetheless, his authoritarian regime allowed no dissent and it took a revolution to remove him from power. It is obvious that any society that emerges from decades of authoritarian rule, will not stop being polarised or fragmented overnight but requires time to heal and process the collective trauma.

Trauma is the experience of intense psychological stress caused by events that exceed an individual's ability to cope, resulting in feeling unsafe, helpless and lacking agency to take control of the situation. Individual trauma can cause chronic mental health problems that may become more severe over time if left untreated. Decades of research in the fields of clinical psychology and psychiatry have contributed to a solid evidence base for different therapeutic approaches and provide guidance for mental health experts in their work with traumatised individuals. Healing trauma is painful but possible. It usually involves participation in an intensive, emotionally challenging regimen of psychotherapy which enables the trauma survivor to make sense of their experiences in the safety of a supportive environment. Under the right circumstances, the healing process may result in post-traumatic growth, allowing the survivor to take control and reframe their trauma as an opportunity for gaining a different outlook on their life (Orejuela-Dávila et al. 2019).

The similarities between individual and collective trauma are more than in name only. Somasundaram (2007) defines collective trauma as the social transformation of a society due to the effects of violent conflict. In the process, various aspects that are considered normal in a functional society and serve as foundation for a collaborative coexistence become dysfunctional. The dysfunctionality extends to social processes, relationships on the micro and macro level, institutions, practices, and other elements of the social fabric. On top of the toll these conditions of extreme stress take on the mental health of individuals, they can lead to diminished intergroup trust and cooperation.

Traumatisation processes are so complex that it is difficult to predict if and how a survivor's mental health will be affected. The intensity and duration of the traumatic event play a key role as well as individual factors such as age, personality, general health, economic security, and genetic predisposition. The existence of strong interpersonal relationships, access to mental health care, and the ability to rely on support from family, friends, or a caring community have an influence on resilience after trauma as well. This illustrates that assessing the extent or predicting the impact of collective trauma is virtually impossible because the response of every member of society would have to be taken into account.

A common reaction to unprocessed collective trauma is the unwillingness of survivors to speak about their experiences to anybody to the point of completely denying that they were present at the time (de Mendelssohn 2008). The guilt of having survived when countless others died can cause an identity crisis centred around the question if it would not have been better to die as well, while trying to protect others. Self-loathing, loss of self-respect, and reduced self-esteem can lead to clinical depression. The effects of diminished mental health of parents on their ability to act as loving caregivers are well documented. A common theme in the family history of children of survivors of genocide, war, or terrorist attacks is a lack of affection during their upbringing, sometimes to the point of neglect. These children have a higher prevalence of behavioural problems and mental illness. Children that yearn for their parents' love in turn develop feelings of guilt for wanting what their parents are not able to give (Felsen 2017).

Another common defence mechanism of survivors is to self-regulate by shutting down their emotions and joke about what has happened. While they might appear to outsiders to have been able to develop a healthy coping mechanism, their lack of emotions also extends to their relationship with their children who in turn are more likely to develop mental health issues themselves. These children carry the additional burden of feeling shame for not having a good relationship with their parents who appear to be well-adjusted to others. The experience of not having been able to protect loved ones can also result in an overprotective parenting style, leaving the children ill-prepared to make their own decisions later in life. Even children who do not develop mental health problems are affected by the unprocessed trauma of their parents and regularly experience marital problems, and report an overall lower satisfaction with their lives (de Mendelssohn 2008).

How well societies are equipped to cope with collective trauma depends on a variety of factors. Significant in this regard are social cohesion, quality of ingroup relations and interpersonal trust, political stability, and the belief in a shared fate. According to Ben-Porath (2012), the mutual investment of citizens in one another is linked to their ability to relate their own fate to the fate of the rest of the nation. In some cases, traumatic events can bring societies temporarily closer together and strengthen the national identity, e.g. large-scale environmental disasters or terrorist attacks.

In the case of Romania, none of the conditions that facilitate resilience to trauma were present. The feared secret police used coercion and blackmail to recruit hundreds of thousands of informants, and spread misinformation to divide the population and prevent collective action by the opposition. However, de Mendelssohn (2008) observed that experiencing trauma is not limited to victims and their descendants, it is also a common occurrence in perpetrators. In the aftermath of violence, perpetrators regularly chose to remain silent and not speak about what they had done out of shame and fear. Their descendants carried this trauma over into the next generation and internalised the shame and guilt. As a result of the massive network of informers in Romania who regularly exaggerated or made up information to satisfy their handlers from the secret police, the distinction between victim and perpetrator was difficult to begin with (Mitroiu 2016). After the revolution, the communist elites remained largely in power. This explains the lack of political will for a reconciliation process and the prosecution of those responsible for the crimes of the regime. Thirty years after the revolution, there has been little progress, and younger generations have been growing up in a post-communist society where the norm has become to condemn the crimes of the communist regime but never to speak about justice or moral responsibility. Attitudes and behaviours that guaranteed the survival in an authoritarian regime such as avoidance of controversy, obedience to authority, silence in the face of injustice, blaming the victim instead of offering solidarity, and many more, have not been critically dissected to analyse their usefulness in a democracy (Gavreliuc & Gavreliuc 2018). The Romanian society has an extremely low tolerance for interpersonal conflict. As a result, difficult conversations are being avoided, completely removing the ability to find an agreeable solution. The unprocessed collective trauma is resulting in collective shame and lowered self-esteem due to perceived personal shortcomings.

The SYMMYS training course provided an opportunity to reflect on the link between visible individual behaviour patterns and their underlying, less noticeable relationship with the collective history. Building on insights of this personal analysis and reflection process, participants were learning skills needed to be assertive and empathic at the same time, both in relation to themselves and to others. The underlying idea was that being able to communicate confidently during challenging situations will contribute to more self-confidence and less conflict-avoidant behaviour in personal and professional settings. This, in turn, would also affect the environment participants are a part of. Aggressive behaviour directed at others and one-self to make up for lowered self-esteem would become unnecessary.

Method

Non-formal education

The training course was designed as an activity based on the non-formal education approach. Unlike formal education, which is used in the formal education system, non-formal education is heavily centred on the individual. A basic principle is that learners participate voluntarily in the process rather than being present only to meet outside expectations as might be the case with university or school settings. By making the individual experiences of participants an essential part of the content that is used to analyse and draw conclusions from, participants are taking ownership of the learning process.

As all PATRIR training courses, the programme was tailored to the needs and expectations of the participants. The application was open to all residents of Romania above the age of 18. During the application process, participants had to outline their personal experiences with conflicts that have materialised in their personal or professional life. The provided information was used to customise the programme and agenda to address the needs identified during the application process.

Holistic learning

While developing the outline, special attention was paid to making the training course as practical as possible and to provide multiple instances of experiential learning. When learning a new competency, the learning process can be broken down into three categories: gaining new knowledge, developing new or honing existing skills, and changing attitudes. A holistic approach means to equally prioritise a change in attitudes, skills, and knowledge as learning outcomes. Whereas knowledge and skills can be acquired comparatively easily, changing attitudes takes time and can be a multi-year process. Of the three categories, measuring attitudinal change is also the most complicated. Knowledge, meaning the cognitive ability to understand and reproduce concepts and facts, can be measured by providing opportunities to discuss the items. Skills, the ability to perform tasks, can be tested by engaging in simulations or exercises where the abilities can be demonstrated. Attitudes, on the other hand, are values and feelings towards a group or a broader theme. They have been formed throughout a lifetime, and people are not even conscious of these attitudes most of the time. Depending on how socially acceptable a value is perceived to be, attitudes may also be suppressed in order not to endanger an individual's social standing. Attitudinal change can be achieved by providing opportunities for experiential learning, i.e. the exposure to situations that can challenge existing social constructs and preconceptions. Youth, for example, are regularly called out by older, established politicians for their lack of political engagement. Quite often that lack of activism does not stem from a lack of ideas or wish for political chance, but from insecurity how to even begin approaching an elected official because they are not perceived as individuals but as their function (e.g. mayor, parliamentarian, etc.). Neither side understands the uninterested or unapproachable impression they make on the other, because *they* know and understand their motivations. A simple, 10-minute role reversal, during which the politician sits at a table with the rest of youth while a young person speaks about a recent project they have been a part of followed by a guided reflection process can result in a greater understanding of the motivations.

The right learning environment is of significance as well. Learners should be able to go beyond their limits and leave their comfort zone while feeling

Table 8.1

Timeslot	Day I	Day II
Morning I	Creating Common Ground – Setting Objectives and Expectations	Empathising at All Cost? Risks and Opportunities of Dialogue
	Lunch Break	
Morning II	Identity and Culture: The Interaction of our Self with our Environment	Empathising at All Cost? Risks and Opportunities of Dialogue
	Lunch Break	
Afternoon I	Core Competencies 1: Reflecting and Empathising	Core Competencies 3: Assertive, not Aggressive
	Coffee Break	
Afternoon II	Core Competencies 2: Active Listening	Making Sense of It All: Practical Applications

they are in a safe space in which they are not being judged or ridiculed for their beliefs. Throughout the learning process, time and space for thorough reflection must be provided to consolidate the new competences.

The training course was split up into eight sessions of 90 minutes each during which different methods were applied. In the following overview, the sessions will be discussed in detail. The agenda itself was presented as a framework that could be adapted depending on the flow of the training course, which resulted in Session 3 and 4 being merged into one (see Table 8.1)

Day 1

SESSION 1

The first session aimed to develop among participants a sense of ownership of the training, a sense of security in expressing their ideas, and a common framework in which to approach the sessions ahead. The Never Again project was introduced – to evoke a sense of purpose and meaning among those attending – before giving each participant the opportunity to introduce themselves and why such a project or initiative was important to them. Several participants shared their perceptions and experiences of living in post-communist Romania, where the rights of minorities such as the LGBTIQ+ or Roma communities were increasingly under threat. The trainers helped to guide discussion, to make sense of these feelings in the wider European context, and to emphasise the importance of Never Again and similar projects.

Participants were subsequently given the opportunity to share what their personal goals were in attending, and what they hoped to achieve. Because they had come from different professional and personal environments, their responses varied. One, a software engineer, wanted to utilise the training to be better able to engage in difficult dialogue with their colleagues, while another who worked in the cultural sector for an NGO wanted to improve their organisational practice.

Introducing the training in this way laid the groundwork for a shared understanding of what was to come, while simultaneously enabling trainers to modify aspects of future sessions to make them more relevant and impactful. Before continuing with further sessions, the final step of developing a common framework of expectation was to establish a jointly created code of conduct, where each participant could contribute. This is a useful tool, as it gives participants a sense of ownership of the social contract between them and the trainers, enabling a safer space for expression and an easier facilitation environment. The code of conduct included contributions such as "listen actively", "don't check phones unless necessary" and "give everyone the chance to speak." The lead trainer emphasised that the space should allow for experiments, that communication be non-judgemental and the content of the discussions absolutely confidential.

SESSION 2

In order to build core competencies related to developing empathy, engaging in dialogue, and maintaining healthy communication, it was important to introduce some theoretical concepts that could help participants understand potential receivers. The trainer introduced the concept of identity from a social psychological perspective beginning with several heuristics through which identity might be understood. Heuristics are mental shortcuts humans subconsciously employ to reduce the required mental energy required for solving problems.

The group explored the "availability heuristic", which states that the expected likelihood of an event or an expected behaviour directly relates to how easy it is to think of examples of the event. Once this heuristic was firmly understood, it was easier to introduce two further heuristics: "accessibility", i.e. the extent to how quickly a concept is brought to mind; and "social categorization", which describes the clustering of people into categories based on readily available common attributes.

The trainer tried to elucidate these heuristics in the minds of the participants by giving the example of negative news reports related to Roma people in Romania – a phenomenon participants could relate to – followed by a short discussion about how they feel about them. Participants very well understood how negative news reports could influence heuristics related to Romani people: increasing the expectation or attribution of "criminal" or "crime", perpetuating negative myths and stereotypes and reinforcing cycles of persecution or marginalisation.

Finally, the trainer introduced the concept of "Social Identity Theory", first described by Tajfel and Turner (1979). According to this theory, social identity is the sense of oneself depending on salient group membership. In order to contextualise the following exercises, the trainer asked them two questions: "how negative news articles, stereotypes, myths and social treatment might affect a group's social identity?" And "how might their identity formation affect other groups' identity formation in turn?"

IDENTITY CIRCLE

To examine the heuristics they apply to themselves, and their relative importance, participants are asked to take ten to 15 minutes to think about elements they consider essential for their own identity. To make what can be an abstract concept more accessible, possible elements were provided according to categories on a presentation slide. It was emphasised that the various categories were not meant to be exhaustive but rather provide examples to work with. Participants were competent at selecting identifiers that went beyond the categories provided – such as ethnicity, religion or occupation – with some defining themselves according to their traits (e.g. kind, creative, analytical), the activities they enjoy (e.g. cooking, making movies, sports) and their socio-economic situations.

Subsequently, participants were asked to write each of the ten most important elements on an index card, and then form two circles, an inner and an outer one, facing each other, so that at any given time each had a partner. Individually, they could choose one element they were willing to "give up" and remove the respective index card from their deck. Each participant was given one minute to reflect with their partner why they chose to discard this specific element before the outer circle was rotated one step to the right, allowing participants to form a new pair.

After ten rounds, participants were left with what they considered the single most important element of their identity. After the group came back together, the trainers facilitated a process of reflection and discussion. Participants reported to be more conscious of the different building blocks of their own identity and some vocalised a realisation of how fragile identity can be. Others spoke of feeling vulnerable when asked to give up an element. Throughout the exercise, participants reported to have empathised with their counterparts and the difficulties of their decision-making process.

The exercise provided a good opportunity to reflect on the significance of the social or personal constructs through which people view themselves, and how context might influence them. Furthermore, the exercise acted as an empathy-building, and ice-breaking, activity – helping participants develop shared compassion and mutual recognition before proceeding further with the two-day training. Each participant demonstrated capacity in connecting the theoretical concepts outlined in the beginning of the session with their lived experiences.

HISTORY MAP

To untangle these self-attributed identifiers in the wider context of their lives, a second exercise was employed for them to map out how certain events – both in their lives as well as in the lives of those before them – might have had an influence. Participants were split into groups of two to three people each. Each group was assigned a separate workstation where each group was able to speak without disturbing others and then spread out three pieces of flipchart paper. The exercise consisted of three key steps:

In the first step, participants were asked to draw a straight timeline on the last two of the connected flip chart papers, beginning on the day the oldest member of the group was born and ending on the present day. They were tasked with marking significant dates and periods in each of their lives: personal and professional highlights, difficult moments, or periods, frustrations, surprises, learning moments, self-discoveries and others that they felt were pertinent. While doing so, participants were encouraged to speak to their group about their documentations – why they added them to the map, why they were important and how they were influential in their everyday lives. Examples of the events outlined included the death of a parent, the conversion of a sibling to a different religion, graduating from school or the birth of a child.

For the second step, participants were asked to come together as one group again to discuss the meaning of the concept "culture" – defined for them by the trainer as the wider societal influences and structures that underpin them. They discussed cultural elements prevalent in their daily lives before returning to their working groups. Their task was to write down all significant cultural elements that affected their documented life events from the previous step, surrounding the timeline and drawing connections with their timelines as they saw fit. Some participants expounded on discussions from previously – for example, how religion has affected personal life positively or negatively; or how a decision to live on their own has been impacted by strong family values.

In the final step, participants used the third piece of flipchart paper, connected at the back to the two from the first step. The purpose was to extend the timeline prior to their birth. In this additional space, participants then marked important events that took place before they were born and explained how these events interacted with the cultural elements outlined in step two, to impact other events and their daily lives. In the case of this group, events ranged from Romania's independence in 1877 to various wars, the end of communism, and Romania becoming a member of the European Union.

Afterwards, participants were asked to take ten minutes to have a look at the work of the other groups before coming together in the big group to reflect. The reactions to this exercise were positive. One participant interestingly reported that they did not believe that culture affected their present life to a significant degree, which was an opportunity for further open discussion amongst the group of the relative importance of external influences on internal perceptions. Another participant reported that he had a newfound respect for the difficult life of his great-grandmother, and how this in turn directly affected the family values that he used to perceive as outdated. There was also a lively discussion about the meaning of national liberation and independence, and the different perspectives Romanians and Hungarians might have on the status of Transylvania – a region in the Northwest of Romania that was once part of the Austro-Hungarian Empire.

As a result of the intense discussions, the facilitators decided to provide a brief introduction to the World Values Survey, a research project that explores beliefs and values in societies across the globe. The results of the survey are clustered according to four categories across two axes: "traditional values" versus "secular-rational values" on the first, and "survival values" versus "self-expression values" on the second. While this categorisation is not without criticism, participants found it a useful tool to explore their position on the graph and how this was affecting their sense of belonging in Romanian society.

SESSION 3 AND 4

Originally, the Identity circle and History map exercises were meant to last a little over one hour. But because of the productivity and liveliness of discussions in the first sessions, the trainers decided to extend their time and condense sessions 3 and 4 into one final session.

This session examined empathy, how it is expressed and why it is important. The purpose of deviating from concepts of identity at this stage was for two reasons: the first was to give participants the opportunity to "mentally refresh" from what had been quite intense discussions and topics, and secondly, to lay the groundwork for combining the first day's sessions on the second day into concrete learning outcomes.

To start, the concept of empathy was discussed and how it directly relates to the ethical and moral beliefs that are often perceived as "normal." Participants then analysed a YouTube video recorded in a store in the United States. In the video, a transgender woman is yelling at a clerk for repeatedly misgendering her by addressing her as a man. While describing the situation, one participant initially dismissed the woman's complaint as unfounded and "hysterical" – the participant felt they were not able to see how this could be hurtful; that the store clerk was only innocently mistaken. The comment sparked a fruitful discussion: one member of the group likened the transgender woman's breakdown to a threat to her personal identity, directly empathising with her situation and connecting it with the content of the morning sessions. After several inputs from other members of the group, the first participant agreed that while he did not understand how this was hurtful, he would not want to feel constantly attacked for his own identity. The session concluded with a review of the basic principles of active listening, exploring how active listening is linked to empathy and how it can evoke empathy in others. Participants were asked to reflect on this as well as the rest of the sessions before returning the following day.

Day 2

SESSION 5

After welcoming participants back to the second day of the training course, the trainers deployed an exercise that aimed to both trigger debate, as well as to help participants reflect on their own empathy skills.

The trainers split participants into two groups under the pretext of wanting to engage in a dialogue regarding controversial opinions they were having. Having noted topics that were particularly important to participants on the previous day, the trainers each moderated the discussion in their relevant groups to focus on these. Intentionally, the trainers, however, did not act in good faith and began to deconstruct and attack the beliefs and values of the participants for 15 minutes to agitate them.

In the context of one group discussion, the trainer spoke about perceived issues with wide-spread corruption in the country and questioned whether Romanians were ready to participate in democratic processes. Both of the trainers were foreigners, and this created tension. Other topics that were chosen related to the rights of the LGBTIQ+ community, foreign immigration to the European Union, and emigration from Romania. In the ensuing heated discussion, the facilitators abused their position of authority by cutting off participants, talking over them, or misrepresenting and ridiculing statements they made. For approximately 15 minutes, the facilitators engaged with their groups to varying levels of success. While in one group participants were able to deduct that the facilitator was not representing his own views and only got moderately annoyed, the discussion on the other group escalated to the point that the participants themselves began to raise their voices.

When the exercise ended, participants came back together in one group and discussed what happened. When asked to reflect on their own emotions and engagement throughout the exercise, participants reported feeling uncomfortable and agitated. When the purpose of the exercise was explained – to both highlight participants' skills at empathy and communication as well as to expose the risks of engaging in dialogue in good faith when another side might act in bad faith, a lively discussion ensued. Participants reported being more aware of the processes and dynamics that took place among themselves and their individual tendencies when a sudden, heated argument ensues.

Feedback for this exercise was very positive. While the setting can without a doubt not be compared to a situation outside of the "classroom", the deception and sudden onset made it a lot more realistic than any simulation could have been. Following the reflection, participants identified lessons learned from engaging in conversations about contested issues.

SESSION 6

In order to apply participants' experiences and lessons from the previous session, the trainers introduced a model which they may themselves deploy to engage in challenging conversations. This three-step model is derived from the approach that "cognitive emotive psychotherapy" takes, which states that feelings are the results of an event combined with thoughts that put the event into context. The three steps are: a) creating a reflective space where more questions can be asked before one's own arguments are posited, b) investigate the interests and needs behind a person's argumentative position rather than looking at the position itself c) practice empathy and be pragmatic, i.e. first actively listening and then choosing if it is worth engaging (otherwise described as "picking one's battle").

To help participants deconstruct argumentative techniques that can be employed when acting in bad faith, trainers listed a series of 15 different rhetorical fallacies and rhetorical devices. These included examples such as ad hominem attacks, strawman arguments, red herrings, and others. They were then shown a video of a debate on US-American politics and asked to identify the different devices that were used. Participants were very astute at identifying them – they were given the chance to write their answers down individually and then to share and discuss. Between them, 13 out of 15 of the techniques were identified in the video clip, and they noted that these were useful devices to be aware of in their daily interactions.

SESSION 7

The penultimate session aimed to improve skills of negotiation and assertiveness when engaging in meaningful dialogue. The session began by asking participants to write down three values they wanted the leader of their country to represent and stand for. Throughout several rounds, participants then had to convince other members of the group to choose the values they selected or come up with new ones that would represent their views. In the end, the whole group had to decide on three values together. In the reflection round, it became apparent that some participants had refused to compromise while others did not manage to make their voice heard. Participants then engaged in various exercises using tools that help to formulate assertive messages (e.g. using nonviolent communication, or finding as much common ground as possible and pointing out moments of learning).

SESSION 8

In the final session, participants explored what having respect means when engaging in dialogue about contested issues. It was pointed out that respect is often a misunderstood concept, as it is used synonymous with words such as "tolerance" or "understanding", but that it was possible to be respectful without agreeing. After looking into how conversations can be managed and how own behaviour can be adapted to ensure a better outcome, participants engaged in a final simulation to put into practice all of the lessons in the brief two days.

In the simulation, two families who have been friends for many years, are meeting for a Christmas dinner. The roles were allocated, and each family was guided in their identities, their values, the timelines of their shared lives and their interactions with the other family, and the respective positions each member of the family must take. Two members of each family, however, were tasked with deploying the techniques they had learned in both de-escalating the conversation as well as guiding others into active listening, empathy development and shared understanding – identifying and countering any rhetorical devices or fallacies they hear.

The exercise was clearly fun, and while participants managed to successfully guide elements of the discussion, there was not enough time to fully transform the conflict at the table. A de-brief with participants highlighted that a major challenge was that skills learned in a two-day workshop cannot easily be deployed under pressure. They were reassured to learn that they are lifetime skills, and must be improved with practice and further reading and training.

Generally speaking, the training course proved to be very impactful. From the feedback survey and post-training evaluation interviews, it became clear that participants were positively surprised to have been challenged so much but also proud of what they achieved. The flexible structure allowed more time to focus on issues that were considered important or relevant to them, and participants left feeling empowered – with a new understanding of how their own identity is a product of the context they are living in, and how threatened identities can lead to violence. The advantage of doing this with a small group is that the facilitators can pay attention to the individual's needs and vulnerabilities. This would have been difficult to achieve in a setting with more than six to eight participants per facilitator.

The training course can contribute to breaking the cycle of violence by building up the ability to understand the needs of other people based on their history, and by honing the ability to empathise.

Further applications

While the training course was developed using the conflict-sensitive do-no-harm principle, there are certain risks associated with applying it in communities that are experiencing or have experienced identity- or ethnic-centred conflicts. Trainers should be aware of the context they are operating in, especially of the sensitivities that exist around contested issues. Identity is directly associated with a feeling of self-worth and a sense of belonging, and challenging assumptions related to it can be perceived as a direct challenge to the legitimacy of a cause.

Many of the methods that have been applied in the SYMMYS training course are long tested and can be considered part of the standard toolbox[1] practitioners have at their disposal, but some have been specifically designed to address the topics of identity and polarisation: identity circle (session 2), history map (session 2), and straight talk (session 5).

Identity circle

The exercise requires a skilled facilitator that can navigate through the different individual sensitivities that arise from opening up to other members about the individual's personal life.

History map

This exercise is similar to the so-called conflict timeline, a tool used in conflict analysis. Depending on the context in which it is used, facilitators have to be aware that it can be impossible for individual and communities to agree on a shared timeline of events. Situations that have contributed to a cycle of violence can be evaluated differently (e.g. the status of Transylvania concerning Hungarian or Romanian nationalism respectively). However, the personal nature of the History map exercise adds additional layers of sensitivity that have to be taken into consideration. The associated risks can be worth the outcome, however, as it allows participants to reflect on their behavioural patterns through a historical and cultural lense.

Straight talk

This exercise requires the facilitators to have an intimate knowledge of the historical context, cultural sensitivities, and potential conflict fault lines as well as the individual members of the group. The exercise itself is very simple in its execution but it also bears great risk when done incorrectly, most significantly the erosion of the trust the group places into the facilitators. It requires deception of the participants, in the beginning, to make the experience as believable as possible.

In the ensuing argument, facilitators are explicitly required to discuss in bad faith, taking advantage of the participants that are engaging in the discussion respectfully. Facilitators are free to abuse their authority to interrupt, raise their voice, misrepresent statements made by participants, etc. Finding the right timing to end the exercise is extremely important and can prove to be difficult. Facilitators should make their intentions clear, and ask participants about what happened and how they felt about the process. It helps if facilitators explain that they are not believing in the points they made and express how they felt having to misrepresent their values and beliefs.

The risks of this exercise are obvious, especially in communities that experienced traumatic conflict. At no point should facilitators attempt to engage issues they consider traumatic, to avoid harming the participants. Instead, the argument should focus on contested issues in the societal or political sphere, overstepping the limits of "political correctness."

Other than risking the relationship between participants and facilitators, there is also a risk of radicalising individuals who idolise the facilitators and their positions or to encourage individuals in the group to share their extremist ideas because they believe these are acceptable to share. In case this happens, facilitators should observe if the group dynamics are strong enough to regulate this, i.e. if there are objections from the group. If there are no objections, facilitators should be ready to transition the exercise to an end and initiate the reflective process.

As a general rule, all exercises that require participants to open up about their values and history should be treated with special care, especially when working with groups that have experienced conflict. Although this provides an opportunity to get to know one another better and discover the humanity in the "other", it also requires a group in which differences in opinions are respected. It is essential to have agreed on rules and guidelines that ensure the personal wellbeing of all and the facilitator must have the authority in the group to enforce these rules if the need arises.

Never again

Rather than addressing a single historical event, the SYMMYS training course addressed the general inability to constructively discuss differences or contested issues. Based on the understanding that this inability to communicate contributes to the most pressing political issue on the European continent, a general polarisation of "liberal" against "conservative" or rather "nationalistic" values, the training course attempted to equip people with the tools required to assertively disagree with other people while not pushing them away. Instead of focusing on WHAT is being said and demanded, we should use the opportunity when we are in conflict to really actively listen to WHY that is. Active listening is difficult because it requires us to inhibit our standard response to immediately react by replying to what is being said. It is particularly difficult if we feel that we have a direct stake in what is being discussed, e.g. if we feel personally attacked/treated unfairly, if what we hear elicits any other strong emotional response, or if our values are affected in any way. In some cases, it can be helpful to take a moment and establish a bit of mental distance by realising that the message is not about us in particular, but about the person who is expressing it. This is the prerequisite of preventing another "great war", which would this time not be fought in the trenches between Germany and France, but on many borders in many countries and cities in Europe.

In Romanian society, there is a clearly established need for some sort of collective process that would allow the victims of the fascist and communist regimes to tell their story, and the rest of society listen to their perspective instead of simply assuming that they know it already. This also includes victims who themselves were perpetrators or collaborators. It is the only way how the shame that is being felt about the collective past can be overcome.

Note

1 The number of excellent resources for trainers and facilitators continues to grow, many toolkits and frameworks are developed in publicly funded projects and made available online for free. Non-formal education has extensively been tested and applied in peace education projects for youth and youth workers and is only slowly being introduced in adult education, where the holistic approach has long not been considered to be a priority. As a result, the available toolkits and methodologies are often targeted at youth work, but this does not mean that they are not suited for working with older participants. The United Network of Young Peacebuilders offers a selection of materials in various languages for free use and adaptation in the resources section at www.unoy.org. The Council of Europe also offers high-quality toolkits including activities and methodologies in their T-Kit series, which can be found at https://pjp-eu.coe.int/en/web/youth-partnership/t-kits.

References

Bar-Tal, D. (2011) *Intergroup Conflicts and Their Resolution*. New York: Psychology Press: 1–39.
Ben-Porath, S. (2012). Citizenship as Shared Fate: Education for Membership in a Diverse Democracy, *Educational Theory*, 62, 381–395. https://doi.org/10.1111/j.1741-5446.2012.00452.x.
Deletant, D. (2001) The Securitate Legacy in Romania. In K. Williams, ed. *Security Intelligence Services in New Democracies*. London: Palgrave Macmillian: 159–210.
Felsen, I. (2017) Adult-Onset Trauma and Intergenerational Transmission: Integrating Empirical Data and Psychoanalytic Theory, *Psychoanalysis, Self and Context*, 12 (1): 60–77.
Galtung, J. (1964) An Editorial, *Journal of Peace Research*, 1 (1): 1–4.
Galtung, J. (1996) *Peace By Peaceful Means*. Thousand Oaks, Calif.: Sage.
Gavreliuc D. & Gavreliuc A. (2018) Generational Belonging and Historical Ruptures: Continuity or Discontinuity of Values and Attitudes in Post-Communist Romania. In N. Lebedeva, R. Dimitrova, & J. Berry, eds. *Changing Values and Identities in the Post-Communist World. Societies and Political Orders in Transition*. Cham: Springer.
de Mendelssohn, F. (2008) Transgenerational Transmission of Trauma: Guilt, Shame, and the "Heroic Dilemma", *International Journal of Group Psychotherapy*, 58 (3): 389–401.

Mitroiu, S. (2016) Recuperative Memory in Romanian Post-Communist Society, *Nationalities Papers*, 44 (5): 751–771.

Nugent, E. (2018) *The Psychology Of Repression In Authoritarian Regimes*. MEI Working Paper [online]. Cambridge: Harvard Kennedy School: 7–10. Available at: https://www.belfercenter.org/sites/default/files/files/publication/2018-01-MEI_RFWP_Nugent.pdf (Accessed 13 June 2020).

Orejuela-Dávila, A., Levens, S., Sagui-Henson, S., Tedeschi, R., & Sheppes, G. (2019) The Relation between Emotion Regulation Choice and Posttraumatic Growth, *Cognition and Emotion*, 33 (8): 1709–1717.

Rouhana, N. (1999) Differentiation in Understanding One's Own and the Adversary's Identity in Protracted Intergroup Conflict: Zionism and Palestinianism, *Journal of Applied Social Psychology*, 29 (10): 1999–2023.

Schiffers, S. & Habersetzer, N. (2018) *Women, Peace And Security: A Chance For Georgia's And Ukraine's Protracted Conflicts?* [online]. Berlin: Polis180 e.V.: 7–8. Available at: https://polis180.org/blog/2018/12/17/womenps-report-women-peace-and-security-in-georgia-and-ukraine/ (Accessed 1 June 2020).

Somasundaram, D. (2007) Collective Trauma in Northern Sri Lanka: A Qualitative Psychosocial-Ecological Study, *International Journal of Mental Health Systems*, 1 (5): 1–27.

Tajfel, H. & Turner, J. (1979) An Integrative Theory of Intergroup Conflict. In W. Austin & S. Worchel, eds. *The Social Psychology of Intergroup Relations*. Monterey: Brooks/Cole: 33–47.

Part III
Using artistic strategies to respond, reflect, and overcome

9 Atomic poetry and active learning: from Japan to Newfoundland

Shoshannah Ganz

Introduction

Canada is a country that has never had a nuclear weapons programme and the impacts of atomic warfare and accidents can seem historically distant and geographically remote. However, the uranium mined and used in the bombs detonated over Hiroshima and Nagasaki was taken from Canadian ground and decimated a generation of Dene (Indigenous) people in Canada's north. Even closer to home, just miles down the road, Newfoundland permitted the American air force base to be a storage place for nuclear weapons. I took the students to the place where these weapons were stored. This allowed the students to see that the distant events of Hiroshima, Nagasaki, and Fukushima have a real-life corollary in their own landscape. This made students more aware of the global and connected impacts of nuclear energy and arms. In preparation for the tour of the Ernest Harmon Air Force Base we read and responded to the writing of Japanese Hibakusha (atomic bomb survivors), Canadian poetry about Hiroshima and Nagasaki, and more recent Japanese writing responding to the events of Fukushima. Finally, we made ethical and historical connections between the atomic bombs and other atrocities during the Second World War including the Canadian internment of Japanese people and the events of the Holocaust. The students responded in every class with their own critical and creative writing connecting local and global histories and the on-going repetition of human rights atrocities in the present.

Background of students

Students in Newfoundland have very little knowledge of Canada's nuclear history or even basic historical knowledge of the events of Hiroshima and Nagasaki. While students study the Holocaust as part of the secondary school curriculum, there is very little attention given to the events of Hiroshima and Nagasaki, such that the average first through fourth year student at Grenfell Campus, Memorial University, when asked in the three English classes I was teaching in the winter of 2019 for what they knew about nuclear weapons and energy, had little to no knowledge of atomic history. As one student wrote in an in-class response to questions about prior knowledge of nuclear history, "Throughout high school, I was never taught about Hiroshima or any of the events that took place involving the devastation."

Course content and objectives

Two of the courses were first-year compulsory writing courses focussed on poetry and drama. The third course was a second-year English course for literature majors. For all courses, the primary objective is developing critical thinking, reading, and writing skills. However, increasingly as an educator I have found that students are not interested or engaged with the reading and the resulting writing demonstrates little connection to the literary work. I thus wanted to find a topic that would interest the students because it was related to their own life and the place they lived, but would also connect them to the larger issues of global history. Thus as a few miles down the road there is the Ernest Harmon Air Force Base, at which atomic weapons were stored; I believed that this local connection would give students a close point of contact to the historical work about Hiroshima and Nagasaki and the on-going impacts of nuclear weapons and energy on Japan and Canada.

I planned at the beginning of the course and the end to teach some poetry and a play on and by Indigenous authors as well as introducing a Holocaust poet. I hoped that the connections between Indigenous issues, so often on the news, and Canada's history of involvement in mining the ore for nuclear weapons and its impact on Indigenous peoples would allow the students to see Canada's historical role as a perpetrator of violence and trauma and thus move beyond the simplistic beliefs and rhetoric of Canada as a peacekeeper. I chose to focus much of our literary reading on the atomic poetry of Japan and Canada following a brief introduction to the atomic literature of Canada and Japan and atomic criticism more broadly. I then went on to show the students two documentaries: one on the mining of the ore in the North West Territories and its connection to Hiroshima and the other on Fukushima. Following our study of the poetry and writing and responding to the poetry, the classes would make a trip to the nearby military base to learn about the sordid atomic history and its impact on the area. Thus there were a number of components to the course that involved what has come to be considered important aspects of experiential learning.

Experiential learning

Jeanne M. McGlinn in "The Impact of Experiential Learning" writes that "[r]eflection is an essential element in learning, as an experience does not automatically lead to the formation of new ideas" (McGlinn 2003, 143). Dewey (1933) and Kolb (1984) likewise argue that reflection is a key aspect of the learning cycle. Thus an essential part of every portion of this course was giving the students opportunities to write about what they were seeing, reading, and experiencing, and thus making a dedicated portion of the class and the grade emphasise reflection. These student "responses" in turn form a portion of this paper and show the reflection of the students on the concepts and experiences that are a part of the class.

Further, as Scott D. Wurdinger and Julie A. Carlson write in their book, *Teaching for Experiential Learning*, there are five approaches to inspire and motivate learners. I was concerned with both the lack of inspiration evidenced in student writing and the lack of motivation. I hoped to remedy this in part through the subject, but also as Wurdinger and Carlson suggest as two of the five approaches, through place-based education (the visit to the nearby base and nuclear storage facility) and through active learning. In the case of active learning, the students collectively and individually contributed to the meaning making and interpretation of the poetry.

Miyamoto and Ross developed a short-term Study Abroad Program, "Hiroshima and Nagasaki in History, Memory, and Discourse", where in the course description the first line makes the primary objective of the course the building of "ethical responses to the atomic bombings of Hiroshima and Nagasaki." Three of the ten objectives of the course overlap with the objectives of the courses I was offering: the development of an ethical framework, historical consciousness, and self-reflection.

Finally, drawing on the burgeoning studies of education and technology, particularly as synthesised in the international journal of *Educational Technology*, advances in technology have had a particular impact on experiential learning allowing educators to "redefine the conception of learning" from an "interaction between instructors and learners in a classroom setting" (Berge & Muilenburg 2008) to a multifaceted experience, in the case of my courses, including real-time footage of what has come to be referred to as the 3/11, the triple disaster of earthquake, tsunami, and damage to a nuclear facility that led to the leak of radioactive material into the Fukushima area.

Toge Sankichi and active learning

The first poet we read and discussed as a class was the hibakusha poet Tōge Sankichi. This poet is part of the collection *Hiroshima: Three Witnesses* edited and translated into English by Richard H. Minear in 1990, thus making Ōta Yōko's *City of Corpses*, along with Hara Tamiki's *Summer Flowers* and the poems I will discuss here by Tōge Sankichi, available for the first time in English. Tōge writes in his poetry about "[t]hat brilliant flash" (Sankichi 1990, 306), and describes what he witnesses and particularly the human suffering in many of his poems. While the suffering of humans is described at length and in detail, there is very little description of the suffering of fellow more-than-human creatures. I pointed this out to the class and discussed this aspect of the poetry at length in order to connect these poems forward to the events of Fukushima and the poems we would be discussing in that context. Therefore I drew attention to the poem "Flames" where he describes "the shroud that mushroomed out/and struck the dome of the sky" (Sankichi 1990, 311) and among the flames he notes "[c]attle bound for the slaughterhouse/avalanche down the riverbank" and "wings drawn in, a single ash-colored pigeon" (Sankichi 1990, 311). The poet continues "countless human beings/on all fours" (Sankichi 1990, 311). Thus, the human and cattle are equally animals "on all fours" trying to escape the "flames that spurt forward" (Sankichi 1990, 311). The "hot rays of uranium" (Sankichi 1990, 312) burned both human and more-than-human animal and "burned the gods/at the stake" (Sankichi 1990, 312). While these poems are almost entirely about the suffering of humans, the mention of the cattle and pigeon is important to thinking ethically about the impacts of human acts of war or accidents on the more-than-human.

After introducing the students to some of the works by Toge Sankichi by reading them aloud and analysing them, I noted all of the human death and suffering recorded by the poet, but then drew attention to the very few places where the poet discusses the suffering of animals and the effects of the bombings on animals. A few of the students wrote about the animals in the poems by Toge Sankichi. One student wrote:

> I aim to respond to the poetry by analyzing the language of the poem "Flames." What first caught my eye was the description of the people who died as "Cattle bound for the slaughterhouse", this is an apt comparison to the industrial meat industry. The people who died that day didn't mean anything to the bombings, they were just a means to an end, ending the war. Likewise, cattle are just a means to an end for most, to have more meat. The line speaks succinctly to the dehumanization of those who died, in the eyes of the western governments. /The description of atomic fire as "pure incandescent hatred", is also meaningful, as how could one cause so much suffering if it wasn't driven by sheer hate?

Another student also comments on the animals writing of "Flames":

> To see the comparisons made between cattle and humans was a bit unsettling at first, but when you realize that both were victims of this horror then it becomes more clear. /During the disaster cattle and human were one in the same since they both had to experience loss, experience pain, and had to live with what they saw for the rest of their lives to haunt them. /To say cattle had gained a bit of humanity (or respect) in the eyes of fellow survivors isn't too much of a stretch, and in a way it may help us remember that not only people are affected by man-made tragedies.

Other students write about the descriptions in the poetry of what happened to the people:

> The poems written by Toge Sankichi show a part of the atomic disasters that should not be forgotten. Throughout the poems, there is a large emphasis on the survivors of Hiroshima dragging themselves to water for some relief from their pain. There is also an emphasis on the eyes of the dead constantly staring at the living, leaving a haunting image in their minds that never goes away. Despite all that is described, however, there is no call for revenge. Rather, there is a warning to not forget the past, lest history repeat itself.

Another student writes, "For example, August 16 describes how people looked after the occurrence. They had raw flesh hanging off of them." Another student writes:

> In the poems read today there are many different perspectives on the devastating events. Some poems had hints of revenge, others focussed more upon remembrance, "how could anyone forget?" and others described the event with detailed imagery. I think the meaning of all these types of poems are a plea for peace and a symbol of remembrance to all; witnesses and survivors of the world.

In a number of student responses the students noted that the atomic bombs were used to end the war and thus save lives. This was not something I was teaching in class and since they had all noted at the beginning of the course that they knew nothing or very little about the atomic bombs I was very curious as to where they were getting this information. It came to light in our discussion that they were discussing the class with their parents and their parents were telling them that the atomic bombs ended the war and thus saved lives. I responded to this inherited belief by reading poems by Al Purdy with the students. One of the poems in his collection about Hiroshima is a found poem that records the responses of visitors in the guest book at the Atomic Bomb museum in Hiroshima. Many of the responses are very racist and suggest that the atomic bombs were a good thing. This gave us an opportunity to discuss and develop our ethical framework about racism, the Second World War era "yellow-peril" politics in Canada and the United States, and historical consciousness and knowledge about the possible and complicated reasons for the Americans dropping the bombs.

Further, I found the student responses focussed on the animals to be interesting for a number of reasons. In the first place, it was interesting that in spite of the fact that the vast majority of the poems discussed human suffering, many of the students focussed their attention on these few instances of animal suffering. Their interpretations were also interesting. That students viewed the cattle as a metaphor as opposed to actual cattle revealed how completely anthropocentric the writing was in its relaying of the events on Hiroshima. Right or wrong, the students were perceiving the writer as unable to really discuss the events of Hiroshima beyond the suffering and witnessing of the human. The students expressed concern and dismay about the neglect of animals and also curiosity about the effects on the animals in the cities of Hiroshima and Nagasaki. This was an interesting and important concern as it looked forward to the consciousness of writers and sufferers in Fukushima. While the official positions on the events of Fukushima were still a disregard for animal suffering, artists and activists gave attention to the more-than-human witnesses of the event. That the students already possessed this ethical awareness and concern and brought this to bear on the historical events where these victims and survivors were overlooked at Hiroshima and Nagasaki showed a remarkable sensitivity. We were able to discuss as a class the changes in human perceptions of suffering and the devastating impacts of anthropocentrism. I learned a great deal from the students about their ethical concerns and awareness, and the course in fact moved in that direction because of the students' more complex understanding of trauma and witnessing that extended the experience to animals and the landscape. These views and ethical concerns anticipated and shaped the direction of the course.

Reflecting on Nuclear Nation: surviving Fukushima

Nuclear Nation, a film by Atsushi Funahashi, is an interesting documentary in part because it does not sensationalise the events of 3/11 or even show much of the footage of the mass destruction; rather, it focusses on the stories and everyday reality of the survivors in their relocated lives. Through these stories it questions the real costs of nuclear energy. Part of the film interviews people about their work in the industry and the effects of the nuclear industry pre-accident. What is made clear is that Fukushima was a very poor area in Japan and that they welcomed the nuclear industry to the area as an industry that would bring financial stability to the region. However, even before the accident almost the opposite was true. Far from making the region wealthy, the area of Fukushima became even poorer and the promises of financial stability and jobs were in the end empty. Like many other industries there was the promise of wealth for the region, but the energy went entirely to other and wealthy regions of Japan and the town was faced with a repetition of the industry cycle of boom and bust. With the region becoming entirely uninhabitable people were living two and three years later in school gymnasiums and still not finding a way to continue on with their lives.

Another part of the film focussed on the animals that were left in the region. In particular, some attention has been given to the cattle and other domestic animals. While the humans were evacuated, the animals were left in the region to suffer and fend for themselves. Many died of starvation.

The government eventually ordered the slaughter of the cows as they were now deemed useless to humans. One man refused to murder his cattle and rather stayed with them claiming that they were witnesses and would stand guard. This act has been the subject of a great deal of art in Japan and we explored this through the work of Keijiro Suga.

However, first I would like to share a few of the responses of the students to the film. The stories told by regular people of the impact on their lives particularly moved the students, and they responded by connecting the events to how it would have felt had it happened to them. I was not expecting this film to have the kind of impact it did on the students and I would like to honour the sensitivity of the students in their responses. The students took on many of the different issues raised by the film and connected these to the problems of nuclear energy. One student wrote:

> Watching this video makes me remind myself how fortunate I actually am. It is so devastating to see these people struggle in not being able to go back home. Watching the part where they actually visit their hometowns was so scary. There was absolutely nothing left in many places and they see pieces of debris and stuff from what used to keep them safe every night. I was also very sad to see them leaving loved ones that they lost before this in the cemetery. Many of them are living in the shelter/refuge homes and are not treated as well as someone who had just lost everything should be treated. Only being allowed to go back to the place you spent all of your life for three hours once a year is extremely sad. Watching videos such as these are very important for understanding the horrible conditions some people have to endure every day.

Another student comments:

> This video is eye opening and emotional. It was that much exposed to radiation that they could not touch anything and had to wear clothes and masks so they wouldn't be exposed to it. Living things were dying. People had to travel and move away from their homes. Graveyards and homes were destroyed. People were trying to save cows… . People were protesting nuclear action and this is the right idea because many things are dying and becoming sick and things are being destroyed.

Active learning and Kejiro Suga poems

Keijiro Suga writes that: "To me, the Great East Japan earthquake was the single most important moment of crisis in post-Second World War Japan and it profoundly affected Japanese society" (Suga 2018, 174). He further notes that the "[t]ragedy [of 3/11] is not limited to humans" (Suga 2018,

176). Keijiro Suga's critical writing and poetry explore the impact of radiation on the more-than-human in the Fukushima area. As a class we read the English translations of ten of his poems on the site Versoteque all of which explore the natural world and many of which note the impacts of radiation. Poem nine in particular reflects on the fate of the cows left in the fallout zone. The poem opens with: "The cows do not dare go out of the fence" because "the humans they are familiar with are not there." Keijiro Suga reflects on how the landscape has changed and the impact on the animals that are still living and have not left. Primarily it is the domestic animals that remain as witnesses.

The students responded to poem nine and other poems by Keijiro Suga on as many as three different occasions including in a class exercise, an in-class essay, and on the final exam. The student responses to the poems also include at times reflections on Keijiro Suga's critical writing, and the events of Fukushima more generally. The students note on a number of occasions the various ways the poet emphasises that "[t]he impact of Fukushima did not only affect the humans, it had a great devastating effect on the animals nearby and the environment as a whole" and further that in poem nine Keijiro Suga "talks about what happened to the animals and how it changed them." One student writes that "[t]o believe that only humans are capable of suffering is a belief that has been influenced by humanity's dominant anthropocentric views in the past, for only in recent years did our egos make way for a view that sympathises for all forms of life." Another student reflects that Keijiro Suga's poem 9 "shows the actions of humans as either cruel, or negligent" and in particular there is an emphasis on the reliance of the domesticated animals on humans for food and shelter and the devastating impact on the cows of being left behind when the humans are evacuated.

Experiencing learning: The Newfoundland connection

I asked the students to write outside of class about the trip to the Ernest Harmon Air Force Base. I did not give them any directives, but rather asked that they reflect on the experience. I then gave the students five specific and guided questions to respond to in class, thus shaping the reflection to respond to concerns of the course and experiential learning more generally. The questions were as follows: 1. Discuss what you were expecting from the trip. How did watching *Village of Widows* contribute to the expectations? 2. Discuss what you think experiential learning is and what should be involved in an experiential learning trip on a course. Discuss how what you experienced and/or learned was or was not in line with what experiential learning should involve. 3. Discuss Tom Rose's discussion of the past and present of Stephenville. Discuss the impacts as he saw them of the Base on Stephenville. What did or do you see as the impacts of the base and its legacy on Stephenville? 4. Discuss the atomic connection. How did what you saw confirm or not the history of storage of atomic weapons at the base?

You may want to discuss the tour and the evasiveness or other responses of the men giving the tour. 5. Discuss any other aspect of the experiential learning trip that you think relevant to the discussion. In particular, feel free to narrate and comment on the trip. You might discuss members of the class, the journey, the drives around town, the lunch, or any other aspects of the trip that you think worthy of note.

The students found evidence for this in the evasion and subterfuge of the men who were designated to show us around the base. At every place they were supposed to give us tours of they came up with reasons including lost keys, not knowing we were supposed to have the tour, security issues, and general ineptitude to keep us out of the various parts of the base that might have been supposed to show us evidence of the atomic history. There was a great deal more security than the students expected on a now defunct base, and this was surprising. Further, the continued security suggested that the base was still in use. The further evidence seemed to come in the high level of military plane activity on the airbase.

The students expected quite a bit from the tour including answers to their questions about the atomic question and evidence in the tour for the storage of weapons. What the students rather experienced was a high level of frustration, lies, evasion, and general ineptitude. This led the students in most cases to confirm suspicions that atomic weapons were still stored at the base and that we were being actively kept by military personnel from seeing anything that might be a security risk. In some ways the experiential learning trip could be viewed as a failure. We did not see or confirm any of the atomic-related history that we were attempting to study. I did ask the students as we drove back if the entire trip and/or course was thus a "bust." We discussed as a class what it meant for us to succeed or fail and what failure in this context meant for me as an educator and them as students. However, to my surprise, the students overall spoke with pleasure about the trip and especially about the time spent driving together and talking.

Again never again?

This course was set up to look at the connections between racist policies and practices across different geographies and historical periods and to explore how these attitudes change and are reproduced in the present. That the students were able to extend these views and attitudes to the more-than-human is evidence that their ethical thinking has developed and moved beyond the pitfalls of the anthropocentric dominance that threatens all forms of life on the planet, human and more-than-human. While I provided readings and historical context, it was again and again the students who extended the meaning and significance well beyond my own thinking on the subjects. I had students write about the reproduction of forms of colonisation, racism, and violence in videogames, the treatment of Indigenous children in foster care, and factory farming.

Students from these courses came at the end of the semester and requested that I teach an upper-year course on Hiroshima and the Holocaust in 2020 and take them on a trip to Auschwitz. This demonstrated to me the ways in which the students saw the application of the concepts of the course beyond the scope of atomic issues to other historical atrocities and other sites of memory and remembering. The students also echoed again and again the necessity, as they saw it, of moving beyond the limits of the classroom and travelling to places where they could see and experience the impacts of history and the attempts to honour memory or, as in the case of our trip, deceive people and hide dark, exploitive relationships with communities. The explorations of these courses more than anything demonstrate to me the deep desire of students to be engaged ethically with the world and to move beyond the easy and repetitive model of education where the professor gives them information and they reproduce the information. The students are hungry and even desperate for real engagement with the world and for the tools and knowledge to fight injustice in the place where they live and beyond.

References

Berge, Z. & Muilenburg, L. (2008) Seamless Learning: An International Perspective on Next-generation Technology-enhanced Learning, *Educational Technology*, 9 (2): 97–121.

Dewey, J. (1933) *How We Think: A Restatement of the Relation of Reflective Thinking to the Educative Process*. D.C. Heath & Co Publishers.

Kolb, D. A. (1984) *Experiential Learning Experiences as the Source of Learning and Development*. Prentice Hall.

McGlinn, J. M. (2003) The Impact of Experiential Learning on Student Teachers, *The Clearing House: A Journal of Educational Strategies, Issues and Ideas*, 76 (3): 143–147.

Minear, R. (ed. and trans.) (1990) *Hiroshima: Three Witnesses*. New Jersey: Princeton University Press.

Nuclear Nation (2013) *[DVD]* Atsushi Funahashi. Japan: First Run Features. (Japanese with English subtitles).

Ōta, Y. (1990) City of Corpses. In R. H. Minear, ed. and trans. *Hiroshima: Three Witnesses*. New Jersey: Princeton University Press: 115–268.

Purdy, A. (1972) *Hiroshima Poems*. New York: The Crossing Press.

Sankichi, T. (1990) Poems of the Atomic Bomb. In R. H. Minear, ed. and trans. *Hiroshima: Three Witnesses*, New Jersey: Princeton University Press: 275–366.

Suga, K. (2018) Invisible Waves: On Some Japanese Artists after March 11, 2011. In H. Wake, K. Suga, & Y. Masami, eds. *Ecocriticism in Japan*. Maryland: Lexington Books: 173–188.

Suga, K. (2018) *9 [Internet]*, Versoteque. Available from: http://www.versoteque.com/authors/keijiro-suga (Accessed December 2018).

Village of Widows (1998). *[DVD]* Peter Blow. Canada: Lindum Films.

Wurdinger, S. D. & Carlson, J. A. (2010) *Teaching for Experiential Learning: Five Approaches that Work*. Maryland: Rowman & Littlefield.

10 "Through the Refugee's Eyes": experiences with the experiential and interactive theatre show

Manca Šetinc Vernik

Introduction

> To read a story is one thing, to hear it first-hand is another, to experience it on your own skin is a class apart! Therefore I now wish these people all the best in life. ~ a young participant from Ptuj high-school.

The project *Through the Refugee's Eyes* by Slovenian NGO Humanitas – Centre for global learning and cooperation (Humanitas) emerged in response to the inhumane and progressively racist asylum policy of "fortress Europe" and the much too often unlawful treatment of people fleeing war, persecution, or poverty. The idea of an experiential interactive theatre play was born in the beginning of 2015. We had no idea that we would soon be observing with our own eyes and before our very own threshold the tragedy of people on the run, who in an organised manner began to cross over through Slovenia, until the refugee corridor was closed in the beginning of 2016. Neither could we possibly have imagined that our country would end up a fenced-in island in the middle of Europe, which will soon be flooded by (new) waves of hate speech and intolerance.

Within the project, which has been carried out in cooperation with friends who have real-life experience of being refugees and who in 2015 and 2016[1] remained in Slovenia and applied for asylum (some have been waiting for five years for a decision!), and with CIES Onlus,[2] an organisation from Italy with a rich history of interactive plays about migration, from which we drew inspiration, a special experiential performance came to be. We have merged all the experiences, pain, and traumas of the people who walked the Balkan route from faraway Afghanistan, Syria, Iran, Iraq, Turkey, and Somalia, as well as our own experiences from the field and those of our members and volunteers in registration centres along the refugee routes. Although in the form of theatre play, *Through the Refugee's Eyes* for us is not a mere play. It is a grim reality; it is something that is at that very moment happening on the shores of Turkey, Libya, Greece, Australia, and many others.

We performed the play *Through the Refugee's Eyes* 68 times in the last four years; mostly for schools, but also for general public. In the play, the (young) audience members suddenly turn into actors, as they, accompanied by our team of performers, travel the uncertain and dangerous path to the heart of the "promised", but unwelcoming Europe, and can thus at least partially imagine what people are experiencing on the run – every day, at this very moment. They suffer violations of the most basic human rights, experience hate speech, hear real police dialogues at borders, those of volunteers in registration centres and "no-man's land", and feel the cold-bloodedness of the bureaucratic apparatus when deciding whether to stay or leave. However, they also get to experience how it is to meet a handful of people who – within this rigid and cold system – still want to lend a warm helping hand. After the show, they meet with people who have travelled the danger-packed refugee path and who have co-created the show, and are confronted with their own prejudices and stereotypes.

During post-performance evaluations, many participants wrote to us, saying that the performance was an incredible experience, a unique one, in fact, that would remain with them for the rest of their lives. In the messages[3] they sent to people, who have experienced refugee life first-hand, they often expressed words of welcome, apologies, and hope – hope for a better future, a future that includes all of us. We dedicated this project to all those who have experienced the life of a refugee. We dedicated it to more than 37,000 souls who died only since 2014, trying to reach safety in Europe and elsewhere in the world (International Organization For Migration (IOM) 2020). In addition, we dedicated it to our family members, who are no longer with us and who have been refugees themselves. The message is that as a society we should never forget.

Global education meets theatre

Dealing with global education for around 20 years now, at Humanitas we believe we have managed to find and creatively design the ultimate transformative educational tool, opening people's minds and hearts for the realities of the world (Council of Europe (COE) 2002), on experiential and maybe even life-changing level. Global education connects head, heart, and hands, meaning that you can understand the issue, but if you do not feel it too, the chances you get motivated to act(ion) are smaller. With this project, our friends with refugee experience who were involved in the making of the play, are showing the society, and especially the pupils we are visiting, that they are not just passive "mascots" of the project but co-actors, co-trainers of the whole module, bringing new perspectives, cultural practices and their own (sometimes very painful) experiences to the process. Some teachers have even called the theatre play revolutionary as well as therapeutic (Humanitas Youtube Channel 2017). Our actors with real refugee experience agree too:

the shift of roles and being able not to play a mere victim after such a long time of degrading and shameful practices on borders across Europe, it means a lot to them to be on the other side of this story for a moment. At the end of this chapter, I include the short interviews with two of our actors with real refugee experience.

At the same time, with the help of the theatre method, we were able to convey these topics on a very symbolic level too. From the use of space, where we set up the scenes of the play in the underground war shelter, to moving from one room to the next to represent a journey, we have also managed to create a gradual shrinking of the physical space. The play begins outside, in the open, continues in the underground war shelter in a bigger room, progressing through many smaller rooms, one of those – at the very end – being only a tiny cell used for holding people before deportations. With such dramatic shrinking of the physical space we wanted to show the actual narrowing the personal field of freedom of the people fleeing to Europe. Using all senses – sight (parts of the play performed in darkness), sound (crying of babies, sounds of the storm at sea, real hate-speech taken from Slovenian media), smell (trash on the ground of the no-mans-land) and touch (people touching cold rough walls of the underground shelter) – we strived toward a true definition of experiential play in terms of a progressive/ radical philosophical approach to learning (Elias and Merriam, 1980, cited in Zinn 1990, 48).

Theatre play with the integral debriefing part at the end, i.e. meeting the real people behind the stories, is a creative and innovative educational approach, which works beyond a mere ratio, in addition to working with the body and the feelings (Brookfield 2004). Using storytelling with people from a refugee background, we eliminated the wall between "them and us" and created real relationships and connections between people. We namely feel it is not possible to deal with increasing hate speech, intolerance, and growing negative attitudes of the general public against refugees and migrants only using the arguments on a rational level. This is being done much too often through countless workshops, seminars, and even scientific symposiums, often speaking about refugees without actually involving them. The project *Through the Refugee's Eyes* takes on a different stance. We believe we cannot speak about refugees without them; everything we do as a society "for" migrants and refugees should be at the same time done "with" and "by" them. We have taken this principle very seriously.[4] And most importantly, with this experiential approach, the participants get an opportunity to recapture the feelings of distress and feel the violation of the rights of people on the run on their own skin, following Mezirow's theory (1991a, 1994b, cited in Kitchenham 2008, 113) which argues that perspective transformation cannot occur without dealing with deep feelings in critical self-reflection. This effectively turns previous convictions of participants upside down and often puts them into question.

From the global education point of view, we could argue that the times of mere identifying of challenges are over; now is the time to take action and envisage and co-create a new world. With the project *Through the Refugee's Eyes* we have tried to do just that: design a transformative educational tool, opening people's minds and hearts for the realities of the world, and to motivate them to take action, to make a change in their local environments with local actions. This means moving from just breaking the borders in their own heads to actually making a difference in peoples' lives too. The project thus motivates the participants towards special and actively engaged movements, so-called local youth actions. With such youth actions or campaigns, we encourage the formation of new possible ways of cooperation of schools/communities of students with the local community, particularly with representatives of the minorities and people with a migrant or refugee experience, and in this way promote creative and respectful intercultural dialogue. Thus, these actions with more globally aware youth contribute to respect for cultural diversity as well as enhance values of solidarity, empathy, and equality in the Slovenian society.

Global education projects should always strive to make this interconnectedness as clear as possible: we are all part of the problem as well as the solution (Andreotti 2006). The participants of our workshops and the theatre show experience first-hand how our everyday consumerist decisions, unsustainable way of living, non-activity towards policy and politics influence what is going on "the other side" of the world (climate change, environmental refugees, migrants in search of better jobs because of destroyed economies and degradation of environment etc.). It also fosters understanding that all humans are equal and deserve equal opportunities, whether it is a neighbour we know or a refugee, migrant, whom we do not know (yet). The participants realise the consequences of their own actions as well as the responsibility to act towards the injustices across the globe and in their own environments. The motto of our activities at Humanitas is "We are all in part of the same world." And it does not really matter how many good things we are doing if we are not at the same time trying to stop the bad ones too. This is why one of the strongest messages we are conveying through the workshops and theatre shows is that by being passive and by looking away or keeping our eyes closed to the realities of the world, we are actually creating borders ourselves.

Educational goals of the initiative

The main target groups of the project were young people, pupils of elementary schools and secondary school students, students, young and other visitors in youth centres, and people with a real refugee experience, currently living with us either in asylum homes or on private addresses. We have also reached the general public, more than half a million were reached through the media reports about the project.

The educational and societal goals of the project were the following:

a. to develop and promote global competencies of young people who truly need them for a life in a rapidly changing world, and equip them with the necessary social skills such as critical thinking, action and cooperation in the group, social engagement and active global citizenship for a life in a multicultural environment;
b. to raise the awareness of young people about the causes and consequences of migration and interdependence of our part of the world and the global South and critically evaluate concepts such as the protection of human rights, unequal distribution of global wealth, climate change (as one of the most acute and most serious questions of our humanity), the severity of the current lack of legal protection of climate refugees and others;
c. to create a (fraction of) experience of refugees and migrants on their difficult journey, and offer the possibility to put oneself in another's shoes, thereby teaching empathy and promoting understanding;
d. to create opportunities to feel the hate speech on your own skin, create possibilities to question xenophobic or even racist prejudices and stereotypes;
e. to raise awareness of the public of the real fates of the refugees living among us, who have been deported because of the negative applications for asylum or are in the process of waiting;
f. to break negative prejudices and stereotypes on the causes of migration and promote critical thinking and critical acceptance of information from the media and society.

The direct beneficiaries of the project were the pupils and students as well as the teachers. With the development of their social skills and global competences, young people are able to better cope with the global challenges of our time and are directly empowered to active and courageous civic actions to benefit themselves first, to benefit the local environment as well as to benefit the wider (and global) society. With the acquired knowledge and skills, they can increase awareness and disseminate knowledge in non-formal education systems, i.e. among their families and friends, thus questioning and possibly breaking many unfair and biased stereotypes and myths about migration and refugees.

The indirect impact of our project and improved awareness of global challenges of migration and sufferings of refugees will lead to a greater level of tolerance, empathy, solidarity, and equality in the local community and the wider society. At the same time, with new methods of youth participation within their local communities and collaboration of representatives of minorities and people with a migrant/refugee background, the project

Figure 10.1 Image from one of the performances – the boat landing scene, in Ljubljana underground shelter, 2016. Photographer: Dani Modrej, archive of Humanitas.

indirectly contributed to nurturing and developing cultural diversity in the country and to strengthening this two-way process of the integration of new fellow citizens from different parts of the world.

The success of the project and its methodology was mentioned in the Global Education Innovation Award Brochure (2018) of the European Global Learning Network GENE and in the Compendium of good practices on Education for Sustainable Lifestyles by Inland Norway University of Applied Sciences (Lederer & Didham 2018) (Figure 10.1).

Why experiential method works and how do we know it does?

It is very easy to judge from the safe shelter of your home, from a comfortable armchair and in front of a huge LCD screen … We are still very closed, we have fences around our houses and even around the whole country, but these fences also exist in our heads. I believe people should see such a play and put themselves in the shoes of a refugee because in such a way they could break down many fences. And when fences fall in our heads, fences around our houses will also fall, and there will be a time when the one around our country will fall as well. ~ A young participant from Zagorje high-school.

After very strong responses both in direct contact and through evaluation made after the performances, we estimate that we have succeeded in breaking down quite many prejudices and presented an opportunity to question many of the generally accepted stereotypes about migration and refugees. We believe the exclamation we have heard after several performances: "Everyone should see this performance!" is very true.

The main change in perception our initiative aims to achieve is that a person with a refugee or migrant background is an individual person with his or her own story and we cannot and we must not generalise as is especially the case in the media, where we read articles about migrants and refugees as a homogenous whole. At the same time, it offers a mirror to recognise one's own responsibility and involvement in today's global issues and that with the privilege to which we are used there comes a price which other people are paying. Young people quickly realise how utterly unfair this is and that we must all together do something about it and change this. It gives an opportunity (maybe for the first time in someone's life if this is a non-empathic person) to at least try to imagine what it would be like to lose a home, possibly even a family, and leave everything behind and set upon a dangerous journey into the unknown.

It shows how global education can have an impact on children, youth as well as adults, in fostering empathy and changing perceptions, especially with the use of simulations and motivating learning environments (Wlodkowski 2004). Teachers we are collaborating with are all saying it should be a part of the curriculum and its themes addressed in the classrooms across Slovenia. We are advocating for the methodology of global education to be systematically used by the teachers. This particular *Through the Refugee's Eyes* project can undoubtedly also be used as an advocacy-tool, motivating people to make a change and become the transformers of the world and taking action against the oppressive elements of reality (Freire, 1970, cited in Kitchenham 2008, 107). The project can also serve as an inspiration for how to approach a co-creation process of working together with the people with migrant or refugee background to create something common and shared, whether it is a theatre play, a workshop or public policy directed towards migrant communities. It also showed us that the participants of the workshops and the theatre play were (in responses) more in favour of hosting refugees in their own town, stating even a clear motivation to do something for and with them.

In the evaluation sheets distributed to participants of the interactive experiential theatre play, we asked them to evaluate the performance and their experience with grades from 1 to 5 (where 1 means very bad and 5 very good mark). The average rating of the performances of all four years is quite remarkable: 4.6 (out of 5). Besides grading the theatre play, we have also asked the participants to write a message that they would send to the person with real refugee experience. Some of the most beautiful messages that the young participants sent were summarised in the publication entitled *When I looked through the refugee's eyes* (Humanitas Youtube Channel 2017). By preparing and publishing a brochure with the personal messages of Slovene children and youth, we wanted to show the people with a refugee experience who were inspiration for the theatre play as well as for the general public another face of the Slovene society and the tolerance of her youngest. We wanted to offer a small counterbalance to hate speech and intolerance, and express the moral support and motivation in the most difficult moments of their lives through the words of their youngest co-inhabitants.

In these messages, the young participants have expressed many emotions, ranging for example from apologies:

> In the name of my country, culture and the people, I would like to apologize for all the bad things you have experienced, and I want you to have a successful life, full of security and warmth. – participant from Ptuj

... and new realisations...:

> After the show, I started to really think about the whole situation, and it seems to me that everyone should attend this play and experience it on their own skin. Perhaps in this way people would be more compassionate not only to refugees but also to all fellow humans. – participant from Nova Gorica

... to powerful resolutions...:

> After this experience, I am going to fight for the human dignity of every refugee. – participant from Ptuj

... and words of comfort:

> I sympathize with you very much and a lot of people wish to help you. There aren't only bad people in this world.... I wish these wars end soon and everyone has their rights – home, family, and peace. – participant from Ljubljana

Responses by the teachers that were on the show are also remarkable.

As one teacher put it, *Through the Refugee's Eyes* really gives you the opportunity to also learn something about yourself, how you would react in uncertain and unknown situations, what things run through your mind at the moment you are being yelled at and humiliated, dehumanised. It gives you the opportunities to realise your own prejudice and stereotypes as they are being served back to you in the form of monologues or dialogues between smugglers, police officers, volunteers, and border patrols.

Another example, in one response, the teacher from Kranj Educational Institute writes:

> On Thursday, 25th of May, previously Day of the Youth, we went to Ljubljana to the underground shelter, to participate at a show that describes what people were experiencing, who for this or that reason were forced to leave their homes, lives, youth, families, friends and simply run elsewhere, anywhere, where they will not live in a fatal fear of war, persecution, hostility. Many of them went through Slovenia, some of them stopped here with us forever. Through the performance we travelled through experiences that were above all dehumanizing, devaluing everything that is important in life, the experience that someone can see in people only dirty numbers, which are irrelevant and unnecessary to him in this world. And until you experience it, you do not imagine what it means.

The teacher from Secondary School Ptuj expressed gratitude:

> Once again, thank you so much for allowing us of being part of the story Through the Refugee's Eyes. We were shocked and enchanted by the show because you found a form through which you address the arrogant and the sensitive at the same time.

One of the most powerful ones, though, came from the teacher from primary school near Ljubljana:

> Movies and other arts can strike the heart, to put it metaphorically. They open up questions for the viewers to answer for themselves. But nothing is more genuine than a living word you can't escape. A story that glues you to a chair due to its authenticity. And nothing is the way it was an hour ago. Changed, you go home. You call, or at least you become aware of the people you love; the freedom that is self-evident to you; economic situation, power ... and you do too little for this world. There is nothing more powerful than a story through the eyes of a refugee. More than words and a story, you hear what he didn't say. And because you've only heard one story, you're afraid to hear more ... (Figure 10.2)

What the experience meant for our friends with refugee experience?

Through the Refugee's Eyes project had another side result besides the ones already mentioned. For our friends, be it the persons with the status of

Figure 10.2 Author with actors Hasan and Payman after the performance in Vienna, September 11th 2018 – Photographer: Boštjan Gretič, archive of Humanitas.

international protection or asylum seekers currently residing in Slovenia, it presented a chance to not only co-create a whole theatre play and be an integral part of its methodology, but also being recognised as a valuable partner in society and as individuals with unique talents and experiences that they brought along. Last but not least, it gave them at least some sort of financial assistance and positive social networks to cope with this gruelling waiting period.

For the purpose of this chapter, I had interviews with two of Humanitas's collaborators with real refugee experience, Hasan from Kurdistan in Iraq, and Payman from Iran, both actors in the *Through the Refugee's Eyes* theatre play. I asked both what it meant to be a real collaborator and to have your story told.

Hasan summarised his experience with these words:

> I had good feelings because for the first time I was explaining my story to the people that I don't know. It was not difficult to act I actually enjoyed it a lot. For me it was painful for the first couple of shows because I was not through this what other guys have been through (the whole Balkan route experience) and it made me feel the reality of it. I believe some people take the show as a joke but when they listen to the

story and realise that it is a true story and it's still happening in real life what ever happened to them through the show, I believe this makes some people change their minds about refugees. I have been in Europe for 5 years before this project and never seen people care so much about refugees and planning to make a story and having theatre show, I am happy to be included in a project like this. The importance of showing and sharing this kind of real life stories to some people who have closed their eyes on everything that happens to us all around the world, this bring peace, it helps us to feel more safe once everyone knows who we are and we are not bad and terrorists. And about Humanitas and all of you, I feel like I'm home with my real brothers and sisters, I feel I have a family and I love you all.

For Payman, the experiences in this project made him express the following:

Honestly, when I started with this project, I did not know much about the goals and targets, however it was working for me at the time financially and emotionally because I did not have any income to travel and meet new people, and most importantly, it gave me a chance to get out of the asylum home. This was certainly good enough reason for me to join the team. When I attended the acting sessions for the first time, and I saw many talented people, I was so scared and I never thought that in few years they would call me a "super star". But the energy of my teammates and also when I found out how important is this show towards the people that were brainwashed by the media and also for the young generation, convinced me to put my 100%. I tried to show the reality to the people that did not know much about us (refugees). I am actually playing a field police officer in the theatre play, who is yelling out curses and hate-speech and being really rude and aggressive towards people. I remember the first few shows, I was still so traumatized and angry, and this role of angry police officer gave me a chance to reverse my role of the victim. But then, as months passed, whenever I had a dialogue as a police man, I pushed myself hard to act as an angry policeman. Because I really am a nice and calm man. It was so hard for me, to this day, but I did it to show the people what really happened in our journey. But honestly, every time the show was over, I had the chance to talk to the people to answer their questions and my first reaction was apologizing to them (for being an angry cop). I am so sorry for all the police officer on the borders who will never have this chance as I did. Through these years I have met a lot of nice people and I am so grateful that I had a chance to share my past experiences and hopes with them. I wish one day we will be experiencing the world with no borders and no hate.

What better way to conclude this chapter than with this Payman's vision of a fairer world.

Notes

1 For more information about this period, facts and numbers, changes in state policies etc., please see also Ladić, M., Vučko, K., Frébutte, M., Kogovšek Šalamon, N., Bajt, V., Pajnik, M., Jalušič, V., Zdravković, L., Kogovšek Šalamon, N., Bajt, V. and Frébutte, M., 2016. Razor – Wired. Ljubljana: Peace Institute. The publication is also available online at: https://www.mirovni-institut.si/wp-content/uploads/2016/03/Razor_wired_publikacija_web.pdf.
2 We are especially grateful to Irene Fisco and Valentina Di Odoardo from CIES Onlus organisation, who gave us the inspiration for this very project and also trained our theatre actors and mentors.
3 We have prepared and published a booklet with most inspiring, positive and also surprising personal messages of Slovenian children and young people, written after the theatre plays and which are intended for people who have experienced refugee life, we wanted to present the other face of Slovenian society and the tolerance of its youngest towards refugees to the latter as well as to the general public. The booklet When I looked through the refugee's eyes was published in 2017.
4 See for example this original set of guidelines entitled «10 things you need to consider if you are an artist – not of the refugee and asylum seeker community- looking to work with our community», prepared by the RISE: Refugees, Survivors and Ex-detainees. Available at: http://riserefugee.org/10-things-you-need-to-consider-if-you-are-an-artist-not-of-the-refugee-and-asylum-seeker-community-looking-to-work-with-our-community/.

References

Andreotti, V. (2006) Soft Versus Critical Global Citizenship Education, *Policy & Practice: A Development Education Review*, 3, Autumn: 40–51.

Brookfield, S. (2004) Discussion. In Michael W. Galbraith, ed. *Golbraith, Adult Learning Methods: A Guide for Effective Instruction*. Florida: Krieger Publishing: 209–226.

Council of Europe (COE) (2002) *European Strategy Framework For Improving and Increasing Global Education In Europe to the Year 2015 (The "Maastricht Global Education Declaration")*. [online] Available at: https://rm.coe.int/168070e540 (Accessed 15 June 2020).

Global Education Network Europe GENE (2018) *Global Education Innovation Award Brochure 2017*. Available at: https://gene.eu/wp-content/uploads/GENE_2 017_Award.pdf (Accessed 15 June 2020).

Humanitas Youtube Channel (2017) *THROUGH THE REFUGEE'S EYES – Humanitas – Recommendation from the teachers* [Video File]. Retrieved from https://www.youtube.com/watch?v=NVmDoNwyl1o&list=PL1cuQD9mi4fE15-1ITWQnOyN3nTVMej6G&index=4&t=0s

International Organization For Migration (IOM) (2020) *Missing Migrants Project*. [online]. Available at: https://missingmigrants.iom.int/ (Accessed 15 June 2020).

Kitchenham, A. (2008) The Evolution of John Mezirow's Transformative Learning Theory, *Journal of Transformative Education*, 6 (2): 104–123.

Lederer, E. & Didham, R. J. (2018) *Education for Sustainable Lifestyles. Learning to live for people, planet and prosperity. Practices from around the world, Vol. 1*. Norway: Inland Norway University of Applied Sciences. Available at: https://www.oneplanetnetwork.org/sites/default/files/esl_good_practices_vol1.pdf (Accessed 15 June 2020).

Šetinc Vernik, M. (ed.) (2017) *Ko Sem Pogledal Skozi Oči Begunca*. Ljubljana: Društvo za človekove pravice in človeku prijazne dejavnosti Humanitas.

Wlodkowski, R. J. (2004) Creating Motivating Learning Environments. In Michael W. Galbraith, ed. *Golbraith, Adult learning methods: A guide for effective instruction*. Florida: Kreiger Publishing: 141–164.

Zinn, L. (1990) Identifying Your Philosophical Orientation. In *Golbraith, Adult Learning Methods: A guide for effective instruction*. Florida: Kreiger Publishing: 39–77.

11 The gestalt of historical research, art, and education: the circus theme and performing arts in remembering the tyranny of the Nazi Regime[1]

Malte Gasche

Introduction

For centuries, European circuses have been run by minority groups (i.e. Sinti and Roma, Jewish), with performers from across the world and of all backgrounds, including people with physical disabilities. As such, circuses have constituted a narrow gateway for the acceptance of otherness. During Nazism, some circuses showed moral courage and hid people during roundups, saving lives; in others, the people in travelling circuses were easy targets for the Nazis and their allies. Despite the significance of this multi-faceted history, we have only scant information about the fates of circus people before, during, and after the Second World War. As such, this chapter aims not only to highlight the potential of studying the history of the circus, but it also seeks to draw attention to the prospects of using research-based performances in educational work and remembrance activities. The deaths of the last survivors of Nazi atrocities make the search for new concepts of memory even more urgent. Moreover, this chapter wants to show the route to gaining and passing on new understanding and insights not only of the past, but also of the living conditions and security strategies of present marginalised communities through a format of combining scholarship with artistic elements.

Research projects "Diverging Fates" and "Forgotten Cosmopolitans"

Recently, two research projects have begun to tackle the widely neglected history of the circus and circus people in Europe during Nazism. One of the first scientific encounters of the project "Diverging Fates: Travelling Circus People in Europe during National Socialism" (2017–2018) involved the utilisation of a biographical approach; it resulted in a collection of 30 short life stories with diverging destinies from different parts of Europe.[2] The aim of the follow-up project "Forgotten Cosmopolitans: Diverging Fates of Europe's Circus People in the Wake of WWII" (2018–2020) was to broaden the study focus, to highlight the cosmopolitan character of the circus milieu, even in Nazi Germany.[3] At the same time, the project pursued a stronger participatory approach by seeking to include members of the circus community and their reflections at all levels of activities. A participatory approach served to give a voice to people who have had fewer opportunities and who would have otherwise remained silent and anonymous.

Circuses as multicultural spaces in the 1930- and 1940s in the Nazi sphere of control

Even in times of crises and war, circuses have remained a popular form of amusement. Likewise, in the Nazi era circuses also attracted audiences hungry for entertainment. Performers from across the world presented their artistic skills in German circuses. Even during the war, foreign circus artists and animal trainers were performing in German-controlled areas. Many of the entertainers, who not only performed in Germany, but also in foreign circuses within the Nazi German sphere of control in Europe, primarily hailed from Hungary, Italy, and Spain during this time. Edit Kleinbarth, once a circus artist herself and whose father worked at the circus Hoppe, remembers in her memoirs and in conversation with the author of this article that a family with an African background and a German-Asian-Arabic artist group travelled with this German circus, even during the war. Russian equestrian groups and Arabic tumbling troupes, which were encountered in Western Europe already before the war, frequently performed in German circus arenas. During the second part of the war, forced foreign labourers, mainly from Eastern Europe, replaced German animal keepers, technicians, and tent workers in German circuses (Kleinbarth 2007; Lewerenz 2017; Koller 2017; Gasche 2019).

In addition, many European circuses had been owned and run by generations of Sinti and Roma, and Jewish families. The most prominent and wealthiest circus family of Sinti origin was and continues to be the Bouglione family, who to this day operates the legendary Cirque d'Hiver (Winter Circus) building in Paris, a locale renowned as one of the most prestigious circus venues in the world. According to Rosa Bouglione, who died at the age of 107 in 2018, the circus company was allowed to travel under Nazi occupation, although the management of the Cirque d'Hiver was handed over briefly to Paula Busch, the owner of the German Circus Busch. As Sinti, the Bouglions were certainly vulnerable during the Nazi occupation of France, though they somehow managed to evade persecution by Nazi German or collaborative authorities. It may well be that their Italian name helped camouflage their origins. In Nazi Germany, members of circus families with a Sinti background who did not have the fortune to have such a distinguished name, e.g. from the families Frank and Lagrin, met with different fates. The scale of racially motivated persecution ranged from forced sterilisation to deportation into concentration camps (Bouglione 2011; Lagrin 2011).

Since medieval times, there had been a distinguished tradition of Jewish itinerant entertainers in Europe. Many of them established circus dynasties, of which some of the most important had settled in Germany, e.g. the circus families Blumenfeld, Lorch, or Strassburger. With the onset of anti-Jewish directives in the Third Reich, the freedom and business opportunities Jewish circus families had hitherto enjoyed in Germany came to an abrupt end. Jewish circuses were Aryanized and changed hands at ridiculous prices. In many cases, performers with a Jewish background went abroad to find employment in more welcoming circus companies (Nissing 1993; Winkler & Winkler 2012).

The circus as shelter for persecuted people

Within the Nazi sphere of control in Europe, circuses as cosmopolitan and mobile spheres with plenty of opportunities to hide and play with different identities could offer refuge to those persecuted by the Nazi regime and their allies. Circus people thus emerged as victims and possible beneficiaries, but also as lifesavers. Protective solidarity within the artist and circus milieu is noticeable in secondary literature, narratives and archival material (Opfermann 2019). The most known case is the survival of the circus artist Irene Bento in the German Circus Althoff during Nazism. Bento, née Danner, was born in 1923. From her mother's side she was a descendant from the famous Lorch family, a Jewish circus family whose roots date back to the 18th century. Until the year 1930, the Lorch family travelled with its own circus in German-speaking areas. Since the persecution against Jewish people in Nazi Germany increased, members of the family were banned from performing, and later put in concentration camps and murdered. When Nazi German authorities came looking for Irene Bento's grandmother Sessie Lorch, who was then deported to the Auschwitz concentration camp in spring 1943, Irene went with her son Peter, her sister Gerda and mother Alice into hiding with the Circus Adolf Althoff, eventually joined by her father Hans. The circus director, for whom Irene's Belgian husband Peter Storms Bento worked as a clown, introduced her as an Italian to others. During a Gestapo operation, the family remained undetected by hiding in a circus wagon with doubled walls. Thanks to the solidarity within the circus community and the unselfish and courageous assistance of the director couple Adolf and Maria Althoff, Irene and her family managed to survive the Nazi tyranny. The story of Irene Bento became known to the wider public through Ingeborg Prior's book *Der Clown und die Zirkusreiterin* (The Clown and the Circus Rider) in 1997 (Prior 1997).

In the Nordic countries, too, circuses emerged as pockets of cultural diversity, thus providing refuge to foreigners deemed racially or politically undesirable by the Nazi regime. The Austrian dissident Alfred Molnar, for instance, on the run from the Nazi Regime found a safe haven as a lion keeper at the Finnish Circus/Tivoli Sariola. In March 1938, Molnar, who had joined the Communist Party of Austria (KPÖ) in 1923, fled from the Vienna SA to

Lithuania. In the spring of 1939, with the help of Jewish relief committees, he continued his escape via Riga and Tallinn to Helsinki, from where he planned to flee by train to the northern Swedish port of Luleå. On the train, he met Alfred Pitsch, an Austrian compatriot. Pitsch was a predator tamer, escape artist, knife thrower, and lasso artist employed by the Tivoli "Sariola", which was a mixture of fairground and circus that travelled all over Finland. Molnar decided to stay on in Finland and helped to build up the Tivoli in Rovaniemi. The international milieu with artists from Estonia, Finland, Latvia, Austria, Sweden, and Hungary welcomed the evader Molnar to their circle. Already in Rovaniemi, he was offered work as a lion guard for the predator tamer Pitsch. His residence and work permit, which "a hundred thousand emigrants fought tooth and nail for", as Molnar wrote in his autobiography *Unstet und flüchtig* (Unsteady and fleeting) from 1982, was arranged by the director of the Tivoli Johan A.F. Sariola. After the outbreak of the Finnish-Russian Winter War in November 1939, Molnar and Pitsch volunteered for the Finnish army, which automatically extended their residence and work permits (Molnar 1982, 104, 110–111, 130–175).

Interplay of research, art and pedagogy: general expectations and activities

Both of the above-mentioned projects aimed to pursue new educational paths. The projects' goals were also to illuminate the synergies between scientific knowledge, the arts, and remembrance. How can history be brought to life when the last survivors of Nazi atrocities' and their points-of-view are, literally, dying out? The projects "Diverging Fates" and "Forgotten Cosmopolitans" aimed to highlight the potential of combining the history of Europe's circus people with artistic/stage storytelling acts in remembering life and repression during Nazism. Moreover, the study of a transnational and marginal culture not only provides information about a society's openness and security, but also about its various forms of oppression. Thus, the performance projects also aimed to address current societal issues and to reduce prejudices against minorities and increase the acceptance of diversity within European societies. Together with the project group "CINS – Circus im Nationalsozialismus", the project "Diverging Fates" arranged an open lecture performance act in the front yard of the Museum Europäischer Kulturen, Staatlicher Museen zu Berlin – Preußischer Kulturbesitz at the International Museum Day, 21 May 2017. In this performance, extracts from Prior's book about Irene Bento's survival of the Holocaust in the circus Althoff were read and visualised with interpretive circus elements such as juggling, pantomimes, and trapeze acts.

During the Second Nordic Challenges Conferences at the University of Helsinki, 7–9 March 2018, the project "Diverging Fates" developed a research-based play in collaboration with the Finnish dramatic advisor Fabian Silén and the Theater Mestola. The open performance was presented at the Think Corner at the University of Helsinki, 8 March 2018. Held in Swedish, the performance

164 *Malte Gasche*

lecture told the story about the Austrian dissident Adolf Molnar, who found a safe place at the Finnish Circus/Tivoli Sariola. The performed act did not only display experiences of discrimination and security strategies of marginalised people with transnational identities, but it also provided a multicultural perspective on Finnish and Nordic history, thus creating a counter-narrative to mainstream interpretations of history in so-called homogeneous societies. The play showed that also in Finland circuses constituted cosmopolitan spaces that offered shelter and protection to those persecuted by the Nazi regime. Moreover, the play referred to the changes and restrictions that international circus colleagues faced within the Nazi sphere of control in Europe. The performance began with an introductory lecture on the theme and ended with an open debate with the audience. The organisers filmed and uploaded the performance on YouTube.[4]

Within the project "Forgotten Cosmopolitans" a teacher-training seminar was arranged at the University College of Teacher Education Burgenland in Eisenstadt (AUT), 4–5 October 2019. The second seminar day was devoted to illuminate the synergies between research, arts, and remembrance and to discuss new pedagogical paths in educational activities. For this last purpose, the project group "CINS" was invited to give a performance on the life of Irene Bento and to share their experiences from previous showings in schools and audience feedback.

Reactions and feedbacks

Eleven viewers, who had either seen the play about Irene Bento or the stage story-telling act about Adolf Molnar, gave feedback on their observations and reflections. Six observers commented on the first mentioned play, five viewers on the second one. In addition, there is a comment from one of the performance artists and co-developers of the act on the life of Irene Bento and a reflection by the dramatic advisor of the Alfred Molnar play. The comments were often given spontaneously and thus unfiltered, and for this reason were left anonymous.[5] The audience present for the piece about Irene Bento, which took place in the courtyard of the Museum of European Cultures in Berlin and at the Burgenland University of Teacher Education in Eisenstadt, was very mixed. Concerning this particular act, comments were made by school teachers, Holocaust-education experts, circus educators, historians, adult education specialists, and one 17-year-old student. The Alfred Molnar act took place within a larger scientific conference. All comments came from professors and other researchers in various humanistic subjects.

This section of the chapter is mainly about general impressions and reactions on the two plays presented above. While the observers generally regarded the interplay between art and historical fact as a positive idea, doubts arose about the circus theme as starting point for such a combination in educational activities. To begin with, the member of the project group

"CINS" wanted to provide a general impression of the responses of the viewers to the performance on the fate of Irene Bento. She described how the play captured the attention of the audience every time without fail and immersed them into the world of the circus. She revealed that the project group usually received an immediate emotional response, for instance, spectators began to cry during the performance. However, more reflective or rational responses usually reached the group shortly after the performance, e.g. in the form of conversation directly after the play or by email. Many have told her that the performance not only has moved them emotionally, but that it also enabled them as viewers to receive and process the new given information.

An experienced researcher, who is studying the genocides of the Roma under the Nazi Regime and who was already familiar with the story of Irene Bento's before taking part in the workshop in Eisenstadt, suggested that the combination of artistic performance and archival knowledge production was unusual and even surprising at first sight. However, experience has shown that this kind of approach can reach students, pupils, and a broader audience more deeply and intensely than can a purely theoretical and historiographical presentation. The multidisciplinary performance of the project group "CINS" concentrated on the fate of Irene Bento in the context of Nazi anti-Jewish laws and persecution. Such an approach would also aptly illustrate the fates of Romani circus artists/groups during Nazism, not to mention their cultural impact on public spaces and their contribution to the formation of cosmopolitanisms in European societies.

An expert from a funding organisation, who saw the play about Irene Bento in Berlin, generally considered performances as an opportunity for marginalised groups in society, such as the Roma, to tell their stories and highlight their contribution to public spaces. She found the biographical focus particularly helpful for connecting individual fates to a complex historical/political topic and reasoned that the interplay between facts and arts could make the plight of today's refugees more concrete to people in the West and thereby increase the majority society's understanding of their needs.

An Austrian social circus educator, who combines artistic training with social inclusion of children, young people, and adults with fewer opportunities, but who is also an artist herself, found the presented format of the project group "CINS" in Eisenstadt, its stage story telling combined with artistry, "great." Nonetheless, she did wonder if younger viewers unfamiliar with the circus or less knowledgeable about history would feel a connection to the piece on Irene Bento. To underline her doubts, she referred to her youth work in Vienna, where most of the teenagers had never been in touch with the circus before.

The youngest participant in Eisenstadt, a student aged 17 from Germany, said that the performance gave him a completely new perspective on the circus. He categorised "the close cohesion in the international and multicultural circus community" as "particularly impressive" and "unique", and

166 *Malte Gasche*

in a certain way "modern." However, he did not see how the circus theme could serve as tool to build an emotional bridge in teaching the tyranny of the Nazi Regime in his age group, simply for the reason that the circus no longer played an important part in his generation's childhood.

As previously mentioned, the Adolf Molnar act was announced as a performance lecture during a bigger conference. According to the Finnish organiser, a university professor and research director,

> there was a positive atmosphere of excitement before the performance, since it was something new and for most not experienced before. [...] After the performance, the audience was still excited and content, and many of the questions and comments touched on how this concept could be developed and used in other similar circumstances.

For this Finnish professor, "combining research with art did provide a leap into something unknown, which generated an enhanced interest, which means that there was an opportunity to get the message across to the audience with much more impact than usual."

Another Finnish history professor, who followed the Adolf Molnar act, remembered that she especially liked the moments when the researcher and actor met and crossed boundaries, such as when the researcher became a lion. She believed that research and the arts could intervene in different ways in a lecture with dramatisation. Although, she acknowledged that it probably take a lot of preparation and work to bring the researcher and the actor to the same level in order to create a format where historical research and drama interact and support each other. Moreover, she expressed with many others in the audience a desire to develop similar performance acts based on their own research/lecture, for instance, as a way to introduce new topics or opening a lecture at historical sites. When discussing circus people as a marginalised group of society, a doctoral student recalled her own and other related research topics, about which there is also a culture of silence lies. Yet she maintained that this silence always finds a way to be broken. In this context, she refers to the lamentation poems of the Eastern Karelians.

Risks, challenges and rewards

This section presents comments that go beyond general impressions and deal with both, the risks and challenges, as well as the gainful perspective of combinations between research and art, for scientific, educational, and remembrance activities. The member of the project group "CINS" draws attention to general ethical hazards and the need for showing respect to circus people, when it comes to research and storytelling projects about this community. She emphasised that this centuries-old form of art with its distinctive way of life is subject to its own rules and its particular social structure. Without knowing these codes, any engagement is at great risk of offending the core values of these people and therefore, consciously or unconsciously, behaving disrespectfully towards them. Nevertheless, she considered research-based performances (or other art forms) seeking to explore the topic on circus people during Nazism or aiming to engage with similar groups, as a more appropriate way to approach this area than with rigid scientific parameters. She points out that circus people, permanently on the move, have always evaded norms and categories. Therefore, alternative engagements with people in the margins have a better chance of capturing more information on these groups and making this new knowledge visible to a greater audience.

From the point of view of an experienced Austrian school teacher in history and organiser of teacher training seminars, who also educated herself at Yad Vashem in "teaching the Holocaust", the "historic background" of productions involving artistic elements "should be really well researched": "I think it is risky if artists, producers, writers etc. too carelessly handle artistic freedom when dealing with history." In this context, she refers to a remake of the German movie "Das Boot", which tells the story about a German submarine during the Second World War. "The new version now on TV misrepresents the historical facts and many younger viewers fail to notice the manipulation in this version." She does nonetheless recognise the value of the interplay between artistic elements and research-based facts: "I think combining art and history is a good way to reach our students, our pupils. For them, the Second World War and the Holocaust are so far away; therefore, films, theatre, and performances are a good way to reach them. And, for a lot of elderly people, it is a good way too." Another school teacher, a specialist in Holocaust education and a maker of two documentary films from Denmark, sees "historical accuracy" as a quality that those seeking to provide artistic perspectives could learn from the research field. For her, this discussion also resonates in the making of historical films. In her view, one of the main challenges of combining research with art is the difference in methods, approaches, audiences, and presenting results – despite common interests and overlapping fields. She also identifies hesitancy about combining these two fields. The dramatic performance about the life of Irene Bento that she attended, however, gave her new ideas regarding what researchers and educators could learn from artistic approaches, "mainly the ability to engage the audience, especially students." At the same time, her "hesitancy" lies "within the dramatic approach itself, as the aim of the drama is to engage the audience through identification or emotions contrary to scholarship, an endeavor that aims at researching/uncovering/conveying topics through scientific methods."

The female Finnish history professor who attended the performance about Adolf Molnar determined that the biggest challenge of using dramatic elements in research presentations is that the audience may perceive dramatisation as something just added on but not fitting well.

For the researcher who wants to use dramatization, it must be clear what he or she wants to accomplish with the drama piece, in what way the dramatization adds something, how it can be a dialogue between two different ways of storytelling, lecture and drama. If you do not do such background thinking, and if you fail to communicate to or discuss what you want and are looking for with the artists, the whole thing can become messy and maybe superficial. The audience must feel that the combination is meaningful.

The director's retrospective contribution about the biggest challenge of his production on the life of Molnar fits these remarks above. He reminded that "writing drama or a dramatic scene always have to be based on an outer or inner conflict." Therefore, the main encounter for him was "to find a conflict that could be in dialogue with the scientific research material." In addition to this debate, an English-Finnish senior researcher, who has attended the act about Adolf Molnar's life, but also other research-based performances, warned about the risk that research interventions, e.g. short lecture contribution with the aim to provide historical facts during the performance, could feel unnecessary and disturb the dramatic element.

The professor and research director, who hosted as conference organiser the performance on Molnar, admitted that there are obvious risks when combining research and arts. "Since art is fiction and research is fact, and in the case shown at the Helsinki Think Corner it was about the life of one man, there is an obvious risk that the research part might be 'damaged' as fiction", he stated. On the other hand, fiction as a tool to discuss societal issues can serve as guiding light towards relevant themes, which researchers have not yet been able to find the right methods to investigate. The finale comment belongs to a retired Finnish research director. Based on his experiences he perceived it as biggest contest to get funding for research-based performance projects. At the same time, he saw the combination of research and art as a chance to open up the rigid positivist conceptual apparatus in conventional research in an emancipator way, especially with regard to atypical individuals in society and their living conditions, about whom we could gain a new perception through such an interdisciplinary interplay.

Conclusion

The projects "Diverging Fates" and "Forgotten Cosmopolitans" on the destinies of Europe's circus people and performers in the shadow of the Third Reich have revealed the potential in combining new scientific knowledge with artistic elements and stage storytelling. The general purpose of such an approach was to re-map and re-imagine the cosmopolitan area of circuses. Dominant national historical and cultural narratives have mostly overlooked this historical fact and have failed to recognise the extent of mutual support, sacrifices made, and life-threatening risks taken for others within the circus community. The circus, a mobile and multinational community replete with hiding places made it possible for persecuted people to find a shelter within it and assume false identities. With the idea of combining new research results with artistic practice in educational and remembrance activities, the projects especially intended to provide wider audiences, especially youth with new perspectives on circus people as a forgotten victim group in the wake of the Second World War. At the same time, the research itself and the interplay of scientific knowledge and the arts aimed to provide a new general view of the living conditions and security strategies of transnational minorities in European societies.

On the whole, the research-based plays performed about the fates of circus people during Nazism at the venues in Helsinki and Eisenstadt met with a largely positive response. Experts in Holocaust-education and history school teachers regarded the circus theme and historical plays as useful in fighting against Holocaust fatigue or teaching the history of Nazism. However, the only representative of the under 18 generation in Eisenstadt pointed out that the circus no longer appeals to his age group and does not conjure up the same kinds of associations that it probably did for members of older cohorts. According to the academic perspective, the interplay between scholarship and the arts holds the potential for a segue into a new and unfamiliar field, both in the researcher's professional works and for the wider public as recipients. Furthermore, the study focus on circus people or similar social groups in combination with research-based plays in public was regarded as a possible way to prepare the ground for disadvantaged and underrepresented communities to leave the margins and publicly speak about their experiences. There were also those who considered the combination of artistic practice and knowledge production as a source for new perspectives, particularly on the cultural contribution of Romani groups to public spaces and their role in the formation of cosmopolitanisms in European societies. All those who shared their views, however, agreed that the interplay between scientific presentation and artistic dramaturgy must fit together in a fluid and complementary way.

Notes

1 This chapter is framed in the project BESTROM, financially supported by the HERA Joint Research Programme (www.heranet.info) which is co-funded by AoF, NCN, AHRC, AEI and the European Commission through Horizon 2020.
2 Available at: http://www.divergingfates.eu (Accessed 12 February 2020).
3 Available at: http://www.forgottencosmopolitans.eu (Accessed 12 February 2020).
4 Available at: https://www.helsinki.fi/en/unitube/video/c968d13c-65e7–43ac-8c48-fe1eb9c752cc (Accessed 12 February 2020).
5 The author received the comments by email in Danish, English, Finnish, German, and Swedish.

References

Bouglione, R. (2011) *Un marriage dans la cage aux lions. La Grande Saga Du Cirque Bouglione*. Neuilly-sur-Seine Cedex: Éditions Michel Lafon.

Gasche, M. (2019) Ein Zirkuskind erlebt die Befreiung 1944 in Luxemburg, *Luxemburger Wort*, 171: 7–8.

Kleinbarth, E. (2007) *Ballerina hevosen selässä*. Vaajakoski: Gummerus Kirjapaino Oy.

Koller, G. (2017) Versteckt im Waggon. 1944 flüchten elf Elefanten, ein Nilpferd und ein Pole vor den Krieg in die Schweiz. *Aargauer Zeitung*. Available at: https://www.aargauerzeitung.ch/panorama/vermischtes/1944-fluechteten-elf-elefanten-ein-nilpferd-und-ein-pole-vor-dem-krieg-in-die-schweiz-132000373 (Accessed 12 February 2020).

Lagrin, P. (2011) *Lebensreise ... Erinnerungen an ein Leben auf dem Drahtseil*. Norderstedt: Books on Demandt.

Lewerenz, S. (2017) *Geteilte Welten. Exotisierte Unterhaltung und Artist*innen of Color in Deutschland 1920–1960*. Köln: Böhlau.

Molnar, A. (1982) *Unstet und Flüchtig. Eine Lebensgeschichte*. Darmstadt: Luchterhand.

Nissing, H. (1993) *Strassburger. Geschichte eines jüdischen Circus*. Dormagen: Circus-Verlag.

Opfermann, U. (2019) "Fahrendes Volk". Binnenmigration in und aus dem alemannischen Raum im 19. und 20. Jahrhundert. In J. Geike & A. Haasis-Berner, eds. *Menschen in Bewegung. Lebenswelten im ländlichen Raum. Historische Erkundungen in Mittel- und Südbaden, Bd. 4*. Heidelberg: Regionalkultur: 189–235.

Prior, I. (1997) Der Clown und die Zirkusreiterin. Berlin: Malik.

Winkler, G. & Winkler, D. (2012) *Die Blumenfelds. Schicksale einer jüdischen Zirkusfamilie*. Gransee: Edition Schwarzdruck.

Part IV
Healing and embodied strategies of learning

12 Utilising the breath as an experiential tool to teach, learn and manage trauma

Anna Walker

> Sleep arrives when a certain voluntary attitude suddenly receives from outside the very confirmation that it was expecting. I breathe slowly and deeply to call forth sleep, and suddenly, one might say my mouth communicates with some immense external lung that calls my breath forth and forces it back. A certain respiratory rhythm, desired by me just a moment ago, becomes my very being (Ponty 2013, 219).

Introduction

In this chapter, I will be addressing experiential methods of managing trauma through an exploration of the 23-minute video, *Breathe Wind into Me, Chapter 1*, 2019, [video] Directed by A. Walker,[1] and Luce Irigaray's and Lenart Skof's notion that we are living in the *Age of Breath* (2013, Ch:14). Donna Haraway, in *Staying with the Trouble, Making Kin in the Chthulucene* (2016), suggests that in the midst of spiralling ecological disaster, and the ensuing suffering we need to find new ways to reconfigure our relationship to each other and to the earth. She formulates ways to stay with the trouble of living and dying together on a damaged earth, where "[b]ecoming-with, not becoming is the name of the game" (12). Reflecting upon the concept of Merleau Ponty's "immense exterior lung" (1992, 167), my intention is to find an alternative approach to rethink the past and confront uncomfortable truths. This project builds upon the past 7-years of arts practice research into trauma and memory, and the challenge trauma poses for individuals, societies, and cultures post 9/11. It is a continuing exploration of the tension where trauma meets memory whether in an attempt to forget or in an effort to remember. Memory in this context is perceived as crucial to understanding oneself socially, culturally, and personally, whilst trauma is understood as an experience borne by the act of leaving wherein the mind's coping mechanism overwhelmed by shocking external events fractures or splits. Trauma from a modernist perspective points to an occurrence that both demands representation and yet refuses to be represented (Roth 2012, 93), the intensity of the experience makes it difficult to remember, impossible to forget, and any form of recollection inadequate.

174 *Anna Walker*

Background

The artwork, *Breath Wind into Me, Chapter 1* (23 mins), was first exhibited as part of a 2-screen and sound installation at Fabrica Arts Gallery, Brighton, UK, in January 2019. Fabrica, a visual arts organisation based in a former Regency church has a high vaulted ceiling and large stained-glass windows. The relationship between the space and spirituality is hard to avoid.[2] Taking this aspect into consideration, but not focusing on it, 2-large 3-meter by 4-meter freestanding screens were positioned on the floor at either end of the gallery space onto which the moving imagery was projected. In a darkened space, the imagery spilled off of the screens into the curves of the ceiling and across the stained glass. Similarly, the voice, sounds, and harmonies travelled across the wooden floors, vibrating through the walls, and bounced off the ceiling, filling the space. When the audience entered the gallery space, they were immediately absorbed by the imagery and sounds. Since then the artwork, *"Breath Wind into Me, Chapter 1"* has been exhibited in three separate locations, the presentation of which, and the audience's responses have informed this essay (Figures 12.1 and 12.2).

Through the work, I was exploring whether it was possible to be sensitive to the needs of the other through our breathing and whether a deepening awareness of one's breath can create the circumstances where we can attend to, not only our bodies, but to the bodies of others, to animals, the oceans,

Figure 12.1 Interior of Fabrica Art Gallery, Brighton. © Fabrica Art Gallery.

Figure 12.2 Interior of Fabrica Art Gallery, Brighton. © Fabrica Art Gallery.

nature, and other cultures. Using this as a theoretical premise I am interested in the relationship of the breath to communicable states of affect within the shared space. Under consideration is a respiratory approach to philosophy, an embodied relationship that extends to physical relations with the enveloping atmosphere: which Kathleen Stewart calls "atmospheric attunement" (2010, 4) and the utilisation of the breath as an experiential resource to address individual and collective trauma. Additionally, in the video, I am seeking to create an interstitial space where traumatic remembering exists on the borders of exposure and concealment, absence, and presence. Far from being completed, the artwork, *Breath Wind into Me, Chapter 1,* and the ensuing critical discussion marks just the beginning of research that links the breath to language and affective resonance.

The text for *Breath Wind into Me, Chapter 1,* was formed out of a series of journal entries: a loosely, flowing, stream of consciousness that questioned what arises physically and philosophically when life is stripped back to the bare essentials – to the breath – and the consequences when the breath is interrupted, or ruptured, as in trauma. The words are layered upon the sounds of breathing, a guided meditation, sounds, music, life, and its various interruptions. The imagery, collected over 2-years, references the ordinariness of moving through one's day that once witnessed and captured on video verges on the extra-ordinary. Contained within the imagery and sounds was the ominous presence of something other, something unknown or unnamed, linking fragments of the past, and historical traumatic traces in the present.

The work begins with the notion of animism, from *anima* in Latin, ("a current of air, wind, breath, the vital principle, life, soul"), sometimes equivalent to animus ("mind"). Animism attributes a living soul in all objects – animals, plants, rocks, rivers, weather-related phenomena, deceased human beings, even words – to be animated is to be alive, possessing distinctive spirits, a presence. At the centre of our existence is our ability to breathe. Our relationship to everything around us is lived through a shared and oxygenated space. All living organisms depend on various types of respiratory processes to maintain life. As Peter Sloterdijk writes:

> Air, the misunderstood element, finds ways and means of advancing to places where no one reckons with its presence; and, more significantly, it makes space on its own strength for strange places where there were previously none. (2016, 28)

It's important to not underestimate the power of the breath or breathing, which most of us so often take for granted. The complexity of the breath as an evolutionary process was millions of years in the making, where the lungs, heart, trachea, bronchial tree, and connecting blood vessels all contribute to the "ingenious breathing system" (Schiefelbein 1986, 132) that brings oxygen to the blood and removes carbon dioxide. Contained within every inhale and exhale is the entire history of humanities' evolution. It is what connects us to each other, to every living thing, and to the world we inhabit. If we could not breathe, we would not be alive. The absence of breath is an absence of life, deadness. I breathe with every living creature, and every living creature breathes through me. Each breath is a memory of the one before, each inhale marked with the trace of the previous one, back to when the first tetrapod emerged from the water 300 million years ago and committed to inhale the sky and the earth. As anthropologist Tim Ingold articulates: "There could be no life, in short, in a world where earth and sky do not mix and mingle" (2010, 6).

So, can an attentiveness to the breath highlight the interaction between states of knowing and not knowing, acceptance and the refusal to acknowledge? Can a listening to the breath, illuminate the relationships between previously unrelated events, structures, perceptions, and actions? Can a breathing into silence create an alternative space of compassion and empathy for the self and for others? And can all of the aforementioned be a method to explore cultural trauma and social responsibility to develop a *just* becoming? (Figures 12.3 and 12.4).[3]

To understand the artwork further and plot a course for this essay, I will be developing four propositions to perceive the world in a respiratory way. Firstly, *Proposition 1: The Spectral Breath*, expands on Derrida's concept of hauntology, a pun on ontology. Secondly, *2: Breathing with The Other*, looks at the shared affective experience as well as, in Škof's words, "an ethics towards two autonomous subjects, based on care and our shared ethical becoming – both as signs of our deepest hospitality towards the other" (2013, 4). Finally, the third proposition, *The Haptic Breath*, continues the previous discussion and expands Laura Marks' concept of haptic visuality, the image that touches, to the idea of one's breath *touching* another. Threaded throughout these propositions are three of Luce Irigaray's philosophical concepts, breath, silence, and listening from the third phase of her

Figure 12.3 Stills from *Breath Wind into Me, Chapter 1* (Walker, 2019).

Figure 12.4 Stills from *Breath Wind into Me, Chapter 1* (Walker, 2019).

philosophy, her envisaging of a culture of breath. Air is not only the material substance that humans and animals breathe but also the invisible, the feminine, the exchange from one to another, it is both physical and metaphysical.

Proposition 1: the spectral breath

The spectral breath is the interrupted breath of traumatic memory, that which haunts us from the past. Here the breath is held, tightened, contracted. It is a ruptured breath layered with remembering both conscious and unconscious, the interrupted breath that has been passed down through generations. It is a concept that builds on Derrida's writings on hauntology, the breath that both haunt the body and is haunted by the body, that holds the traces of the past, the traumatic memories. The Derridean notion of spectrality – the anachronistic spectre, outside of time and place – exists between life and death, absence and presence, as Derrida writes "a trace always referring to another whose eyes can never be met" (1993, 84). The spectral for Derrida arises from the concept of a future absence. "To haunt does not mean to be present, and it is necessary to introduce haunting into the very construction of a concept. Of every concept, beginning with the concepts of being and time" (Derrida 1993, 13). This notion of "hauntology", links being, presence and absence. Through the figure of the ghost, the past and present are indistinguishable. Embodied in the spectral the past is brought to life.

In *Specters of Marx* (1993), Derrida considers this conflict between presence and absence, inside and outside. He suggests cinema as an appropriate medium for spectrality, which sets in motion for the viewer, communication with some work of the unconscious that, by definition, can be compared with the work of haunting, the Freudian notion of the "uncanny" (unheimlich) (2015, 26). Derrida argues that the true logic of uncanniness is a phantom-logic, a necessity of learning to live with ghosts, phantoms, and spirits, because "there is no Dasein without the uncanniness, without the strange familiarity [Unheimlichkeit] of some spectre" (1993, 125). It is a state of being that is to be always and everywhere haunted by ghosts, phantoms or spirits: the "visibility of the invisible" (125). Spectral logic is the presence related to the otherness of the self, or the self that is found within the other (whether person, place, or time). In honour of Barthes, he writes: "Ghosts: the concept of the other in the same, the punctum in the studium, the completely other, dead, living in me" (Derrida 2001, 42). This ghostly punctum is linked to the voice of the other, it is the "accompaniment, the song, the accord" (2001, 43). It is the breath of the other.

The breath leaves the body, leaves a trace before returning, through my body, through the body of the other, of every living creature. For Derrida, "this trace is the opening of the first exteriority in general, the enigmatic relationship of the living to its other and of an inside to an outside: spacing" (1974, 71). In the sounds of *Breathe Wind into me, Chapter 1*, the breath is audible, it travels alongside the narrating voice, and then spills into the exhibition space. It enters the space from multiple sources. There is the original breath, mine, now disconnected from my body, the technological recording of the breath, at times distorted, and the audience's breath all of which contribute to this shared space outside of the self. There is no control over how the voice, my voice is heard or received, or even how my breath is received. The voice, the sound of breathing, the breath, all are divorced entities existing in their own right no longer attached to my body. As Steven Connor explains:

> Voices do not merely drift apart from their origins [...] nor are they inadvertently lost: they are ripped or wrested. A voice without a body suggests some prior act of mutilation: for every unbodied voice, it seems, there is always some more-or-less violently muted body. (Connor 2012, 1)

There are a multitude of dissociated voices embedded into the imagery of *Breath Wind into Me, Chapter 1,* which, in Connor's words, seem to "summon in their wake the phantasm of some originating body, effect convening cause" (2012). It is, to quote Holzman & Rousey, a "complex confrontation experience' brought about by the 'loss of anchorage'... [and] loss of the cathected familiar" (1966; Connor 2000, 84). Listening, I experience hearing my voice, as a part of me that has been disembodied but still retains life a way of "being me in my going out from myself" (Connor 2000, 4).

Lisa Blackman, in *Immaterial Bodies* (2012), writes about the paradoxical voice that is neither entirely inside nor outside, self or other, material or immaterial. "It is neither fully defined by matter nor completely beyond it. It is matter in circulation" (138). Listening, also, is not confined to the interior. We are both inside and outside in the process of listening. The external sounds finding their way into the body, subsequently means to be open without as well as within. Listening brings us into proximity with the other and vice versa. It connects us and establishes the interconnected space of relation.

The breath does something similar, especially when it is audible. It leaves the body, enters the shared space. It is both inside and outside, mine and others. I hear my breath and it is as if I bring something old, known and familiar but forgotten into the space. Invisible, the breath crosses borders, moves from one to the other. If it is tight and constricted with anxiety or fear, the shared space heightens, crackling with trepidation. Anxiety restricts the respiratory process, changing the quality of space inside and out of the body. Constricting the breathing space inside the body is also to constrict it on the outside. Alongside the anxious other we participate in the tightening of space, share the other's anxiety, sometimes knowingly, mostly unknowingly. It is a place of neurobiological and chemical interaction; it is shared intensity. In *The Autonomy of the Affect* (1995), Brian Massumi explores the concept of two different systems, one a conscious automatic system and the other an intensity system that exists outside of normal physiological sequencing, beyond narration, and therefore incapable of integrating into normal functioning systems. He describes a hormonal meeting of the past and the present, a physicality of existence that comes into being from an event or series of events from the past: "the embodied event of a life re-gathering in recoil. [This is] life self-enfolding in affective vitality" (2010, 4).

Teresa Brennan approaches the shared experience in The *Transmission of Affect* (2004) as an olfactory exchange. She suggests that:

> pheromones are pollenlike chemicals that when emitted by one creature have some effect on other members of the same species. One detects pheromones by touch or smell, but smell is more common. To smell pheromones is also in a sense to consume them. But the point here is that no direct physical contact is necessary for a transmission to take place. Pheromones are literally in the air. (69)

The hypothesis, therefore, is that all it would take is one member of a group in a communal space (whether classroom, cinema, or theatre) to generate the scent of fear, triggered through a re-living of traumatic memories, and the pheromones would ripple invisibly through all of those present spreading the *affect* of fear and trauma. Though controversial (Marks 2000), the connection between pheromones and hormones is well established: a pheromone in one may cause a hormone to be secreted in the blood of another (Brennan 2004, 69). Pheromones speak directly to the most primitive part of the brain, the hypothalamus, without ever making contact with consciousness (Marks 2000, 115). Similarly Laura Marks, in her notes on *The Logic of Smell* (2000), writes;

> Science popularisers argue that pheromones are received by the vomeronasal organ or Organ of Jacobson, high up in the nose. These substances produce effects more profound and intractable than any collectively understood image. (228)

More recently, The Stowers Lab, have produced research that would indicate some value in the above theory:

> The second class is specialized and activates neural circuits "pre-programmed" with meaning, as is the case for pheromones. The sniff of specialized odors has a high probability to generate the same behavior across individuals, with limited flexibility (sic). (Stowers & Logan 2010/ 2016)

Marks likens smell to Deleuze's concept of a fossil image, or the kind of an image that contains within it the material trace of the past (2000, 114). Scent is a powerful means to connect to the past, when we smell something familiar, we give our bodies over to the past, to memories that often cannot be comprehended in any other form. The scent acts on our bodies before we're even conscious of it. The sense of smell requires physical contact with the world, and forces not only a sensory communication between bodies, but also a dialogue with our own body in the interaction.

Smell is so closely intertwined with the processing of traumatic events and thereafter the remembering (Vermetten & Bremner 2003, 202). Physiologically, scent hits the olfactory bulb, where some neurons travel to the thalamus and others travel straight to the cortex and the limbic system, the parts of the brain that demand instinctual and immediate responses. For Marks, "smell has a privileged connection to emotion and memory that the other senses do not" (2000, 120), the symbolisation of which requires cognitive discrimination and the language centre of the brain (Marks 2000, 122). As Brennan writes:

> Discernment begins with considered sensing (by smell, or listening, as well as observation)-the process of feeling that also operates, or seems to operate, as the gateway to emotional response. When we do not feel, we open the gates to all kinds of affective flotsam, being unaware of its passage or its significance. We cease to discern the transmission of affect. (2004, 96)

Stewart's concept of "atmospheric attunement" (2010) is another way of perceiving the invisible connections between us and the haunted spaces. As she suggests:

> An atmospheric attunement is an alerted sense that something is happening and an attachment to sensing out whatever it is. It takes place within a world of some sort and it is itself a generative, compositional worlding' [...] Atmospheric attunements, then, attend to the quickening of nascent forms, marking their significance in sounds and sights and the feel of something's touch or something penetrating. It's like a sixth sense. It turns a potentiality into a threshold to the real. (4)

Affect theorists Gregg and Seigworth frame *attunement* as the first feel of an atmosphere as you enter, the angle of arrival (2010), weighted with what existed before the arrival, alive with sensory imperatives. When one is attentive to such attunements, when one can hone such a fine sense of listening in and to the atmosphere, time and space shift. Breathing is our most basic condition of nature, our most primordial level of adjustment to the environment we inhabit. Awareness of the space around us, and those who enter, and leave activated through our own breath, and those breathing around us begins to illuminate the non-duality and fundamental openness of one breathing body to another, which brings me to the next proposition.

Proposition 2: breathing with the other

In the process of researching the violence of trauma on the body, how the body responds to overwhelming traumatic situations and how it reorganises itself to cope with or manage the trauma I have also been considering the role of breathing with the other as an exercise or tool to soothe not only oneself but the other. This concept expands upon Irigaray's investigation of breath and inter-subjectivity. Once we inhabit space with another, occupy the atmosphere, we share breath. As Irigaray writes:

> Something has happened – an event, or an advent – an encounter between humans. A breath or soul has been born, brought forth by two others. There are now living beings for whom we lack the ways of approaching, the gestures and words for drawing nearer to one another, for exchanging. (2008, 31)

If it is possible to sense the other's state of being through contracted or restricted space that affects our relationship to space and therefore the breath, it is equally possible to affect the other in reverse; to calm the other down through centred and focused breathing. It is a concept or philosophy of breathing to manage and organise the trauma whether our own or that of others, a fine balance between consciousness, awareness, and compassion. It means to negotiate and understand the traumatic trigger and come to terms with how to live alongside each other and the trauma.

Conscious breathing is to be in the shared rhythm with not just the other, but with everything that breathes in the world. For Irigaray, the breath is "the first autonomous gesture of the living human being" (3). In the third phase of her philosophy she links the breath with silence and listening and argues for an ethical becoming to direct us towards respect for ourselves, each other and the world we live in. It is a silence that is attentive to others. The original place in our bodies and selves, reserved for the welcome of the other, for respect for the other despite our differences. Silence is the inner speaking of the threshold. The inner listening to the breath.

In "I love to you", she writes:

> This touching upon asks for silence. [...] This touching upon needs attentiveness to the sensible qualities of speech, to voice tone, to the modulations and rhythm of discourse, to the semantic and phonic choice of words. [...] The touching upon cannot be appropriation, capture, seduction – to me, toward me, in me – nor envelopment. Rather it is to be the other's awakening to him/her and a call to co-exist, to act together and dialogue (1996, 125)[4]

Breathing with the other requires attentive listening to firstly our own bodies, our breath in response to the other, followed by listening to and for the breath of the other. This listening is deep listening, a comprehension and understanding of the body that is both in breath and out of breath. It requires a slowing down and stepping outside of all that we have inherited to find over and over the first breath. It means divining what is out of sync and why, while addressing how it interrupts the coming together. It involves asking how difference can be addressed while deciphering alternate rhythms to breathe with and realign the breath to the other. It means constantly being attentive to one's breath, and to the breath of the other. Karen Barad eloquently articulates this in her paper *On Touching – The Inhuman That Therefore I Am (v1.1)*:

> All touching entails an infinite alterity, so that touching the other is touching all others, including the "self", and touching the "self" entails touching the strangers within. Even the smallest bits of matter are an unfathomable multitude. Each "individual" always already includes all possible intra-actions with "itself" through all the virtual others, including those that are non-contemporaneous with "itself." That is, every finite being is always already threaded through with an infinite alterity diffracted through being and time (2012, 7).

Breathe Wind into Me, Chapter 1 came out of this enquiry around ways we touch each other. Through the making I become one with the work. The toil of my breath is embedded within the sounds and the imagery. I impart my breath to the audience, to share, to breathe with. Trauma is the ruptured breath, the interrupted breath, I listen to where mine is interrupted, pause, realign, begin again. The viewer follows, alerted perhaps through the imagery, the other familiar sounds that are woven through the narrating voice. There is laughter, singing, the rumble of something in the distance, but still I breathe. Is it possible then that an alternative world could rest on a new culture of breath as the basic element of inter-connectedness, one, where we breathe with the other, breathe through our differences? Can a video such as *Breathe Wind into Me, Chapter 1* guide an audience into a deeper relationship with themselves, with others? These were the questions I was considering in the early stages of making. As the work progressed, so to, did my breath. The work developed in complexity, as did my understanding of what it is to tend to the self while listening to others. There was a constant layering of the memory of the original breath, with the breathing of the digital footage and the breath of the one (me) who was now editing, trimming, repairing, and preparing the footage for an audience. In this way I was also tending to my breath, to how my breath would be received. Reparation was taking place in the making, on a conscious and unconscious level.

The experience of trauma creates a tension in the body that ruptures the functioning of *normal* memory schemas, whether in an attempt to forget or an effort to remember. Dissociation not only exists as a coping mechanism to deal with trauma on an individual level but also collectively, i.e. culturally and societally. Remembering requires a reclaiming of the dissociated parts. Parts that could be described as frozen, or outside of the system. Integrating these aspects on an individual and collective level firstly involves recognising these fragments exist. The nature of dissociation is a numbing to that which is uncomfortable or denying that one is affected by such traumas. Denial can be complicated. It can be social, reinforced in communities, in conversations and in the media, and over time it gets passed down through generations. Psychological, deeply rooted in how we respond to the world, denial at its worst is absolute, a pretence that *this,* (whatever this is), does not exist and therefore "I" or "we" will not look – it is a refusal to face the reality of what has happened. But at the opposite end of the spectrum, denial is the beginning of a process to move towards clarity, realisation, and change. In *States of Denial* (2001), Stanley Cohen asks what does it mean to acknowledge atrocity and suffering? What do we do with our knowledge about the suffering of others, and what does this knowledge do to us? So, I ask, does a collective dissociation contribute to the difficulties of responding to the ecological crisis, to the convenient amnesia and forgotten histories that play a role in the migration disaster and the rise of the right wing? Why have we conveniently forgotten? What is this collective amnesia and therefore desire for the "better" past, the idealised notion of what once was, this feigned nostalgia.

Proposition 3: the haptic breath, creating a new narrative through sense

Which brings me to the concept of *the haptic breath*, derived from Marks, and Deleuze's notion of *haptic visuality*, as a way of seeing or knowing that exceeds sensory conventions. The haptic breath moves deeper into breathing with the other to the breath that both touches the self and touches the other, it is a coming into contact with the "exteriority within", a realisation of the active embodiment of matter, of "being in the world in its dynamic specificity." (Barad 2007, 377). It is the concept of breath that has the potential to embody the other and their experiences, to know oneself and the other through coming into contact with another through one's breath and vice versa. In the instance of the video *Breathe Wind into Me, Chapter 1*, the haptic breath extends beyond the *skin of the film* (Marks 2000) to the sensual interaction of breathing with the film and within the body. It is taking the film into the body through the breath. Approaching the work in this way is to reframe ocularcentrism in support of Haraway's feminist argument against the primacy of sight in the hierarchy of senses.[5]

The etymological root of *haptic* in Greek is *haptein* – to take hold of an object, fasten onto, or to touch it. Marks developed the concept of *haptic visuality* as a way of seeing or knowing that which exceeds sensory conventions, which looks at the distinction between haptic and optical images as vision that is tactile, "as though one were touching a film with one's eyes"

(Marks 2000, xi). Marks goes on to describe haptic as mimetic, pressing up to the object and taking its shape.

> Mimesis is a form of representation based on getting close enough to the other thing to become it. Again, the point is not to replace symbolisation, a form of representation that requires distance, with mimesis. Rather it is to maintain a robust flow between sensuous closeness and symbolic distance. (2002, xiii)

She emphasises the tactile and contagious quality of cinema as something viewers brush up against like another body. "The words contact, contingent, and contagion all share the Latin root contingere, 'to have contact with; pollute; befall'" (Marks 2000, xii). In phenomenological terms the haptic is a form of the visual that muddies intersubjective boundaries whilst psycho-analytically it is an aspect of the visual that moves between identification and immersion. As she comments: "The engagement of the haptic viewer occurs not simply in psychic registers but in the sensorium" (18). Haptic vision is the close-to-the-body form of perception of film as skin, which moves the work into "circulation among different audiences, all of which mark it with their presence" (Marks 2000, xi), "the eyes themselves function like organs of touch", and "move over the surface of its object to discern texture", (62) thereby taking in, or absorbing the imagery into the body. The haptic visual does not depend on the viewer identifying with a recognisable figure or character but on a more sensuous bodily relationship between the viewer and the subject, "haptic images and haptic visuality encourage a subjective position of intimacy and mutual entanglement between viewer and viewed." (Marks 2015, 227)

The installation of *Breathe Wind into Me, Chapter 1,* exhibited at Fabrica Gallery, in which the video was projected onto screens larger than the human form, encased the viewer. She/he stepped into the imagery, and into the sound. Seeing and hearing became an active process of immersion. If the sound of breath, of someone breathing has the potential for contagion, a realigning of patterns of breathing to those that breathe, so then *Breathe Wind into Me, Chapter 1* creates the space for the viewer to mimic that which moves through the video. And so, by accessing the haptic visual, and therefore the haptic breath we begin to re-evaluate our relationship to space, and those inhabiting it. Through conscious engagement with the haptic visual the possibility is created for an increased awareness of one's body, of its physicality, and the interaction with what is on the screen. This naturally extends to an increased consciousness between what one is seeing and the sounds of breathing. Sound, Marks writes, can also be haptic where the uncanniness of sound impacts the listener in ways that are not easy to explain (2000, xvi). Sound comes into "play insofar as it is experienced kinaesthetically; for example, the booming in the chest caused by deep bass tones, or the complex effects of rhythm on the body" (Marks 2000, xvi). The viewer, submerged in the sounds of another breathing, will activate both conscious and unconscious responses and interrupts a purely visual experience.

Shifting attention away from the purely visual to activate other senses is also a recurring theme in Haraway's work. She, like Irigaray continually questions the patriarchal language and primacy of sight in Western culture,

> the eyes have been used to signify a perverse capacity – honed to perfection in the history of science tied to militarism, capitalism, colonialism and male supremacy – to distance the knowing subject from everybody and everything in the interests of unfettered power (1988, 581).

In her book, *Staying with the Trouble, Making Kin in the Chthulucene* (2016), Haraway devises new ways to question patriarchal constructs. Through replacing the idea of relationships with kin, where making kin is connecting, she creates a multispecies that embraces all diversity. She calls on feminists to exercise leadership, brings art into the entanglement of biology and activism, and emphasises the power of storytelling and the need to radically alter the kinds of stories we tell. In *Staying with the Trouble* we begin to imagine ourselves as participants in collective world-making.

> I also insist that we need a name for the dynamic ongoing symchthonic forces and powers of which people are a part, within which ongoingness is at stake. (Haraway 2016, 100)

The breath is what connects all living species. I suggest making kin as a useful way to breath together.

> My purpose is to make "kin" mean something other/more than entities tied by ancestry or genealogy. The gently defamiliarizing move might seem for a while to be just a mistake, but then (with luck) appear as correct all along. Kin making is making persons, not necessarily as individuals or as humans. (2016, 102)

Through strong feminine figures and science fiction we begin to create alternative worlds that do not depend on a recycling of the past. This creates an interesting process of revisiting the past, from the future, a way to perceive history while taking responsibility, a way to reframe the present as a state of emergency. Put simply, a matter of restitution and apology while making plans for the future where trauma, shame and/or guilt are not the foundation for creating future narratives.

> If there is to be multispecies ecojustice, which can also embrace diverse human people, it is high time that feminists exercise leadership in imagination, theory, and action to unravel the ties of both genealogy and kin, and kin and species. (103)

Utilising the breath as an experiential tool to teach 187

Easier said than done, but nevertheless a consideration if we are to move forward. The breath and breathing are important to this development, a way to encourage honourable relations between human beings. To return to Irigaray:

> Breathing in a conscious and free manner is equivalent to taking charge of our life, to cutting the umbilical cord in order to respect and cultivate life for ourselves and for others. (2010, 4)

To breathe into the future, is to be aware and therefore responsible for each breath. It is to know when one's breath is tight or constricted. It is to feel when one's breath is not forthcoming. It is to take charge of all matters to do with one's body. This concept of the haptic breath emerges out of affect as a disruptive energy that escapes the restrictions of mind, reason, and cognition. Affect, (after Spinoza), is the capacity to affect and be affected. It invests strongly in a Deleuzian inspired model of intensities and locates affect in encounters in the world, rather than the interiority of the psychological. As such, emotion is the interiorization of affect towards psychological expression, situated in an unconscious "zone of indistinction" or "zone of indeterminacy" between thought and action (2015, 204). Attentiveness to affect, creates space. A gap opens up between cognition and affect, existing as an in-between state of either potential or foreclosure. This is the in-between space where the breath can be held, contained or released, the place of hope or alternatively, despair. It is the place of intention. To grasp it though, requires listening beyond the immediacy of a syncopated rhythm to a deeper sense of self, and readjusting to hold simultaneously what is in and out of breath. It is a becoming where each breath counts.

This links back to Haraway's *Staying with the Trouble* (2016), the commitment to "living and dying with response-ability in unexpected company of creating a new future based on fiction. Such living and dying have the best chance of cultivating conditions for ongoingness" (38). Quoting ethnographer Thomas van Dooren, she places mourning as intrinsic to cultivating response-ability. "Outside the dubious privileges of human exceptionalism, thinking people must learn to grieve-with" *(ibid)*, because we are all part of this undoing. "Without sustained remembrance, we cannot learn to live with ghosts and so cannot think" (39). The mimetic model of spectatorship creates entry into *Staying with the Trouble*, it generates a deepening awareness of the breath in relationship to the other, turns one's whole system into an interaction with inside and out. We breathe with our whole bodies and as Haraway asks why should our bodies end at the skin? (1991, 178).

At every stage of making *Breathe Wind into Me, Chapter 1*, I was aware of the relationship of haptic visuality to the positioning of the skin as a vast visual organ, thereby sensitising an audience to witnessing the work from a plurality of perspectives. The engagement of the whole body as a tool for seeing shifts the gaze to inhabit an exterior as well as an interior space. In The Tactile Eye

(2009), Jennifer Barker writes about muscular empathy, where viewers empathise with the body of a film so much so that they can experience and "grasp", the imagery in their muscles and tendons the exhilaration of the "close call" or the intimacy of a closeup. The viewer is *open out* and therefore *open to* absorb the sounds and the visuals on a complexity of levels. The body responds. In the process of sensing, seeing or hearing copy and contact are part of the same process (Taussig 1992, 2). A listening can be a contraction, a discomfort, or alternatively a softening, a coming into the space and into being with and beyond the *skin* of the film and to the relationship of the self and of the other. Breathing links up the visual to the body where the information is carried on the wave of each breath. The breath is in communication.

Michael Taussig insists that "what is crucial in the resurgence of the mimetic faculty" is precisely the "palpable, sensuous, connection between the very body of the perceiver and the perceived" (1992, 2). Mimesis ties the perceiver to the event, where copy and contact are steps in the same process. On this line of reasoning contact and copy merge with each other to become virtually identical, different moments of the one process of sensing; seeing something or hearing something is to be in contact with that something (Taussig 1992, 2). So, it would follow, the mimetic breath ties us together, to events, to *response-ability*.

Taussig also goes on to write about the depth and the complexity of the relationship between the image and the bodily involvement of the perceiver. A complexity we too easily regard as non-mysterious with terms that simultaneously "depend upon and erase all that is powerful and obscure in the network of associations conjured by the notion of the mimetic" (1992, 2). Here, mimesis is arrived at through three considerations: alterity, primitivism, and the link between mimesis and modernity. This notion of resurfacing primitivism "as a direct result of modernity" is based on the assumption and the importance of mimesis to ritualistic practices of ancient societies; mimesis triggered by "the revelation of the optical unconscious made possible by mimetic machinery like the camera and the movies" (Taussig 1992, 1). Taussig suggests, mass culture: "both stimulates and is predicated upon mimetic modes of perception in which spontaneity, animation of objects, and a language of the body combining thought with action, sensuousness with intellection, is paramount" (1992, 1).

The interconnected breath, breathing in union, in communion, with all of its ruptured interruptions is about embracing the tension between the concrete and speculative, sensing and knowing. It means being in touch with oneself, the other, the world. It is expanding the awareness of how the breath touches the other, while engaging actively with the embodiment of perception, affect, thinking and caring. It is making kin through the breath.

For Martia Puig de la Bellacasa, "Embodiment, relationality, and engagement are all themes that have marked feminist epistemology and knowledge politics" (2017, 97). Being *in touch* with how the visual and the aural penetrates one's body is to consciously be aware of the breath.

Questioning the affect is to re-appropriate, in Haraway's words, the "persistence of vision." As she writes, "I would like to insist on the embodied nature of all vision, and so reclaim the sensory system that has been used to signify a leap out of the marked body and into a conquering gaze from nowhere" (1988). Bringing awareness to the breath and how it touches us expands Haraway's "situated knowledge", to embrace a *knowledge* beyond *knowing*. It is to participate in Puig de la Bellacasa's reclamation of touch as a form of "caring knowing", thinking with touch as a means to question anew (2017, 98).

Breath Wind into Me, Chapter 1, is about caring, it extends the concept of the breath as touching upon and with the visual, and it links a complex interplay of affect and sensation to reframe Bergson's concept of attentive recognition through a feminist epistemology. It is creating afresh "not only the object perceived, but also the ever-widening systems with which it maybe bound up" (Marks 2000, 48). It is an effort to cultivate and nurture the breath as a method of communication that goes beyond the surface, an endeavour in support of Irigaray's philosophy:

> Not only does our culture not teach us how to cultivate breathing to assure our existence in an autonomous way, but it does not make known to us that becoming spiritual amounts to transforming our elemental vital breath into a more subtle breath at the service of loving, of speaking and hearing, of thinking (Irigaray 2010, 4).

Finally

It is important to be affected, to be outraged, to correspond to political forces of oppression and power. Even in the absence of actions, passions are present, which in turn may manifest in chance, or aleatory encounters and assemblages of experiences. It is the collective, the interactive encounter that links becoming to becoming-with and the potential to create community and spaces for breathing. But it is equally important to listen, to breath, to perceive with the whole body.

In *Air and Dreams* (1943), Gaston Bachelard writes, "breath ... is ... the premier phenomenon of silence of being", that is, there is "the silence that breathes" (193). In the silence we attend to ourselves, to each other and to the inside and outside of the self. In our attentiveness we receive ourselves and each other. Self-affection is based on our inchoate receptivity for the needs of the other, thus we can critically engage the idea of an ethical becoming. Our affective capacity defines the body in action. Deleuze suggests it is impossible to know ahead of time "the affects one is capable of" (Deleuze 1988, 125). But if we are practised and alert to our breath, our patterns of breathing, and the breath of the other, we can start to forge a knowing, a practical wisdom.

Breath Wind into Me, Chapter 1, is but the first step of research in an ongoing enquiry in how to move forward from trauma. It is thinking through making, staying open to the emergent properties of the intrapsychic as well as the intersubjective. The aim is to find a balance between the individual and the collective. A space for reflection, contemplation, and difficult conversations, while addressing far-reaching and collective issues. Using film, sound technology and text the intention is to transfer these spaces for breathing from the community to moving imagery and sound installations, and to the internet. As Stewart reflects: "A world can whisper from a half-lived sensibility. It can demand collective attunement and a more adequate description of how things make sense" (2010, 6).

Notes

1 https://www.anna-walker-research.com/chapter-1.html
2 See Fig. 1/2.
3 Here, what I mean by *just*, is a becoming that honours difference that doesn't deviate into hierarchical structures.
4 Here, she leaves a critique of patriarchy to the development of a foundation for a possible inter-subjectivity between the two sexes. She poses the question: how can we move to a new era of sexual difference in which women and men establish lasting relations with one another without reducing the other to the status of object? She argues for what she calls "sexed rights" and a right of persons based on the right to life, not the right to property.
5 Also see Laura Mulvey's original article on the phallocentrism of visual pleasure: *Visual Pleasure of Narrative Cinema* (1989).

References

Bachelard, G. (1943) *Air and Dreams, An Essay on the Imagination of Movement*. Trans. Edith R. Farrell & C. Frederick Farrell. Dallas, US: The Dallas Institute Publications.
Barad, K. (2007) *Meeting the Universe Halfway, Quantum Physics and the Entanglement of Matter and Meaning*. London: Duke University Press.
Barad, K. (2012) On Touching – The Inhuman That Therefore I Am, *The Politics of Materiality*, edited by Susanne Witzgall, 23 (3): 206–223.
Barker, J. (2009) *The Tactile Eye, Touch and the Cinematic Experience*. California: University of California Press.
Bergson, H. (2004) *Matter and Memory*. Mineola, New York: Dover Publications, Inc.
Blackman, L. (2012) *Immaterial Bodies, Affect, embodiment, Mediation*. London: Sage Publications Inc.
Brennan, T. (2004) *The Transmission of Affect*. Ithaca and London: Cornell University Press.
Cohen, S. (2001) *States of Denial: Knowing About Atrocities and Suffering*. Cambridge: Polity Press.
Conner, S. (2000) *Dumbstruck: A Cultural History of Ventriloquism*. New York: Oxford University Press.

Connor, S. (2012) *Panophonia*. Talk given at the Pompidou Centre, 22nd February 2012.
Deleuze, G. & Guattari, F. (1988) *A Thousand Plateaus: Capitalism and schizophrenia II*. Trans. B. Massumi. London: The Athlone Press.
Derrida, J. (1993/1994) *Specters of Marx*. Trans. P. Kamuf. New York: Routledge [etc.].
Derrida, J. (2001) *The Work of Mourning*. Trans. P. A. Brault & M. Naas. Chicago: The University of Chicago Press [etc.].
Derrida, J. (2007) *Psyche, Inventions of the Other*, Volume 1. Trans. P. Kamuf & E. Rottenber. California: Stanford University Press.
Derrida, J. & Chakravorty Spivak, G. (1974) Linguistics and Grammatology, *SubStance*, 4 (10) (Autumn, 1974): 127–181.
Freud, S. (1919) *The Uncanny*. http://web.mit.edu/allanmc/www/freud1.pdf (Accessed 1 December 2015).
Freud, S. (1950 [1895]) *Nachtraglichkeit – Project for a Scientific Psychology*. http://www.lacanianworks.net/?p=401 (Accessed 25 June 2015).
Gregg, M. & Seigworth, G. J. (eds.) (2010) *The Affect Theory Reader*. Durham, NC: Duke University Press.
Haraway, D. (1988) Situated Knowledges: The Science Question in Feminism and the Privilege of Partial Perspective, *Feminist Studies*, 14 (3) (Autumn, 1988): 575–599. Published by: Feminist Studies. https://www.jstor.org/stable/3178066
Haraway, D. (1991) A Cyborg Manifesto: Science, Technology, and Socialist-feminism in the 1980s. In Linda Nicholson, ed. *Feminism/Postmodernism*. New York: Routledge.
Haraway, D. (1998) The Persistence of Vision. In Nicholas Mirzeoff, ed. *The Visual Culture Reader*. London and New York: Routledge: 191–198.
Haraway, D. (2016) *Staying with the Trouble, Making Kin in the Chthulucene*. Durham/London: Duke University Press.
Ingold, T. (2010) Bringing Things to Life: Creative Entanglement in a World of Materials. *NCRM Working Paper Series, ESRC National Centre for Research Methodologies*. Manchester.
Irigaray, L. (1996) *I Love to You: Sketch for a Felicity within History*. Routledge.
Irigaray, L. (1999) *The Forgetting of Air in Martin Heidegger*. London: Athlon Press.
Irigaray, L. (2001) From *The Forgetting of Air to To Be two*. In N. Holland & P. Huntington, eds. *Feminist Interpretations of Martin Heidegger*. Pennsylvania: Pennsylvania State University Press.
Irigaray, L. (2010) Ethical gestures toward the other, *Poligrafi*, 15 (57): 3–23.
Irigaray, L. (2013) To Begin with Breathung Anew'. In L. Skof & E. A. Holmes, eds. *Towards Breathing with Luce Irigaray*. London: Bloomsbury Academic.
Marks, L. U. (2000) *The Skin of the Film: Intercultural Cinema, Embodiment, and the Senses*. Durham and London: Duke University Press.
Marks, L. U. (2002) *Touch, Sensuous Theory and Multisensory Media*. London [etc.]. University of Minnesota Press.
Marks, L. U. (2015) *Hanan al-cinema, Affections for the Moving Image*. Cambridge, MA: MIT.
Massumi, B. (1998) Event Horizon. In Joke Brouwer, ed. *From The Art of the Accident*. Rotterdam: Dutch Architecture Institute/V2: 154–168.

Massumi, B. (2010) The Future Birth of the Affective Fact: The Political Ontology of Threat. In M. Gregg & G. J. Seigworth, eds. *The Affect Theory Reader*. Durham, NC + London, UK: Duke University Press: 52–70.

Merleau-Ponty, M. (1992) *The Merleau-Ponty Aesthetics Reader.* In Galen A. Johnson, ed., Michael B. Smith, trans. Evanstong, IL: Northwestern Universoty Press.

Merleau-Ponty, M. (2013) *Phenomenology of the Perception*. Trans. Donald A. Landes. London/ NY: Routledge.

Mulvey L. (1989) *Visual Pleasure and Narrative Cinema.* In: Visual and Other Pleasures. Language, Discourse, Society, London: Palgrave Macmillan. Available at: https://luxonline.org.uk/articles/visual_pleasure_and_narrative_cinema(printversion).html (Accessed 17 April 2007).

Puig de la Bellacasa, P. (2017) *Matters of Care*. Minneapolis: University of Minnesota Press.

Roth, M. S. (2012) *Memory, Trauma, and History: Essays on Living with the Past*. New York: Columbia University Press.

Schiefelbein, S. (1986) *The Incredible Machine*. Washington, D.C.: National Geographic Society.

Skof, L. & Berndtson, P. (2019) *Atmospheres of Breathing*. New York: State of New York Press.

Skof, L. & Holmes, E. A. (2013) *Breathing with Luce Irigaray*. London: Bloomsbury Academic.

Sloterdijk, P. (2016) *Foams*, Spheres Volume III: Plural Spherology, Trans. Wieland Hoban. Semiotext(e) / Foreign Agent Series. Cambridge, MA: MIT.

Stewart, K. (2010) Atmospheric Attunements. *Rubric*, Issue 1, Writing from UNSW. https://s3.amazonaws.com/arena-attachments/525663/aa329a589b83cbc-48a4793e3102569fe.pdf

Stowers Lab (2016) *Vomeronasal organ (VNO)*. Available at: http://www.scripps.edu/stowers/ (Accessed 17 April 2016).

Taussig, M. (1992) *Terror as Usual: Walter Benjamin's Theory of History as a State of Seige. Social Text*, 23, 3–20. Available at: http://www.jstor.org/stable/466418 (Accessed 24 August 2011).

Vermetten, Eric A. U., Bremner, James P. Y. (2003) Olfaction as a Traumatic Reminder in Posttraumatic Stress Disorder: Case Reports and Review. *The Journal of Clinical Psychiatry*, 64: 202–207. https://doi.org/10.4088/JCP.v64n0214

13 Art therapy and integral education with traumatised youths in Bosnia-Herzegovina

Anna Druka and Hannah Scaramella

Introduction

The experience to which we refer in this chapter was born with the aim to give psychological support to the young generations after the war in Bosnia-Herzegovina. The project took place in Tuzla, Bosnia-Herzegovina from 2007 to 2009 and involved around 30 teenagers and preteens divided into three groups. They used art materials to explore their feelings and later shared this in a circle format. The participants were chosen by the adults of reference, including the psychologists of the orphanage. The most significant experiences were with three groups of adolescents and preadolescents, from the orphanage and refugee camp. The project was supported by a local association in Tuzla, which cares for children without families, as well as by the orphanages and the refugees camp in Tuzla. Financially, there was aid provided by an elaborate list of sponsors. After each meeting, feedback was given to the sponsors. There was also individual psychological support during the process.

The settings of work in the group

The settings of work in the group were based on the Integral Education method and on these following elements:

1. Creating a safe environment, based on trust and on a non-judgemental attitude, that would facilitate the expression and sharing of feelings.
2. Participants were free to choose between classic and recyclable art materials (leaves, stones, beads, etc.).
3. The topics of the meetings, based on which the images were created, emerged mostly spontaneously from the moods expressed by the participants at the beginning of the meeting.
4. Representations of feelings such as anger, desires, etc. – the images or small sculptures were individual, or group works on large common sheets.

The process and the results are based on observations of the behaviour of the youths in their daily environment for the duration of the project – an orphanage and a refugee camp. The beginning of the work with the youths was characterised by strong resistance to the proposed environment. The features of relationships between the youths at the beginning included: fear of others; acting out; bullying; aggression and hostility; avoidance of contact and connection with others; low tolerance of other people; inability to recognise and respect their emotions; inability to trust each other; inability to be in a group. Above the resistance, fear, shame, and all the negative feelings that initially dominated the relations between them, gradually, during group meetings the youths began to develop a taste for the new type of environment. They were welcomed with love, listened to and respected despite what they said or drew, and this was something that opened a door for them and allowed them to begin feeling a new pleasure in being with others.

After the first months of weekly meetings with the three groups, their way of relating to each other began to change radically and it was possible for them to express themselves and listen to the experiences and feelings of the members of the group, to identify with them and to start trusting the group. It seemed as if a new reality was formed in the relationships between them and through the insights they expressed with the group. Towards the end of the project, a 14-year-old boy wrote, "*My reward has been to feel part of this group.*" The statement shows that a value has been placed on the experience and an understanding of the need for a supportive environment has emerged. A 14-year-old girl wrote, "*Everyone has given something to me of himself and I have been able to give something of myself to the others: after this experience, I feel richer within and I bring to my house a lot of red fruits.*" This statement also expresses a value being placed on emotional ties and healthy social interaction. The author of the comment also shows an awareness of the personal growth she gained during the experience. At the end of the project, some of the participants drew a joint mutual conclusion: *"The secret to creating peace is to be united."* This comment expresses the sum value of what the participants experienced and understood during the project. From the scars of a reality of war, violence and hatred with no means of control or self-regulation, the participants of the project learned to find comfort in each other and in themselves, eventually, re-discovering hope and the possibility of healing

Although it can be argued that recovery and healing are a part of human nature and in a sense, we are drawn to heal or cope in whatever way possible, tailored and thought out intervention allows for the healing process to happen faster and on a deeper level. What contributed to the changes that took place in the dynamics of the group of participants were various factors, implemented, monitored, and adjusted by the leading staff of the project.

Elements that contributed to the change in relations among the youths

In light of this experience, it seems important for us to reflect also on the possibility of implementing these elements in similar social contexts. What we have learned during these years of experience is how crucial it is to educate ourselves as human beings about the necessity and meaning of mutual connection and responsibility as well as the necessity to shape this as a contribution to forestall repetition of social clashes and wars. This is because "Our wellbeing is inextricably intertwined with that of strangers from around the globe… . At some point, we'll have to move beyond fighting mode and adapt to our interconnectedness" (Laitman & Ulianov 2012).

Albert Einstein thought that a human being is part of the whole called by us "universe." We experience ourselves, our thoughts, and feelings as something separate from the rest, a kind of optical delusion of consciousness (Popova 2011).

> It's not the trauma itself that causes the most long-term damage; it is how the trauma wreaks havoc on the psyche and prevents reintegration into a normal, healthy life where other people and unknown situations are seen as benevolent. The foremost pillar of happiness is a sense of belonging and purpose. Cultures that are more communal are more mentally healthy as a whole. People who are alone often die earlier and get sicker before they do. We are a tribal species. There is no way around this despite what many highly individualistic cultures may want us to believe. No person is an island unto themselves. We are born through connection, and it is through connection to others that we accomplish virtually everything else in life. We do not just prefer healthy relationships; we need them. (Wiest 2018)

About the method used

The method consisted of five elements which were interwoven into a framework adapted to suit the needs and pace of the recipients. The environment was created to be such that it provides an example of attitudes, actions and interactions. The workshops were tailored to allow to scrutinise deeper questions about one's life and learn to lean on peers for support and scrutiny. Group work was there to provide a framework and a sense of discipline among peers to develop a natural, healthy sense of discipline based on the pleasant feelings they begun to feel between themselves. Through group work, they began to contribute to the environment by taking care of emotions. Group work also acted as a framework for socialising. Art therapy was used to allow each member of the project to acknowledge and process his or her emotions individually. The focus on connection allowed to create deep bonding, acceptance, compassion for oneself and one's peers.

The main factor that played a crucial role was the connection that was created in the group, which complemented and resulted from the other elements already mentioned. The Connection Circle (CC) is the most commonly used tool in Integral Education (IE) for adults and youths. It is a simple and effective form of discussion that creates warmth and harmony among people, whether they know each other or have just met. The circle is a unique shape: it has no angles, and no beginning or end. You cannot sit at the head of a circular table because a circle doesn't have a head; all of its points are equally removed from the centre. King Arthur's Knights of the Round Table knew this and conducted their discussions precisely around such a table to emphasise that they had reached their decisions together, without any one knight imposing his views on the others.

Because of its unique qualities, the circle symbolises equality. People seated in a circle tend to feel equally worthy. This allows them to both contribute to the rest of the people in the circle and receive from them without the need to protect themselves from the other people's criticism. To maintain that atmosphere, many people who conduct CCs make it a rule that putting someone down is strictly forbidden. As soon as criticism enters the circle, harmony and warmth fly out the window. We learned the method of Integral Education from the ARI Institute, which teaches students in many countries across the world.

In short, the values of Integral Education answer to the fact that we are all living in trying times, confronted by personal, environmental, and social crises. These crises are occurring because humankind has been unable to perceive the interconnectedness and interdependence among us and between humanity and nature. By providing information to the public through a rich environment, we act as a catalyst to shift human behaviour towards a more sustainable model. We advocate a solution to the current global challenges and promote it through our unique educational content. Through extensive research and public activities, ARI Institute offers a clear, coherent understanding of the natural development of the events and societal degradation that have led to the current state of affairs in our global, integral world (Laitman 2015).

Reflecting on the methodology

When considering the topic of connection, we find that it is important and beneficial to look at it in very broad terms across a wide spectrum. It is hard to define connection or connectedness on a human level, since it is intangible by nature. We are talking largely about feelings, but not necessarily emotions. We are talking about communication, but not necessarily word choice, speaking, or listening skills. We are talking about mutual respect, but not necessarily politeness. We are talking about empathy, but not necessarily being sensitive; we are talking about being sensitive, but not necessarily sentimental. It is difficult to pin down what connection really is and how to establish it in a group setting, yet it proves itself as such a natural and deeply ingrained part of being human and belonging to the dynamic system of existence that we know as life.

As far as neuroscience is concerned, there are studies conducted by Dr. Daniel J. Siegel, notably of which "The Neurobiology of We" talks specifically about the way our brain is wired for connection. According to Siegel, connection is biologically and chemically ingrained in us and benefits our development, thus providing the much-needed scientific proof and motivation to continue with this work at times when individuality and personal wellbeing seems to dominate the popular culture (Siegel 2008). In the field of psychology, the need to focus on connection is becoming increasingly more recognised. Authors such as Johann Hari claim to have discovered the single greatest cause of depression: separateness or disconnection in its varying forms (Hari 2018). In the field of communication, public relations and politics, the notion of connectedness has long been used and abused. Today, we see an inclination towards better understanding, truthfulness, patience, awareness, and inclusion. Non-violent communication is becoming a more widely recognised form of communication norm while dismissing the notion of an unrealistic world where everyone gets along with everyone. It is as if we are finally ready to stop trying to like each other and be liked, and instead are beginning to work on understanding each other and being understood in our most genuine, specific and honest needs, desires and values which make us human. A wonderful book about this topic is "Collaborating With The Enemy" by Adam Kahane (Kahane 2017).

A clearer picture emerges once we look at the notion of connection and its essence in various contexts. One may need to use slightly different language and information base when engaging with traumatised children or with opposing politicians, but nonetheless, the essence of creating connection and its importance remains the same. It appears for every form of conflict, disagreement, separateness, and disconnection there is a form of connection, togetherness, understanding, and agreement to be discovered. All that remains to do, is to learn how.

Repeating and replicating the methodology

The method which was used in this project can be repeated and replicated elsewhere by combining the various elements and adjusting them to suit the present circumstances. For example, an intense, week-long rehabilitation retreat may require more focused and intense workshops right from the beginning than a therapeutic process lasting several months or more. It is important for the moderators and facilitators of the method to think about the ways in which each of the elements of the method will influence and contribute to the healing of the receivers of the method. This does not necessarily mean that the facilitators and moderators of the method need to be exquisitely skilled in each of the areas contained in the method. Rather, they themselves must be willing to use parts of the method to think deeply about the true needs of their subjects. Some training in conducting workshops is essential as it involves skills unique to the method. Risks in repeating and replicating the implementation of the method may include making premature assumptions about the effects or the results of the process. Lack of proper guidance during crucial points in the process may also contribute to the risk of having to go back a few steps, thus slowing down the process. Appropriate training and experience in working with the method and adapting it to different settings provide the confidence, skills, and ability to reduce risk. The following section provides guidelines for the implementation of the method and adapting it to various settings.

Guidelines for implementing the method

To implement the method in a practical way, having guidelines, rather than rules will determine the success of the outcome. The facilitator's attitude and flexibility will set the tone for the resulting outcomes of each session as well as the overall result. It is recommended that the facilitators are trained in and use the method themselves, however, what is even more important than long term experience and knowledge in the field, is genuine engagement with the recipients of the method. The facilitator must be willing to share of themselves genuinely and fully while maintaining the tone of conversation and purposeful guidance during the process. There are what are known as "rules of the workshop", which serve as the guidelines for conducting conversations or workshops in a circle. It is important to ensure that all participants – facilitators and receivers of the method – adhere to these rules by gentle guidance rather than strict order. This can be achieved most effectively by taking the time to discuss the importance and reasons for having such "rules." Rules of the workshop include four main points to remember, which can be elaborated upon and discussed in the circle. Discussion about the necessity of the rules and the importance of their implementation helps to build a foundation for a framework of communication aimed at healing. The first rule is that no one is more important or less important. Everyone is equal and very important. This rule is there to help develop a culture of listening, where the ability to listen, hear and be heard becomes a possibility despite differing opinions or experience.

The second rule implies that we don't reject opinions or negate, but only collaborate. This rule serves the purpose of directing the flow of the conversation to the optimal direction and lessens the chances of meaningless discussion which can lead to hostility and deterioration of the therapeutic environment.

The third rule implies that the real solution won't come from knowledge or verbal perfection, but only from our connection. This rule helps to tear down socially and culturally conditioned responses to status and assumed opinions about someone's importance or unimportance and value of opinion based on their skills or status. The fourth rule asks to speak shortly and from the heart. This is an additional rule to the original three, to keep the conversation heart-focused and flowing, which ensures equal participation between those with greater and lesser inclination to express themselves verbally as well as maintain a good balance between speaking and listening. As described by Michael Laitman,

> the heart and soul of the Connection Circle is the workshop. This is where we connect! Once people are ready to open their hearts a little, you can switch to workshop mode and ask your first question. Remember, the purpose of the workshop is to make people enjoy the connection! It is great to have a good time with friends doing something you all like. But here we are talking about another level of happiness. When people feel connected, they feel confident, relaxed, and optimistic. They feel this because they are connecting to the fundamental quality of connection (Laitman 2015).

Replacing the cycle of violence with a circle of love

It is not always easy to put the ego aside, engage with and open to connection with fellow human beings. To do that, especially for adults, there needs to be a choice, a desire or a necessity to heal. Often this comes at a time of crises when all other options have been drained of their merit. Too often it takes a family crisis, a tragedy or the breakout of a war to realise that the humble acceptance of the presence, words and thoughts of the other is the key to finding the freedom, safety and peace so many of us dream of.

In his book, "It Didn't Start with You: How Inherited Family Trauma Shapes Who We Are and How to End the Cycle", author Mark Wolynn describes his own struggles, research and healing techniques used to overcome inherited family trauma, which spread across generations. Wolynn discovered, like many others, that the ultimate cure lies in a connection to those closest to us, or if that is not a possibility, to seek out a way to create a connection with others, who will become close as mutual healing takes place (Wolynn 2016).

Wolynn also makes a point that trauma, which is not healed looks for opportunities to be healed in later generations. Trauma keeps repeating itself until healing is brought about. Although it is not evident to what extent inherited trauma or trauma from experience affects us as individuals, communities or the society at large, there never seems to be a lack of the need for healing (Wolynn 2016). The global culture provides a means for pressures to display individual qualities and strive for solitary achievement and detachment while hiding vulnerability and our true needs for closeness. We still have a long way to go until the system we live in becomes truly suitable for these needs, however, it is our responsibility to aid in creating spaces, mechanisms and ultimately systems for human connection.

Conclusions on the experience with adolescents in Bosnia

The experience with youth groups has taught us a lot – adults as well as children. We have come to know a new quality of relationship between us, based on a new type of reciprocity, in which we have recognised ourselves in others and others in ourselves. Through this specularity and the sense of mutual responsibility that was born in the groups, a very powerful connection was created, capable of defeating fears and healing the internal wounds consequent to the trauma suffered during the war. We have felt the strength of the network of connections between us as humans and found this to be something that acts in a subtle and profound form, an influence we are not usually aware of. It is as if every human being belongs to a unique and invisible system, an organism similar to the human body, in which each of us is an organ that makes life possible through mutual interaction. In return, each of us is dependent on the health of this organism – the state of health of our society depends on the relationships between us, and from this point of view, each of us is responsible for others and vice versa, none excluded.

In conclusion, during this experience, we felt the importance of educating ourselves, both adults and children, about how much we depend on each other. If starting from school and Preschool levels, we would cultivate the values of mutual responsibility, rather than competition and if our human interactions were based on respect and mutual good, just like the interactions between the organs of the human body, then our society could become an environment in which not only those who have suffered terrible trauma would find the safe and protected refuge they need, but probably the causes of trauma and wars themselves will no longer have reason to exist.

References

Hari, J. (2018) *Lost Connections: Uncovering The Real Causes Of Depression – And The Unexpected Solutions*. USA: Bloomsbury.
Kahane, A. (2017) *Collaborating With The Enemy: How To Work With People You Don't Agree With Or Like Or Trust*. Berrett-Koehler Publishers.
Laitman, M. (2015) *Completing the Circle: An Empirically Proven Method for Finding Peace and Harmony in Life*. Toronto, New York: ARI Publishers.
Laitman, M. & Ulianov, A. (2012) *A Guide to the New World: Why Mutual Guarantee is the Key to our Recovery from the Global Crisis*. Toronto, New York: ARI Publishers.

Popova, M. (2011) *The Quantum and the Lotus: A Journey to the Frontiers Where Science and Buddhism Meet.* New York, NY: The Three Rivers press.

Rosenberg, M. B. (2015) *Nonviolent Communication: A Language of Life.* Encinitas, CA: PuddleDancer Press.

Siegel, D. J. (2008) *The Neurobiology of "We": How Relationships, the Mind, and the Brain Interact to Shape Who We Are.* Audio CD: Sounds True.

Wiest, B. (2018) *Connection Is a Core Human Need, But We Are Terrible at It.* Medium.

Wolynn, M. (2016) *It Didn't Start with You: How Inherited Family Trauma Shapes Who We Are and How to End the Cycle.* New York: Penguin Books.

14 Poetry against Trump: shared experience and creative resistance

Adam Beardsworth

On 16 June 2015, then business mogul Donald Trump descended the golden elevator of his eponymous New York tower and announced his Presidential bid to a few dozen supporters, many of whom, it would later emerge, were paid $50 each by the Trump campaign to attend the event. From a small temporary stage, Trump kicked off his campaign with remarks aimed at garnering the support of an increasingly vocal, and predominantly white, American populist base by identifying immigration, and racialised minorities, as threats to both the physical and economic security of white Middle America. For instance, in his now notoriously divisive style, Trump announced his entrance into the presidential race with overtly racist comments aimed at securing the support of his xenophobic followers:

> When Mexico sends its people, they're not sending their best, they're sending people that have lots of problems, and they're bringing those problems with us [sic]. They're bringing drugs, they're bringing crime, they're rapists. And some, I assume, are good people.

From that point on, Trump's Presidential campaign was characterised by a litany of inflammatory remarks aimed at racialised minorities, immigrants, and women. With the public support of several Alt-right mouthpieces, including Steve Bannon, Alex Jones, and even the KKK's David Duke, it became clear that Trump's racist and misogynist comments were more than the musings of an ignorant candidate; they were campaign strategies aimed at further inflaming the already volatile constituencies of a conservative, white America deeply concerned about threats to what it perceived as fundamental American values.

For most candidates, being caught on tape claiming that when you're a star you can do anything to women, even "grab 'em by the pussy", would spell the end of a Presidential run. However, Trump's penchant for xenophobic, racist, anti-trans, and misogynistic comments seemed to strengthen his campaign, making him the straight-talking, no-nonsense candidate for the millions of Americans who shared his troubling (and troubled) views. On 8 November 2016, when Trump became only the fifth President to win the election while simultaneously losing the popular vote, the slow process of consecrating his troubled private opinions into public policy began, a process that has sought to delegitimise, victimise, and even vilify the millions of Americans whose gender, race, and politics do not fit the President's pseudo-nostalgic, and wholly mythical, vision of a "Great" America.

Trump's election highlighted longstanding divides in American culture and politics. Since then, his habit of taking direct, public aim at immigrants and minorities, both through his Twitter account and through the isolationist policies that he heralds, has simultaneously legitimised and normalised the currents of xenophobia, racism, and misogyny that have been bubbling beneath the American mainstream for decades. For many of the millions of Americans who did not vote for Trump, his inflammatory tweets, racist barbs, and reckless boasting have been a source of frustration, anxiety, and even fear. Immigrants from many nations, though most particularly those from majority Muslim or Latin American backgrounds, fear political persecution borne along racialised lines. Women and their families fear the repeal of long fought-for rights as conservative judges revisit *Roe vs. Wade*, a decision which has protected American women's right to choose since 1973. African American, Latino, and Jewish communities have grown anxious about the President's unwillingness to denounce white supremacist and anti-Semitic groups even after outbreaks of racially motivated violence, and in spite of both public outcry and demands from other politicians that the President uphold the civic and moral values demanded of his office. Indeed, Trump's unwillingness to condemn the persecution of minority groups, which for many of his far-right leaning supporters is as good as an endorsement of their views, has left many innocent Americans afraid that his attitudes can only lead to increased violence in American culture. Further, Trump's climate denialism, diplomatic tantrums, and deliberate courting of trade (and military) wars appear to jeopardise, on nearly a daily basis, the economic, political, and even existential security of a once-proud nation.

For many Americans, and indeed for many citizens around the world, the uncertainty cultivated by Trump's rhetoric and policies are a source of physical, symbolic, and rhetorical violence. In the contemporary North American university classroom, the effects of what has been referred to as "Trump trauma" in the popular media are routinely visible. Increased instances of student anxiety, pervasive feelings of helplessness in the face of political volatility, fears about future careers, relationships, and child-bearing, and frustration over the normalisation of racist, anti-Semitic, and misogynist behavior are all common student responses when discussions of contemporary politics arise in the classroom. The purpose of this chapter is to discuss experiential learning strategies for combatting the impact of Trump trauma in the contemporary English literature classroom. In particular, I will show how experiential learning activities that require imagination and ingenuity combined with critical self-reflection can create a shared vulnerability that foregrounds the power of witness and testimony as powerful means of contextualising, and coming to terms with, the traumatic fallout of their current political moment. Finally, I will discuss how teaching poetry, and political poetry, in particular, extends this shared vulnerability by allowing students to embrace the poetic as an unassimilable space of witnessing both past and future traumas and providing guidance for forging their own discourses of resistance.

Teaching Trump in context: affective politics

Before considering effective means of teaching Trump in relation to the context of post-Second World War American politics, it is important to establish the context of my own pedagogical situation. The classes with whom I worked on establishing shared vulnerability through poetry as an effective means of contending with Trump Trauma were first-year English classes at my institution in Western Newfoundland, Canada. While Trump bears no tangible political control over Canada, his overbearing personality, as well as his threats to global security, have an intangible impact over the daily lives of our predominantly Canadian students. Whether through news media, social media, memes, or late-night comedians, the shadow cast by Trump's Presidency extends well beyond national borders. As Chaiya Heller argues, there are real psychological implications for those of us exposed to Trump's "reality by decree" (2017, 9):

> Since his presidential win, there has been ubiquitous discussion of the impact of a Trump presidency on survivors of social trauma: this is because social trauma rests on a distortion of reality.... Trump purposefully manipulates the truth like a street performer twists balloons into animals. With each new bizarre and menacing decree, trauma survivors feel unable to hold onto a vision of a rational and just world where people wielding tremendous authority are held accountable for their words and actions (2017, 9).

Trump is a president who refers to women as pigs and dogs and appoints Supreme Court nominees who, like the President, have been accused of sexual assault by several women. He is a president who has attempted to ban trans and non-binary people from the military and who signs executive orders to enforce travel bans against Muslim countries; he is a president who mingles with the Alt-right and defends racially motivated violence. He is a president who authorises the detention of children and the fracturing of families as a form of deterrence at the Mexican border. For trauma survivors in particular, and for rational citizens in general, the manner in which Trump's actions destabilise any belief in the possibility of a "rational and just world" is at once deeply unsettling and has the potential for inflicting further trauma. From a pedagogical perspective, it is important to provide students with the intellectual tools necessary for recognising Trump's rhetoric as a form of discursive politics specifically aimed at fracturing social solidarity and alienating subjects, most specifically those from minority backgrounds. Providing these tools is, at least in part, a matter of helping students place Trump's presidency within a wider historical context that demonstrates its affiliations with a long history of fear-based political initiatives.

For many of my first-year English students, whose general knowledge of history and politics tends to be fairly rudimentary, Trump's presidency, along with its hate-filled rhetoric, seems to be a frightening anomaly that lacks any historical context. Without that context, their existence in the Trump era can feel overwhelming given the daily barrage of anxiety-inducing news. In other words, my Canadian students, who are exposed daily to newsfeeds, television reports, and podcasts repeating Trump's divisive rhetoric and making predictions and declarations of their own, are victims of an affective politics aimed precisely at keeping them anxious and fearful – of foreign threats, immigrant incursions, and domestic disputes fought along racialised lines. While Canada is one step removed from the immediate political situation of the United States, the pervasive anxiety propagated by American media, as well as by the American President himself, knows no national boundaries.

To this effect, I chose to administer a short, anonymous survey to students enrolled in my first-year critical reading and writing classes in order to better understand the level of anxiety they felt in relation to their contemporary political situation. The survey unanimously confirmed that many of them do indeed suffer from anxiety related to issues that have frequently been inflamed by Trump's grandstanding. Students overwhelmingly responded in ways that confirmed their feelings of anxiety over issues such as racialised violence, gun violence, homophobia and transphobia, and climate change. They predominantly commented that they received their news through social media and other online sources. When they were asked to comment about whether or not they felt hope for the future, they said things like "the future seems scary to me", "I feel nervous and scared but I try to be hopeful", "I'm worried about the world my children will grow up in", "I wonder if it is even worth having children", and "the world is only going to get worse."

Within the context of Trump's tumultuous presidency, it is natural for students to feel traumatised. As Cathy Caruth argues, "to be traumatized is precisely to be possessed by an image or event" (1991, 3). Trump's exploitation of America's traumatic past (and present) means that many citizens are forced to carry within them the "symptom of a history that they cannot entirely possess" (1991, 4). When a world leader such as Trump uses rhetoric both to trigger trauma and to disavow it by pronouncing whatever does not fit his discourse fake, it demeans survivor experience while simultaneously undercutting the possibility of testimony. Trump's persistent rhetoric of disaster has helped shape contemporary America as what E. Anne Kaplan calls a trauma culture, or "a culture in which discourses, and especially images, about catastrophic events proliferate, often 'managed' by government; these discourses overtake public discussion of other things, dominating the social atmosphere" (2013, 54). Recognising the impact of cultural trauma, and finding ways of addressing it, is a fundamental pedagogical responsibility when faced with groups of students seeking means of witnessing, and contextualising the uncertainty of their era.

After reading the students' survey responses, I felt that it was important to help them find ways of expressing vulnerabilities. As Elizabeth Dutro and Antero Garcia assert, in the wake of Trump's election,

> Enacting witness depends on the presence of testimony, a sharing of experience by another. In classrooms, testimony to experience is always present, whether explicitly invited or authorized, as the bodies of teachers and students tell stories of connection, disconnection, care, dismissal, belonging, and exclusion. Thus as literacy scholars have argued, classrooms should be spaces of intentional invitation and opportunity for students to testify to and engage with their experiences and histories. (2018, 379)

However, creating this space of witnessing in a classroom where students often struggle to situate cultural trauma within a wider historical and political context poses a challenge. As Kaplan argues, "[w]itnessing in the ethical sense has to address not just the individual but the social collectivity as well. It involves taking responsibility of injustices in the past, and… preventing future human-based catastrophe. It is a position in which one acts as a member of a collectivity or culture" (2013, 54). It, therefore, seemed crucial to help students in my classes understand the trauma of their current cultural moment within a wider culture of trauma that extends back to the early Cold War.

While there is little doubt that the Trump era has, to date, created a remarkable degree of social and political divisiveness and uncertainty, the deliberate cultivation of anxiety is by no means new to American politics. As Joseph Masco argues, the deployment of effect as a political strategy dates back at least to the beginning of the Cold War:

> [T]error has a specific American logic and domestic history, one that since 1945 has drawn on the destructive capacities of nuclear weapons to focus social energies, unlock resources, and build things. In the twentieth century, the United States remade itself through the atomic bomb, using nuclear fear as a coordinating principle for U.S. institutions, citizen-state relations, and geopolitics alike. (2014, 7)

In the United States, the deliberate political cultivation of anxiety as an affective scenario can be traced to a National Security Council policy document submitted to then President Harry Truman in 1950. Known as NSC 68, the document outlined far-reaching measures to ensure that the United States would emerge victorious in its stand-off with the Soviet Union. While the document was extensive, it suggested in part that Americans could be mobilised against the Soviet menace if the government were to foster a climate of fear and uncertainty. As Masco contends, after the presentation of NSC 68, the White House recognised that "nuclear fear was... to be not only the basis of American military power, but also a means of installing a new normative reality in the United States, one that could consolidate political power at the federal level by reaching into the internal lives of citizens" (2014, 48). The deployment of this new reality was propagated through government bodies such as the Federal Civil Defense Administration and the Atomic Energy Commission. These bodies were responsible for the creation and dissemination of what are the now notorious pamphlets, advertisements, and broadcasts aimed at educating Americans about issues such as surviving nuclear attacks, living with the fallout, and spotting communists in public. These Cold War campaigns were deployed to help both contain and control the profound epistemological uncertainty born in tandem with the United States' development of atomic – and later hydrogen – bombs, as well as to manage fears of communist invasion. While the threat of nuclear war and, to a lesser extent, communist invasion was real, it also provided an unprecedented political opportunity, one where the fear of an uncertain future could be packaged, marketed, and regulated by the government as a means of managing domestic populations.

From a pedagogical perspective, analysing the cultural artifacts of the early Cold War era has proven an effective means of establishing the relationship between government propaganda and social anxiety. From the contemporary perspective, many of these relics appear alarmist, inflammatory, and even factually incorrect. Students, for instance, are often astonished to learn that in the 1950s Saturday morning cartoons were accompanied by regular, Civil Defense sponsored advertisements featuring Bert the Turtle, whose cheery song taught children the correct way to duck and cover in case of a nuclear attack. Or they are intrigued to learn that the Civil Defense office distributed its *Survival Under Atomic Attack* booklet to millions of American households, and that citizens in American cities would have regularly been confronted by bold, colourful advertisements asking them to purchase fallout shelters or to learn how to spot the communists in their midst. For students examining these historical events from a contemporary perspective, the atomic and communist hysteria of the early Cold War era seems out of proportion with the actual threat. Familiarising students with this sometimes fascinating era of American history provides an opportunity to demonstrate how the government worked hard to keep these threats at the forefront of the American consciousness, thereby making citizens more likely to consent to repressive and aggressive policies, both foreign and domestic. The threat posed to American civil liberties by

McCarthyist witch hunts and the investigations of the House UnAmerican Activities Committee, for instance, show students that there are fairly recent and equally outrageous precedents for the similar attacks against American liberties made by the Patriot Act post 9/11, or by Trump's victimisation of immigrants, many of whom are legal immigrants, through the work of bureaucratic enforcement agencies such as US Immigration and Customs Enforcement (ICE).

The goal of teaching this Cold War history is to demonstrate to students that Trump's deliberate cultivation of anxiety and divisiveness amongst the domestic population is not new. In fact, the United States has a long history of tying the propagation of fear to official policy. Brian Massumi argues that when nations deliberately raise the specter of future disaster in a fashion that keeps citizens in a state of permanent anxiety, they are governing by a "political ontology of threat" (2009, 52). According to Massumi, for many citizens exposed to the daily regimen of anxiety-inducing spectacles exemplified by, for instance, early Cold War America, "The felt reality of threat legitimates preemptive action, once and for all. Any action taken to preempt a threat from emerging into a clear and present danger is legitimated by the affective fact of fear, actual facts aside. Preemptive action will always have been right" (2009, 54). Put in simpler terms, the pervasive anxiety experienced both during the Cold War and during the Trump presidency is not merely the product of a random, if unfortunate, political climate. It is instead linked directly to policy initiatives aimed at generating fear within the public as a means of legitimating political agendas that may otherwise be met with resistance.

One thing I try to make clear to my students is that if the Cold War invented affective politics as an ontology of threat, the post 9/11 war on terror has extended that strategy in unprecedented ways. In the wake of 9/11, President Bush, VP Cheney, and Secretary of State Donald Rumsfeld helped usher in a new political era, one where military action could be justified in order to preempt a threat from emerging. In this scenario, the truth took a back seat to the supposed facts, such as the notion that Iraq held stockpiles of weapons of mass destruction. What was most important was the anxiety generated by the thought Iraq may have weapons of mass destruction was enough to help sway both public and political opinion. Indeed, Rumsfeld's infamous speech about acting on "unknown unknowns" appears to precipitate the fake news era of Donald Trump. Just as examples from the early Cold War era showed students how the production of fear became an effective political management strategy, examining the post-9/11 era shows how those methods have become normalised to the extent that absurd claims such as Rumsfeld's stand as justifications for war.

The constant sense of threat ushered in by the post-9/11 era and its concomitant policy documents such as the Patriot Act has helped establish fear, suspicion, and surveillance as what Kathleen Stewart calls "ordinary affects", or feelings that structure the atmosphere of everyday life. They may not be recognised in an overt way; rather, they may persist in the background by calling our attention to small threats, such as unattended luggage, or they may be triggered by more overt signs, such as Homeland Security Advisory Codes, severe weather warnings, lockdowns, or even disaster films. Either way, they codify threat as a part of the conscious and unconscious experience that impacts everyday life whether we recognise it overtly or not. For many of my students, most of whom were born in the year 2000, their everyday lives have always been structured by ordinary affects that frequently project the possibility of future danger. Helping them recognise this fact, along with its connection to a wider history of US-effective politics, was meant to be a source of empowerment. By providing students with this brief historical context, they were able to see that Trump's manipulation of the truth for political gain, along with his deliberate (and constant) fear-mongering amongst the US populace, is by no means unique. It also helps them recognise a method to Trump's actions. While this methodology cannot help explain the logic (or lack thereof) behind Trump's divisive actions, it can help students recognise that the fear he routinely stokes is meant to keep people reacting to that fear rather than resisting political policy. From this perspective, it can help students detach themselves from the fear, confusion, anxiety, and frustration generated by Trump's rhetoric, and focus instead on how to live with less political anxiety and, hopefully, find ways to voice resistance and dissent to a pervasive ontology of threat.

The art of resistance: a shared vulnerability exercise

In order to help nurture a relationship between understanding affective politics and voicing resistance, I designed an experiential learning exercise aimed at allowing students to simultaneously confront their Trump-era anxiety and to publicly voice dissent. The assignment was straightforward: each student was asked to use an art form of their choice to represent and challenge a contemporary issue that they experienced as a source of anxiety in their daily lives. They were also asked to write a brief expository essay from a third-person perspective that imagined themselves as the analyst of their own work. The purpose was to give the students the opportunity to relate their own fears and anxieties in an experiential, rather than analytical, format.

Going into the assignment, my expectations were, admittedly, low. I assumed a handful of students, particularly those who had already chosen English or Fine Arts as their majors, would submit the creative assignment and the majority would choose the safer alternative, which I also offered, of writing a conventional academic essay. On the day the assignments were due, however, I was overwhelmed by both the number of students who chose to submit the creative assignment and the amount of careful and detailed work they put into it. It was immediately clear that the students took a pride in their creative responses that is often absent from more conventional assignments. It was also immediately clear that, for them, Trump trauma is a real thing that not only impacts their daily lives, but that motivates them to find means of expressing anxiety, dissent, and resistance. My office soon became a small gallery housing oil paintings, sculptures, collages, photomontages, and sheaves of poetry devoted to challenging the affective politics of the contemporary world. Trump himself made it into several of the works, and in others, his presence was felt based on the issues the students chose to engage. For example, several of the women in the class chose to create works that aligned with the politics of the #METOO movement, which came to prominence in 2017 following a number of high-profile allegations of sexual assault against men in powerful positions. Trump, of course, has frequently been accused of sexual assault and sexual impropriety, and for many women, his misogynistic attitude exemplifies why the #METOO movement is so urgently needed. One particular example of a work that expressed solidarity with #METOO was an oil painting that featured the faces of three women, each of whom had a piece of duct tape slowly being removed from their lips in order to signify that they will no longer remain silent. Another student made a large collage of news articles and images of Trump in order to protest his proposal to ban transgendered individuals from the American military. Several students represented their anxieties over the climate crisis in a variety of ways. One student sculpted a turtle and tangled it in plastic waste; others produced oil paintings of humans and wildlife in compromised scenarios. One student created a political cartoon featuring Canadian Prime Minister Justin Trudeau that demonstrated the impact of oil pipelines on both nature and indigenous communities. Both gun violence and racialised violence were also represented by several students. One student went as far as recording a four-minute rap song devoted to the memory of the victims of American gun violence. Examples such as these demonstrate the serious manner in which many of my students approached the assignment. Their work, while often varying in quality, nevertheless revealed that they are at once politically engaged and looking for ways of speaking their minds. While I was not prepared for the intensity of their response, I was immensely proud of the work they put into their projects, which demonstrated the importance of allowing them to express themselves from an experiential, rather than strictly academic, perspective.

Once the projects were submitted I immediately recognised that they created the perfect opportunity to help the students recognise their shared sense of vulnerability. Achieving this understanding came simply from having students share and discuss their work in class. While many of them found this intimidating at first, they soon saw that their peers were experiencing the same sorts of anxieties, or shared deep concerns about the same issues. In effect, it helped create a sense of solidarity that demonstrated how each student who participated was victimised by an affective politics that legitimises anxiety as a mode of being. Speaking about this process helped them recognise that without forging a response to the crises of the current climate, they allow the politics of threat, fear, and violence to control their affective lives. While admittedly this was little more than a first step towards a more nuanced political standpoint for many of the students, recognising that they were not alone in their anxiety and outrage helped empower their feelings of dissent. More importantly, they were learning about other areas of political concern from their peers, and seeing that their private anxieties looked much like the anxieties experienced privately by those around them. Learning these lessons through sharing their respective vulnerabilities, rather than being told by their professor that they ought to fear the contemporary political climate, helped them experience a more tangible and self-motivated sense of the power of using aesthetics as a form of political resistance.

By creating an atmosphere of shared vulnerability, each student was able to testify to the impact of contemporary political crises – and the affective politics that often drives those crises – in their own unique way. Each student was also able to witness how such political turmoil impacts their peers, and to better understand how specific crises and concerns impact people of different socioeconomic backgrounds, genders and races. In short, it helped them recognise how their emotions are not merely private; rather they are both the product of their political climate and the starting point for forging voices of dissent.

Poetry against Trump

The final strategy for teaching students the relationship between art and resistance was to expose them to a work of contemporary poetry that exemplifies how art, and in this specific case poetry, seeks unique ways of understanding, and responding to, political turmoil. My basic pedagogical strategy was to help the students recognise their own artistic responses to Trump trauma in the same terms as the responses made by a notable American author. Specifically, I hoped that the students' newfound sense of shared vulnerability would lead them to see themselves, at least in a fledgling way, as part of a lineage of artists who use their work to express dissent. Furthermore, I hoped that their interest in the poems, given that poetry is often a hard sell to students in compulsory literature courses, would improve in light of the fact that the students had recently had to make similar choices about content, form, and politics in relation to their own artistic works.

For these two first-year classes the book I chose to explore was Terrance Hayes's *American Sonnets for My Past and Future Assassin* (2018). Hayes's book was, as the dustjacket says, "written during the first two hundred days of the Trump Presidency" and is "haunted by the countries past and future eras and errors." The book is primarily an examination of the continuing legacy of physical, social, and psychological violence against African Americans, and particularly African American male, bodies in the United

States. Over the course of the book's eighty sonnets, Hayes connects the cultural trauma of the Trump era – both vicarious and actual – with the cultural memory of trauma experienced by African Americans, and with the future-tense trauma of the increasingly reckless politics of Trump. As such, his book explores trauma as the product of a violent effective politics, one that aims at the continued subjugation of African Americans, but that also speaks to the biopolitical management of all American subjects by a perpetual rhetoric of fear and panic. To emphasise this sense of affective politics, Hayes uses the metaphorical figure of a nameless assassin, who has exerted his violent authority over the past, but whose presence lingers as a source of constant fear and agitation. This assassin takes various shapes over the course of the collection, often mirroring the sitting American president.

In various poems in the collection, my students were able to identify the figure of Trump as both threat and fool. In the book, Hayes compares Trump's skin tone with Homeland Security threat advisories and links the President to the arrogant and absurd terrorism of Caligula. After positioning Trump as a threat to Americans, and in particular to black Americans, Hayes carries on only to suggest that Trump's threatening behaviours exemplifies the damage done to marginalised groups when a politics of fear is used to assert a political agenda. While Hayes sees through the act, he also acknowledges that it is hurtful for those who are oppressed by Trump's tyranny.

Reading Hayes's collection in the wake of completing their own creative assignments on political resistance allowed my students to better understand and appreciate the purpose of his work. Given that they had recently grappled, to one extent or another, with the difficulty of expressing dissent against a powerful political system wherein terms such as safety, security, and normalcy are bound up with political conformity, many students began to see on a nascent level that aesthetics offers a means of carving out small spaces of resistance. In reading Hayes's collection, and with some pedagogical guidance, they began to see poetry as that which embraces the often paradoxical and inexplicable nature of contemporary politics, and that asserts the intensity of its own affective experience against the seemingly solid structures of political affect. In other words, it becomes a counter-discourse that intervenes and can help us resist, the politics of fear that shape contemporary experience. Making a connection between their own efforts at political art and the complex work of an established contemporary political artist such as Hayes proved to be an invaluable teaching tool insofar as it helped students recognise that their instincts about affective politics, even if they could not precisely put those instincts into words, corresponded with those of an acclaimed writer such as Hayes. It also helped them see that using art to capture the intensity of their feelings of fear, protest, or frustration, rather than trying to respond logically to an illogical political scenario, offered them new avenues for defining themselves against the political ontology of threat. Therefore, the exercise allowed at least some of the students to gain enough confidence in their own voices and opinions to begin asserting those opinions as forms of protest.

For the past several years, I have coordinated *Paper Mill Press*, our campus's creative arts journal. Last winter I was very pleased to see that several of the students who completed the assignment on aesthetic resistance either submitted works they composed for my class, or new works altogether, to the journal. While it is possible that many of these students would have submitted work regardless of the exercise in my class, I would like to think that for at least some of them the exercise, by contextualising affective politics, giving students the opportunity to voice resistance, and connecting their works to a study of contemporary political poetry, cultivated the necessary combination of engagement, outrage, and aesthetic confidence to encourage future courses of political action.

References

Caruth, C. (1991) Introduction, *American Imago*, 48 (1): 1–12.
Dutro, E. (2013) Towards a Pedagogy of the Incomprehensible: Trauma and the Imperative of Critical Witness in the Literacy Classroom, *Pedagogies: An International Journal*, 8 (4): 301–315.
Garcia, A. & Dutro, E. (2018) Electing to Heal: Trauma, Healing, and Politics in Classrooms, *English Education*, 5 (9): 375–383.
Hayes, T. (2018) *American Sonnets for My Past and Future Assassin*. New York: Penguin.
Heller, C. (2017) Trump Trauma: Where Reality TV Meets 'Reality by Decree', *Tikkun*, 32 (2): 9–20.
Kaplan, E. A. (2013) Trauma Studies Moving Forward: Interdisciplinary Perspectives, *Journal of Dramatic Theory and Criticism*, 27 (2): 53–65.
Masco, J. (2014) *Theater of Operations*. Raleigh, NC: Duke University Press.
Massumi, B. (2010) The Future Birth of the Affective Fact. In Greg and Siegworth, eds. *The Affect Theory Reader*. Raleigh, NC: Duke University Press: 52–70.

Part V
Playing (with) the past, rehearsing (for) the future

15 Performative experiential learning strategies: reenacting the historical, enacting the everyday

Ger Duijzings, Frederik Lange, and Eva-Maria Walther

Introduction

In this chapter, we will compare different performative modes through which the past, including traumatic experiences and their legacies and resonances today, can be reenacted. Reflecting on the two self-standing activities that we organised in Regensburg in January 2019, this is the overarching theme that has emerged. The first event consisted of a screening of the film *"I Do Not Care If We Go Down in History as Barbarians"* (2018) by Romanian director Radu Jude, which captures the half-real, half-scripted rehearsals for a historical reenactment of the 1941 massacre of the Jewish population of Odessa by Romanian troops. The actual reenactment that is shown at the end of the film consists of a grandiose spectacle held on one of the largest public squares in the very center of the Romanian capital Bucharest in the presence of an audience. We organised a simultaneous and trans-local screening of this movie both in Regensburg and Cluj-Napoca (Romania), a transnational experiment with our Romanian partner PATRIR.[1] The simultaneous screening across borders was followed by small-group conversations between viewers from both cities, facilitated by half a dozen video connections. The second event which we organised a week later formed a counterpoint to the spectacular historical reenactment staged and choreographed by Radu Jude: it consisted of a performative intervention in public space, on a small square in Regensburg's historical center, where participants built up metal bunk beds from the recently dismantled nuclear bunker of the city, and carried out mundane activities such as folding, arranging and hanging bedsheets – representing normality – and then ripping them apart – suggesting rupture and crisis. The lack of any clear historical reference left it to the imagination of passers-by and onlookers to come up with their own associations, entering into conversation with the performers.

Here we will not describe these two events in detail, which we did in two blog posts for the website of the project Again Never Again.[2] We will focus instead on what connects the two events, that is, the employment of two contrasting performative strategies, on the one hand, a largely scripted, rehearsed, and choreographed reenactment of a historical event (with a full mise-en-scène including actors, music, battles, uniforms, and speeches) as in Jude's film, and on the other, the relatively inconspicuous, unscripted and improvised enactment of everyday activities on a small square using props that are only vaguely reminiscent of historical traumas. Hence what we will offer here is a comparative analysis of these two formats: a theatrical performance or spectacle carried out on a stage in front of an audience, and a relatively unassuming enactment of domestic mundane activities in public space, using everyday objects without a clear reference to traumatic events.

Historical reenactments have become a widely practiced and popular type of performance, attracting large numbers of spectators. During these happenings, important events from a more or less distant past are reenacted, ideally using the appropriate costumes and props. Such reenactments have become an effective extra-mural "teaching" and "learning" format to acquaint people with past epochs and episodes key to our history and identity.[3] In his book *The Idea of History*, published posthumously in 1946, the English philosopher and historian Robin G. Collingwood insisted that historical research and understanding always requires a reenactment of past experiences of some sort (Dray 1999, 32; see also Giannachi 2017, 116). While Collingwood's understanding of a historical "reenactment" refers primarily to the need for every historian to put themselves somehow in the position of their subjects to acquire a better understanding of the past from textual relics, rehearsing their subjects' deeds and thoughts, in today's era this type of hermeneutic understanding is often achieved through forms of physical reenactment (Cook 2004, 491). Reenactments span different media and history-themed genres like theatrical performances, historical dramas in film and television, living history events or television shows (Agnew 2004, 327). As examples may serve the American Civil War reenactments in the US, the reenactments of the 1968 Berlin student protests in Germany (Hinz 2011) or of the two World Wars in England, but one may also think of popular medieval fairs and workshops for Roman and medieval craftsmanship, TV shows like *The 1900 House* and its international broadcast sequels.

While reenacting past events by following the footsteps of their predecessors or by restaging past military battles (without applying real force or violence of course), costumed performers and audiences of these spectacles claim to learn something about history which is "less accessible using conventional methods for studying the past" (Cook 2004, 487). Scholars on the other hand tend to emphasise that the reenactments' epistemological contribution lays more in the expression of reactions to a conflicted present (Agnew 2004, 328). Instead of seeing them as a rendering of a relevant past-as-the-present in funny costumes, they bring about a "clash of contemporary values and expectations with the conditions and rules of the historical situation" (Cook 2004, 493). Therefore, reenactments tell us more about the present than about the collective past as they document the ongoing engagement with the past and the participants' and visitors' desire for historical understanding (Cook 2004, 495). Collective remembering has to be understood as firmly embedded in the present, and the same is true for reenactments, which demonstrate how contemporary generations deal with the past. In the following, we will not primarily look at the reenacted past itself, or what is claimed to be transmitted, but at the format of the historical reenactment itself, as an act of remembering in the present.

One key characteristic of historical reenactments is that they are choreographed spectacles, with an audience that watches and occasionally engages with the actors. This is also the case in Jude's film, which shows the tumultuous rehearsals and subsequent actual reenactment of the massacre of the Jewish population of Odessa in 1941, in which 18.000 Jews were killed by Romanian troops. Jude's film engages with Romania's role in the Holocaust in a rather confrontational and subversive manner by addressing head-on one of the darkest episodes in the country's history through a choreographed historical spectacle on a central square in Bucharest in front of an unsuspecting audience. Spectators see a realistic and captivating reenactment (including Soviet, German, and Romanian armies marching in military gear and involving in battle scenes) and applaud when listening to the anti-Semitic speeches of Romania's wartime leader, Marshal Ion Antonescu, forcefully rendered by a professional actor.[4]

Although Jude adopts the conventional format of a reenactment (where important events in the history of the nation are staged and celebrated) he subverts this format by thematising a very controversial topic (if not a taboo theme) in contemporary Romania, one which is largely ignored by local historians and forgotten in public remembrance: the complicity of Romania and of Romanians in the Holocaust. In other words, Jude brings back something that "is actually known but has been repressed, from whence it returns" (Arns quoted in Giannachi 2017, 121). His staged reenactment brings masterfully Romania's current refusal to face its own problematic past to the surface, putting the audience in a position not just as viewers of an interesting spectacle, but as actors in a play: as onlookers and bystanders who do nothing whatsoever to prevent a massacre, applaud when hearing Antonescu's anti-Semitic speeches, and even assist the perpetrators. Jude eliminates the safe distance between the audience and the reenacted tragedy, creating hybrid, uncanny, and 'ambiguous mixed states' (Lütticken quoted in Giannachi 2017, 116). One may argue that Jude sets up a trap for the audience, which, in this staged and scripted setting, becomes complicit in the massacre by condoning the brutal concluding scenes where the Jewish population of Odessa is brought to a shed that is put on fire. The film triggered angry responses from nationalists who are highly critical both of the film and the filmmaker, depicting him with the yellow star and the label "Jude" (using his surname, which in German means "Jew", as an anti-Semitic insult) on extreme right websites.

As viewers of the movie in Regensburg and Cluj, we were onlookers of the second degree, a position that comes with its own moral dilemmas. Are we, as passive outsiders, entitled to shame and blame certain protagonists of the film, or their real-life counterparts, and extend our sympathy to others? Is it ethically questionable to involve an unsuspecting audience by triggering a reaction using hidden actors prompting the audience to respond with applause to anti-Semitic speeches and the brutal and violent scenes at the end? Using the experimental method of transnational online video connections, we facilitated a public exchange after the film was simultaneously screened in both cities, and we could observe that this form of proxy-testimony influenced conversations in several ways (Figure 15.1).

We asked participants to rally in front of pre-installed computers or their own smartphones in groups of two or three and use video links that had been set up prior to the event. Participants thus suddenly found themselves in conversation with a stranger they knew nothing about, but with the experience of having seen the same film and a list of topics they could talk about as the starting point. As many visitors in both locations were expats from respectively Germany or Romania, as well as from other countries, these transnational conversations rarely evolved as straightforward juxtapositions of German and Romanian perspectives, they were actually strongly influenced by the mixed or "international" composition of the two audiences. Also, as Romanians (under Nazi-German auspices) were the perpetrators of the Odessa massacre, and contributed to numerous other atrocious crimes against Jewish populations in Romania throughout the Second World War, discussions quickly turned to questions of shared guilt

Figure 15.1 Participants in Regensburg in conversation with viewers in Cluj-Napoca.

and identity, and the remembrance of victims and perpetrators in the contemporary collective memory. On the other hand, not being directly exposed to the physical experience of watching a performance, viewers quickly abstracted the message of the film from its immediate context and came to reflect on their own life story. Participants exchanged how the Second World War and the Holocaust are being remembered in their own towns, villages, and families, and discussed common controversies in their respective local memory politics.

The spatial and temporal distance between the performative event and its reception, as shown and condensed into the film, also allows for a critical evaluation of the properness of the setup. An aspect that remains unclear to the viewer of the movie is which roles are scripted, and which capture actual responses of uninvolved visitors. It is also impossible from the edited material to judge whether people are applauding the lynching, or perhaps the great performance of the actors, or do what one normally does at a spectacle, give a round of applause, whether the performance is good or not. Some of us were of the opinion that it is ethically problematic to make the public unwittingly part of such a performance. We may respond like this because of our own disciplinary codes of ethical conduct, as Kathy Brown suggests: academics, when doing "experiments" involving human subjects, are expected to obey strict ethical principles, while artists "may entrap, exploit, or even abuse individuals in a way that can damage the trust between the artist and his or her audience" (Brown 2014, 10).

It is from the locally and nationally embedded perspective of viewers in Regensburg and Cluj-Napoca that Jude's pedagogical aspirations were also controversially discussed. One may question whether his goal of raising people's historical awareness through theatrical stimuli, hoping to trigger forms of self-reflection, was successful at all. Some of those who had just seen the film argued that the reenactment apparently did not stimulate genuine cognitive engagement in the audience, in the worst case it confirmed existing stereotypes. In case the artist hopes for some kind of "behavior modification", and awaken people's political responsibility, one may wonder whether this was indeed the best way of achieving it (Brown 2014, 10). Is the provocative and confrontational style really the best way to "reach people", and would one not be better advised in a context like the Romanian, to apply a more cautious approach, making sure that the target groups are allowed to maintain their cherished national identity while helping them to acknowledge some uncomfortable historical truths. A possible "lesson learned" from Jude's reenactment is that it shows all of us, if we want it or not, that no safe and comfortable distance exists between the perpetrators of a crime and its onlookers. Spectators can quickly become entrapped in the dubious role of bystanders, also against their own will. Realising that we may very easily fall into this trap may be a "lesson learned". As Tzvetan Todorov argues: "The memory of the past serves no purpose if it is used to build an impassable wall between evil and us" (Todorov 2009, 461). People

222 *Ger Duijzings et al.*

shout "never again!" but they better realise that we may all be capable of such acts. We will only be able to tame evil, as Todorov argues, when we realise that "The 'foul beast' is not in some remote place outside us: it is within" (Todorov 2009, 461). Either way, Jude's main intention to spark controversy about the darkest episodes of our past and our failure to address them, but also about how we can perhaps develop appropriate ways to represent and commemorate them, was definitely accomplished.

The performance that we carried out a week later, on a cold but sunny January day, differed from the spectacle that Jude had organised in Bucharest. It was rather small-scale and similar to a live art performance where historical references to traumatic events were far less explicit and direct. It consisted of a public intervention on a small square in the pedestrian zone of the old center of Regensburg, with mundane "micro-performances" carried out around bunk beds taken from a former local nuclear shelter, thematising the human need for rest, protection, and sanctuary. We did not define any clear theme, such as the "Holocaust", "refugees" or "nuclear war", and had no explicit didactic content that we wanted to convey, no banners with slogans, just bunk beds meant to trigger various associations amongst the onlookers, who could come up with their own interpretations and personal stories. Having no clear message to bring across, we were open to others and learned more. We connected with people's individual lives, in their own local context. Through our intervention, the square became a space for communication and exchange.

Confronted with these beds, which looked like metal scaffolds, onlookers shared their thoughts with the performers, virtually all of them being students from the University of Regensburg. The students wrote snippets of statements they had heard from passers-by on patches of bed sheets which they had previously folded – symbolising normality – and then ripped apart – symbolising rupture – during the performance.[5] At a separate table, we offered coffee and tea to the people who entered into a conversation with us (Figure 15.2).

The two bunk beds were taken from a former (and never used) fallout shelter located beneath the Thon-Dittmer-Palais (next to the town hall of Regensburg), offering 2.400 citizens a place to sleep in case of Cold War air raids or nuclear attacks. The idea to use these bunk beds for our performance came from a member of the local contemporary art organisation *donumenta*, Hans Simon-Pelanda, who knew the beds were about to be discarded because the shelter was in the process of being dismantled. They had been employed already by the Bosnian (Roma) artist Selma Selman who had used them as props in her video installation *I Wish I Had a German Passport* (2018), addressing the fate of war refugees, in an installation in an indoor venue in the center of Regensburg. Simon-Pelanda, an academic and local memory activist had assisted the Bosnian artist and also became closely involved in our activity. We mobilised, as already mentioned before, a dozen students, most of them members of the "Southeast" student association

Performative experiential learning strategies 223

Figure 15.2 Image from the public intervention in Regensburg on 31 January 2019.

(*Fachschaft Südost*) studying the Southeast and East European studies degrees. We contacted the city authorities, who provided us with two such bunk beds, including the original bed covers, we stored them, and only then started to think and brainstorm what to do with these objects. What crystallised was the idea to use them as symbols of (relative) safety in abnormal times, a safe refuge in "extraordinary" times of war, homelessness, illness, or other forms of adversity. We realised of course that in public space they would seem out-of-place: beds as taken-for-granted everyday objects stand for privacy and intimacy but by putting them up on a public square we would expose them to the gaze of numerous unknown others, creating a somehow "uncanny" situation, for which the German language provides the more appropriate and evocative adjective *unheimlich* ("unhomely").

We held a preparation meeting with all the participants, who were briefed about the concept, the site of the intervention, and they also received practical instructions from us on how to make the event more performative. What we provided was a kind of "event score": general verbal instructions that constitute a set framework for a performance or "do-it-yourself" artwork (Dezeuze 2016, 218). The participants received oral and written instructions on how to start conversations, what questions to ask, how to perform roles, and create "situations" that would trigger a response from the audience. They were also made aware of various categories of people they were likely to encounter during the event, such as elderly Germans with their own experiences of war, violence, and displacement, specifically *Vertriebene* (expellees from the eastern territories of the Third Reich, after Germany lost the war) and *Aussiedler* (ethnic Germans who relocated from parts of eastern Europe during the 1980s and 1990s). In addition, we anticipated encountering homeless people, migrants from Eastern Europe, Syrian refugees, and sympathisers of the extreme right.

We conceived the performative situation partly as a "fieldwork" setting, blurring the boundaries between performance and anthropological research. We thought of this beforehand and told all the participants that, above all, we were there to listen, to capture other people's voices, and not to vent our own opinions or contradict collocutors. We respected ethical principles normally applied by anthropologists in fieldwork situations, which artists, ostensibly assuming the role of "ethnographers" – representing and working in the name of "cultural (or economic) others" – sometimes ignore (Foster 1996). We also thought of the intervention the other way around, as fieldwork bleeding into performance. As has been pointed out by the anthropologists Arnd Schneider and George Marcus, anthropological research can indeed be thought of as staged and performative, as a mise-en-scène that "allows, indeed demands the intervention of research subjects and others into its processual construction" (Schneider 2016, 195–196; see also Duijzings 2018). We took this one step further, assuming as ethnographers and historians the role of performance artists. This is, as Aileen Burns, Johan Lundh, and Tara McDowell argue, not so uncommon and unthinkable anymore: "The space of art is, to its great credit, increasingly capacious and hospitable" (Burns et al. 2018, 10).

Throughout the day, we performed various "everyday" domestic activities: folding bed sheets, arranging the covers on the beds, wrapping ourselves in these sheets and covers (a welcome protection against the freezing cold), and hanging the variously colored sheets on a washing line drawn between a tree and the fountain located on the square. Because of these mundane activities, the performance looked like a slice of ordinary life "out-of-place", reminiscent of other art performances involving commonplace activities like cooking and eating (Dezeuze 2016, 215), with the difference that our intervention was rather *unheimlich* because what we performed were domestic activities fully exposed to the public eye. Even though we did not want to shock or provoke – applying a conversational rather than a confrontational mode (Dezeuze 2016, 230) – the performance disoriented and destabilised onlookers. There was not enough "spectacle" there for them to conclude that they were watching street theatre. Rather it was a "situation" as defined by Situationist principles: a moment of ordinary life concretely and deliberately constructed (Theodoropoulou 2016, 78) (Figure 15.3).

The most provocative part of our performance (getting closer to becoming a spectacle) was the ripping apart and scissoring sheets into small patches on which we wrote brief statements of passers-by who talked to us and shared their ideas. At the end of the day, the two beds had multiple patches with

Figure 15.3 Example of a textile patch quoting from a conversation.

inscriptions hanging on them, snippets from the conversations we had heard.[6] These inscribed patches of textile visibly changed the display of the installation and added meanings to it which we had not scripted beforehand. The consecutive alterations then changed how the site was experienced and interpreted by others arriving later. Our work became as it were a process of exchange between us, the performers, the everyday objects (beds) and materials (bed sheets) we were using, and passers-by and onlookers (Brown 2014, 4–5). By inviting the latter to enter into a dialogic situation, to interact and contribute to the work, the boundaries between us as performers and the audience became blurred. Without realising it at that point, we practiced what in art theory is called "relational aesthetics", showing similarities with how anthropological knowledge is produced through the dialogic exchange (Schneider 2016, 196).[7] We also followed certain Situationist principles as defined in the Situationist Manifesto, such as "against unilateral art", "an art of dialogue", "an art of interaction" (Theodoropoulou 2016, 77). Through the creation of "situations", one may offer spaces where social experiments can happen and micro-communities can emerge, as long as it is not exhibited in, or sequestered into, established art institutions and galleries (Brown 2014, 1; Theodoropoulou 2016, 86) (Figure 15.4).

We intentionally offered few immediate clues for passers-by of what we were doing except for a small poster with an image of a bed placed in a destroyed and dystopian landscape with an accompanying text, and an

226 *Ger Duijzings et al.*

Figure 15.4 The accompanying poster and flyer, designed by Matej Máthé.

identical flyer for people to take away.[8] People were forced to get closer to the poster (if they noticed it at all) and enter into conversations to understand what was happening, and what kind of higher cause we were defending. This was indeed our intention: to trigger spontaneous conversations and open-ended exchanges of ideas. People had all sorts of associations after seeing us doing "things" around these "undefined" objects in public space: many assumed that they were scaffolds, and were surprised to hear that they belonged to a nuclear shelter and that people were supposed to sleep on them, others thought almost immediately of (psychiatric) hospital beds, army beds, prison or concentration camp beds. Youngsters had more positive and adventurous associations such as youth hostel beds. A small child was exasperated that the cuddly animals were missing. In a way, we created something that Michel de Certeau once called *lieux de parole* (sites of speech), platforms in public spaces for small voices to be heard (Dezeuze 2016, 227).

The beds and our micro-performances triggered non-verbal and verbal responses as well as conversations, which we captured and shared through WhatsApp group sound recordings after they had taken place.[9] Some people just stopped, watched, read the poster or flyer, nodding affirmatively or shrugging shoulders, and moved on without entering into a conversation. Others approached us with questions or comments. Some elderly people knew about the nuclear bomb shelter, but younger people were generally unaware.

Quite a few people shared their own tiny or not-so-tiny personal traumas. Two young women told the story of how they had been left stranded at night in an unknown city; they went to the train station to sleep there. A man told he had slept in various collective facilities, such as in army barracks or at an official night shelter for the homeless at the train station: he deplored these situations because of the humiliating lack of privacy. Another man told he had been hospitalised in several psychiatric wards, where, according to him, the beds are generally much worse. An elderly lady told us she had slept on the floor after she had quarreled with her husband, and yet another mentioned her divorce and how she lives in a small apartment estranged from her family. Many seemed absorbed by a general feeling of defeatism: many things go wrong in life and in the world around us, and one never stops confronting numerous issues. After seeing the beds, they immediately switched to their own adversarial experiences and the various other problems of this world.

Some homeless people assumed that we were students or activists protesting against homelessness, the lack of affordable housing, rent increases, and the privatisation of social housing. A shabby looking elderly woman carrying plastic bags with belongings told us that homelessness is a serious feat and that people cannot really help it when they end up in such a dire situation. She complained about her tiny pension and the cuts to social security, calling Germany a *Verbrecherstaat* (criminal state), a term commonly used in extreme-right circles. She claimed to have a home but also said she was anxious to become homeless. As expected, some had had their own experiences of war and displacement. There was a young Syrian couple jogging through the pedestrianised center of the town, who had fled the war in their country and now tried to build up new lives in Germany. They refused to talk about their war experiences. A frail woman in her eighties, with a son of sixty-something, had had her own experience as a refugee in 1945. They both considered our intervention to be rather silly and demonstratively refused to take the flyer. They claimed to know what it meant to be refugees and did not want to be compared with the Syrian refugees, "who receive all the support they desire". She claimed that she had never had received any assistance whatsoever: at the end of the Second World War, the situation had been far more brutal, and hence she felt offended that we saw these two situations as comparable.

Others told of their political engagement. One man presented himself as a *Reichsbürger*, a self-designation of people on the right political fringe who believe that the German state is a farce, and who strive to construct their own alternative legal order. Although these ideas are usually associated with the extreme right, he denied being part of such circles because he had married a foreigner. A woman who had been active in the anti-war movement claimed that nowadays, people have no clue what it means, war and violence: had they known they would show more empathy for refugees. During the so-called "refugee crisis" of 2015–2016, she had sheltered a refugee family in her home, which had been challenging, to be sure, but she still thought this had to be done. Two teenage girls dropped by at the table and asked for two cups of tea for the homeless people sitting around the corner.

The students that participated in the activity thought our intervention had also been a process of discovery for ourselves. The only way to create genuine occasions for exchange, we concluded afterwards, is by approaching passers-by and onlookers in a gentle and inoffensive manner, giving them enough time to watch, read, think and respond. Yet it was difficult for most of us to keep going for hours: it was intense, and most of us became over-saturated with impressions, suffering from mental exhaustion. We all developed our own strategies how to conduct such conversations, some of which had been unpleasant or bizarre. What became clear is that "the" public does not exist; it should be thought of as essentially multi-vocal, fragmented, and even polarised. Audiences can refuse their role, and turn down invitations to participate. During our event too, some passers-by declined to conform to the notion of the ideal participant, rendering the work unstable (Brown 2014, 4). In many ways, this made the performance more unpredictable and exhausting, but at the same time also more exciting and epistemologically productive than our first event. During the screening and the ensuing online discussion, the audience had a clearer idea of what was awaiting them (a film and a discussion on a particular historical topic) and what was expected of them (passive reception during the film, active engagement in the conversation). For us as organisers, it was easier to instruct the already informed participants, and anticipate what was going to happen during the evening, not least because the type of person who might attend a screening in an arthouse cinema dealing with a difficult historical topic can be expected to be open and willing and able to debate in a self-conscious but civilised manner. The benefits of the street performance were that we left and moved out of our academic-intellectual bubble, encountered a broader audience, and needed to keep ourselves on our toes and open to reactions and interpretations we had not foreseen.

Part of the discussions we had after the event revolved around the question of whether the performative element could have been stronger and whether we should have conveyed a stronger message, as in Radu Jude's reenactment of a historical event. This way, people would have been able to watch something more eye-catching. A problem one may discern is that spectacles turn people into passive spectators, not participants or active *viveurs* as the Situationists argued (Theodoropoulou 2016, 79). Consumerist society is already dominated by too many 'passive' leisure activities, entertainment, and spectacles, which are scripted, have a more or less fixed duration, and do not allow for much participation and input from the audience. Skeptics of the reenactment of the Odessa massacre presumed that audiences relied too much on their familiar role of the detached spectator and did not necessarily engage with the critical and thought-provoking aspects of the project in the aftermath. Following this line of reasoning, if our intervention had been more "theatrical", people would possibly not have entered into conversations with us, which indeed was the thing we wanted to achieve, how unpredictable and unexpected the results were to be in the end. The micro-performances were actually by far the easiest thing to do, as it allowed us to kill time and beat the cold by wrapping the sheets and bed covers around us. It was fun performing these activities, whereas approaching people was more difficult.

What we also learned through this intervention was to exercise tolerance: it is not possible or even desirable to attempt to convince others that our public intervention is meaningful. We encountered emotional responses, and that helped to increase the affective attachment to what we were doing, achieving better and deeper learning. There are also certain risks attached to approaching unknown others and entering into conversations with them. Receiving numerous unexpected responses, one is always forced out of one's own comfort zone. Theoretically, the conversations after the film screening, which all took place in virtual space, were of a similar character: participants met with strangers and had to start a conversation with hardly any cues about their counterpart's beliefs or value systems, or political opinions and affiliations. This type of online encounter is an exercise in probing empathetic communicative strategies, of getting to know the other in a respectful manner while allowing nevertheless for some level of disagreement. It was surprising to see that very quickly, collocutors shared personal and intimate details of their lives with unknown others on the other side of the connection, like family histories or political socialisations. The difference between encountering a stranger online versus meeting one in a public space is one in degree, not in kind. However, the face-to-face encounters on a city square seemed to be of a far more memorable and "experiential" kind since they marked a starker digression from the participants' habitual modes of social exchange with others. In this era of social media, we have less and less actual experience negotiating viewpoints with others in real-time and non-virtual space. Video conversations, as well as debates with strangers online, are more readily part of our day to day lives than unprompted exchanges with strangers in the street. For most of us, it was remarkable to see how easy it was to have such conversations and how little it takes to learn from them.

We also reflected on whether this kind of intervention could be repeated as a didactic course at university, or could be institutionalised as a model for schooling and learning, but students were all of the opinion that it would not, as all spontaneity would be lost: they would be too much preoccupied with getting their credit points, fulfilling the course requirements, and the marks they would get for their work, introducing elements of stress, pressure, hierarchy, and asymmetry. Although they reported that they had enjoyed interacting with strangers in public and had learned a lot from the experience, they concluded that it would not work in a more formalised university context, where their rehearsed endeavor to "perform" well for grades and meet pre-set expectations would have led the free and playful nature of the activity ad absurdum. In order for this type of experiential

230 *Ger Duijzings et al.*

learning experiment to work in a setting of institutionalised schooling, both the will and infrastructural resources to overcome existing conventional forms of teaching and learning would be necessary – a challenging proposition. This does not mean that such an intervention and performance, in this particular format (with beds or other objects) cannot be done again elsewhere. The performance could be multiplied and become, as Jonah Westerman has argued for performative art interventions, "a networked conductor that connects different moments, each one voicing a new facet of the work's significance in a new situation, with a new audience" (Westerman 2017, 19). And one of its key benefits would indeed be "a breaking of the boundary between the educational institution and the world" (Johnson 2015, 10, quoting Paul Thompson).

Notes

1 *"I Do Not Care If We Go Down in History as Barbarians"* (dir. Radu Jude, 2018). Screened simultaneously on 24 January 2019 in Regensburg (FilmGalerie – Kino im Leeren Beutel) and Cluj-Napoca (Urania Palace) followed by trans-local video link conversations. The event was organised, on the Regensburg side, by Ger Duijzings, Frederik Lange, and Eva-Maria Walther, all three associated with the Graduate School for East and Southeast European Studies of the Universität Regensburg, and on the Cluj-Napoca side by Benedikt Hielscher and Silvia Spurigan of the Peace Action, Training and Research Institute of Romania (PATRIR). In Regensburg, the event was organised in collaboration with *donumenta*, a contemporary art organisation and local partner.
2 See https://againneveragain.eu/article-item/15/ and https://againneveragain.eu/article-item/21/.
3 One should distinguish between historical and artistic reenactments. The first are reenactments of historical events, by artists or non-artists, the latter are repeat performances by artists in which some first "original" art performance is performed once again. An example of the first is Felix Gmelin's *Colour Test, Red Flag II* (2002) where an activist protest in 1968 Berlin is reenacted, or Enri Shala's film *Intervista (Interview)* (1998), in which the artist, with the help of lip readers, reconstructs his mother's spoken words in silent film footage from the 1977 Albanian communist youth congress (Giannachi 2017, 116). An example of the second is Marina Abramović's *Seven Easy Pieces* (2005), performed on seven consecutive nights in New York's Guggenheim Museum. She reenacted performances both by herself and other well-known and established performance artists.
4 Radu Jude's most recent films all address Romania's troubled past: his film *Aferim!* (2015) depicts slavery of the Roma population in the Romanian principalities in the 19th-century, revealing the roots of anti-Roma prejudice and racism, while *Scarred Hearts* (2016) and *The Dead Nation* (2017) address anti-Semitism and the Holocaust in Romania. *Aferim!* won the Silver Bear at the Berlinale and *"I Do Not Care If We Go Down in History as Barbarians"* won the Prize for the Best Film in the Karlovy Vary Film Festival.
5 *Dreams and Nightmares: Beds in Normal and Extraordinary Times.* Public performance and art intervention on the Viereimerplatz, Regensburg, 31 January 2019. The organising team consisted of Ger Duijzings, Frederik Lange, Hans Simon-Pelanda, and Eva-Maria Walther, with the participation of the student association *Fachschaft Südost*.

6 English translations of inscriptions on the textile patches:

- We are fine, we have nothing to complain about
- One should always have a small suitcase prepared just in case
- These look almost like hospital beds
- Unworthy for humans
- When I have no bed, I sleep at the train station
- The world is still unsafe
- If you die (in the war), you go to Paradise
- This reminds me of my time in the army
- The worst thing is the indifference
- There are still lots of things going wrong
- Sometimes it's just naked survival that is at stake
- When time comes, time comes
- I often lay in my cozy bed thinking, "how many people don't have this!?"
- There were five of us in one room – nobody helped us, but that was '45
- It is important to be aware of how well we are doing!
- The cuddly animals are missing

7 A seminal work is Nicolas Bourriaud's book *Relational Aesthetics* (2002, originally published in 1998 in French). In anthropology, a key reference is Alfred Gell's *Art and Agency* (1998), which draws the attention away from art as "objects" and emphasises the role of human relations and social agency in the making and subsequent use of artworks (Schneider 2016, 201).

8 English translation of the poster and flyer text: For most of us, beds are normal everyday objects that we take for granted. In these beds we have a well-deserved rest, we sleep and dream, processing all experiences from a busy day that has just passed. Sometimes we may have a nightmare too, but when we wake up, we find ourselves in our own bed in the protected environment of our home. For some people, a safe and comfortable bed is something they can only dream of. They do not have one, as they have become homeless or have had to flee a natural disaster or a man-made tragedy or war. In our intervention, we show beds that are fifty years old and have been taken out of the former air-raid shelter of the city of Regensburg, which was located under the Old Town Hall, providing a place to sleep for around 2.400 citizens in case of an air raid during the Cold War. These beds resemble those in contemporary refugee centers, where people find a place to rest and recover after a war that destroyed their homes, or a dangerous trip in which they did not see a bed for months. Normally beds stand for safety, privacy, and intimacy, but this can change suddenly and unexpectedly. Beds in hospitals, psychiatric wards, prisons, refugee centers, army barracks, or concentration camps may be far from pleasant places to dwell. Beds displayed in public space are a contradiction in terms, they show that objects that we take for granted in our everyday lives can become rather uncanny (*unheimlich*), and represent a nightmare that is a bitter reality for many people worldwide. Bosnian artist Selma Selman had used the unused beds from a nuclear bunker underneath the town hall of Regensburg in a video and sound installation for the Danube Art Lab in Maximilianstraße, which served as an inspiration for the action on the Viereimerplatz. The activity takes place in the framework of the Never Again Project which is co-financed by the EU's "Europe for Citizens" program. Eight organisations in eight countries use experience-based learning tools to stimulate a critical reflection of traumatic events in European history.

9 Another method of capturing and documenting our performance for future access was through photographs, whereby we were careful not to shoot the faces of people who entered into a conversation with us.

References

Agnew, V. (2004) Introduction: What Is Reenactment? *Criticism*, 46 (3): 327–339.
Arns, I. & Horn, G. (2008) *History Will Repeat Itself*. Dortmund: Hartware Medien Kunstverein / Berlin: KW Institute for Contemporary Art.
Bourriaud, N. (2002) (1998) *Relational Aesthetics*. Dijon: Les presses du réel.
Brown, K. (2014) Introduction. In K. Brown, ed. *Interactive Contemporary Art. Participation in Practice*. New York: I.B. Tauris: 1–14.
Burns, A., Johan L., & McDowell, T. (2018) *The Artist As*. Berlin: Sternberg Press.
Cook, A. (2004) The Use and Abuse of Historical Reenactment: Thoughts on Recent Trends in Public History, *Criticism*, 46 (3): 487–496.
Dezeuze, A. (2016) *Habitable*: Spectator Participation in Everyday Life. In S. Bianchini & E. Verhagen, eds. *Practicable: From Participation to Interaction in Contemporary Art*. Cambridge, Mass: MIT Press: 215–234.
Dray, W. H. (1999) *History As Re-enactment: R. G. Collingwood's Idea of History*. Oxford: Oxford University Press.
Duijzings, G. (2018) Transforming a Totalitarian Edifice: Artistic and Ethnographic Engagements with the House of the People in Bucharest. In C. Raudvere, ed. *Nostalgia, Loss and Creativity in South-East Europe. Political and Cultural Representations of the Past*. Cham: Palgrave Macmillan: 11–36.
Foster, H. (1996) The Artist as Ethnographer? In H. Foster, ed. *The Return of the Real*. Cambridge, Mass: MIT Press: 302–309.
Giannachi, G. (2017) At the Edge of the "Living Present". Re-enactments and Re-interpretations for the Preservation of Performance and New Media Art. In G. Giannachi & J. Westerman, eds. *Histories of Performance Documentation. Museum, Artistic, and Scholarly Practices*. London: Routledge: 115–131.
Hinz, M. (2011) *Die Schlacht am Tegeler Weg. Ein 68er-Reenactment*, URL: https://www.bpb.de/gesellschaft/bildung/kulturelle-bildung/60278/reenactment (Last Accessed on 15 July 2020).
Johnson, D. (2015) *The Art of Living. An Oral History of Performance Art*. London: Palgrave.
Schneider, A. (2016) Art/Anthropology Interventions. In S. Bianchini & E. Verhagen, eds. *Practicable: From Participation to Interaction in Contemporary Art*. Cambridge, Mass: MIT Press: 195–213.
Theodoropoulou, V. (2016) Against the Spectacle: The Construction of Situations. In S. Bianchini & E. Verhagen, eds. *Practicable: From Participation to Interaction in Contemporary Art*. Cambridge, Mass: MIT Press: 77–89.
Todorov, T. (2009) Memory as Remedy for Evil, *Journal of International Criminal Justice*, 7 (3): 447–462.
Westerman, J. (2017) Introduction. Practical Histories: How We Do Things with Performance. In G. Giannachi & J. Westerman, eds. *Histories of Performance Documentation. Museum, Artistic, and Scholarly Practices*. London: Routledge: 1–12.

16 Escaping the Thucydides Trap in IR class

Mikael Mattlin

Introduction[1]

International relations, especially between Great Powers, has historically been a ruthless affair. The emergence of new Great Powers has often ushered in turbulence, conflict, and war. From the point of view of Structural Realists in the field of international relations, this is a timeless and natural state of affairs, known to thinkers since Thucydides famously wrote about Sparta's fear of the rise of Athenian power in the *History of the Pelopennesian War*. With the seemingly inexorable rise of China and intensified strategic rivalry between the United States and China, Graham Allison (2017) coined the concept Thucydides Trap, as a novel description for this age-old dilemma, whereby a rising power causes fear in the dominant power that leads to arms races and conflict. More generally, this is known as the security dilemma: one side's actions to increase its own security are interpreted as threatening by others, thus decreasing their sense of security, which then may lead to a cycle of actions that decreases everyone's security. Not so long ago, Allison's restatement of this ancient theory would hardly have gained much traction in international relations. Yet, given the recent changes in world politics, Allison clearly hit a nerve. Allison's book is already widely cited, and journal special issues have been produced on it.

More generally, international relations teaching, especially in the major powers themselves, tends to convey, and thus perpetuate, the Realist worldview among students. Yet it need not be so. In a course concept that I have developed and taught over several years in two different universities, I adapt a board game and negotiation simulation that, in its original form, is very much steeped in Structural Realism. However, through a series of adaptations to gameplay and win rules, the game – and by extension also the learning experience – has been transformed. From an exercise in seeking dominance, sowing distrust, and betrayal, the game has been turned into an exercise in building more peaceful outcomes, in the process enhancing communal aspects in the classroom. While the notions of "friend" and "enemy" are very basic and crude categories, they are still among the most fundamental structuring features in contemporary world politics, as Carl Schmitt famously argued (Mouffe 1999; Wendt 2010, 260–263). Given the great importance and topicality of how we handle China's rise—the topic of the course—this novel method has global relevance in international relations teaching.

I have taught the course at two universities in Finland, at the University of Turku and at the University of Helsinki. I first taught the course in Finnish under the general title *Diplomacy –game course*. The basic course concept has been described in previous articles (Mattlin 2018, 2021). In the last three courses, I have more specifically focused on the topic of how we handle China's rise, and also continued to improve on the course concept, based on student feedback and teaching experiences. The course name was thus changed to *China's rise, diplomacy and the future of international relations*, and I have taught the course in English the last three times. The course concept and structure are still essentially the same, although the syllabus contents and some of the discussions have been continuously modified. In this chapter, I will focus on discussing how the concept relates to the theme of this book.

The relevance of the course concept for transcending collective histories

While the course is taught primarily to students of international relations, political science, and political history, it is open to students also from other disciplines. The course merges insights from several related disciplines and sub-disciplines: international relations, political history, diplomatic studies, foreign policy studies, political psychology, and China studies.

The course utilises the classical board game *Diplomacy* as a teaching method and pedagogical platform. *Diplomacy* is set in the context of early 20th century European Great Power politics and thus deals with how Europe ended up fighting what was at the time the bloodiest war that humankind had ever seen – First World War. The war ended, similarly to the Second World War, with calls for its horrors never again to be repeated. It also marked the end, not only of four European empires but also of Europe as being at the center of world affairs. The war also gave rise to the academic discipline of International Relations, with the first chair within the discipline being established in Aberystwyth in Wales in 1919. We have thus just celebrated the centennial of the discipline's founding. While the discipline has seen extraordinary expansion over the last decades, becoming a truly global field, many of the basic features of international relations – questions of order, security, power and restraint, freedom, and equality – have remained broadly the same (Bain 2019). The war loomed large in early IR scholarship. Many early scholars were driven by a desire to prevent a repeat of the war. The first generation of scholars have been called Idealists. After the Second World War, IR scholars turned more pessimistic – including several who harboured liberal inclinations. Classical Realist scholarship took over, and dominated discussions until the late 1970s, which saw the emergence of important works offering alternative readings of international relations. However, as a recent book argues, even the Realist tradition maintained a liberal and normative core, although it often rejected blind faith in democracy and law, as well as crusading in the name of Western liberal values and universalism (Reichwein 2020).

Using this particular board game therefore in a way "returns to the crime scene" of when the discipline was born, examining from various angles what led to the war. The question of the causes for the outbreak of the First World War is one of the most studied questions in political history, as well as a classical exam question (which I have also had to answer as an undergraduate student). The course, however, does not just dwell on this perennial question passively through reading books. Instead, students get to re-enact the events themselves, yet in a way that does not necessarily end in general mayhem, but may even lead to the amicable and peaceful resolution of conflicts. This dovetails with the recent call by Peter L. Hahn in his presidential address to *The Society for Historians of American Foreign Policy* on diversifying instructional methodologies. According to Hahn, it is "worth considering such pedagogical approaches as role-playing and simulations that replace the passive learning in a traditional lecture format with assignments to research a historical figure and then act the part in a re-enactment of a consequential historical moment" (Hahn 2019, 21). Games and simulations have previously been used in international relations theory, e.g., to simulate history (Weir & Baranowski 2011), protracted conflicts (Kirschner 2018), as well as the foreign-policy decision-making process (Loggins 2009). They have also been used to simulate more specific event-sequences, such as the 1945 Yalta Conference or the NATO expansion decision in 1993 (Hahn 2019, 21). Re-enacting historical situations and political decision-making in them has also been used in educational larps (Servetnik & Fedoseev 2016).

While knowing about the sequence of events that led to the First World War is important in itself for students of international relations and political history, it is important also because some observers perceive that there are distinct parallels between the international circumstances then and today, especially between the role of a rising Germany in the early 20th century and recent global events in relation to the role of a rising China (Kelly 2014). Yet, history does not simply repeat itself, although some parts of it may rhyme, as the saying goes. Normatively, it is also important that the evolution of history and international relations is regarded as open-ended (Mattlin 2018, 2021; Bain 2019), rather than pre-ordained, e.g., towards inevitable conflict between the leading power United States and a rising China, as Graham Allison and John Mearsheimer would suggest. History is neither entirely deterministic, nor is it wholly contingent (Carr 1961; Lebow 2010). Just because there appear to be some similarities between China's rise now and Germany's rise a century ago, we need not necessarily end up in a major war, or even a Cold War, although such a view currently seems to be becoming increasingly prevalent.

In order to maintain the open-ended nature of history in IR teaching, I have adapted the original *Diplomacy* game in several ways, to accommodate for the possibility of more peaceful outcomes. In the original game version, the game objective is eventually domination of the game board. While one cannot win the game without cooperation, forming alliances, and hence excelling in social interactions and "diplomatic" negotiations, eventually in order to win the game, one has to betray one's allies (or "backstab" them, in *Diplomacy* parlance).

My application of *Diplomacy* for teaching purposes allows students to choose which game strategy they want to play. There are three basic strategies – corresponding to three major theoretical paradigms in international relations: the Hobbesian, Lockean/Grotian, and Kantian paradigms (Bull 1977; Wight 1991; Wendt, 2010). The game may still end in a domination win, as in the original game, although this is exceedingly difficult to achieve (as it would be in reality). Alternatively, it may end in a negotiated and mediated peace agreement (facilitated by a dedicated peace mediator team), or it may end in the successful establishment of a "Zone of Peace" by some of the remaining teams. The specific requirements are described in detail in another recently published article (Mattlin, 2021).

How the game is played

Diplomacy is a board game, but also a negotiation simulation. Players represent the major early 19th-century European countries (randomly drawn or assigned) with the objective to negotiate their way through the game to victory. While the game requires a strategic eye, it is not purely a strategy game, rather the interpersonal interaction and communicative aspects of it are emphasised, which by itself may be considered an educational advantage, as university students these days tend to spend much time glued to small screens, rather than communicating in person with each other (cf. Hahn 2019, 21–22).

Negotiations are strictly timed, but during that time anyone can negotiate with anyone else about anything they wish to talk about. Following each round of negotiations, orders are written down on a piece of paper. Orders are resolved simultaneously by the game master. One of the features of the game is that there is no requirement to stick to any negotiated agreements. This mimics what is arguably the most fundamental difference between domestic affairs and international relations. In international relations, there is ultimately no higher authority and arbiter than nation-states (no supranational government). Although the international community has made repeated attempts at creating such institutions – the League of Nations, the UN and its Security Council, the Permanent Court of Arbitration, and the International Criminal Court – ultimately, if a sovereign nation decides to ignore these institutions, it can often get away with it, especially if it is a major power. So, e.g. when the Permanent Court of Arbitration in 2016 ruled in favor of the Philippines' position in the Sino-Philippine dispute over the Scarborough Shoal, China simply rejected the arbitration procedure, as well as its outcome (Pemmaraju 2016). Similarly, other major powers, foremost the United States, often do not accept that such international institutions have jurisdiction over them.

Although the backdrop of the game is martial and revolves around questions of war and peace, I emphasise to students the importance of not thinking of the game as only about conflict and war. Rather it should be understood as a simulation of any negotiation situation, where different parties have at least partially incompatible interests (e.g. trade or climate negotiations), and need to negotiate their way to some kind of outcome despite this.

The innovative aspects of my experiential teaching method are on two levels. The first level relates to several adaptations to gameplay itself that, I believe, make it more useful for IR teaching purposes. These adaptations are the altered win conditions, team-play, the use of dedicated peace mediators, and the possibility of using "public diplomacy" within the online learning environment (Moodle). The second set of innovative aspects relates to how the game is integrated into the rest of the teaching. The game forms an integral part of the whole teaching process (time-wise 30–50 % of the course's contact teaching hours), and it is interwoven into the rest of the teaching so that game-related phenomena are reflected upon also in class, in small group and online discussions, as well as by reading the compulsory course literature. Finally, the course ends in extensive debriefing and feedback, after which students complete the course by returning a learning diary in which they should interweave the various elements and reflect upon their learning process (a more extensive description of these course elements has been provided in Mattlin (2018)). This use of the *Diplomacy* game differs from how other IR university teachers have used the game, where the game typically has formed a smaller part of the class, or as only one game among other games that are used to illustrate theories, e.g. to reflect on Realism and the "rules of the game" in IR (Asal 2005; cf. Hirst 2019 on the use of "play" in IR teaching), or game-sessions that take place outside of class in an online environment (Rittinger 2018; Bridge & Radford 2014).

So far, the main lessons learned from teaching the course concept can be summarised as two points. Firstly, students have highly (and consistently) appreciated the teaching concept, based on numerical, written, and oral feedback collected over several years. Secondly, the adaptations introduced by me to the game have fairly dramatically altered the way students play the game, with outcomes now typically ending in either a Zone of Peace or a negotiated outcome. This already suggests that the game has educative potential beyond just teaching Realism as one IR theory (or serving as a platform to reflect upon Realism). This would also seem to point to the potential for the game to assist in breaking the cycle of conflict and violence, in this case by providing students with some hands-on experience in peaceful negotiations and resolving of interest-related differences. Seen from a *long dureé* perspective of history, the general trend in human history and international relations has been towards a reduction in militarism and wars (Harari 2016; Jervis 2005), so why teach IR in a way that takes conflict as the normal state?

In this context, it is interesting to note that there may also be some cultural elements involved. When I discussed using *Diplomacy* as a teaching tool with one of the pioneers of using the game in IR teaching, Victor Asal, he shared with me that in his classrooms in the United States, students tend to be very Realist.[2] In contrast, my own experience of using the game in Finland with Finnish and foreign students (from a broad range of countries), has been quite different. Very few of my students have professed to being strongly Realist in their thinking. This may also reflect the fact that Realism is currently not a strong element in IR teaching in Northern Europe.

As for whether the game concept is a more effective way to teach international relations theories, the jury is still out. In general, studies have shown that games can be effective in IR teaching (e.g. Lee & Shirkey 2017). Subjectively, students overwhelmingly perceive the teaching concept to be a better way to learn than more traditional lecturing or independent book reading (see Mattlin (2018) for some data). However, whether improved learning results can also be objectively measured, is more challenging. Methodologically , one of the difficulties is that there is no clear point of comparison (control group), i.e., a course where the exact same contents would be taught in a more traditional way (lecture course, reading, and exam). We recently presented preliminary data from a plausibility probe study that indicated positive changes both in students' learning of discipline-specific theory, as well as acquisition of future skills (Kruskopf et al. 2021).

Are there any drawbacks or disadvantages to this method of teaching then? One small drawback is that the teaching concept requires more effort from the teacher than a regular lecture course, especially initially. For example, the teacher has to familiarise her/himself with the game rules (as the teacher acts as a game master in the game). Student assessment is also continuous throughout the course, which requires the teacher to be very attentive to students' performance. The course concept may thus not be suitable for instructors, who are very busy or who do not have an interest in going beyond the normal teaching requirements.

The open-ended nature of the game events and current real-world events (which I often bring into the discussion), also means that teachers have to retain some flexibility to change their teaching (or at least its sequence), to better align with the game and real-world events. Finally, there is a small technical challenge related to the number of students taking the course. Because of the nature of the course and the designated roles students have in the game, the course is designed for 14–16 students (seven two-player teams

+ peace mediators), and students should preferably be present all the time, or at least almost all of the time, otherwise the concept will not work well. Course attendance is therefore compulsory. Students are informed about this in advance, and eventually, things have worked out, with very low absence rates (2–10 %). However, before the start of the course, there is always some to-and-fro, with some students informing the teacher very late that they will not be able to attend all teaching sessions, or not realising the required time-commitment until the course starts. To solve this challenge, it is advantageous to have an oversubscribed course registration, and reminding registered students about the compulsory nature of the course and the required time commitment.

Finally, one potential drawback is that because no final exam is used to gauge student learning, and students themselves have an active role in producing their own learning experience, it is possible that some students slip through in the sense that they do not fully require the body of theoretical knowledge in a systematic way. On the other hand, as students' performance assessment in this course concept is continuous and uses multiple methods (class and small group activity, online discussions, game performance, and course diary), the teacher will more easily notice if someone has not read the required literature. In this teaching concept, the teacher gets to know all the students better than in traditional lecturing, including learning all of their names by the end of the course.

Although student evaluations of the course already are at a level that is hard to further improve, from the teacher's perspective, I still see some further room for improvement. One of the areas that can still be improved on, is the balance in the adaptations introduced into the game's win conditions. One of the main purposes of the game adaptations is that the game should simulate real-world negotiations as realistically as possible. So far, the adaptations introduced have made the game more peaceful, with fewer betrayals and fewer eliminations of other players from the game. The last three games all ended in a peaceful resolution (the establishment of a Zone of Peace). In the most recent course, none of the playing teams was even close to being eliminated from the game, even after six hours of gameplay, which is rather unusual for the board game version of *Diplomacy*. However, in keeping with the aim of making the game more realistic, it should also not be *too* easy to achieve a peaceful solution. After all, real-world peace negotiations and mediations are seldom easy (Mattlin 2021).

Can the teaching concept be replicated elsewhere?

In principle, the course concept is replicable, which is also part of the reason why I have presented the concept in detail in earlier academic publications. There are two levels to this. The suggested game adaptations can be relatively easily adopted also by other university teachers, especially instructors who are already familiar with the game from before. Several colleagues around the world have already been in contact about the teaching concept, and drawn inspiration from it for their own teaching. The board game itself is also widely available for purchase, and relatively affordable. The whole course concept may, however, be more difficult to copy as such, as it brings together several elements, such as relevant course literature and an online learning environment (Moodle) that may not be available in other teaching contexts. The concept also relies on an active and dedicated teacher, who is committed to improving teaching and ready to spend a bit more time on it than otherwise required. Every teacher will also bring their own emphases to the teaching situation. The adapted board game is versatile enough to accommodate this.

If this teaching method is used in other contexts, instructors are advised to familiarise themselves very well with the game and game rules in advance. The instructor also acts as an impartial game-master, and should therefore know the rules at least as well as the students. Typically, very few students have played the game before, which means that especially at the beginning of the game, there may be many questions directed towards the game master related to game rules. Often inexperienced players also write their game orders incorrectly, which according to the game rules, voids the order. If not explained properly beforehand, this may cause some disappointment among students.

Another thing to note is that the *Diplomacy* game is infamous for bringing out emotions, sometimes even strong ones. Because the game revolves so much around interpersonal relations, communication, trust (and betrayal of trust),[3] players are sometimes – and only half-jokingly – advised to avoid playing with their friends, if they want to remain friends. The adaptations that I have made to the game somewhat ameliorates this problem. However, one element that is still present is the time-pressure due to the tightly timed game turns. This in turn causes some stress and anxiety, which most students report feeling, at least to some extent. On the other hand, almost all students also report feelings of joy associated with the game. Less commonly reported are feelings of fear and grief.

Although the vast majority of students have reported high appreciation for the learning experience at the end of the course, this aspect of the game needs to be considered by instructors. Students should be warned prior to the course that the course is both time-consuming and may also be stressful and emotionally taxing. This may also indicate that there are additional risks associated with using the game in contexts where participants are recovering from acute trauma related to conflicts and violence, or what Anthony Oberschall refers to as a cognitive "crisis frame" (Oberschall 2000). Teachers need to be mentally prepared to cope with students, who show disappointed or even angry reactions when trust has been broken and they feel betrayed by their fellow students.

Conclusions

The adapted version of the *Diplomacy* game is promising as a more interactive method to teach international relations, that can be fruitfully used also by other adjacent disciplines, e.g. political history. The original version of the game is, however, not conducive to breaking cycles of conflict and violence, as it may even attenuate a world-view that others cannot be trusted, interests are zero-sum, betrayal is to be expected, and other people are out to destroy you. In the original version of *Diplomacy*, players need to pay continuous attention to hedging their bets, as letting down one's guard will quickly result in other players taking advantage of the opportunity. Keating and Ruzicka (2014) have suggested that in real-world international relations, the absence or removal of hedging strategies is one of the best indicators of a trusting relationship. The adapted version of the game that this chapter reports on can overcome many of these problems. While issues of trust are still present, it offers students a chance to reflect, through their own experiences, on what causes people to lose trust in each other, how easily trust can be lost, and how to build trust under circumstances where it is lacking, e.g. because of a shared history of antagonism and conflict. The game and teaching concept may thus be useful also under circumstances of dealing with collective historical traumas.

Observers of international relations and human history have in recent years noted a trend of declining militarism and wars as a defining characteristic of the human condition. In his best-selling book, Yuval Noah Harari notes this changing nature of international politics, and especially the declining role of war (Harari 2016). Previously, Jervis (2005) has also noted that shifts in identity reflect a sharp decline in militarism and nationalism, as well as growing compatibility in values among the most advanced major powers, although global events after the global financial crisis has thrown the latter in doubt. Nevertheless, based on the experience of teaching this course concept, it is tempting to conjecture that university students will often prefer to build peace rather than wage endless war if only they are given the chance to do so.

Notes

1 The idea for this paper was born, and the chapter was written, while the author was employed as Collegium researcher in the Turku Institute for Advanced Studies (TIAS).
2 Author's correspondence with professor Victor Asal from Albany University in July-August 2018.
3 Trust research has recently been prominent in International Relations (Ruzicka & Keating 2015).

References

Allison, G. (2017) *Destined for War: Can America and China Escape Thucydides's Trap?* Boston and New York: Houghton Mifflin Harcourt.

Asal, V. (2005) Playing Games with International Relations, *International Studies Perspectives*, 6: 359–373. https://doi.org/10.1111/j.1528-3577.2005.00213.x

Bain, W. (2019) Continuity and Change in International Relations, 1919–2019, *International Relations*, 33 (2): 132–141.

Bull, H. (1977 [1995]) *The Anarchical Society. A Study of Order in World Politics*, 2nd ed. New York, NY: Columbia University Press.

Bridge, D. & Radford. S. (2014) Teaching Diplomacy by Other Means: Using and Outside-of-class Simulation to Teach International Relations Theory, *International Studies Perspectives*, 15 (4): 423–437. https://doi.org/10.1111.insp.12017

Carr, E. (1961) *What Is History?* Harmondsworth: Pelican Books.

Hahn, P. (2019) The Authority of Academics in a Time of Turbulence, *Diplomatic History*, 43 (1): 1–30.

Harari, Y. (2016) *Homo Deus. A Brief History of Tomorrow*. London: Harvill Secker.

Hirst, A. (2019) Play In(g) International Theory, *Review of International Studies*, 45 (5): 891–914. https://doi.org/10.1017/S0260210519000160

Jervis, R. (2005) *American Foreign Policy in a New Era*. New York: Routledge.

Keating, V. & Ruzicka, J. (2014) Trusting Relationships in International Politics: No Need to Hedge, *Review of International Studies*, 40: 753–770. https://doi.org/10.1017/S0260210514000059

Kelly, R. (2014) Comparing China and the Kaiser's Germany (part 1), *The Interpreter*. Available at: https://www.lowyinstitute.org/the-interpreter/comparing-china-and-kaisersgermany-part-1-similarities

Kirschner, S. (2018) Simulating Negotiation in Protracted Conflicts, *Journal of Political Science Education*. https://doi.org/10.1080/15512169.2018.1530122

Kruskopf, M., Ketonen, E., & Mattlin, M. (2021). Playing Out Diplomacy: Gamified Reinforcement of Future Skills and Discipline-specific Theory. *European Political Science*. https://doi.org/10.1057/s41304-020-00305-7

Lebow, R. (2010) *Forbidden Fruit. Counterfactuals and International Relations*. Princeton and Oxford: Princeton University Press.

Lee, M. & Shirkey, Z. (2017) Going Beyond the existing *Consensus*: the use of games in international relations education, *PS: Political Science & Politics*, 571–575. https://doi.org/10.1017/S1049096516003218

Loggins, J. (2009) Simulating the Foreign-policy Decision-making Process in the Undergraduate Classroom, *PS: Political Science & Politics*, 42 (2): 401–407. https://doi.org/10.1017/S1049096509090544

Mattlin, M. (2018) Adapting the DIPLOMACY Board Game Concept for 21st Century International Relations Teaching, *Simulation & Gaming*, 49 (6): 735–750. https://doi.org/10.1177/1046878118 7889

Mattlin, M. (2021) Anarchy Is What Students Make Of It: Playing Out Wendt's Three Cultures of Anarchy, *Journal of Political Science Education*. https://doi.org/10.1080/15512169.2020.1861457

Mouffe, C. (1999) Carl Schmitt and the Paradox of Liberal Democracy. In C. Mouffe, ed. *The Challenge of Carl Schmitt*. London & New York: Verso: 38–53.

Oberschall, A. (2000) The Manipulation of Ethnicity: From Ethnic Cooperation to Violence and War in Yugoslavia, *Ethnic and Racial Studies*, 23 (6): 982–1001. https://doi.org/10.1080/014198700750018388

Pemmaraju, A. (2016) The South China Sea Arbitration (The Philippines v. China): Assessment of the Award on Jurisdiction and Admissibility, *Chinese Journal of International Law*, 15 (2): 265–307. https://doi.org/10.1093/chinesejil/jmw019

Reichwein, A. (2020) Introduction: Realism—A Primarily European Tradition Emigrating to the U.S. In A. Reichwein & F. Rösch, eds. *Realism: A Distinctively 20th Century European Tradition*. London: Palgrave Pivot: 1–12. https://doi.org/10.1007/978-3-030-58455-9_1.

Rittinger, E. (2018) Inspiring Students to Think Theoretically about International Relations through the Game of Diplomacy, *Journal of Political Science Education*, 16 (1): 41–56. https://doi.org/10.1080/15512169.2018.1516556

Ruzicka, J. & Keating, V. (2015) Going Global: Trust Research and International Relations, *Journal of Trust Research*, 5 (1): 8–26. https://doi.org/10.1080/21515581.2015.1009082

Servetnik, V. & Fedoseev, A. (2016) Educational Larps for Political Studies. In K. Kangas, M. Loponen, & J. Särkijärvi, eds. *Larp Politics: Systems, Theory and Gender in Action*. Solmukohta: 65–71.

Weir, K. & Baranowski, M. (2011) Simulating History to Understand International Politics, *Simulation & Gaming*, 42 (4): 441–461. https://doi.org/10.1177/1046878108325442

Wendt, A. (1999 [2010]) *Social Theory of International Politics*, 13th ed. Cambridge: Cambridge University Press.

Wight, M. (1991) The Three Traditions of International Theory. In G. Wight & N. Porter, eds. *International Theory: The Three Traditions*. Leicester: Leicester University Press: 7–24.

17 Designing videogames for teaching about transmission of historical traumas: a case study of *Memory Gliders*

Nena Močnik

Introduction

Though as researchers we are called to produce new knowledge and/or creative and innovative reinterpretations of existing ontological connections, the vast majority of us who (must) also engage in teaching invest little to no time in learning, developing, and exploring new, progressive, interactive, and/or experiential pedagogical practices that would respond to the needs of the contemporary classroom and learners. More than ever before, the new generations call for participatory culture in the classroom that would extend beyond simple lecturing and the passive transmission of information from teachers to students. Particularly due to the rapid intervention of digital technologies in our lives, we can no longer deny our students' increased intellectual readiness for and technical fluency in the different modes of e-learning, including interactive platforms and videogames.

Since the beginning of my teaching career, I have been lucky to have opportunities to deliver courses that I could also design, both in terms of my pedagogical approach and the contents. Consequently, I have been able to follow the didactic trends in teaching and to challenge the tradition of the limited and discipline-oriented perspectives. Together with my students (or, in the context of non-formal education, with the workshop participants), I was furthermore able to experiment with different methods and to test and evaluate different learning practices. Although the students' response to the dialogical, experiential teaching was usually positive, I got the impression that the interactive, embodied, or art-based practices that I used were rather unusual and uncommon in tertiary education. In some cases, it took me quite some energy and time to "unprogram" the previously adopted learning styles: from a hierarchical to a non-hierarchical teacher-student relationship; from a one-way-only teaching-learning process to a mutual *edu-learning* exchange; from a passive delivering-consuming practice of knowledge transmission to the active modes of searching, questioning, and critically reflecting; and, last but not least, from a cognitive to an embodied and emotional interpretation and comprehension of complex, intersectional social problems.

While I was relatively free in designing my courses as an individual, to systematically introduce novel pedagogical practices in tertiary education is a very slow process. This is particularly the case when seizing new opportunities and engaging with skills and forms of knowledge that interrupt our classroom dynamics with digital technologies. The digitalisation of teaching practices regarding the intergenerational effects of trauma transmission in history classes often finds lecturers in tertiary education ill-prepared, both in terms of *content-related skills* (how to deal with potential traumatic ruptures and triggers) as well as the *technical skills* required to incorporate, explore, and benefit from the digital tools for stimulating learner engagement. As a *digital immigrant* (Prensky 2001), an occasional user of digital devices and apps, I am curious about the potential of digital technologies for teaching among the *digital natives* and how those can enrich and benefit the learning exchange between educators and learners. For me as a teacher, the pervasiveness of technologies primarily means reflecting on my physical presence and role in the classroom and on the need for new (adjusted) foundations for our own profession. However, though the omnipresence of easily accessible information does not equal knowledge: the technology impacts how we teach the information that is accessible with a single click, and how students place it in relation to other sources available beyond the authority of the teacher. While for digital immigrants the ban on using smartphones during class may appear logical as these devices can interrupt the pedagogical process, for digital natives the participatory culture enabled by digital devices in terms of creating content and having agency over that content is taken for granted in their daily lives – why, therefore, would such culture not be allowed in the school?

In this chapter, I reflect on my attempts to adopt the online education trends designing a videogame on the topic of the transmission of historical traumas. Due to my interest in embodied teaching practices, I will first draw some correlations between the various dualities that structure our learning experience, such as the "physical/virtual", "real/imaginary", and "immersed/embodied." Then, I will tackle the difficulties involved in converting a very conceptual and intangible topic (i.e., trauma transmission) into the videogame format that requires a simple, concise, and understandable scenario. By discussing the making of *Memory Gliders*,[1] I will raise questions related not only to the transmission of collective traumas but to the institutional pressure to incorporate more information and communication technologies (ICTs) into our teaching practices without being offered any proper training in online content design and using ICT. Using the case of *Memory Gliders*, I question the paradigmatic discrepancy between the digital natives and the digital immigrants as elaborated by Marc Prensky (2001) when it comes to understanding how and why (if at all) we should incorporate videogames in the learning process. I focus particularly on the actual skills and capabilities that a digital immigrant – for example, a teacher who is (almost) completely foreign to videogames (and ICTs in general) and has no experiences and theoretical background either as a creator or a user – should obtain to successfully use such contents in teaching. Reflecting on my own experience of collaborating in designing a videogame, I summarise this chapter by reflecting on the limited resources that go beyond the teacher's enthusiasm and personal skills, such as time and funding, that would support transforming analogue topics into digital language. I claim that such limitations can further marginalise some already unmotivated teachers who are digital immigrants and slow down the process of the digitalisation of education.

The virtual/real/imaginary and the digitalisation of embodiment

Despite the continuous discussion by education scholars on the role of the body and the multiple applications of "whole person learning" (Merriam 2008) in the early years of schooling, tertiary education in the Western schooling system follows the pedagogies that prioritise cognitive understanding over embodied experience. However, with the rich scholarship on the connection between the body and trauma and on the importance of the body in the trauma healing process, one cannot envision an impactful understanding of the trauma and intergenerational effects without inquiring into one's own body and the body in communication with others. Trauma is often caused by abusive relationships, and building trust in others, who are present as embodied subjects – think of family members in the case of domestic violence or school peers in the case of bullying – is crucial in establishing new, posttraumatic interpersonal dynamics. Our bodies store our histories as much as our minds do, and therefore, the body's multiple levels of experiencing the world – besides the intellectual, there are also the physical and sensual as well as the emotional and spiritual forms of experience – and the diverse ways that these experiences are defined and changed when we engage in relationships with other learners might all be sites for pedagogical practice. When addressing the question of (collective) traumas in the context of historical transmission, our learning bodies often cross zones of comforts; through their embodied performance, one does not only respond to the injustices of today but becomes aware of the patterns and values that correspond to traumatic legacies. Within and across different social groups, historical traumas continue existing in different discursive and ideological social constructions of today, manifesting in the lived realities of individuals and the privileges and/or opportunities that individuals are granted.

Including the emotional, embodied, and non-cognitive aspects of trauma transmission in (history) education, particularly in relation to the current forms of social oppression and injustice, means looking for transformative opportunities in breaking the cycles of violence by working on one's own body in relation to the bodies of others. The teacher-student and student-student dynamics are crucial in one's reaction to traumatic content and self-connection or/and self-reflection. Furthermore, the very presence of the learners' bodies in the physical spaces gives the impression that the risk of emotionally loaded and potentially traumatic topics can be mitigated with the support of fellow members of the learning community.

The empathic immersion in the experiences of others, and thus the relationships in which we engage when physically present in the classroom, is a crucial means of communication in working with collective traumas and exploring the effects of intergenerational transmissions in families and communities (Saul 2013; Sajnani & Johnson 2014; Reimann & König 2017). Designing a videogame where both the immersion of and the relationship between the players happen on a different level confronted me with the issues of (1) *vertical* and (2) *horizontal* transmission of knowledge in the classroom. With the *vertical transmission of knowledge*, I refer to peer-to-peer exchange, which today importantly includes also sharing the content over different social media platforms and communication tools. In this chapter, however, I want to focus more on the *vertical transmission of knowledge*, the kind of transfer that happens from generation to generation. The gap that exists between the two age groups is a gap in terms of worldviews, which are affected by the knowledge that is accumulated, challenged, and evaluated by each new generation (Zemke et al. 2000; Billings 2004; Reeves & Oh 2007; Kirschner & De Bruyckere 2017). Therefore, my digital-immigrant mindset is, perhaps, not skilled enough to adequately consider the topic that was so distant from me, both in terms of physicality and relationality, as is the case with videogames. The immersion and the embodiment that are rooted in our experience of the physical world have different characteristics: during the human-to-human interaction, *we use the created world*, whereas in the human-computer interaction, *we participate in the created world* (Slater & Sanchez-Vives 2016, 3). Consequently, the digital natives, who are continuously exposed to multisensory simulations (visual, auditory, tactile, kinesthetic, etc.) that generate "illusory realities, mostly related to the self (and body), in order to get the mind to believe (and accept) the virtual as real" (Perez-Marcos 2018, 2), are also better skilled in using and not just participating in the created virtual worlds. Through the exposure and immersion that starts from an early age, the digital natives create new worlds, meaning, and relationships, and, for them, these worlds are not more or "less" real than what is known as our physical everyday world. While digital natives are able to create parallel, coexisting worlds that, in a way, merge in the holistic worldview, digital immigrants are more likely to refer the content of the "imaginary" videogame back to the "real world."

Such traditional division between physical, that is "more real", and virtual, that is "constructed", reality put to question many experiential learning methods, particularly the principles of embodied education, that were positively promoted and used long before the emergence of ICT. In his anthropological account, Tom Boellstorff (2008) aimed to understand the transformative possibilities that occur when humans, with their physical bodies and cognitive sense, interact with technology – not in the sense of two divided and separate worlds but in terms of how humans and technology are simultaneously inspired and impacted. Although they operate under different principles, the intersecting worlds also create a new understanding and positioning of the embodied identity of the player. In sophisticated videogames or virtual reality, the body and senses (emotions) engage with *the virtual body of the avatar* and sometimes with the bodies of other present avatars. However, this apparently individual experience is enhanced once it is united with other *physical bodies* in *physical (actual) reality*. Therefore, the experience of the virtual is "real" and stays with the physical in the aftermath. Adding the virtual world and merging and overlapping it with actual reality allows us to experience situations and emotions that our physical bodies are not capable of providing. In addition, social contracts are very often limiting the full expression of individuals and collectives.

Teaching with videogames, similarly to any other embodied engaged pedagogy, encourages students to envision and create spaces, situations, emotions, and, therefore, simulations of the worlds that are not necessarily in existence (yet). As with in situ learning or the pedagogy of hope (Freire 1994), for instance, virtual realities build on the potential of "on-spot" immersion that involves the physical and mental participation of individuals and collectives (Carù & Cova 2006). Scholars have considered the immersion process, whereby senses can be isolated sufficiently "to make a person feel transported to another place" (Boellstorff 2008, 20), to be a defining characteristic in teaching the emphatic connection." In the context of trauma transmission, the effort involved in taking on different identities, such as "getting into the shoes of the other" or belonging momentarily to the very specific time- and place-limited context (Hansen & Mossberg 2013, 212), is crucial in preventing further traumatisation and/or breaking the cycles of violence (Sallberg & Grand 2016). However, "living the experiences of 'the Other'" through the empathic connection can only be done as a performative, constructed, imaginary, and, therefore, "virtual" act.

However, even if practices like the formation of empathic connections, are merely virtual in the actual world, the knowledge that is generated in and for the pre-virtual context cannot simply be moved to the "virtual" format. This brings us to my second concern regarding the *vertical transmission of knowledge*, which I understand as the direct, body-to-body interaction between the learners. While such interaction, not only between learners but generally, is an essential social practice for the well-being of people and for achieving full integration with the other members of society, the scholars are yet to reach an agreement what is the capacity of the videogames to nurture the physical, spiritual, and emotional interactions among humans. However, extensive scholarship on prosocial videogames has shown positive short- and long-term effects of prosocial actions as well as changes in beliefs, attitudes, emotional responses, and empathy, and enhanced interpersonal relations (for sources, see Boduszek et al. 2019). While creating *Memory Gliders*, I focused (or should I say "was fixated"?) on the idea that we need to incorporate the already recorded benefits of the embodied and emotional aspects in learning in a videogame about trauma transmission. However, what if the principles of embodied teaching provide benefits and learning impacts in the very particular context of physical spaces and are also generationally conditioned, meaning that they could lose their impact when used by the new/next generation? Does the embodiment even have the same importance for the digital natives, who are supposedly born into the digital world and have, therefore, a different experience than we, the digital immigrants, do? Or does the embodiment gain new dimensions in the virtual world? While from the theoretical and empirical points of view, I can strongly argue for the importance of embodied and emotional experience in teaching about the transmission of trauma and breaking the cycles of violence in the classroom, but I am not knowledgeable and experienced enough to recognise whether there are other (more) important cognitive and/or sensorial features that a simple, low-budget videogame can offer to the learner. Moreover, other issues with translating the physical experience into the virtual kind came up once we embarked on the process of videogame creation.

Conceptualising trauma transmission in a videogame

When creating a videogame, before deciding on the concrete narrative and the visuals that go with it, one has to decide what the target group and the goals are. As the project focused on transforming the traditional pedagogical methods to develop and promote more inclusive, participatory, and experiential approaches, particularly in tertiary education, the main target group was not hard to define. We wanted the game to be played in our university classrooms by our students, meaning primarily by young adults between 18 and 25 years of age. Most of the game designers today create educational games that help develop skills important for 21st-century employees, such as science and mathematics skills, creativity, information, and communication skills, and the ability to solve multi-layered and complex problems (World Economic Forum 2016). Teachers in primary and secondary schools most often see the advantages in enhancing logic, memory, problem-solving, critical thinking, visualisation, and, sometimes, team-building skills (Annetta 2008, 231). But what are the particular skills that today's university students need to learn in history classes, and how can such skills be taught through videogames?

Crogan (2003, 296) listed several games that embody "the classic task given to historical discourse" in preventing violent history from repeating itself. The creators are often given the freedom to appropriate historical events for the sake of clarity on behalf of the player, which usually involves separating the characters between the good and the bad and events between peace and war. While with *Memory Gliders* we wanted to avoid reenacting and/or representing concrete historical events, the game still featured some of the specific elements unique to the format of videogames. Among such features, immersion and the first-person perspective within the interactive space (Hess 2007, 345) respond to what in the classroom is achieved through embodied activities. In comparison to the videogames that are based on some very concrete historical events, for instance, *Attentat 1942* or *Call of Duty: World War II*, one of the initial goals in creating *Memory Gliders* was to create a videogame that could be played by the learners all around the world. We strove to create a game that (1) minimises the connections with specific historical and socio-political contexts, (2) addresses identity politics in the widest sense possible, and (3) leaves an open space for learners to form their own interpretations and conclusions rather than setting concrete learning goals. The game was meant to tackle the topic of intergenerational trauma transmission in a very broad sense and to possibly raise questions and provoke discussions, but, contrary to the general idea of "educational" games that pre-set the learning objectives for the players, we hoped that Memory Gliders can leave enough room for the teachers and learners to define specific learning goals that are important for their own context. To give a parallel example, while there are some universal learning points in history education that we can all take away from the experience of the Holocaust, there are also very contextually specific (ethical) perspectives on the Holocaust that differ from one case to another, for instance, political dynamics, current events in the context where the game is played, etc. With the Memory Gliders, therefore educators can decide very freely whether they want to address the topic of intergeneration trauma as a broad concept or apply it to historical events that affect the current socio-political context.

In order to leave the game open to various interpretations and uses in different contexts, we refrained from portraying real or concrete historical situations and used a very simple yet conceptually designed script. This means that no particular place or community was mentioned, no references to historical events were suggested, and the level of immersion did not depend on either the very private family or collective experiences of the player. However, this "abstract" approach to the game content, the characters, and the setting did not make the decisions on the symbolical meaning and representations any easier. Due to limitations in terms of time, finances, and human resources, we agreed on a combination of animals and humans for the main characters, which turned out to be a tricky decision. Most animals have strong symbolic connotations, not only as part of the culture but particularly in the processes of group ostracism and discrimination (see Mayersen 2018), meaning that the use of animal characters or symbols to narrate the story on political violence can be highly problematic. While there were serious concerns regarding the use of animals (in the case of *Memory Gliders*, birds), particularly from my side, I also wanted to encourage the creative and artistic expression of the game designers. Although visual representations and semiotics are a very important component of videogames, it is impossible to create or include visuals that would be free of cultural meanings and the (harmful) narratives and ideologies attached to them. Furthermore, the imagery used does not necessarily just reflect the "realities" of the past but can actively construct new meanings and participates in the sense-making of important historical events and the present identity-building. Being knowledgeable about the power of representations, narratives, and (visual) semiotics of cultural artifacts can make the process of videogame design extremely more complex.

Another important component, the game's narrative, is a central feature that is used to immerse players in the game world and, in the context of educational games, to navigate the learning objectives. The narrative, along with the visuals, gives meaning to the player's actions, but it also grants them the power of decision-making. Every dialogue has several potential outcomes that depend on the player's choice, which corresponds to what Seixas and Morton (2013) called "plural histories": the need to provide opportunities to evaluate competing historical claims. The past, according to their argument, comprises everything that has ever happened overall time, including the (re-)interpretations of events, and is therefore not a fully formed singular story. Therefore, giving the learners the opportunity (or the responsibility) to navigate the flow of the game narration importantly emphasises the "variations" of history and how, similarly to a videogame, a "single situation" (i.e., a single historical event) has "different variations" (different interpretations of the same historical event in the present) depending on the player's choices and decisions (the players in the creation of historical narratives can be different, such as state institutions, survivors, political bodies, journalists, historians, etc.). In line with Seixa's arguments on "Postmodern History", *Memory Gliders* aims to encourage students not to rely on conclusions by history scholars but to establish their own positions when interpreting the past. This is not to say that the historical evidence is inaccurate or that historical evidence and/or knowledge is completely open to interpretations because histories are simply "stories we tell about the past" (Seixas & Morton 2013, 1). In fact, as its narrative is so broad and, to a certain extent, abstract (i.e., it does not refer to any specific historical event), the question is whether *Memory Gliders* is a "history game" at all. Seixas and some other scholars that deal with the concepts of plural histories and multiperspectivity have emphasised the importance of recognising the role of history in our current social structures and dynamics as well as our own (individual or collective) reflection of the concepts and the ways in which our world is represented and understood through the history stories. As I mentioned at the beginning of this chapter, history teachers are not necessarily trained in such a dialogical, conversational, and multi-interpretational idea of history teaching. Engaging with historical traumas demands a specific set of skills, at least those that would prevent trauma triggers and/or the re-traumatisation of the learners. This means that history teachers should eventually be skilled in trauma-informed principles, which means understanding how violence, victimisation, and other traumatic experiences shape the lives of the learners and ensuring the safety of the learning experience to accommodate the needs of potentially traumatised learners (Butler et al. 2011; Harris & Fallot 2001). The narrative of *Memory Gliders*, therefore, extends beyond the idea that history can be interpreted and understood through multiple perspectives and that the long-term consequences of traumatic historical events might shape our current realities. Most importantly, the development of the narrative, subject to the player's decisions, shows that no matter what interpretations and how many of them are attached to a single historical event, and regardless of the fact that we only have limited control and/or power over the past, one can always decide how to handle this legacy in the present. The very fact of creating an "educational" game, a game that supposedly teaches (about) something, leaves little room to create value-free content and narrative. However, as opposed to some other videogames on violent histories, *Memory Gliders* does not question any of the historical truths and does not strive to contest official histories by teaching pluralism and multiperspectivity. It simply acknowledges that violent past events might have long-term, intergenerational effects, and though there is little to no chance to change this, individuals can, nonetheless, take a proactive step in handling such traumatic legacies either individually or collectively.

Understanding histories as "lived experiences" is another aspect of the game that brings back my concerns about embodiment. The structure of the storyline encourages learners to cognitively (and emotionally) process the experiences and knowledge that are grounded in the embodied actions of their everyday life. The game does not ask the learners to empathically connect with the histories of the temporally, spatially, and culturally distant communities but to focus their attention on how the violent pasts are embodied in the learners' own communities. While the physical classroom enables us to "rehearse" certain real-life situations by including breath, movement, feelings, and non-verbal communication, in the end, it is still, like a virtual space, an artificial and pre-prepared methodology with the goal of learning. Similarly to the videogame, the "narrative" in the classroom is prepared in advance and exercised in a safe environment. Both of these learning principles encourage our changed participation in the world; however, a learner still needs to ground their learning outcomes in the actual mobilisation of "being in the world" and "shaping the world" (Merleau-Ponty in Schwarz-Franco 2016, 454). The body has different modes of action, but "being in the world" replaces passive observation with the functionally defined, concrete act as the "relation of the subject to the world" (Merleau-Ponty in Schwarz-Franco 2016, 454). While *Memory Gliders* does not involve the body in the learning process in the same, traditional way as does embodied (physical) learning in the classroom, the most ambitious learning goal of this game was to change attitudes towards the body – that is, to use the game as a tool and an initiator to mobilise the bodies of the learners in actively changing and shaping the realities of the lived experiences in the physical world.

As *Memory Gliders* was one of the outputs of the project *#Never Again: Teaching Transmission of Trauma and Remembrance through Experiential*

Learning (see the Introduction), the game designers and other project participants were extremely limited in how they could approach the creation of the game. To respond to the needs of the participatory classroom, ideally, the game development would be followed up by long-term research on the users, collecting the materials, reflections, ideas, and needs of the digital natives, and then reflecting on these data with the new players and repeating this cycle several times before integrating all the outcomes, evidence, and feedback into the product to be used and distributed. Unfortunately, such a process is rather difficult to afford in terms of the temporal, financial, and human resources, especially given the pressure for rapid and massive knowledge production within the present academic structures.

However, assuming the intergenerational gap in both the learning methods and the many world perspectives, it is highly possible that a teacher creating a game without students' input will fail to deliver the content at least at some level, be it either in terms of entertainment and/or engagement, the comprehension of the topic as such, the importance of the topic, or the contextualisation of the topic in real life. Engaging students in the creation of the game would, therefore, already be an interactive pedagogical process that would enable students to contribute using their very particular and personal family histories and also to close the potential technical gaps that occur in the understanding and practicing/using ICTs and navigating the life between the virtual and actual worlds. Moreover, students' ideas on how to create a videogame with this specific topic would challenge the transmission of knowledge in the traditional classroom, where the teacher still has the power to decide which topics and perspectives to prioritise and to emphasise in their curricula. But, in this concrete case of an 18-months-long project that also involved numerous other challenges, this ideal, bottom-up, and participatory approach toward creating the videogame was neither realistic nor (financially) feasible.

Conclusion

Including conceptual videogames in history, education demands certain changes in traditional objectives and disciplinary paradigms of the history discipline as such. One of the most important issues would be to consider the topic of trauma and the long-term traumatic impacts of collective/political violence and the potential presence of this same trauma in the classroom. Second, to include the connections between historical traumas and current socio-political structure, the teacher training should incorporate comprehension of broader sociological concepts. Third, as the game is designed very broadly, it responds to the calls for "inclusive classrooms", meaning that students are invited to share their family histories and very personal connections in relation to collective historical events. In today's classrooms, the multicultural background of the learner's demands not only to understand that diverse historical traumas can span multiple generations or be very recent, but also that the history taught should reconsider the eurocentric (Western) narratives and provide the content from multiple geopolitical regions instead. History education a part of an ideological state apparatus very often covers different past events in unequal proportions and uses very limited ethnocentric perspectives. The issue of what is included in contemporary history education (which periods, what events, which world regions, what communities, what perspectives?) is now being discussed within postcolonial and indigenous studies. For me, one of the most important values is establishing dialogue and engaging in conversations rather than holding instructor-focused lessons, and *Memory Gliders* can be a great way to invite learners to create their own sets of values, to develop intimate relationships with their (painful) family histories, and reflect on the intergenerational structural violence occurring in their own realities. The game creates an environment where the player's excitement is based on their own decision-making and the responsibilities that come with the development of the plot. In this way, Memory Gliders responds to the notion that knowledge should no longer be "deposited", as termed by Paolo Freire, but constructed, in the individual mind of the learner and in active exchange with other learners, teacher, and the broader environment (see Papert & Harel 1991).

As several negative stereotypes are still attached to videogames (particularly those to do with violence), in this chapter I mostly focused on the benefits of videogames and how, as digital immigrants, we can use the potential of videogames to respond to the needs of contemporary digitally native learners. However, "playing with trauma" can present some serious risks if the issue is not approached carefully and with sufficient preparation. As much as this game provides a platform for critical reflection and the impulse to act in real life for the betterment of society, it can also enhance the negative feelings, trauma, and pessimistic views regarding the repetition of historical events. However, removing as many references to the actual world as possible in creating a videogame means that the topic of trauma transmission can be grasped from very different perspectives depending on the teacher's knowledge and skills in the multidisciplinary approach. I argue that staying away from the "concrete" brings students closer to understanding the overwhelming complexity of traumatic events like wars or mass atrocities that go beyond the limited narratives of the official (national) histories that primarily serve the goal of nation-building and social cohesion. In addition, the impact of transmitted collective traumas on persistent identity-based violence (specifically racism) is still very rarely addressed within history teaching. If Memory Gliders can bring this topic to the classroom and spark a discussion on how historical traumas are experienced, lived, and manifested in the lives of students and teachers, this process (playing the game and reflecting on it collectively) potentially emphasise also the point that many forms of violence are rooted in history and that, in order to break the vicious cycles, we need to actively address the traumas related to historical violence. The list of the "most important skills for the 21st-century worker" as defined during the Business-Higher Education Forum in 2005 needs to include critical reflection on violent histories by taking an active and responsible role in dealing constructively with the legacies expressed as an individual or collective traumas and experienced as different forms of identity-based violence. Such a skill is crucial if we want to establish a less malevolent and more welcoming social order.

Note

1 The videogame has been created in the frame of the project *#NeverAgain: Teaching Transmission of Trauma and Remembrance through Experiential Learning*, funded by European Comissions – European Remembrance programme.

References

Ahonen, S. (2005) Historical Consciousness: A Viable Paradigm for History Education? *Journal of Curriculum Studies*, 37: 697–708.

Annetta, L. A. (2008) Video Games in Education. Why They should be Used and How They are Being Used, *Theory into Practice*, 47 (3): 229–239.

Billings, D. (2004) Teaching Learners From Varied Generations, *The Journal of Continuing Education in Nursing*, 35 (3): 104–105.

Boduszek, D., Debowska. A., Jones, A., Ma, M., Smith, D. Willmott, D., Tortman J., Da Breo, H., & Kirkman, G. (2019) Prosocial Video Game as an Intimate Partner Violence Prevention Tool among Youth: A Randomized Controlled Trial, *Computers in Human Behavior*, 93: 260–266.

Boellstorff, T. (2008) *Coming of Age in Second Life: An Anthropologist Explores the Virtually Human*. Princeton: Princeton University Press.

Butler, L. D., Critelli, F. M., & Rinfrette, E. S. (2011) Trauma-informed care and mental health, *Directions in Psychiatry*, 31: 197–210.

Carù, A. & Cova, B. (2006) How to Facilitate Immersion in a Consumption Experience: Appropriation Operations and Service Elements, *Journal of Consumer Behaviour*, 5 (1): 4–14.

Crogan, P. (2003) Gametime: History, Narrative, and Temporality in Combat Flight Simulator 2. In M. J. P. Wolf & B. Perron, eds. *The Video Game Theory Reader*. New York: Routledge: 303–314.

Freire, P. (1994) *Pedagogy of Hope: Reliving Pedagogy of the Oppressed*. New York: Continuum.

Hansen, A. H. & Mossberg, L. (2013) Consumer Immersion: A Key to Extraordinary Experiences. In J. Sundbo & F. Sørensen, eds. *Handbook on the Experience Economy*. Cheltenham, UK: Edward Elgar: 209–227.

Harris, M. & Fallot, R. D. (eds.) (2001) *New Directions for Mental Health Services. Using Trauma Theory to Design Service Systems*. Jossey-Bass/Wiley.

Hawkey, K. (2012) History and Super Diversity, *Educational Sciences*, 2: 165–179.

Hess, A. (2007) You Don't Play, You Volunteer. Narrative Public Memory Construction in Medalo of Honor: Rising Sun, *Critical Studies in Media Communication*, 24 (4): 339–356.

Kirschner, P. & De Bruyckere, P. (2017) The Myths of Digital Natives and the Multitasker, *Teaching and Teacher Education*, 67: 135–142.

Mayersen, D. (2018) Cockroaches, Cows and "Canines of the Hebrew Faith": Exploring Animal Imagery in Graphic Novels about Genocide, *Genocide Studies and Prevention: An International Journal*, 12 (2): 165–178.

Merriam, S. (2008) Adult Learning Theory for the Twenty-first Century. *Special Issue: Third Update on Adult Learning Theory*, 119: 93–98.

Papert, S. & Harel, I. (1991) *Constructionism*. Norwood, NJ: Ablex Publishing.

Perez-Marcos, D. (2018) Virtual Reality Experiences, Embodiment, Videogames and Their Dimensions in Neurorehabilitation, *Journal of NeuroEngineering and Rehabilitation*, 15 (113): 1–8.

Prensky, M. (2001) Digital Natives, Digital Immigrants Part 1, *On the Horizon*, 9 (5): 1–6.

Reeves, T. C. & Oh, E. (2007) Generational differences. In M. Spector, M. D. Merrill & M. J. Bishop, eds. *Handbook of Research on Educational Communications and Technology*. New York: Taylor & Francis Group, LLC: 295–303.

Reimann, C. & König, U. (2017) Collective Trauma and Resilience. Key Concepts in Transforming War-related Identities. Comment on: Transforming War-related Identities. In B. Austin & M. Fischer, eds. *Berghof Handbook Dialogue Series No. 11*. Berlin: Berghof Foundation.

Sajnani, N. & Johnson, D. R. (eds.) (2014) *Trauma-Informed Drama Therapy: Transforming Clinics, Classrooms, and Communities*. Springfield, IL: Charles C. Thomas.

Sallberg, J. & Grand, S. (2016) *Wounds of History: Repair and Resilience in the Trans-Generational Transmission of Trauma*. New York: Routledge.

Saul, J. (2013) *Collective Trauma, Collective Healing: Promoting Community Resilience in the Aftermath of Disaster*. New York: Routledge.

Schwarz-Franco, O. (2016) Touching the Challenge: Embodied Solutions Enabling Humanistic Moral Education, *Journal of Moral Education*, 45 (4): 449–464.

Seixas, P. & Morton, T. (2013) *The Big Six Historical Thinking Concepts*. Toronto, ON: Nelson Education.

Slater, M. & Sanchez-Vives, M. (2016) Enhancing Our Lives with Immersive Virtual Reality, *Frontiers in Robotics and AI*, 3 (74): 1–47.

World Economic Forum (2016) *New Vision for Education: Fostering Social and Emotional Learning Through Technology*.

Zemke, R., Raines, C., & Filipczak, B. (2000) *Generations at Work: Managing the Class of Veterans, Boomers, Xers, and Nexters in Your Workplace*. New York: Performance Research Associates, Inc.

18 In memory of *Memory Gliders*: preservation of EU-funded serious games as digital heritage

Maria B. Garda and Jaakko Suominen

Introduction

This chapter investigates preservation strategies related to educational game-based software in general, and serious games specifically. We are focusing on a case study of *Memory Gliders* (Ulric Games 2019). *Memory Gliders* (*MG*) is a non-profit research intervention that is using the narrative potential of videogames to explore new ways of communicating the complex issues related to trauma transmission. The educational potential of digital games has been recognised even before their mainstream success in the late 1970s (see Abt 1966). During the microcomputer era of the 1980s, educational games became a popular type of commercial software, and by the early 2000s, there were already established media franchises focused on games for children, such as *Reader Rabbit* or *JumpStart* (for a more detailed historical overview, see: Games & Squire 2011). As of today, the digital game industry is the biggest entertainment market, larger than the movie and music industries combined, and studies show that games are played by the majority of Millenials (Entertainment Software Association 2019). Interestingly, even some of the highest-grossing games, especially those with historical settings, are intentionally designed to include educational elements (e.g. the Discovery Tour in the *Assassin's Creed* series). Furthermore, there is a growing number of game-based, or gamified,[1] solutions being developed with the sole purpose of educational use. Applying any new media for educational purposes has its challenges, for example, the requirement that educators constantly develop their transmedia literacy (Scolari 2019). Yet in order to engage with younger audiences, it seems only reasonable to employ the media of their preference.[2]

Sara de Freitas (2018) points out that the existing literature on educational games is very fragmented and dispersed among various disciplines, ranging from the area of human-computer interaction to environmental awareness-raising, or advertising and marketing. As she continues, "[o]ne challenge with the literature so scattered is that not all researchers acknowledge the breadth of the area and range of applications, and therefore miss vital academic contributions by looking too narrowly at the literature-base" (de Freitas 2018,

74). In our opinion, this is an important observation, as this fragmentation and the resulting limited interdisciplinary communication can affect the overall sustainability of projects such as *MG*. This chapter is written from the perspective of the cultural history of games in relation to game studies and heritage studies. We set out to answer a simple research question: what will happen to *MG* after the #NeverAgain project is over? Then, we aim to explore short-term solutions for reinforcing the academic and societal impact of the game, as well as long-term solutions for its preservation as a digital heritage artefact. Because of the funding structure and institutional embeddedness of *MG*, this chapter focuses on the European context of digital preservation, which involves specific measures not necessarily applicable worldwide. Furthermore, special attention is given to solutions available on a national level in Finland, where the project management is located, and in Poland, where the game development studio is based.

Memory Gliders as a serious game

In this section, we investigate the characteristics of *MG* that are important to a game historian interested in the preservation of educational game-based software. *MG* can be described as a serious game. Simon Egenfeldt-Nielsen (2005, 262; see also Abt 1966, 5) defines serious games as a "concept (…) used to describe the overarching perspective of games for something else than just entertainment". *MG* uses the storytelling tools developed by videogames in order to engage the players with the three levels of trauma transmission: (1) personal story, (2) social circle and (3) historical perspective. The game follows a story of bird-like creatures, descendants of space refugees escaping an unspecified trauma from the past. The flock is struggling to settle on a new planet while trying to retain their identity. *MG* is an interactive adventure game, which is a genre typical for edutainment software dating back to the famous *Where in the World Is Carmen Sandiego?* (Broderbund 1985). While playing, the player develops deep relationships with various members of the flock, uncovering a complex set of interdependencies and internal tensions. This way players learn multiperspectivity, an important notion in understanding the historical process involved in trauma transmission. To better understand how unique the design concept behind *MG* is, it is useful to compare it to a serious game with an almost directly opposite strategy in representing history.

Attentat 1942 (Charles Games 2017) is according to the official description "a historically-accurate adventure told through the eyes of World War 2 survivors" (Steam 2020). Vit Šisler (2019), lead game designer of *Attentat 1942* and a game studies scholar, defines the project as a *critical war game* (a subset of serious games) that "through its procedural rhetoric and/or narrative frames challenges the established design practices and generic conventions that dominate the representation of war in videogames" (Šisler 2019, 202)[3]. According to Šisler (2019), "[t]he civilian perspective, casualties and the trauma of war are typically missing in war-themed videogames" (Šisler 2019, 201), and numerous examples of franchises support that claim (e.g. *Call of Duty* or *Total War*). The gameplay of *Attentat 1942* starts in 2001 when the player takes on the role of a grandchild trying to understand what happened to their grandfather after the assassination of a top Nazi official in Prague in 1942. Even though the main characters and storyline are fictitious, they are "based on real testimonies and historical research" (ibidem, 214) and the in-game encyclopedia offers detailed historical contextualisation. Furthermore, contemporary scenes are fashioned as oral history interviews with survivors, recorded on camera with actors. As we can see, the *Attentat 1942* team is striving for authenticity, realism, and historical accuracy.

Clearly, the science-fiction setting and the unspecified nature of the historical trauma faced by the characters in *MG*, make it a very different experience. Yet the educational premise of *MG* was to reach as diverse audiences as possible, and that could have only been achieved by not anchoring the story world in any particular cultural setting. This decontextualised approach does not mean that the game is not critically engaging with representations of war and trauma in the popular media. It is important to remember that *MG* is not a commercially sold game based on almost a decade of development and iteration, as *Attentat 1942*, but a research intervention developed for experimental purposes. The aim of *MG* is to innovate, to explore the educational advantages (and disadvantages) of its design concept.

From a game historian's perspective, preservation of projects, such as *MG*, is important for at least two main reasons. First of all, the preservation of serious games helps to maintain the diversity of collections meant to safeguard our ludic and popular culture heritage for future generations (e.g. in public museums and libraries). These archives should not focus only on entertainment games but also acknowledge other uses of digital games. Secondly, serious games should be preserved for reasons related to their non-entertainment purposes, such as learning and education. Future researchers and educators should be able to rely on historical sources, in the case of *MG*, related to experiential learning in the area of trauma transmission. In the next section, we discuss what actually preservation of digital games entails.

Memory Gliders as a born-digital artefact

The term born-digital refers to "digital content that originated as a digital product" (FAGDI 2020) and is meant to differentiate it from the content that was only digitised at some point after its creation (e.g. scans of printed books uploaded to online libraries). Digital games are complex born-digital artifacts which makes them especially challenging to preserve. In the case of the aforementioned book scans, we are usually dealing with a single file format (e.g. JPG or PDF). In the case of digital games, we are facing a multileveled directory involving hundreds of files coming in a variety of formats, many of them created with a specific gaming platform (e.g. a model of a console) in mind and thus becoming obsolete as the given hardware becomes replaced with a newer product. The designed obsolescence and ever shorter life cycles of modern technology, as well as dependence on always online network infrastructure and constant updating (see Švelch 2019), are making the situation even more complicated.

Digital games as born-digital artefacts are vulnerable to phenomena such as digital decay (also called bit rot). The notion of digital decay describes the ongoing loss of readability that affects digital artefacts (see Swalwell 2009, 265–266; Newman 2012, 16–19).[4] We have to remember that all of the born-digital content produced by our civilisation has to be physically stored somewhere. Usually on a dedicated device, such as a hard drive, server (e.g. cloud storage services), or cartridge (i.e. in case of older games). As we can see, digital games are complex artefacts made of various components, both digital (software) and material (hardware) that might require customised preservation strategies.

Barwick et al. (2011) have described three main strategies of digital preservation in the context of digital games: (1) technological preservation, (2) migration, and (3) emulation. The first approach refers to the collection, conservation, and maintenance of original hardware, hence it underscores the physical aspect of games. The second method focuses on porting the games to other platforms, which are perhaps more accessible or just newer. In the long-term perspective, this requires continuous porting, as contemporary hardware and software become obsolete. Finally, the third option is to emulate the original platform on a newer operating system environment. The second and third strategies may seem similar at first, but migration requires access to the source code (which is not always possible). However, emulation presents a more significant challenge, as it is often illegal. It might be also worth noting that emulators are born-digital artefacts themselves, so they need to be periodically ported or updated to work with newer operating systems. From today's perspective, what is missing from the Barwick et al. (2011) overview, is an in-depth reflection on the environmental cost of digital preservation. However, these pressing issues are addressed by newer publications on the topic (Pendergrass et al. 2019) and hopefully, the emerging debates on the sustainability of game preservation (Garda et al. 2020) will lead to new developments in this area in not so distant future.

Apart from these technological considerations, there are some other fundamental challenges regarding the preservation of games. What are we preserving? Are we just preserving the material remnants of digital games (tangible heritage), or rather the cultural practices related to play (intangible heritage)?[5] The ongoing academic discussions on digital games as heritage have moved in the last decade towards the inclusion of the latter. James Newman (2012, 153) suggests that "games as playable entities may have a limited lifespan and that the objective of game preservation need not be to artificially extend this perpetuity, but rather, should be to document the period of the game's existence". At the same time, "games as playable entities" are important to player communities. As Melanie Swalwell (2017, 214) observes:

> a desire for the 'original experience' is strongly evident in much contemporary writing about game history and preservation. We often read accounts of historic game exhibitions, a trip to a specialist arcade, or reports of playing an emulated game in which the author reflects on the experience of play, only to note that it was (or was not) the same as it used to be, just like the original (or not).

In fact, a closer look at the accessibility status of some earlier projects of similar scope may give us an informative perspective on the preservation problem. We would like to showcase two projects that – just like the *MG* – were funded by the EU, only earlier in time: in the 1990s and 2000s.

The Playground Project (1998–2001), funded by and hosted by the Knowledge Lab UCL[6], was meant to "iteratively design and evaluate a computational playground where children aged 4–8 can play and create their own games." The Playground website is still active but the created games are not easily accessible, and you need to install an emulator in order to make them work via a browser. In addition, various linked documents and websites of project partners are no longer available. It has not even been 20 years and the Playground project outcomes are best preserved in secondary-sources, such as descriptions in post-project publications (e.g. Noss & Hoyles 2006).

Another useful example is the *Europe 2045* game developed by Vit Šisler and his team in the 2000s (Šisler & Brom 2008). After the funding has finished, the game kept running thanks to scholarships provided by Charles University to students working on the service maintenance. Nonetheless, in 2018 and after 10 years of extended lifetime, the title was finally discontinued by its creators. As Šisler (2020) explains, the causes were twofold: firstly, the technology became obsolete, and secondly, the game's content – reflecting on issues topical for the future of European policies in 2008 – was no longer relevant. Simply put, it would be easier to create a new game than maintain (or potentially update) the old one. Unfortunately, as the title was an online multiplayer game, hence interdependent on server infrastructure, it has not been archived as a playable entity. What prevails, again like in the case of the Playground project, are mostly the articles documenting the educational testing of the tool.

What happens to *Memory Gliders* after the funding period is over?

MG was produced by the Games Research Association of Poland, established in 2004, and hence the oldest Polish academic association focused on game research. The developer was Ulric Games, which is a young independent studio from Poland but the team itself has many years of experience in game design, including Live Action Role-Playing Games (LARPs). From a technological standpoint, *MG* is not ideally optimised for preservation purposes as it uses dedicated solutions and technology that has already proven difficult to sustain. For example, the game uses a combination of middleware tools, such as the flash-based Starling engine for rendering its graphics and elements of Citrus engine for scene management. In addition, a lot of the source code has been modified for compatibility with newer libraries (e.g. the DragonBones animation library). Preserving *MG*, as a born-digital artefact, could be easier if it applied a more popular game engine, especially an open-ended solution (e.g. Unreal Engine).

From an aesthetic perspective, *MG* is a rather timeless production, at least in the temporal context of videogame art. The comics-inspired graphic style of the game is more resistant to obsolescence than the mainstream photo-realism known from high-production-value digital game franchises, and which gets outdated with every update of the graphics processing hardware.

From an educational standpoint, *MG* is as lasting as any other learning tool depending heavily on technology. However, extending the *MG's* lifecycle has limited advantages, as we have to remember the primary purpose of the game. *MG* is a research intervention that was never meant to compete with the commercial off-the-shelf games, it has a different purpose. We suggest that the preservation of its gameplay is not a priority, as the more important part is the project documentation and post-project retrospective analysis, as it was in the case of the early Charles Games projects.

Because *MG* is intentionally designed not to relate to any specific cultural context, it might be challenging to preserve, as there is no single topical memory institution interested in its preservation. On the other hand, the atypical theoretical concept behind the design of *MG* makes it potentially interesting to a large number of preservation institutions, not to mention involved stakeholders. As earlier studies of game heritage communities have shown that engagement of a wide range of heritage actors in the process is the most desirable approach to preservation (Suominen & Sivula 2016; Suominen et al. 2018). In the next sections, we offer a brief overview of these stakeholders, dividing them into three categories based on the main actor(s) behind the preservation effort: (1) users, (2) developers, and (3) academic and memory institutions.

User-driven preservation

As a serious game, *MG* does not have the same fan and hobbyist following as popular entertainment games. One of the reasons for this is that games played in institutional contexts are less likely to evoke the nostalgia effect, e.g. towards players' experiences than the ones played in leisure time (see Swalwell 2009; Suominen 2008; Garda 2013). According to Games and Squire (2011, 38), even the most popular serious games reach audiences no bigger than 20,000 users. For comparison, the most popular games of today attract over 100 million players (e.g. *Fortnite*).The users are thus unlikely to play a significant role in the preservation of this particular game. It is an impediment as user-driven efforts are still at the forefront of the game heritage process.

MG is available on the project's website (www.againneveragain.eu), free of charge. This is a popular solution for this kind of project, as it complies with the EU's open data policy. However, it also has its downsides, at least from the preservation perspective. Because it will not be distributed on any major game-oriented digital distribution platform (e.g. Steam), it is rather unlikely it will be spotted by hobbyists and catalogued in one of the videogames archives, such as MobyGames. Although the long-term sustainability of services like Moby Games could be questioned itself, it is more likely that the big archives will somehow be preserved, at least as data sets kept by the retrogaming enthusiasts.

Developer-driven preservation

Since Henry Lowood (2009, 1) tried to alarm the attendees of the International Game Developers Association conference that in a few decades there might be not much left from their productions, the developers are definitely more aware of the necessity of preservation. Yet archiving procedures are time and money consuming and not every game development studio can afford it. So far, only the biggest videogame companies, such as Nintendo or Microsoft, have developed archiving strategies (Andersen 2011) or legacy policies (Suominen 2008). Yet if a developer wants to engage in preservation, there are white papers providing best practices, such as the final report from the *Preserving Virtual Worlds* project (McDonough et al. 2010). In brief, basic preservation would involve archiving all source code and source data, as well as compiled and release versions of the executable software. This, together with development documentation, will make later migrations to newer platforms possible.

The website of *MG* is managed by the game developer. From the preservation perspective, it is important that they make a copy of the server data, since various institutional reasons may cause the discontinuation of the project's original site. There should be a mirror and the site should be saved manually on the Wayback Machine (Internet Archive) to make sure the service is preserved. Unfortunately, preserving the website alone only ensures the continued visibility of the game as a project deliverable. It does not, however, ensure that the game itself can be played. This is why the steps described above are not sufficient.

Preservation is usually not addressed, at least not in the first place, when a serious game such as *MG* is being developed. Limited financial and time resources are the developer's main concerns, as they try to deliver a working product on time, fulfilling the project's objective. This is why preservation should be addressed and enforced on a formal, bureaucratic level. It might be beneficial to introduce clear guidelines on the documentation to the EU recommendations. Ideally, these should address the specific needs of the medium and genre in question. In the case of serious games, a walkthrough produced by the developer and later uploaded to a service such as an online video sharing platform (e.g. YouTube) might be the most promising way of documenting the gameplay, and at the same time accessible to wider audiences then documentation intended for game developers and other IT professionals. A well-prepared walkthrough could reach other practitioners and educators. Niklas Nylund (2015) has explored the use of the popular in the gaming culture, streaming format called let's play. These recorded playthroughs rely on the performative aspect of gameplay and "make much use of contemporary *gamer talk*" (ibid, pp. 62). Yet if recorded in collaboration with academic experts, who can make sure that the discourse is relevant to the intended audience (e.g. educators), this kind of documentation could be a useful educational material itself.

Institutional preservation: an overview

In the same way, the educational research literature is fragmented, the responsibility to preserve educational games can be delegated to various entities effectively sharing that duty. Historically, institutional preservation of videogames centred on specific titles that belonged to the emerging game historical cannon, as in the case of the US Library of Congress initiative (see Anthony 2007). However, in the last decade or so, the debate on game preservation has moved on to include gameplay and the broadly understood game cultures in the preservation efforts. Yet in our chapter, we focus on games themselves, as they are not discussed enough in the context of educational tools produced in EU funded projects.

The stakeholders that are the most invested in the longevity and lasting impact of *MG* as an educational tool are, of course, the institutional parties involved in the project, such as the University of Turku in Finland.[7] In the following sections, we highlight three further types of institutions that can participate in the preservation efforts: (1) game-specialised institutions, (2) institutions that do not focus on games, and (3) European Union institutions and policies.

Preservation by game-specialised institutions

Starting from the late 1990s, we see a slow emergence of different kinds of memory institutions that work specifically in the field of videogame preservation. In addition to specialised research centres (i.e. CoE Game Cult) and memory institutions, such as national museums. In that area, Finland is one of the most advanced countries. Currently, several Finnish institutions are working together on a holistic national preservation strategy, including the internationally recognised Finnish Museum of Games in Tampere.[8]

Unfortunately, the *MG* is not technically published in Finland, and the developer is not a Finnish entity. As such it will not be a part of the Tampere's museum priority acquisitions, yet it most likely will be preserved because of its connections to the University of Turku. In Poland, there are several private museums of videogames focused on hardware, and no public institution specialised in that area.

Another type of game-specialised institution that might be relevant here, are various game research associations that have proven to be interested in the preservation of games and other ludic objects associated with their operations. For example, in 2014, the International Simulation and Gaming Association (ISAGA) has funded the "Time Capsule of Game Simulation" exhibition where numerous historical simulation games were presented and even reconstructed, and some of them for the reason of being connected to ISAGA operations (Kriz 2014). Because the producer of *MG* is the Games Research Association of Poland, it is very likely this scientific association will preserve the game as part of its own societal impact.

Preservation by institutions that do not focus on games

We have focused so far on the preservation of *MG* as a ludic object, part of the local game culture. However, given the complex and hybrid nature of this digital artefact and various cultural contexts in which it operates, there are also other possible heritage actors to be involved in the preservation process. For example, as an educational tool, *MG* may be of interest to memory institutions focused on the history of education. In Finland, since the 1990s there is no national museum dedicated to education. The collections of the former Finnish School Museum are stored at the Vapriikki Museum Centre in Tampere but no new acquisitions are being made. There are, however, several operating museums with a similar scope. Yet, given the prototype nature of the game, an educational research institution might be a better fit. In Finland, there are various academic departments focused on education, as well as researchers' communities gathered around related scientific periodicals, such as the "Kasvatus ja aika". Potential collaboration with these groups and institutions, or their counterparts in other countries involved in the project, seems like a worthwhile effort.

Furthermore, in most of the EU countries, there is the so-called legal deposit, which means that every publisher is legally required to submit their publications to selected libraries. Various national institutions should be interested in upholding this requirement with regard to videogames. In Finland, respective institutions include the National Library and the University of Turku Library. In Poland, the legal deposit legislation covers all publications including software and videogames (see Garda 2014). According to this law, at least hypothetically, each game published in Poland should be placed in all of the entitled libraries (in total 17). Unfortunately, to our knowledge, only a minority of game publishers follow that rule and due to a lack of resources, it is not enforced in practice. Even more regrettably, this reflects the global situation in regard to game preservation in public libraries.

Preservation by European Union institutions and policies

MG was funded by the European Union which has previously financed game-based tools for educational purposes, including serious games. Although, it is hard to establish even an estimate, let alone the exact number of such projects. The structure of various databases managed by the EU Publications Office (e.g. CORDIS) makes it not easy to estimate the number of educational games (or game-based tools) that were reported as projects' deliverables. As far as we know, the number can easily be in thousands.[9] The European Commission grant agreement itself does not address the issues of sustainability, nor preservation. Yet all EU funded projects have to follow general guidelines regarding open access and data management.

As a part of the Europe for Citizens program, AgainNeverAgain project is under the supervision of the European Commission's Education, Audiovisual, and Culture Executive Agency. Since 2014, the EU recognises cultural heritage as "resources inherited from the past in all forms and aspects – tangible, intangible and digital (born-digital and digitised)" (2014/C 183/08). Although this definition includes digital games (as born-digital artefacts), there is still a lot to be done regarding the preservation of gaming software and hardware. For example, videogames are only a marginal part of the Europeana Collections. However, the new Copyright Directive of the Official Journal of the European Union (2019) includes an exemption for cultural heritage preservation purposes that can be applied also in cases related to videogames. Thanks to initiatives such as the European Federation of Game Archives, Museums and Preservation Projects (EFGAMP), videogames are becoming recognised as a part of joint European heritage.

Although we do not know the exact scale of the problem, it would be beneficial for the community of practice around educational games research and development to revise the European Research Data Management implementation policies (see Science Europe 2020), so the domain-specific best practices would better accommodate the sustainability of projects producing serious games as their deliverables. This could potentially improve the lasting impact of these projects and interdisciplinary communication within the field of game research focused on education.

Conclusion

The date when the project funding ends is rarely the end of the dissemination process of this project's results, nor it should be. Even more so, research projects that focus on education and involve the development of digital game-based learning tools are meant to have an academic and societal impact after the project's administrative ending. Usually, the EU guidelines expect the accessibility of the results to be secured by open-access publications or datasets. A project's visibility is then achieved by the creation of a website and press coverage of project-related events. However, these provisions are of a very general nature and if the results comprise of a more unique born-digital artefact, such a serious game, there is little institutional support. In this chapter, we provided a preliminary survey of the possible short-term and long-term solutions for ensuring longevity and preservation of a EU-funded deliverable such as *MG*.

Our main findings are that the preservation of *MG's* gameplay is not a priority, as more important is the project documentation and post-project retrospective analysis. First of all, the game relies on proprietary technological solutions that are difficult to sustain. Ideally, in order to facilitate long-term sustainable preservation, such a project should rely on popular open-source software ecosystems, as a large and apt user base can, at least in theory, result in longer technical support. Secondly, *MG* is an experimental serious game whose main contribution is its culture agnostic treatment of trauma. This intervention can be preserved without the need to maintain *MG* as a playable entity. However, it is a good practice to document the game development processes, as well as to publish a walkthrough video that discusses the main pedagogical ideas behind the game. This documentation will be useful to researchers interested in the specific educational solutions of the game, and to educators that would like to implement it in their work.

We propose that the first several years after the end of the project are the most important period for an exploratory research intervention to have a direct impact on the academic field of educational games. First of all, it is important to reach the community of practitioners which can be achieved via close collaboration with a diverse group of stakeholders. We suggest identifying cultural heritage and memory institutions, as well as research communities and repositories, that would be best fitted for preserving the specific digital artefact as early as possible, at the very beginning of a project, or preferably even at the proposal level. This will allow them to engage directly in the dissemination of project results. Rather surprisingly, it might be beneficial to have a small number of physical copies of the game and distribute them to memory institutions to make use of the existing legal deposit policies, which are in force in most of the EU member states.

Acknowledgements

This research was supported by the Academy of Finland project Centre of Excellence in Game Culture Studies (CoE-GameCult, [312396]). We would like to thank all participants of the Remembrance, Trauma, and Experiential Learning Conference, held on 26–27th May 2019 in Turku, for thought-provoking conversations. We also would like to thank Stanisław Krawczyk, Michał Staniszewski, and Jan Švelch for their valuable comments that improved this chapter substantially.

Notes

1 Gamification is the application of game-design elements and game principles in non-game contexts (see Huotari & Hamari 2012).
2 Similar challenges were faced by educators in the early 20th century, at the time when cinema was a new medium (see Fiadotau et al. 2019, 61–62).
3 A seminal work on procedural rhetoric defines it as "the art of persuasion through rule-based representations and interactions rather than the spoken word, writing, images, or moving pictures" (Bogost 2007, ix).
4 Rather intriguingly, newer technologies are more prone to digital decay than older ones. For example, decades-old tape memories are more resilient to bit rot than modern flash drives.
5 Videogame preservation should also take into account numerous artefacts related to the physical copy of the game and the cultural practices related to its reception.
6 http://playground.ioe.ac.uk/gameplace/index.html (the quotation in the text is from the "About" section on the website).
7 There is no existing digital preservation policy at the University of Turku. Yet, the SELMA online archives will be maintained by the UTU and preserved by the UTU's library.
8 In 2018, Finnish Museum of Games received the prestigious Dibner Award for Excellence in Museum Exhibits given annually by the International Society for History of Technology.
9 CORDIS keyword search (28.03.2020): 140653 results for "game-based", 35673 results for "game-based" "educational", 18014 results for "game-based" "learning", 2817 results for "game" (for project deliverables).

References

Abt, C. C. (1966) *Games for Learning. Occasional Paper No. 7*. Cambridge, MA: Educational Services.
Andersen, J. (2011) Where Games Go To Sleep: The Game Preservation Crisis, Part 3, *Gamasutra*, 10 March, https://www.gamasutra.com/view/feature/134671/where_games_go_to_sleep_the_game_php (Accessed 10 July 2020).
Anthony, J. (2007) The Computer Game Canon, *The Guardian*, 15 March https://www.theguardian.com/artanddesign/artblog/2007/mar/15/thecomputergamescanon1 (Accessed 10 July 2020).
Barwick, J., Dearnley, J., & Muir, A. (2011) Playing Games With Cultural Heritage: A Comparative Case Study Analysis of the Current Status of Digital Game Preservation, *Games and Culture*, 6 (4): 373–390.
Bogost, I. (2007) *Persuasive Games: The Expressive Power of Videogames*. Cambridge, MA, and London: MIT Press.
Broderbund (2007) Where in the World Is Carmen Sandiego? Digital game by Dane Bigham, Gene Portwood and Lauren Elliott, published by Broderbund.
Burn, A. & Durran, J. (2007) *Media Literacy in Schools: Practice, Production and Progression*. Sage.
Charles Games (2017) *Attentat 1942*. Digital game designed by Vít Šisler, Lukáš Kolek & David Vávra, published by Charles Games.
de Freitas, S. (2018) Are Games Effective Learning Tools? A Review of Educational Games, *Journal of Educational Technology & Society*, 21 (2): 74–84.
Egenfeldt-Nielsen, S. (2005) *Beyond Edutainment: Exploring the Educational Potential of Computer Games*. Unpublished PhD. Copenhagen: IT-University of Copenhagen.

Available at: https://www.researchgate.net/publication/245584260_Beyond_Edutainment_Exploring_the_Educational_Potential_of_Computer_Games

Entertainment Software Association (2019) Essential Facts About the Computer and Video Game Industry, *ESA*, https://www.theesa.com/esa-research/2019-essential-facts-about-the-computer-and-video-game-industry/ (Accessed 10 July 2020).

European Commission (2018) Cultural Heritage: Digitisation, Online Accessibility and Digital Preservation: Consolidated Progress Report on the Implementation of Commission Recommendation (2011/711/EU) 2015–2017, *Open-Heritage.eu*, 4 June 2019, https://www.open-heritage.eu/implementation-of-commission-recommendation-on-the-digitisation-and-online-accessibility-of-cultural-material-and-digital-preservation/ (Accessed 10 July 2020).

Federal Agencies Digital Guidelines Initiative (2020) "Born digital". http://www.digitizationguidelines.gov/term.php?term=borndigital (Accessed 10 July 2020).

Fiadotau, M., Sillaots, M., & Ibrus, I. (2019) Education on Screens: Histories of Co-innovation and Convergence between Audiovisual Media and Education Sectors. In *Emergence of Cross-innovation Systems*. Emerald Publishing Limited: 61–69.

Games, A. & Squire, K. D. (2011) Searching for the Fun in Learning: A Historical Perspective on the Evolution of Educational Videogames. In S. Tobias & J. D. Fletcher, eds. *Computer Games and Instruction*. Charlotte, NC: Information Age: 17–46.

Garda, M. B. (2013) Nostalgia in Retro Game Design. In *DiGRA '13 – Proceedings of the 2013 DiGRA International Conference: DeFragging Game Studies*, http://www.digra.org/digital-library/publications/nostalgia-in-retro-game-design/ (Accessed 10 July 2020).

Garda, M. B. (2014) Gry komputerowe jako dziedzictwo kulturowe, *Replay*, 1 (1): 119–127.

Garda, M. B., Nylund, N., Sivula, A. & Suominen, J. (2020) Preservation of Digital Games and the Questions of Cultural Sustainability, *DiGRA 2020: Proceedings of the Digital Games Research Association conference*.

Huotari, K. & Hamari, J. (2012) Defining Gamification: A Service Marketing Perspective', *MindTrek '12, Proceeding of the 16th International Academic MindTrek Conference*: 17–22, https://people.uta.fi/~kljuham/2012-huotari&hamari-defining_gamification_a_service_marketing_perspective.pdf (Accessed 10 July 2020).

Kriz, W. (2014) 250 Jahre Planspiel. Wie alles begann, *Wirtschaft + Weiterbildung*, 26 (5): 50–52.

Lowood, H. (2009) Before It Is Too Late: A Digital Game Preservation White Paper, *American Journal of Play*, 2 (2): 139–166.

McDonough, J. P., Olendorf, R., Kirschenbaum, M., Kraus, K., Reside, D., Donahue, R., Phelps, A., Egert, C., Lowood, H., & Rojo, S. (2010) *Preserving Virtual Worlds: Final Report*, 20 September, https://www.ideals.illinois.edu/handle/2142/17097 (Accessed 10 July 2020).

Newman, J. (2012) *Best Before: Videogames, Supersession and Obsolescence*. London and New York: Routledge.

Noss, R. & Hoyles, C. (2006) *Exploring Mathematics Through Construction and Collaboration*. In K. R. Sawyer, ed. *Cambridge Handbook of the Learning Sciences*. Cambridge: Cambridge University Press: 389–405.

Nylund, N. (2015) Walkthrough and Let's Play: Evaluating Preservation Methods for Digital Games, *Proceedings of the 19th International Academic Mindtrek Conference*: 55–62.

Official Journal of the European Union (2019) *DIRECTIVE (EU) 2019/790 OF THE EUROPEAN PARLIAMENT AND OF THE COUNCIL of 17 April 2019 on Copyright and Related Rights in the Digital Single Market and Amending Directives 96/9/EC and 2001/29/EC*, https://eur-lex.europa.eu/eli/dir/2019/790/oj (Accessed 10 July 2020).

Pendergrass, K. L., Sampson, W., Walsh, T., & Alagna, L. (2019) Toward Environmentally Sustainable Digital Preservation, *The American Archivist*, 82 (1): 165–206.

Prensky, M. (2007) *Digital Game-Based Learning*. New York: McGraw-Hill.

Science Europe (2020) Implementing Research Data Management Policies Across Europe: Experiences from Science Europe Member Organisations, *Science Europe*, 29 January, https://www.scienceeurope.org/our-resources/implementing-research-data-management-policies-across-europe/ (Accessed 10 July 2020).

Scolari, C. A. (2019) Beyond the Myth of the "Digital Native". Adolescents, Collaborative Cultures and Transmedia Skills, *Nordic Journal of Digital Literacy*, 14 (3–4): 164–174.

Steam (2020) Attentat 1942: About this game, https://store.steampowered.com/app/676630/Attentat_1942/ (Accessed 10 July 2020).

Suominen, J. (2008) The Past As the Future? Nostalgia and Retrogaming in Digital Culture. In *Proceedings of perthDAC2007. The 7th International Digital Arts and Cultures Conference. The Future of Digital Media Culture* (vol. 15).

Suominen, J. & Sivula, A. (2016) Participatory Historians in Digital Cultural Heritage Process – Monumentalization of the First Finnish Commercial Computer Game, *Refractory – Australian Journal of Entertainment Media*, 27, themed issue: *Born Digital Cultural Heritage*.

Suominen, J., Sivula, A., & Garda, M. B. (2018) Incorporating Curator, Collector and Player Credibilities: Crowdfunding Campaign for the Finnish Museum of Games and the Creation of Game Heritage Community, *Kinephanos*, special issue: *Preserving play / Préserver le jeu*.

Swalwell, M. (2009) Towards the Preservation of Local Computer Game Software Challenges, Strategies, Reflections, *Convergence: The International Journal of Research into New Media Technologies*, 15 (3): 263–279.

Swalwell, M. (2017) Moving on from the Original Experience: Philosophies of Preservation and Dis/play in Game History. In M. Swalwell, A. Ndalianis, & H. Stuckey, eds. *Fans and Videogames: Histories, Fandom, Archives*. New York: Routledge: 213–233.

Šisler 2020 Šisler, V. (2020) Interview with Maria B. Garda conducted online.

Šisler, V. (2019) Critical War Game Development: Lessons Learned from Attentat 1942. In P. Hammond & H. Pötzsch, eds. New York: Bloomsbury Academic: 201–222.

Šisler, V. & Brom, C. (2008) Designing an Educational Game: Case Study of "Europe 2045". In Z. Pan, A. D. Cheok, W. Müller & A. El Rhabili, eds. *Transactions of Edutainment I*. Berlin: Springer-Verlag: 1–16.

Švelch, J. (2019) Resisting the Perpetual Update: Struggles against Protocological Power in Video Games, New Media & Society, 21 (7): 1594–1612. https://doi.org/10.1177/1461444819828987.

Ulric Games (2019) *Memory Gliders*. Digital game produced by Krzysztof Chmielewski and Michał Stawski. Available at: https://againneveragain.eu/

Index

A
active listening 2, 59, 63, 123, 128, 132
aesthetic(s) 5, 9, 48, 185, 211–213, 262; relational 225, 231
affect 175, 180, 187, 208, 212
affective 62, 229; politics 9, 204–205, 208–212, 220
African American 203, 211
Allison, Graham 233
Alpine front 71, 74, 77, 80
Alt-right 202, 204
American Sonnets for My Past and Future Assassin 212
anti-Gypsyism 99
anti-Semitic 90, 203, 219
art 160, 168, 193, 209, 224; therapy 193, 195
artistic 160, 167, 211, 250; practice 169
artwork 174, 223
atomic 138, 140, 145, 207; bomb 59, 137, 206; poetry 137; warfare 137
Atomic Energy Commission 207
atrocities 59, 137; Nazi 160; mass 98, 254
Attentat 1942 250, 259
Asal, Victor 2
asylum 8, 147, 150, 156–157
audience 66, 83, 148, 161, 174, 217, 259, 264
Austria-Hungary 36, 72
authoritarian 34, 116

B
Balkan 23, 25, 73, 83; route 147, 156
Bannon, Steve 202
Battisti, Cesare 72
Bert the Turtle 207
biopolitical 212
blackboard method 35
body-to-body 248

borderland 71
borders 25, 72, 74, 112, 133, 148–151, 175, 179, 204, 217
Bosnia-Herzegovina 22, 59, 73, 193, 200, 222
breath, breathing 9, 173–190, 252
bunk beds 217, 222
bunker 217, 231
Bush, George B. 208
bystander 98, 219, 221

C
campaign 25, 90–91, 150, 202, 207
Canada 8, 137–138, 141, 204
cause – effect thinking 34
cemetery 74, 87, 144
change 11, 20, 27, 194; attitudinal 115, 121
Cheney, Dick 208
children 48, 67, 92, 95, 109, 112, 120, 145, 153, 158, 165, 193, 197, 200, 204, 205, 207
China 233
circus 160; people 162, 163, 165, 167, 169
citizens 19, 120, 204; Soviet 86
civic 10, 33, 151, 203
classroom 4, 42, 60, 99, 129, 146, 203, 244; moving 59
climate 207, 210, 237; change 151, 205; denialism 203
Cluj 217, 220, 230
co-creation 8, 153
Codes of ethical conduct 221
cognitive 4, 20, 63, 104, 108, 110, 117, 129, 181, 221, 240, 244, 252
Cold War 208, 222, 236
Collingwood, Robin G. 218
comfort zone 96, 122, 229
commemorations 74, 90–98

272 *Index*

community 86, 116, 150; micro- 225; circus 161
communist 38, 94, 103, 118, 162, 207
Communist Party 89, 162
comparison 18, 38, 140, 238, 250, 263; social 118
conflict 36, 51, 60, 71, 74, 94, 116, 131, 178, 234
Connerton, Paul 19, 87, 88
control group 238
construction 91, 178, 224, 247
cosmopolitan 161
critical thinking 11, 43, 138, 151, 249
crisis 120, 143, 183, 199, 217; climate 210; frame 240; refugee 240
Croatia 22, 32, 103
curricula 4, 32, 61, 108; national 104

D
debate 26, 43, 62, 66, 73, 128, 164, 219
deconstruction 36, 104
Dene 137
Denmark 17, 26, 167
deportation 18, 149, 161
descendants 61, 121, 162, 254
dialogue 47, 56, 63, 88, 115, 123, 150, 168, 181, 226, 254
diary 50, 76, 96, 237
didactic 10, 20, 222, 229, 244
digital 245, 258; *born-digital* 259; games 260; immigrants 264; natives 247
digitalisation 245–246
diversity 49, 107, 163, 186, 259; cultural 150, 152
diplomacy 238; Diplomacy [game] 234
divergent thinking 62
division 1, 24
donumenta 223, 230
Duke, David 202
dynamics (group) 132, 194, 245, 250

E
Earnest Harmon Air Force Base 137
Eastern 73, 103, 107, 166, 224; Europe 32, 93, 117, 161, 224; Slavonia 104, 112
education 59, 103, 146, 164; global 148; history 2, 10, 250; Holocaust 99, 167; integral 193; non-formal 121, 133, 151, 244; peace 62, 104, 110; remembrance 96; tertiary 245, 249
Einsatzkommando 9 89
embodied 98, 178, 244

emotional 20, 621 71, 87, 107, 119, 143, 165, 181, 195, 229, 240, 244
emotions 51, 63, 88, 97, 108, 110, 120, 128, 154, 167, 194, 196, 212, 240, 248
empathy 18, 59, 63, 71, 124, 150, 176, 196, 227, 248; historical 19
encounter 47, 63, 182, 223, 229; face-to-face 229
engagement 21, 122, 128, 146, 151, 167, 185, 213, 228, 245, 253; emotional 26, 29; political 122, 227
entertainment 24, 161, 229, 257, 259, 262
Erll, Astrid 19
ethical 71, 127, 137, 139, 167, 176, 182, 189, 200, 250; principles 221, 224
ethnic 25, 39, 62, 99, 112, 115, 131, 224
ethnofiction 46
Euroclio 60
Europe 116, 149, 161, 224, 234, 245, 261; fortress 147
Europe for Citizens 5, 231, 267
European 17, 32, 71, 75, 83, 104, 116, 123, 161, 165, 231, 234, 258, 261
European Union (EU) 36, 116, 126, 128, 264, 266
experiential learning *see* learning
experience 7, 20, 42, 46, 56, 60, 71, 105, 119, 121, 147, 173, 188, 194, 200, 206, 224, 246, 261; intergenerational 45; learning 19, 97, 234, 239, 251; lived 125; refugee *see* refugee
experimental 20, 47, 80, 83, 124, 217, 220, 221, 225, 230, 244, 259, 267

F
facilitate 23, 33, 57, 66, 125, 193, 217, 220, 236
fact-checkers 79
fake news 79
family tree 45–57
Farber, Yuri 92, 95
fascist 17, 22, 39, 90, 118, 133
Federal Civil Defense Administration 207
Feigus, Hilaris 94
field 5, 148, 157, 198, 223
film 46–57, 142, 167, 184–188; screening 115, 218–220
filmmaking 52; participatory 47
Finland 5, 46, 163, 234, 258, 264
forced labour 73, 94, 117
Foucault, Michel 104–105, 110

Index 273

fragmented 95, 118, 175, 184, 228, 257, 264
Fukushima 8, 137–144

G
game 50, 59, 173, 250, 253; board 234–241; interactive 65–66; master 237; strategy 236; video *see* videogames
generations 3, 43, 45, 61, 66, 96, 103, 121, 166, 178, 184, 193, 219, 234, 244, 247, 249, 259
genius loci 87–88, 98
Genocide and Resistance Research Centre of Lithuania 93
Germany 39, 93, 133, 161, 220
ghetto 94
gli ultimi 77
Great War 72, 133
group 19, 47, 55, 79, 89, 117, 126, 151, 162, 194, 200, 220; inter- 117; minority 20, 203; out- 118; social 17, 90, 169, 246; work 22, 24, 52, 56, 126, 193, 195, 239

H
Habsburg 33, 43; Empire 33–36, 72
Halbwachs, Maurice 86
Haraway, Donna 173, 185
hate 110, 140, 205; speech 147–158
Hayes, Terrance 211–212
healing 2, 9, 46, 60, 119, 194, 197–200, 246
hedging strategies 241
heritage 46, 56, 64, 87, 97, 117, 258; cultural 266, 268; game 262
Hibakusha 60, 137, 140
Hiroshima 138
Hiroshima Three Witnesses 139
historical 18, 22, 32, 57, 71, 131, 138, 167, 205, 217, 235, 249, 258; empathy 19, 29, 63; events 20, 32, 35, 48, 52, 56, 75, 83, 104, 142, 208, 217, 250; narratives 19, 42, 60, 104, 251; places 64, 86, 96; trauma *see* trauma
history; as a school subject 1, 28, 42; family 57, 120; political 33, 234; teaching 19, 32, 60, 63, 108, 169, 251
Hobbesian 236
Holocaust 22, 87, 98, 115, 137, 163, 167, 221; fatigue 169
Homeland Security Advisory Codes 209
Homeland War 32, 103–104, 107

homeless 224, 227
homelessness 223, 227
homophobia 205
hooks, bell 4
House UnAmerican Activities Committee (HUAC) 208
Human Rights 137, 148, 151

I
I do not care if we go down in history as barbarians 115, 217, 230
ICOMOS (International Council of Monuments and Sites) 88
ICTY (International Criminal Tribunal of the Former Yugoslavia) 22
Idealists 234
identity 61, 87, 117, 124, 218, 248; national 6, 30, 41, 120, 221; social 117, 120, 125
imaginary 55, 245, 247
immersive 6
in situ 7, 87, 89, 99, 248
indigenous 5, 137–138, 145, 210, 254
information 22, 47, 73, 79, 92, 95, 97, 103, 109, 115, 120, 146, 151, 160, 167, 188, 196, 244
injustice 1, 37, 62, 90, 117, 121, 146, 150, 206, 246
innovative 3, 149, 236
interactive 3, 64–65, 241, 244, 253; theatre play 147–153
intergenerational 2, 45, 245, 252
International Court of Arbitration 236
International Relations (IR) 96 10, 233–238
International Roma Holocaust Remembrance Day 96
intervention 115, 168, 194, 217, 222, 224, 258
Irigaray, Luce 173, 182, 186
Irredentist 72
Italy 71, 73, 78, 79, 147, 161

J
Jagomastas, Enzis 93–94
Japan 137–138, 142–143
Jewish 86–88, 91, 119, 160, 203, 217, 219
Jews 22, 60, 86, 91, 95, 219
Jude, Radu 115, 217
justice 1, 121; transitional 103, 111, 112

K
Kantian 236

Index

Keijiro Suga 143
KKK 202
knowledge 4, 18, 20, 28, 45, 79, 83, 96–97, 104, 110, 122, 138, 151, 165, 184, 189, 244, 247, 252
Kolb, David 3, 20, 28, 138
Krstajić, Mladen 22

L

League of Nations 236
learning; active 139; experiential 3, 20, 55, 59, 98, 104, 108, 110, 122, 138, 144, 203, 209, 230, 248; global 147; holistic 122; *shared* 56; *Spiral of learning* 20
legacy 32, 41–42, 146, 211, 252, 263
librarians 96, 99
lieux de parole 227
literature 138, 204, 211; atomic 139
Lithuania 7, 86, 88, 89, 90, 91, 92, 93, 94, 95, 96, 99, 163
Lockean/Grotian 236

M

marginal 18, 117, 124, 160, 212, 246
Massumi, Brian 180, 208
McCarthyist 208
Mearsheimer, John 235
media 18, 24, 41, 57, 71, 77, 83, 149, 184, 204, 229, 147
meditation 175
memes 26, 204
Memorial Centre of the Homeland War Vukovar 103
memorialisation 32, 72
memory 19, 72, 74, 77, 86–88, 91, 96, 105, 173; collective 86–88, 221; cultural 19, 88, 212; historical 17, 87; institutional 263–265; my-their 61
Memory Gliders 245–254
Middle America 220
militarism 186, 238, 241
military 39–40, 107, 138, 145, 203–204, 207, 210, 218, 220
misogynist 203, 210
model 20, 60, 79, 117, 129, 187, 230; needs-based 64; of experiential learning 3, 111
more-than-human 139–140, 142, 144–145
movement 34, 150, 210, 228; anti-war 227; political 40; #METOO 210
multiperspectivity 32, 62, 251
multisensory 247

multi-vocal 228
museum 62, 71, 87, 90–98, 142, 163, 264, 266; industry 59, 64
muslim 18, 203

N

Nagasaki 60, 137, 142
narratives 19, 36, 60, 72, 83, 104, 162, 184, 249, 251; counter- 164; master- 32, 34, 42
nationalist 24, 32, 41, 67, 132, 219
Nazism 160, 165
negotiation 129, 233, 236
Newfoundland 138, 144, 204
non-violent 62, 197
normality 217, 222
NSC 68, 207
nuclear 137, 142, 205, 222, 227; fear 207; weapons 137, 206

O

Oberschall, Anthony 241
occupation (occupied) 54, 91, 125, 182, 229; Nazi 89, 161; Soviet 87, 89, 96; territory 105–107
Odessa 9, 217, 219, 220, 228
Ongari, Dante 73
onlookers 217, 219–222, 228
oppressive 36, 117, 153, 163, 189, 212, 246
Othering 1, 18; The Other 84, 76
out-of-place 223

P

pain 43, 67, 108, 140, 147
Paludan, Rasmus 18, 27
Paneriai (memorial) 88–100
paramilitary 22, 107
participatory 46, 54, 83, 161, 244
Patriot Act 208
patriotism 65, 67, 108
Pasierbska, Helena 93
passers-by 217, 222, 224–225, 228
past 2, 17, 20, 29, 36, 42, 46, 52, 66, 71, 82, 86, 173, 178, 212–213; socialist 38; traumatic 3, 27, 46, 60, 61, 96, 100, 103, 117, 133, 147, 251, 258; violent 108–110, 253
peace 62, 107, 109, 116, 157, 194, 241, 249; mediators 236; *Zone of Peace* 239
peacebuilding 115
pedagogy 32, 63, 163; engaged 4, 248; of hope 2

performance 147, 153, 163, 218, 221, 230, 239, 246; micro- 226, 229; research-based 160, 167
performative 105, 217, 248, 264
persecution 119, 124, 147, 161, 204
perspective 32, 62, 83, 98, 133, 165, 209, 221, 238, 249; taking 65; recognition 20
Philippines, the 237
pluralism 252
poetry 138, 202, 211
polarised 119, 228
policy 36, 86, 111, 147, 150, 153, 203, 207–209, 235, 263
Ponarska, Rodzina 92–93
predecessors 116, 219
Prensky, Marc 245
preservation 80, 257
psychotherapy 119, 129
public 17, 35, 46, 71, 76, 83, 115, 148, 153, 162, 196, 203, 208; school 35; space 72, 165, 169, 217, 223, 227

R
racism, racist 141, 145, 147, 151, 202, 203, 230, 254
radiation 144
Realism 237
reconstruction 110, 112
Red Army 90, 91, 94
reenactment 217, 235
reflection 18, 21, 25, 46, 52, 55, 60, 67, 121, 129, 144, 161, 190, 231, 251, 254; self- 11, 139, 149, 203, 221, 246
refugees 22, 87, 98, 115, 137, 163, 167, 221; experience 148, 150, 153, 156
Regensburg 217
Reichsbürger 227
remembrance 97, 160, 187, 219
reunification 72
research 19, 23, 26, 43, 47, 60, 64, 67, 71, 73, 77, 90, 103, 105, 110, 119, 127, 160, 164, 166, 167, 196, 224, 259, 267; anthropological 224; -based performances/plays 8, 160, 167–169
Retrospection 104–108
risk 18, 25, 27, 71, 123, 128, 132, 166, 198, 240, 246
Roe vs. Wade 203
Roma 22, 89, 95, 119, 124, 160, 165, 222, 23
Romania 115, 217
Rumsfeld, Donald 208
rupture 175, 217, 221, 245; ruptured breath 178, 183

Russians 72

S
safe 48, 88, 119, 148, 157, 200, 212, 219, 231, 251; environment 50, 60, 193; space 47, 56, 63, 123, 164, 252
school 17, 26, 28, 42, 56, 59, 78, 103, 148, 164, 200, 245; primary 59, 104, 155; teacher 19, 23, 164, 167
School of Peace 103, 104, 108
security 93, 117, 119, 123, 145, 154, 160, 202, 227, 234
Selman, Selma 222, 231
sensual 184, 247
Serbia 19, 22, 36, 41, 71, 110; Minority 110
Serbs 22, 37, 73
sexual assault 204, 210
shelter 73, 143–144, 152, 162, 164, 169, 222, 227; war 149
Sicherheitspolizei 89
silence 41, 46, 93, 121, 166, 176, 182, 189
simulation 4, 122, 130, 153, 233, 247, 265
Sinti 160
site 64, 72, 75, 87, 91, 103, 166, 246; mass killing 88, 90, 91, 98, 99; memory 87, 64, 90, 104, 164; of intervention 223
situationists 224
Slovenia 36, 38, 41, 147, 149, 150, 153, 155, 156
smartphones 220
solidarity 74, 121, 150, 162, 205, 2010
Sonderkommando 1005A 95
South Tyrol 71–85
Soviet Union 90, 91, 119, 207
spectacle 218, 222, 224
spectator 165, 218, 228; passive 228
stigma 3, 18
Stolpersteine 79
storytelling 33, 45, 52, 149, 166, 186, 288
Stram Kurs 18, 27
students 2, 19, 22, 32, 45, 59, 72, 80, 103, 137, 204, 222, 235, 244; high school 21
supremacist 203
Survival Under Atomic Attack 207
Syria 147, 224, 227

Š
Šimunić, Josip 22–26

T
teacher 2, 43, 47, 54, 59–67, 96–97, 105–110, 148, 153, 167, 238, 244, 246;

high school 19, 23, 28; history 3, 66, 251
teaching 5, 11, 17, 26, 28, 34, 38, 42, 63, 78, 96–98, 108, 141, 151, 166, 204, 208, 218, 230, 234–239; concept 237–241; history *see* history; history of Nazism 169; IR 236–238; method 234, 238, 240; pack 19, 22–23; problem-oriented 98
technology 64, 139, 190, 245, 260, 262
teens, teenagers 5, 9, 17, 18, 20, 24, 28, 165, 193
tertiary (education) *see* education
textbooks 19, 43, 60, 66–67, 99
The International Commission for the Evaluation of Nazi and Soviet Occupation Regimes in Lithuania 96
theatre 147–158
theatrical 218, 221, 229
think tank 71
Third Reich 162, 169, 224
Thucydides Trap 233–243
Todorov, Tzvetan 221–222
Tōge, Sankichi 139–140
tolerance 107–109, 121, 130, 148, 184, 194, 229
transfer of burden 46
transformative 29, 99, 148, 150, 246, 248
training 11, 60, 115, 121–132, 164, 167, 198, 245, 254
transgender 127, 210
transphobia 205
trauma 3, 46, 60, 71, 121, 147, 173, 199, 267; collective 5, 104, 117, 120, 175, 245; culture 206; historical 51, 218, 241, 244; informed 2, 251; transmission 57, 245, 249, 257; vicarious 3, 212
traumatic 4, 6, 9, 46, 57, 83, 86, 132, 175, 178, 204; event 7, 60, 87, 119, 120, 181, 218, 222, 231, 245, 255; experience 2, 57, 60, 61, 87, 91, 217, 252; past *see* past
trigger 2, 5, 36, 115, 128, 180, 182, 189, 205, 209, 219, 221, 222–226, 245, 251
Trudeau, Justin 210
Truman, Harry 207
Trump, Donald 9, 202–212; trauma 203, 210
trust 50, 63, 104, 118, 131, 193, 221, 240–241, 246

U
uranium 137, 140
Ustasha 22, 39–41
US Immigration and Customs Enforcement (ICE) 208

V
Verbrecherstaat 227
victimhood 71
victims 32, 41, 59, 61, 65, 67, 74, 77, 79, 86–98, 118, 133, 140, 142, 149, 157, 163, 169, 203, 210, 221; blaming 116; of Fascist Terror 90
videogames 244–245, 247–250, 252–254, 258–259
Village of Widows 144
Vilna Gaon State Jewish Museum 90, 92–94, 96, 98
violence 46, 60, 71, 78, 116–119, 145, 182, 194, 203, 211, 224; cycles of 6, 130, 199; cultural 116; gender-based 66, 116; gun 205, 210; mass 18, 20–22, 27–28; racialised 205, 210; structural 10, 11, 116, 254
virtual 78, 183, 229, 246, 248, 252
voice 56, 62, 128, 161, 174, 179, 209, 211, 213, 224, 226
volunteers 78–79, 89, 147, 155, 163
vulnerability 7, 55, 199, 203, 204, 209, 211; shared 203, 205

W
War 46, 51, 59, 66, 71; crimes 23; First World War 72, 234; Yugoslav 21, 32, 65; prisoners of 73, 80, 90, 95; Second World War 21, 38, 40, 86, 95, 104, 137, 143
Western 141, 161, 186, 204, 235, 246, 254
WhatsApp 226
whole person learning 246
Wikipedia 72, 77, 80
witness 77, 88, 98, 141, 175, 204, 211
workshop 45, 59, 65, 72, 80, 130, 149, 196, 244
worldview 20, 233, 247

Y
Yugoslavia 21, 25, 33, 36
1991 Vukovar battle 103–113
9/11 208
IV Hague Convention 73

Ingram Content Group UK Ltd.
Milton Keynes UK
UKHW022113040523
421267UK00007B/90